MARS
マース

2

惣領冬実

ALSO AVAILABLE FROM TOKYOPOP®

REALITY CHECK
REBIRTH
REBOUND
REMOTE June 2004
RISING STARS OF MANGA December 2003
SABER MARIONETTE J
SAILOR MOON
SAINT TAIL
SAIYUKI
SAMURAI DEEPER KYO
SAMURAI GIRL REAL BOUT HIGH SCHOOL
SCRYED
SGT. FROG March 2004
SHAOLIN SISTERS
SHIRAHIME-SYO: SNOW GODDESS TALES December 2004
SHUTTERBOX
SNOW DROP January 2004
SOKORA REFUGEES May 2004
SORCEROR HUNTERS
SUIKODEN May 2004
SUKI February 2004
THE CANDIDATE FOR GODDESS April 2004
THE DEMON ORORON April 2004
THE LEGEND OF CHUN HYANG
THE SKULL MAN
THE VISION OF ESCAFLOWNE
TOKYO MEW MEW
TREASURE CHESS March 2004
UNDER THE GLASS MOON
VAMPIRE GAME
WILD ACT
WISH
WORLD OF HARTZ
X-DAY
ZODIAC P.I.

NOVELS

KARMA CLUB APRIL 2004
SAILOR MOON

ART BOOKS

CARDCAPTOR SAKURA
MAGIC KNIGHT RAYEARTH
PEACH GIRL ART BOOK April 2004

ANIME GUIDES

COWBOY BEBOP ANIME GUIDES
GUNDAM TECHNICAL MANUALS
SAILOR MOON SCOUT GUIDES

CINE-MANGA™

CARDCAPTORS
FAIRLY ODD PARENTS MARCH 2004
FINDING NEMO
G.I. JOE SPY TROOPS
JACKIE CHAN ADVENTURES
KIM POSSIBLE
LIZZIE MCGUIRE
POWER RANGERS: NINJA STORM
SPONGEBOB SQUAREPANTS
SPY KIDS
SPY KIDS 3-D March 2004
THE ADVENTURES OF JIMMY NEUTRON: BOY GENIUS
TRANSFORMERS: ARMADA
TRANSFORMERS: ENERGON May 2004

TOKYOPOP KIDS

STRAY SHEEP

For more
information visit
www.TOKYOPOP.com

ALSO AVAILABLE FROM 🔊TOKYOPOP®

MANGA

.HACK//LEGEND OF THE TWILIGHT
@LARGE
A.I. LOVE YOU February 2004
AI YORI AOSHI January 2004
ANGELIC LAYER
BABY BIRTH
BATTLE ROYALE
BATTLE VIXENS April 2004
BIRTH May 2004
BRAIN POWERED
BRIGADOON
B'TX January 2004
CARDCAPTOR SAKURA
CARDCAPTOR SAKURA: MASTER OF THE CLOW
CARDCAPTOR SAKURA: BOXED SET COLLECTION 1
CARDCAPTOR SAKURA: BOXED SET COLLECTION 2
  March 2004
CHOBITS
CHRONICLES OF THE CURSED SWORD
CLAMP SCHOOL DETECTIVES
CLOVER
COMIC PARTY June 2004
CONFIDENTIAL CONFESSIONS
CORRECTOR YUI
COWBOY BEBOP: BOXED SET THE COMPLETE
  COLLECTION
CRESCENT MOON May 2004
CREST OF THE STARS June 2004
CYBORG 009
DEMON DIARY
DIGIMON
DIGIMON SERIES 3 April 2004
DIGIMON ZERO TWO February 2004
DNANGEL April 2004
DOLL May 2004
DRAGON HUNTER
DRAGON KNIGHTS
DUKLYON: CLAMP SCHOOL DEFENDERS
DV June 2004
ERICA SAKURAZAWA
FAERIES' LANDING January 2004
FAKE
FLCL
FORBIDDEN DANCE
FRUITS BASKET February 2004
G GUNDAM
GATEKEEPERS
GETBACKERS February 2004
GHOST! March 2004
GIRL GOT GAME January 2004
GRAVITATION
GTO

GUNDAM WING
GUNDAM WING: BATTLEFIELD OF PACIFISTS
GUNDAM WING: ENDLESS WALTZ
GUNDAM WING: THE LAST OUTPOST
HAPPY MANIA
HARLEM BEAT
I.N.V.U.
INITIAL D
ISLAND
JING: KING OF BANDITS
JULINE
JUROR 13 March 2004
KARE KANO
KILL ME, KISS ME February 2004
KINDAICHI CASE FILES, THE
KING OF HELL
KODOCHA: SANA'S STAGE
LAMENT OF THE LAMB May 2004
LES BIJOUX February 2004
LIZZIE MCGUIRE
LOVE HINA
LUPIN III
LUPIN III SERIES 2
MAGIC KNIGHT RAYEARTH I
MAGIC KNIGHT RAYEARTH II February 2004
MAHOROMATIC: AUTOMATIC MAIDEN May 2004
MAN OF MANY FACES
MARMALADE BOY
MARS
METEOR METHUSELA June 2004
METROID June 2004
MINK April 2004
MIRACLE GIRLS
MIYUKI-CHAN IN WONDERLAND
MODEL May 2004
NELLY MUSIC MANGA April 2004
ONE April 2004
PARADISE KISS
PARASYTE
PEACH GIRL
PEACH GIRL CHANGE OF HEART
PEACH GIRL RELAUNCH BOX SET
PET SHOP OF HORRORS
PITA-TEN January 2004
PLANET LADDER February 2004
PLANETES
PRIEST
PRINCESS AI April 2004
PSYCHIC ACADEMY March 2004
RAGNAROK
RAGNAROK: BOXED SET COLLECTION 1
RAVE MASTER
RAVE MASTER: BOXED SET March 2004

Translator – Shirley Kubo
Retouch Artist – Roselyn Santos
Graphic Designer – Thea Willis
Production Specialist – Dolly Chan
Editor – Paul Morrissey
Associate Editors – Trisha Kunimoto and Robert Coyner

Senior Editor – Jake Forbes
Reprint Editor – Mark Paniccia
Managing Editor - Jill Freshney
Production Coordinator - Antonio DePietro
Production Managers - Jennifer Miller, Mutsumi Miyazaki
Art Director - Matt Alford
Editorial Director - Jeremy Ross
VP of Production - Ron Klamert
President & C.O.O. - John Parker
Publisher & C.E.O. - Stuart Levy

Email: editor@TOKYOPOP.com
Come visit us online at www.TOKYOPOP.com

A ⦿TOKYOPOP® book
TOKYOPOP Inc.
5900 Wilshire Blvd. Ste 2000
Los Angeles, CA 90036

Mars Vol. 2

© 1996 Fuyumi Soryo.
First published in 1996 by Kodansha Ltd., Tokyo.
English publication rights arranged through Kodansha Ltd.

English text © 2003 TOKYOPOP Inc.

ISBN: 1-931514-59-3

First TOKYOPOP® printing: June 2002

10 9 8 7 6 5 4

Printed in the USA

Volume 2
By Fuyumi Soryo

LOS ANGELES • TOKYO • LONDON

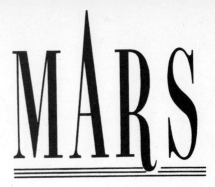

MARS

LEGEND OF MARS

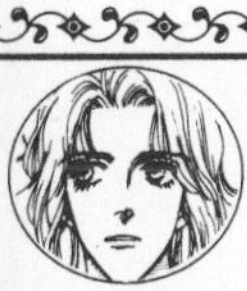

Rei Kashino:
He's a high school student with a love for motorcycle racing. He is blown away by Kira's drawings. He lives for the moment and is not afraid of anything.

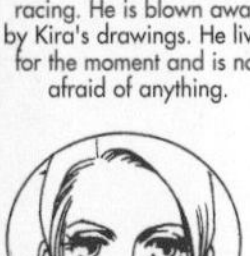

Harumi:
She's in love with Rei. She sees Kira as her enemy and bullies her mercilessly.

Our story up to now...

Kira is crushing hard on Rei after she saw him smooch a statue of Mars in her school's art studio. (How sweet!) After Rei saw Kira's amazing sketch of a mother and child, he can't get her off his mind. Rei is super excited when Kira promises to give him her painting of the mother and child when she's finished with it. In return, Rei promises to protect her from anything and everything. Then Kira asks Rei to model for her...and sparks fly.

Harumi, Rei's former fling, becomes insanely jealous of Kira. She pulls Kira into the gym and threatens to crush her fingers unless she agrees to give up on Rei. Kira refuses and realizes for the first time that she might truly be in love with him. Harumi is heartbroken when she realizes how much Kira and Rei actually like each other. In a jealous rage, she issues a warning to Kira: "For your own sake, I wouldn't get too serious about Rei...you might die sooner than you think." What could Harumi mean by that?!

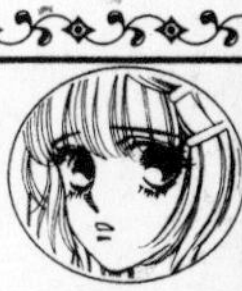

Kira Aso:
She's a shy student with an amazing talent for art. She asks Rei to model for her and begins to fall in love with him. She's always been timid, but Rei helps her find her hidden strength.

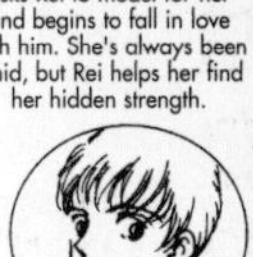

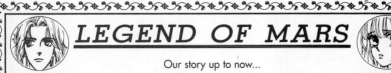

Tatsuya:
Rei's best friend. He used to have feelings for Kira, but how does he feel now?!

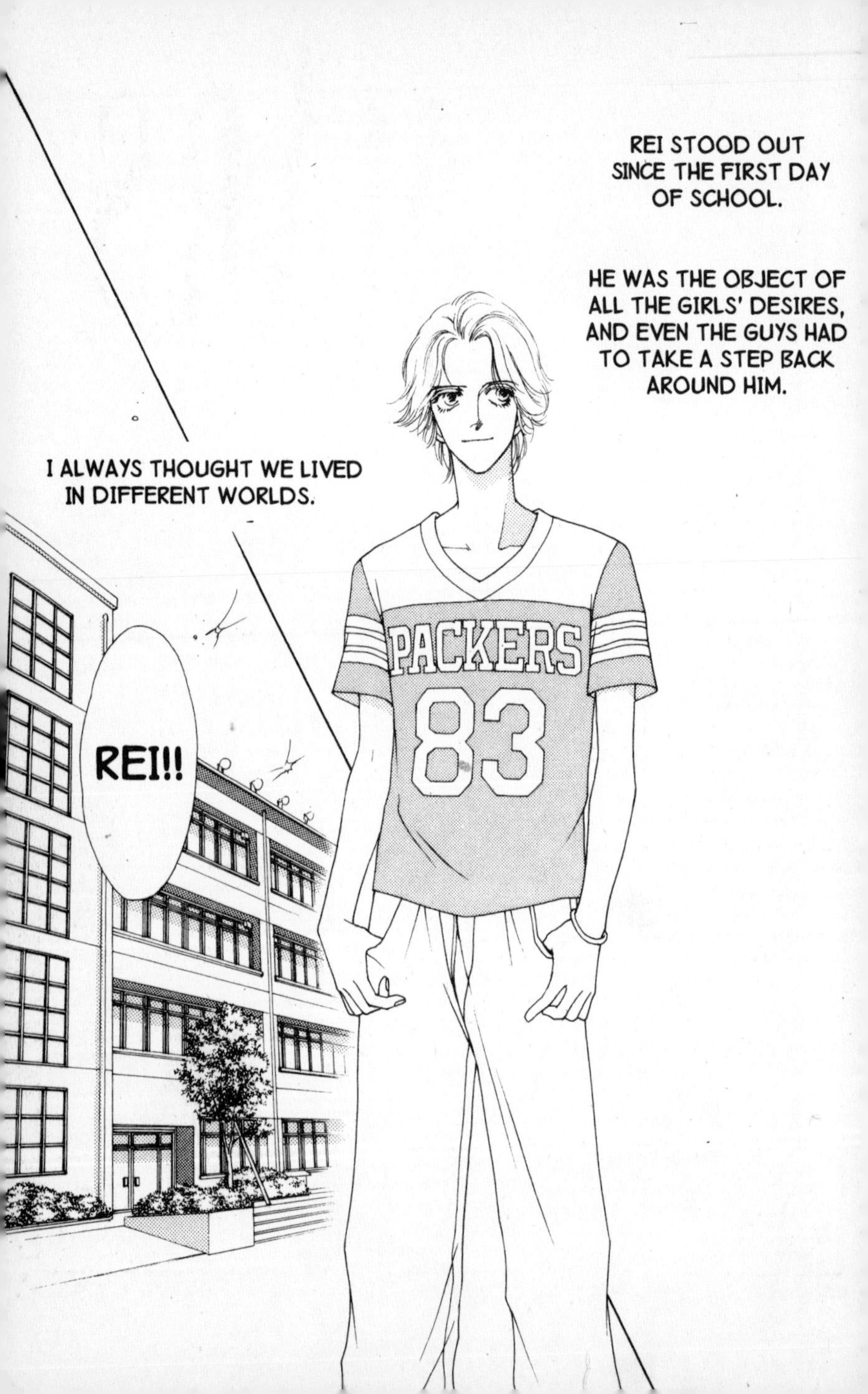
REI STOOD OUT SINCE THE FIRST DAY OF SCHOOL.
HE WAS THE OBJECT OF ALL THE GIRLS' DESIRES, AND EVEN THE GUYS HAD TO TAKE A STEP BACK AROUND HIM.
I ALWAYS THOUGHT WE LIVED IN DIFFERENT WORLDS.
REI!!
PACKERS
83

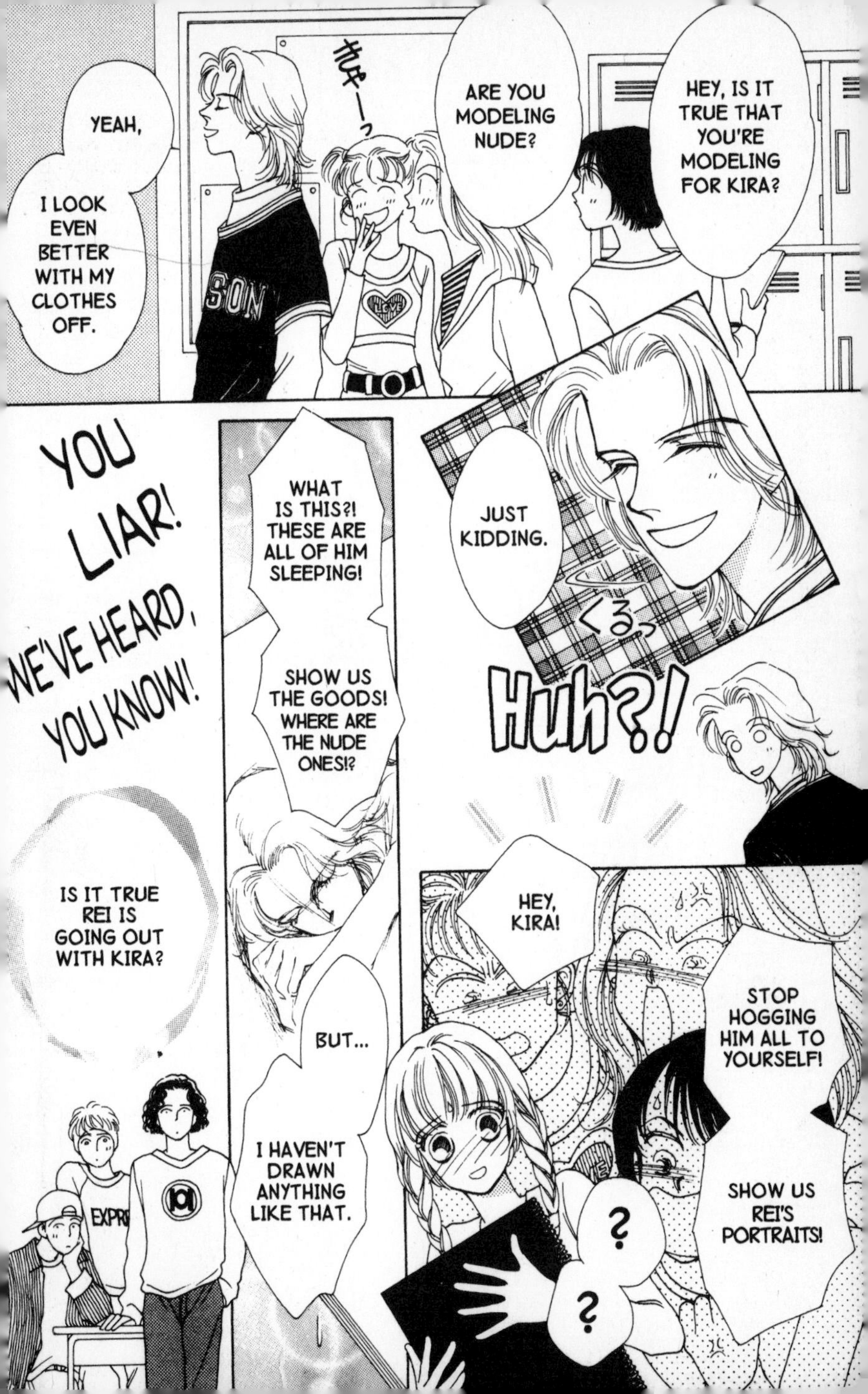
HEY, IS IT TRUE THAT YOU'RE MODELING FOR KIRA?
ARE YOU MODELING NUDE?
きゃーっ
YEAH,
I LOOK EVEN BETTER WITH MY CLOTHES OFF.
JUST KIDDING.
くるっ
Huh?!
HEY, KIRA!
STOP HOGGING HIM ALL TO YOURSELF!
SHOW US REI'S PORTRAITS!
?
?
WHAT IS THIS?! THESE ARE ALL OF HIM SLEEPING!
SHOW US THE GOODS! WHERE ARE THE NUDE ONES!?
BUT...
I HAVEN'T DRAWN ANYTHING LIKE THAT.
YOU LIAR!
WE'VE HEARD, YOU KNOW!
IS IT TRUE REI IS GOING OUT WITH KIRA?

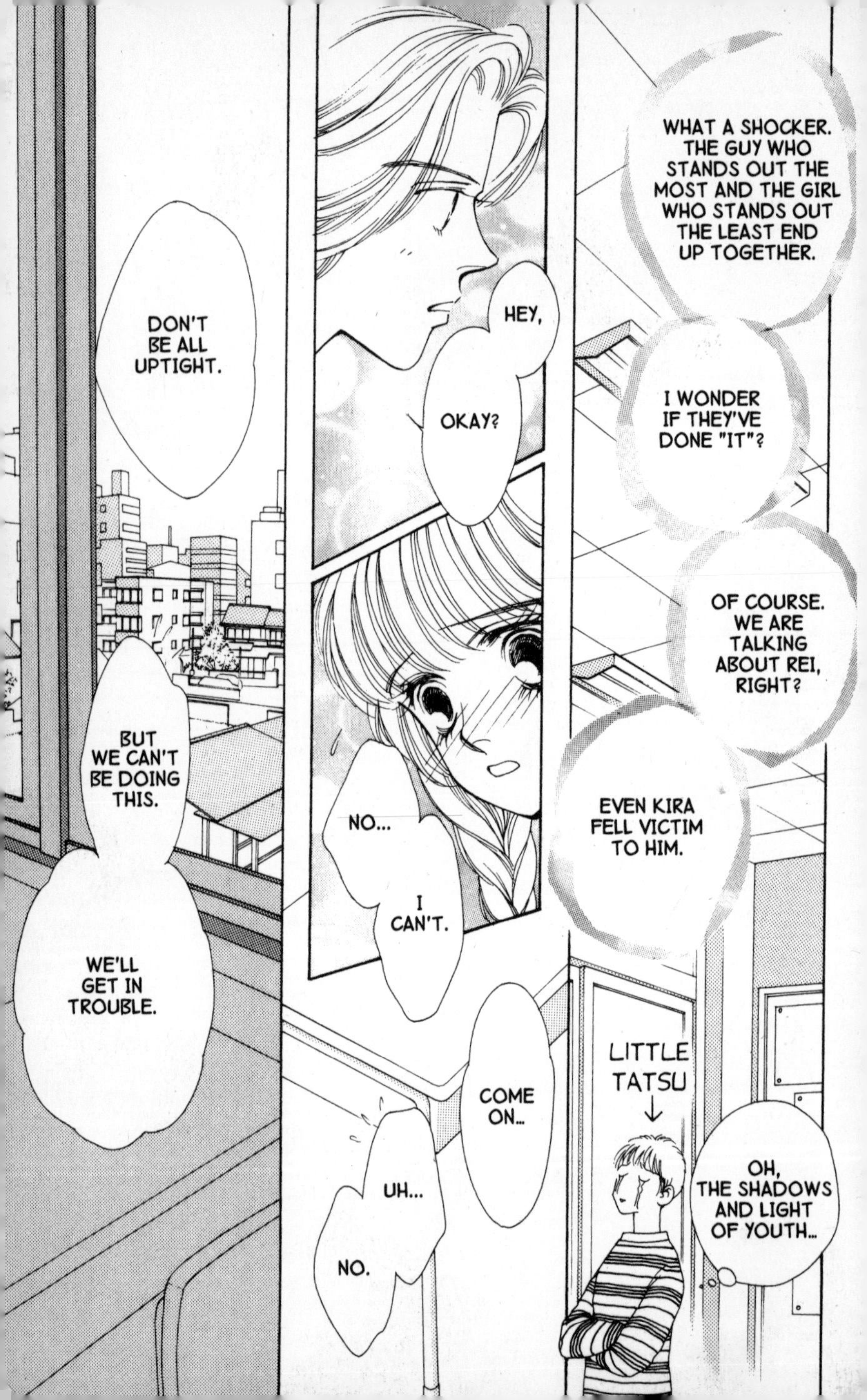
WHAT A SHOCKER. THE GUY WHO STANDS OUT THE MOST AND THE GIRL WHO STANDS OUT THE LEAST END UP TOGETHER.
I WONDER IF THEY'VE DONE "IT"?
OF COURSE. WE ARE TALKING ABOUT REI, RIGHT?
EVEN KIRA FELL VICTIM TO HIM.
LITTLE TATSU ↓
OH, THE SHADOWS AND LIGHT OF YOUTH...
HEY,
OKAY?
NO...
I CAN'T.
COME ON...
UH...
NO.
DON'T BE ALL UPTIGHT.
BUT WE CAN'T BE DOING THIS.
WE'LL GET IN TROUBLE.

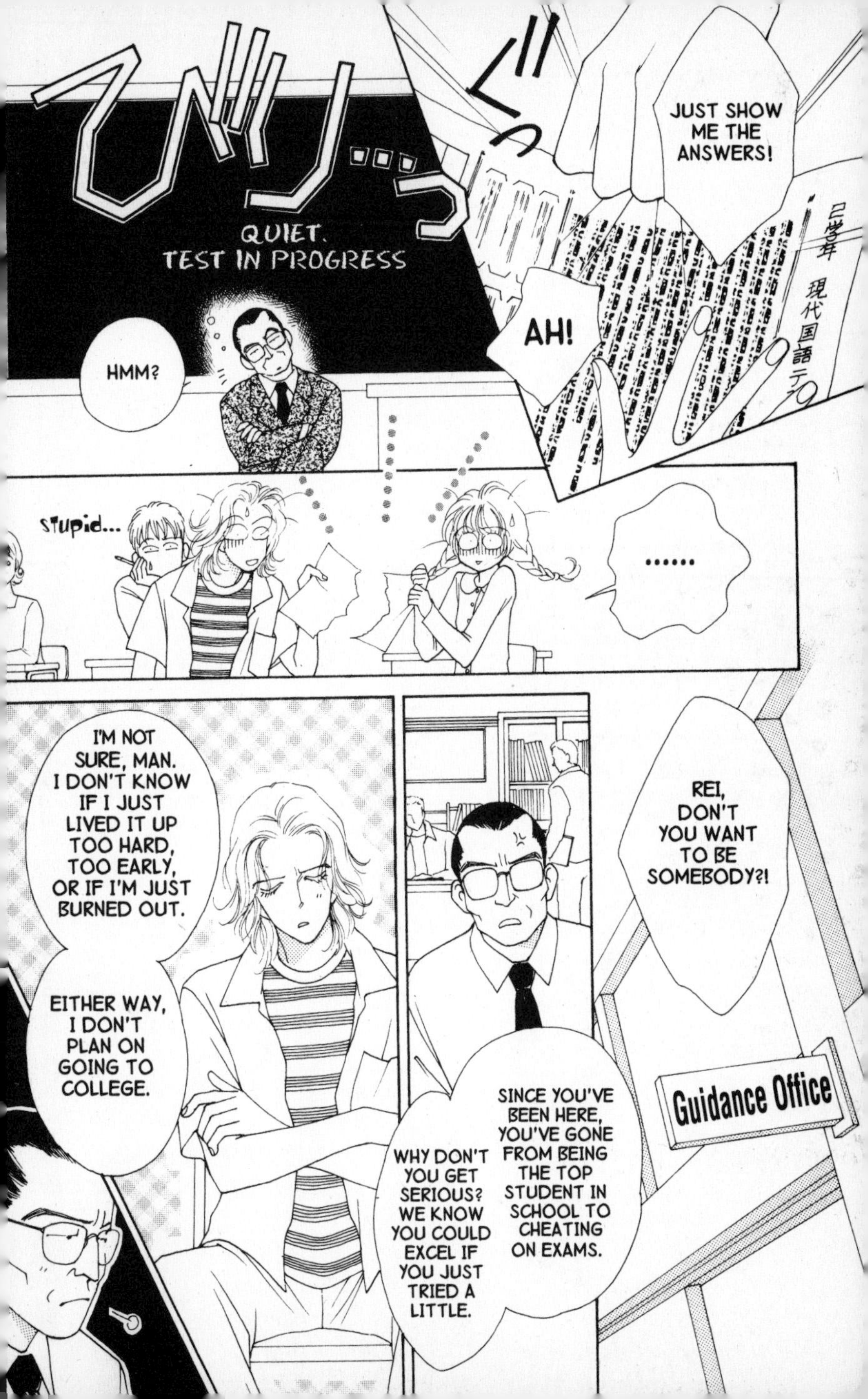
JUST SHOW ME THE ANSWERS!
AH!
2学年 現代国語テ
QUIET. TEST IN PROGRESS
HMM?
......
stupid...
REI, DON'T YOU WANT TO BE SOMEBODY?!
Guidance Office
SINCE YOU'VE BEEN HERE, YOU'VE GONE FROM BEING THE TOP STUDENT IN SCHOOL TO CHEATING ON EXAMS.
WHY DON'T YOU GET SERIOUS? WE KNOW YOU COULD EXCEL IF YOU JUST TRIED A LITTLE.
I'M NOT SURE, MAN. I DON'T KNOW IF I JUST LIVED IT UP TOO HARD, TOO EARLY, OR IF I'M JUST BURNED OUT.
EITHER WAY, I DON'T PLAN ON GOING TO COLLEGE.

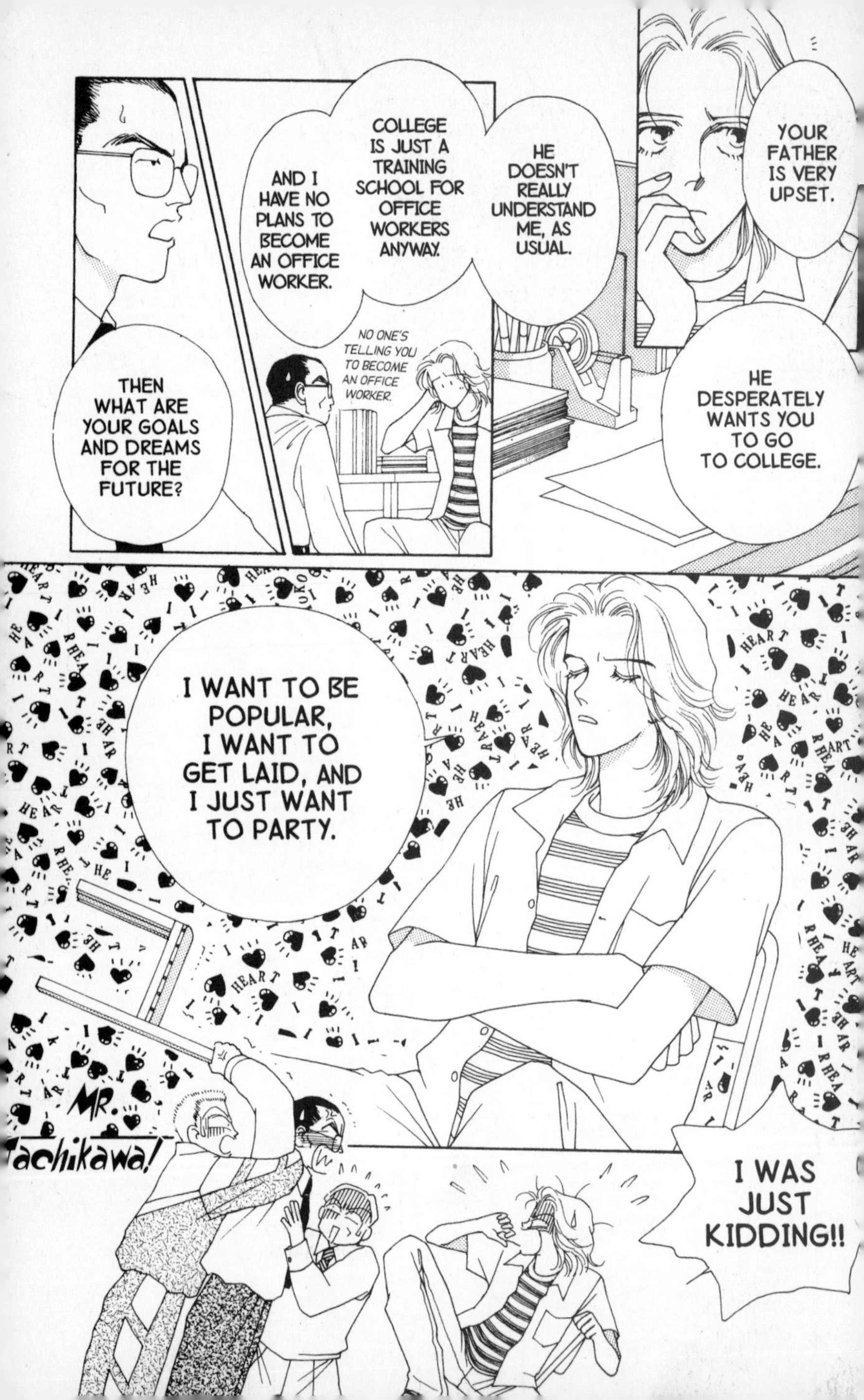
YOUR FATHER IS VERY UPSET.
HE DESPERATELY WANTS YOU TO GO TO COLLEGE.
HE DOESN'T REALLY UNDERSTAND ME, AS USUAL.
COLLEGE IS JUST A TRAINING SCHOOL FOR OFFICE WORKERS ANYWAY.
AND I HAVE NO PLANS TO BECOME AN OFFICE WORKER.
NO ONE'S TELLING YOU TO BECOME AN OFFICE WORKER.
THEN WHAT ARE YOUR GOALS AND DREAMS FOR THE FUTURE?
I WANT TO BE POPULAR, I WANT TO GET LAID, AND I JUST WANT TO PARTY.
I WAS JUST KIDDING!!
MR. Tachikawa!

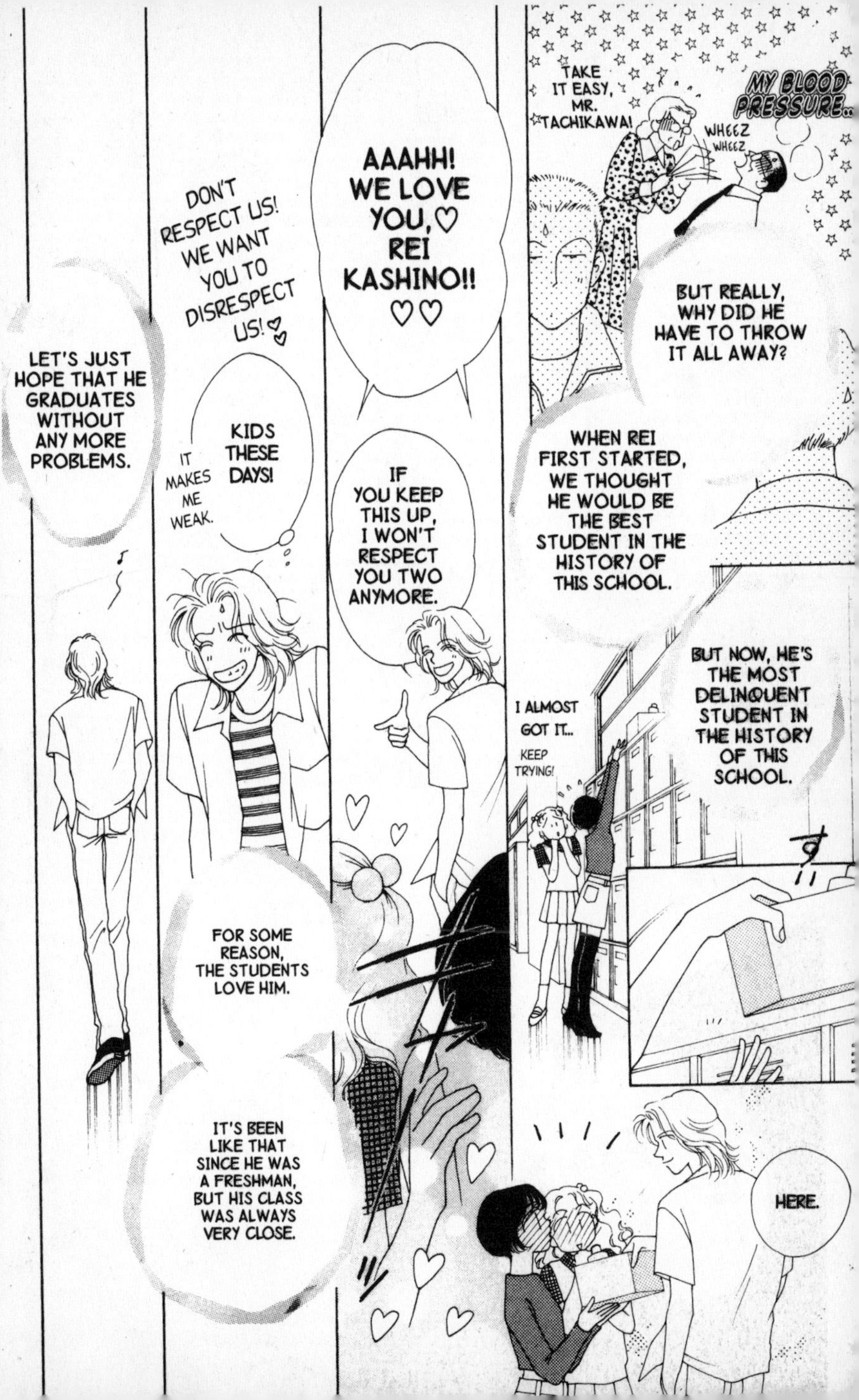
MY BLOOD PRESSURE..
WHEEZ WHEEZ
TAKE IT EASY, MR. TACHIKAWA!
BUT REALLY, WHY DID HE HAVE TO THROW IT ALL AWAY?
WHEN REI FIRST STARTED, WE THOUGHT HE WOULD BE THE BEST STUDENT IN THE HISTORY OF THIS SCHOOL.
BUT NOW, HE'S THE MOST DELINQUENT STUDENT IN THE HISTORY OF THIS SCHOOL.
I ALMOST GOT IT..
KEEP TRYING!
HERE.
AAAHH! WE LOVE YOU, ♡ REI KASHINO!! ♡♡
IF YOU KEEP THIS UP, I WON'T RESPECT YOU TWO ANYMORE.
DON'T RESPECT US! WE WANT YOU TO DISRESPECT US! ♡
KIDS THESE DAYS!
IT MAKES ME WEAK.
FOR SOME REASON, THE STUDENTS LOVE HIM.
IT'S BEEN LIKE THAT SINCE HE WAS A FRESHMAN, BUT HIS CLASS WAS ALWAYS VERY CLOSE.
LET'S JUST HOPE THAT HE GRADUATES WITHOUT ANY MORE PROBLEMS.

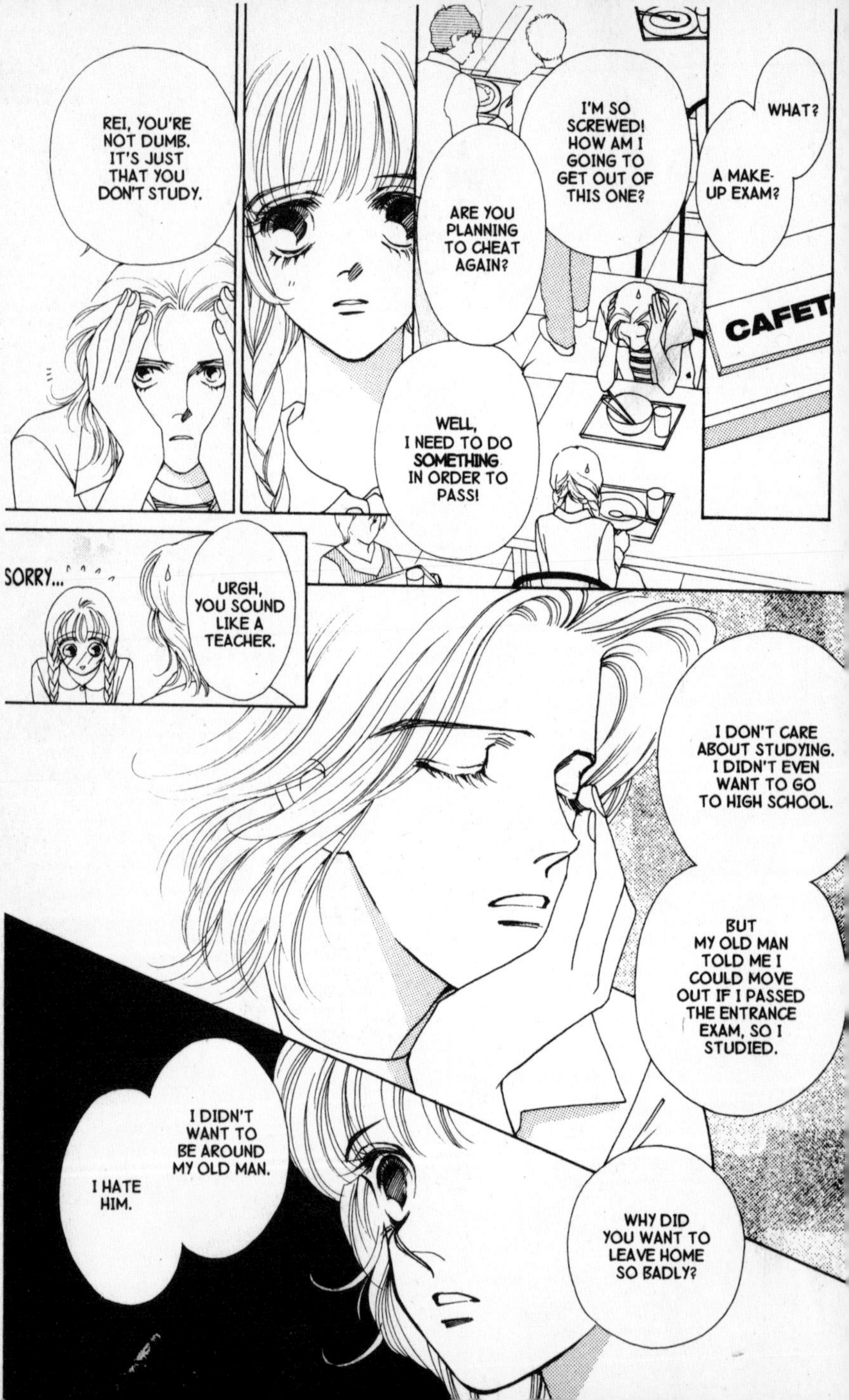
WHAT?
A MAKE-UP EXAM?
CAFET
I'M SO SCREWED! HOW AM I GOING TO GET OUT OF THIS ONE?
ARE YOU PLANNING TO CHEAT AGAIN?
WELL, I NEED TO DO SOMETHING IN ORDER TO PASS!
REI, YOU'RE NOT DUMB. IT'S JUST THAT YOU DON'T STUDY.
URGH, YOU SOUND LIKE A TEACHER.
SORRY...
I DON'T CARE ABOUT STUDYING. I DIDN'T EVEN WANT TO GO TO HIGH SCHOOL.
BUT MY OLD MAN TOLD ME I COULD MOVE OUT IF I PASSED THE ENTRANCE EXAM, SO I STUDIED.
WHY DID YOU WANT TO LEAVE HOME SO BADLY?
I DIDN'T WANT TO BE AROUND MY OLD MAN.
I HATE HIM.

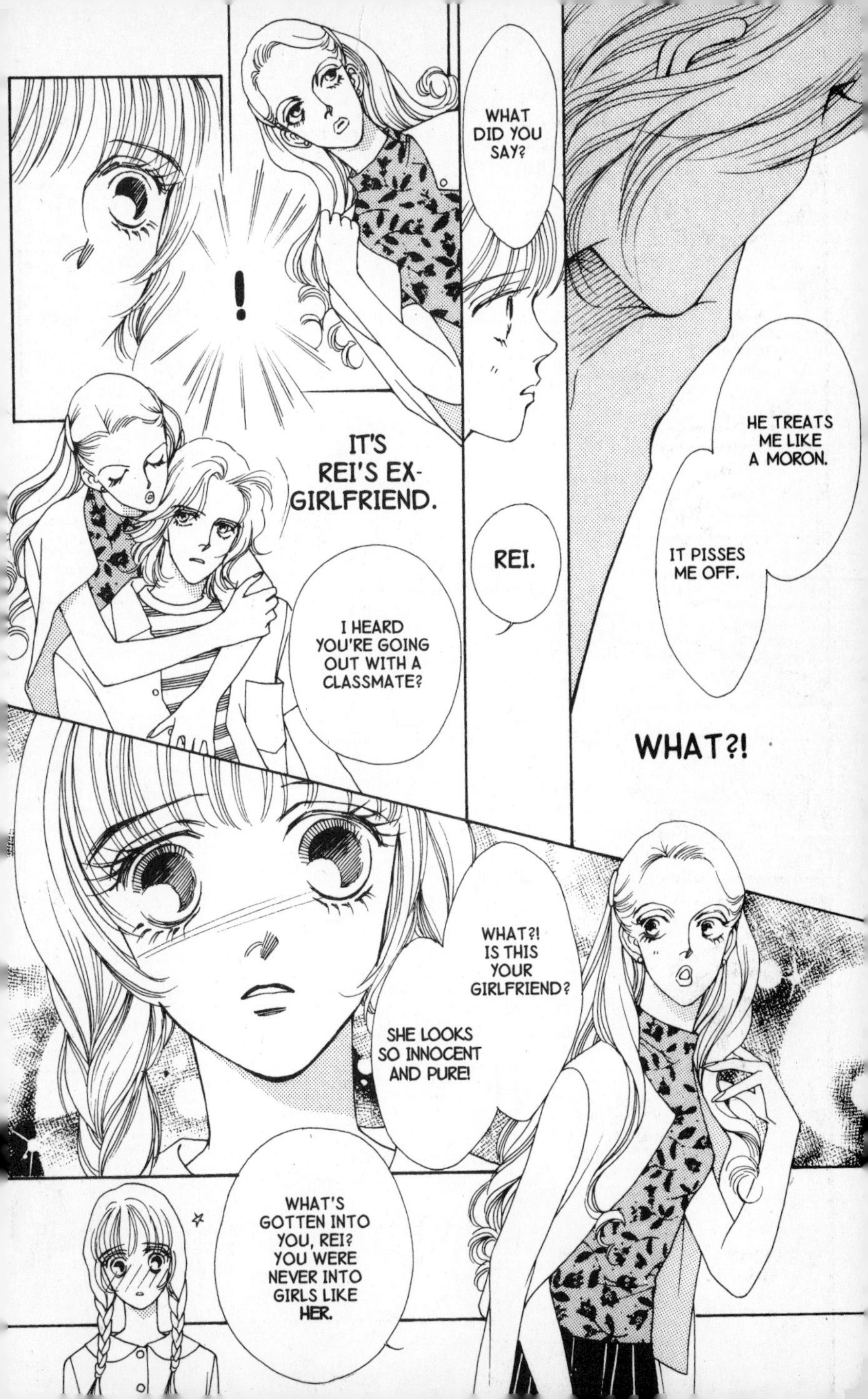

HE TREATS ME LIKE A MORON.
IT PISSES ME OFF.
WHAT?!
WHAT DID YOU SAY?
REI.
!
IT'S REI'S EX-GIRLFRIEND.
I HEARD YOU'RE GOING OUT WITH A CLASSMATE?
WHAT?! IS THIS YOUR GIRLFRIEND?
SHE LOOKS SO INNOCENT AND PURE!
WHAT'S GOTTEN INTO YOU, REI? YOU WERE NEVER INTO GIRLS LIKE HER.

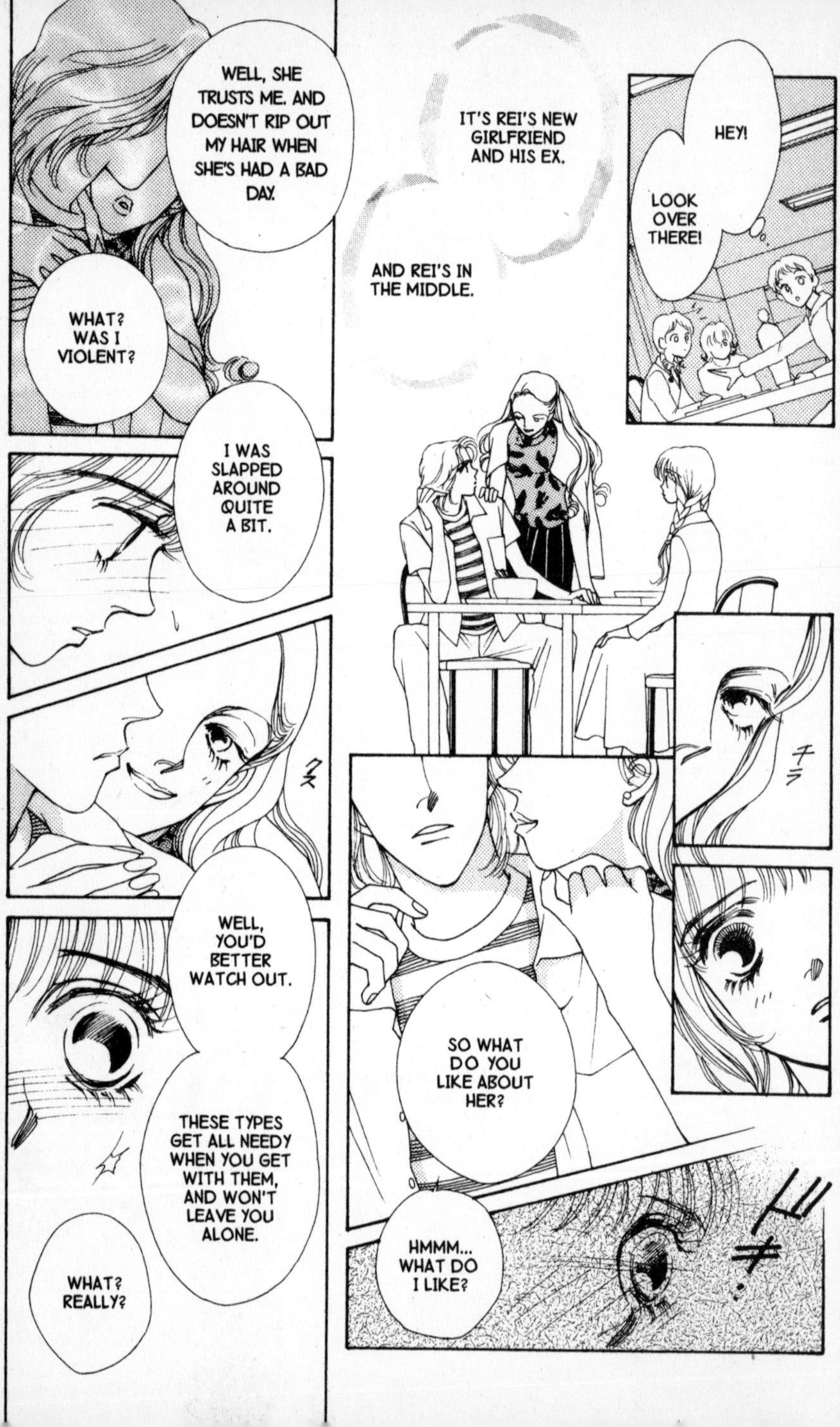
HEY!
LOOK OVER THERE!
IT'S REI'S NEW GIRLFRIEND AND HIS EX.
AND REI'S IN THE MIDDLE.
チラ
SO WHAT DO YOU LIKE ABOUT HER?
HMMM... WHAT DO I LIKE?
WELL, SHE TRUSTS ME. AND DOESN'T RIP OUT MY HAIR WHEN SHE'S HAD A BAD DAY.
WHAT? WAS I VIOLENT?
I WAS SLAPPED AROUND QUITE A BIT.
クス
WELL, YOU'D BETTER WATCH OUT.
THESE TYPES GET ALL NEEDY WHEN YOU GET WITH THEM, AND WON'T LEAVE YOU ALONE.
WHAT? REALLY?

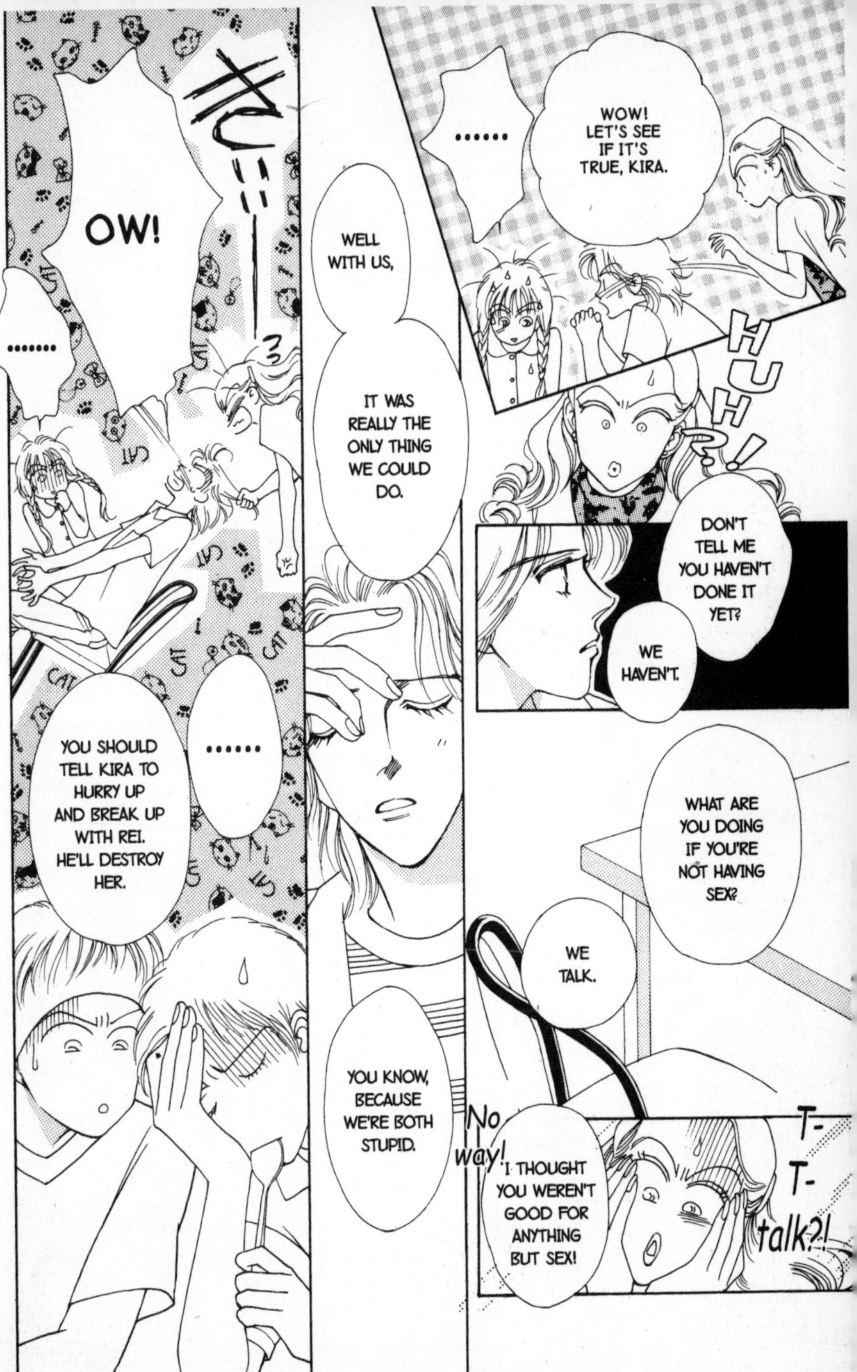
WOW! LET'S SEE IF IT'S TRUE, KIRA.
......
HUH?!
DON'T TELL ME YOU HAVEN'T DONE IT YET?
WE HAVEN'T.
WHAT ARE YOU DOING IF YOU'RE NOT HAVING SEX?
WE TALK.
T-T-talk?!
No way!
I THOUGHT YOU WEREN'T GOOD FOR ANYTHING BUT SEX!
WELL WITH US,
IT WAS REALLY THE ONLY THING WE COULD DO.
YOU KNOW, BECAUSE WE'RE BOTH STUPID.
OW!
......
......
YOU SHOULD TELL KIRA TO HURRY UP AND BREAK UP WITH REI. HE'LL DESTROY HER.

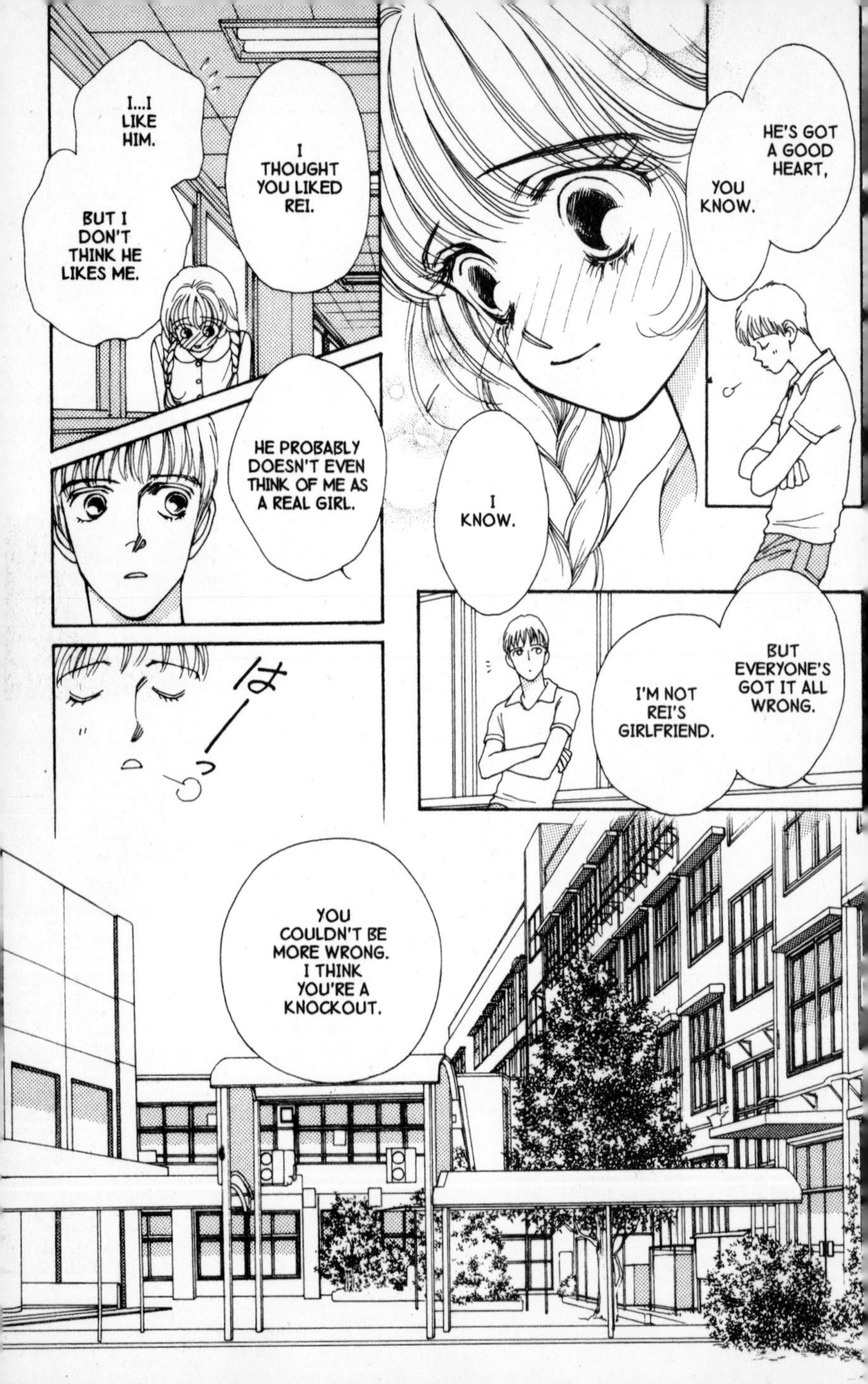
HE'S GOT A GOOD HEART, YOU KNOW.
I KNOW.
BUT EVERYONE'S GOT IT ALL WRONG.
I'M NOT REI'S GIRLFRIEND.
I THOUGHT YOU LIKED REI.
I...I LIKE HIM.
BUT I DON'T THINK HE LIKES ME.
HE PROBABLY DOESN'T EVEN THINK OF ME AS A REAL GIRL.
は一っ
YOU COULDN'T BE MORE WRONG. I THINK YOU'RE A KNOCKOUT.

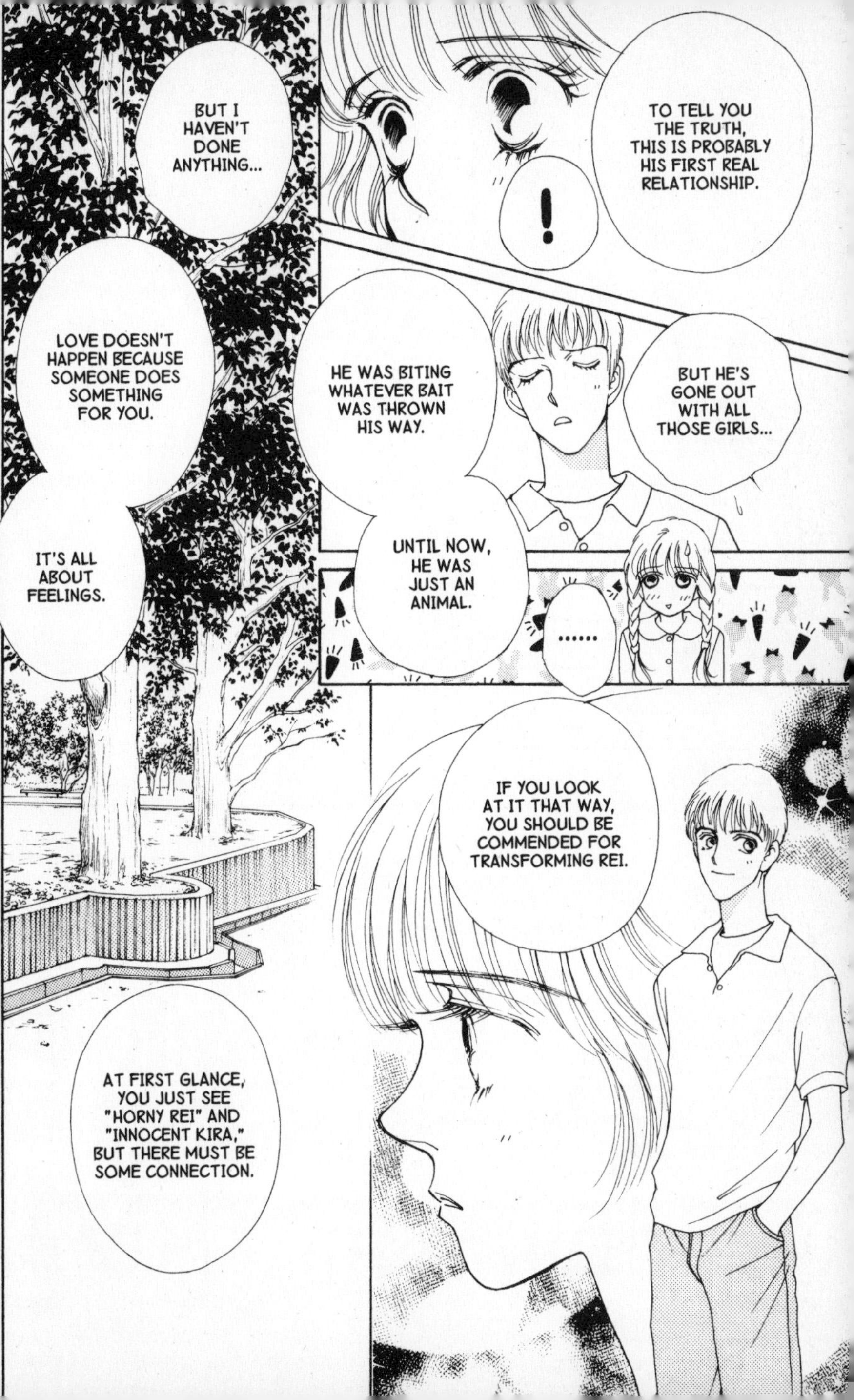
TO TELL YOU THE TRUTH, THIS IS PROBABLY HIS FIRST REAL RELATIONSHIP.
!
BUT HE'S GONE OUT WITH ALL THOSE GIRLS...
HE WAS BITING WHATEVER BAIT WAS THROWN HIS WAY.
UNTIL NOW, HE WAS JUST AN ANIMAL.
......
IF YOU LOOK AT IT THAT WAY, YOU SHOULD BE COMMENDED FOR TRANSFORMING REI.
BUT I HAVEN'T DONE ANYTHING...
LOVE DOESN'T HAPPEN BECAUSE SOMEONE DOES SOMETHING FOR YOU.
IT'S ALL ABOUT FEELINGS.
AT FIRST GLANCE, YOU JUST SEE "HORNY REI" AND "INNOCENT KIRA," BUT THERE MUST BE SOME CONNECTION.

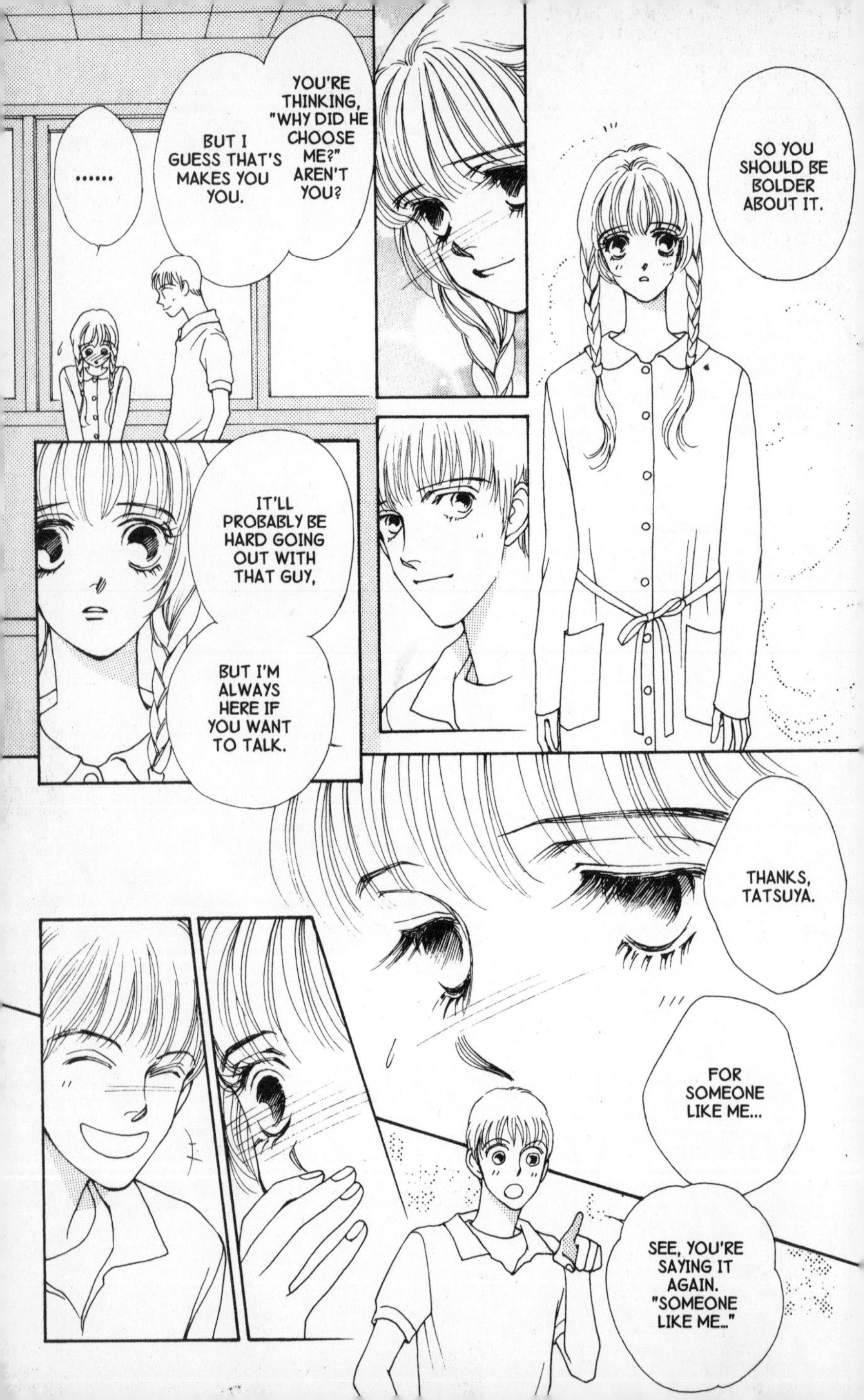
SO YOU SHOULD BE BOLDER ABOUT IT.
YOU'RE THINKING, "WHY DID HE CHOOSE ME?" AREN'T YOU?
BUT I GUESS THAT'S MAKES YOU YOU.
......
IT'LL PROBABLY BE HARD GOING OUT WITH THAT GUY,
BUT I'M ALWAYS HERE IF YOU WANT TO TALK.
THANKS, TATSUYA.
FOR SOMEONE LIKE ME...
SEE, YOU'RE SAYING IT AGAIN. "SOMEONE LIKE ME..."

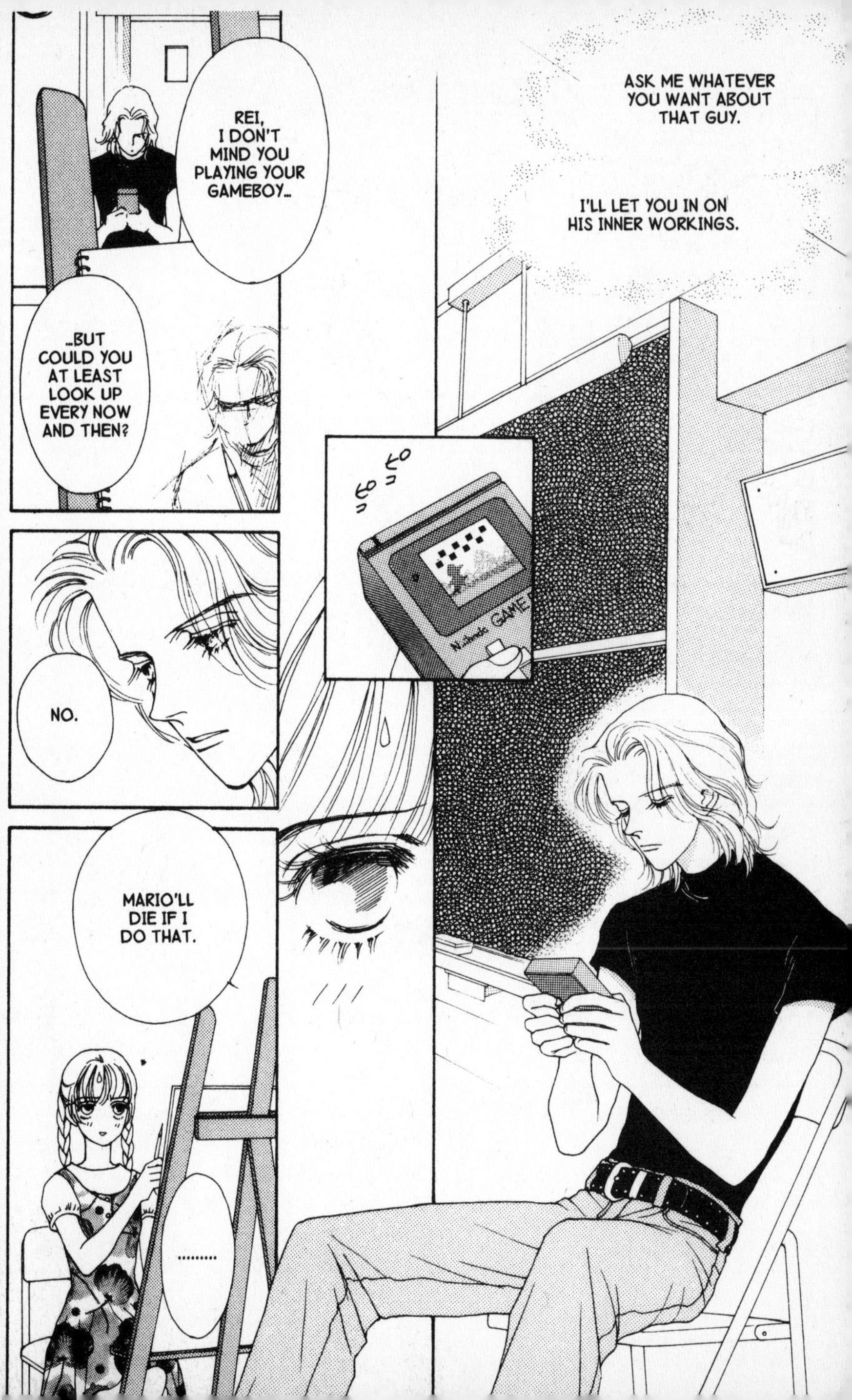
ASK ME WHATEVER YOU WANT ABOUT THAT GUY.
I'LL LET YOU IN ON HIS INNER WORKINGS.
REI, I DON'T MIND YOU PLAYING YOUR GAMEBOY...
...BUT COULD YOU AT LEAST LOOK UP EVERY NOW AND THEN?
NO.
MARIO'LL DIE IF I DO THAT.
....

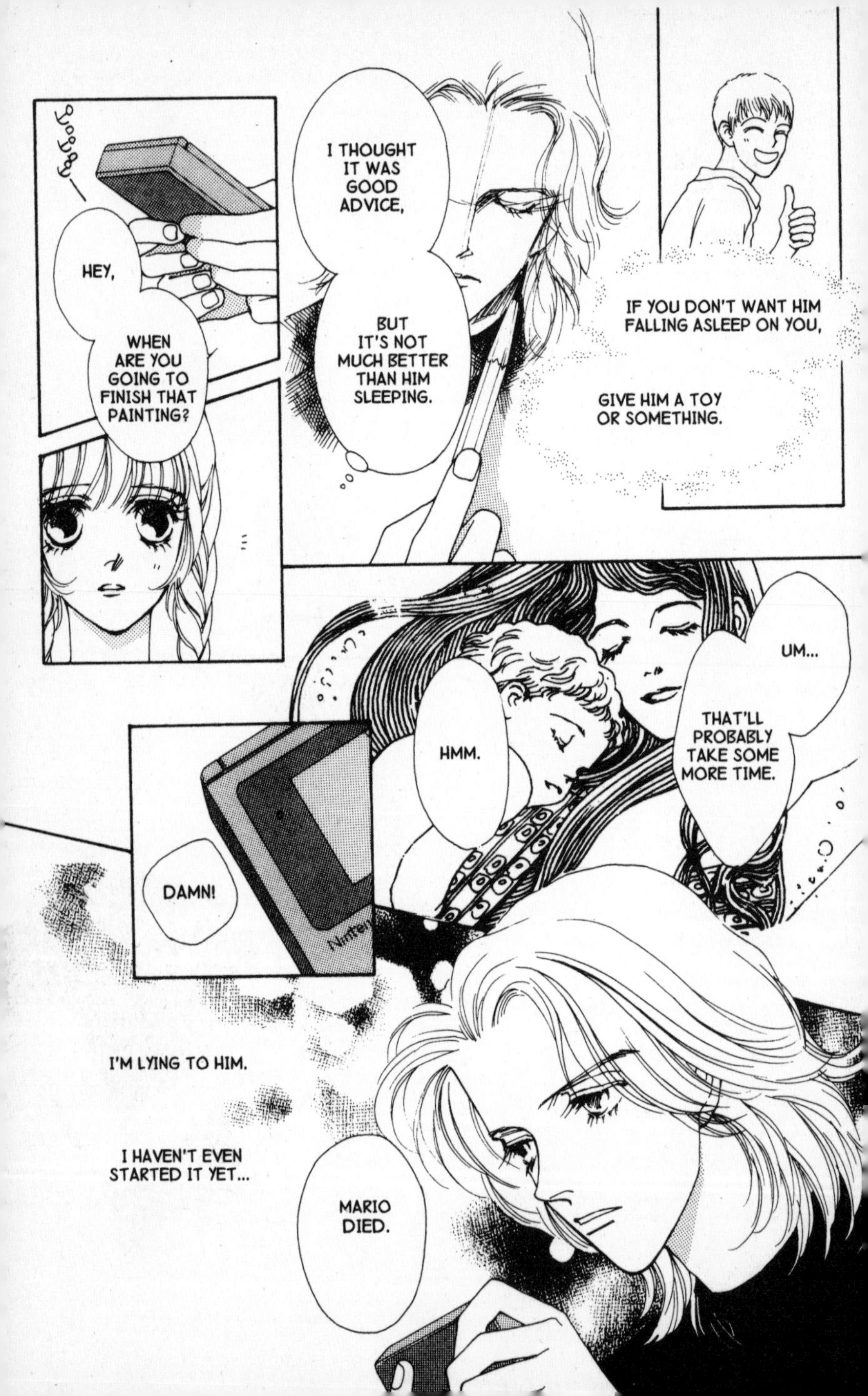
IF YOU DON'T WANT HIM FALLING ASLEEP ON YOU,
GIVE HIM A TOY OR SOMETHING.
I THOUGHT IT WAS GOOD ADVICE,
BUT IT'S NOT MUCH BETTER THAN HIM SLEEPING.
HEY,
WHEN ARE YOU GOING TO FINISH THAT PAINTING?
UM...
THAT'LL PROBABLY TAKE SOME MORE TIME.
HMM.
DAMN!
MARIO DIED.
I'M LYING TO HIM.
I HAVEN'T EVEN STARTED IT YET...

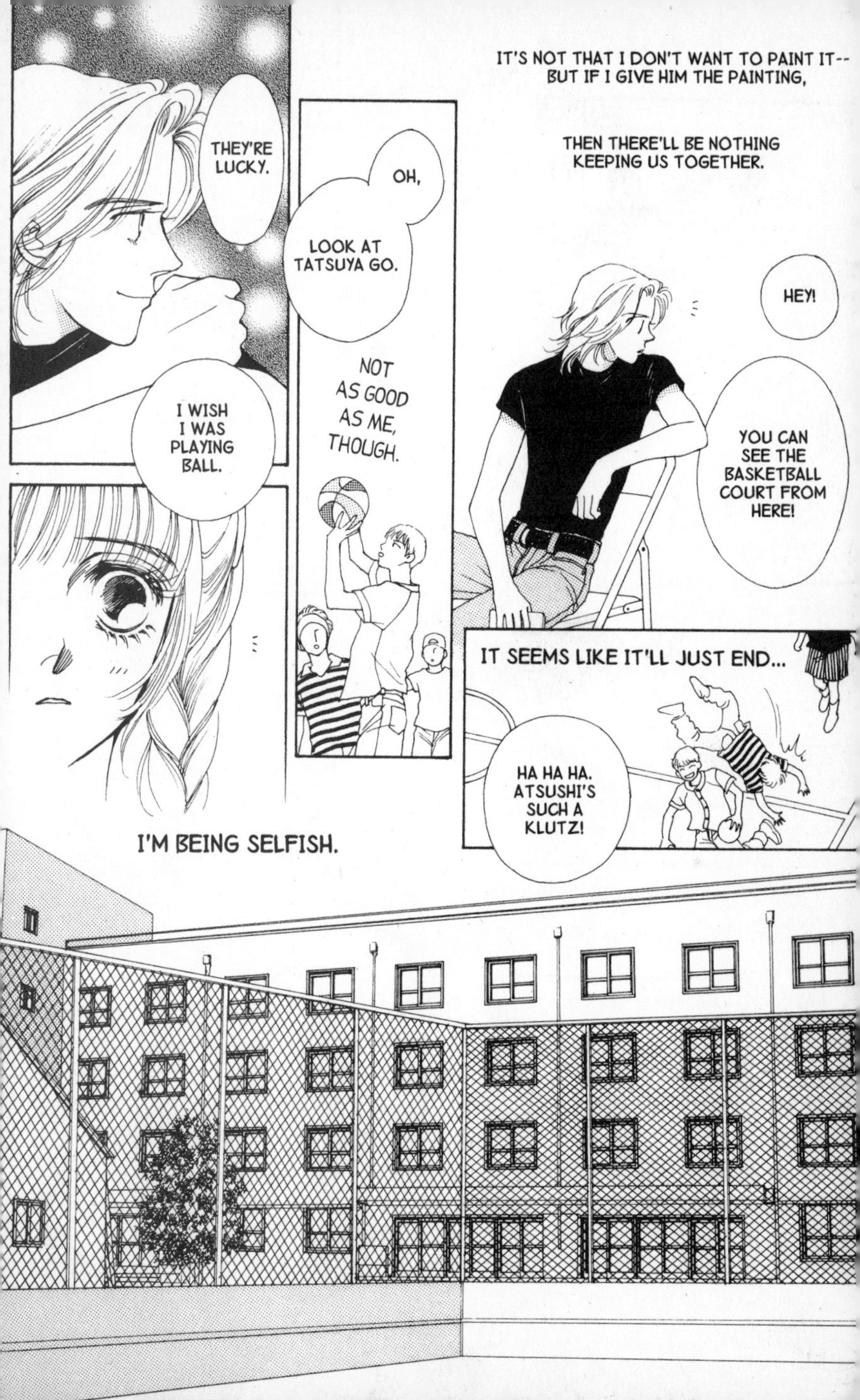
IT'S NOT THAT I DON'T WANT TO PAINT IT-- BUT IF I GIVE HIM THE PAINTING,
THEN THERE'LL BE NOTHING KEEPING US TOGETHER.
HEY!
YOU CAN SEE THE BASKETBALL COURT FROM HERE!
IT SEEMS LIKE IT'LL JUST END...
HA HA HA. ATSUSHI'S SUCH A KLUTZ!
OH,
LOOK AT TATSUYA GO.
NOT AS GOOD AS ME, THOUGH.
THEY'RE LUCKY.
I WISH I WAS PLAYING BALL.
I'M BEING SELFISH.

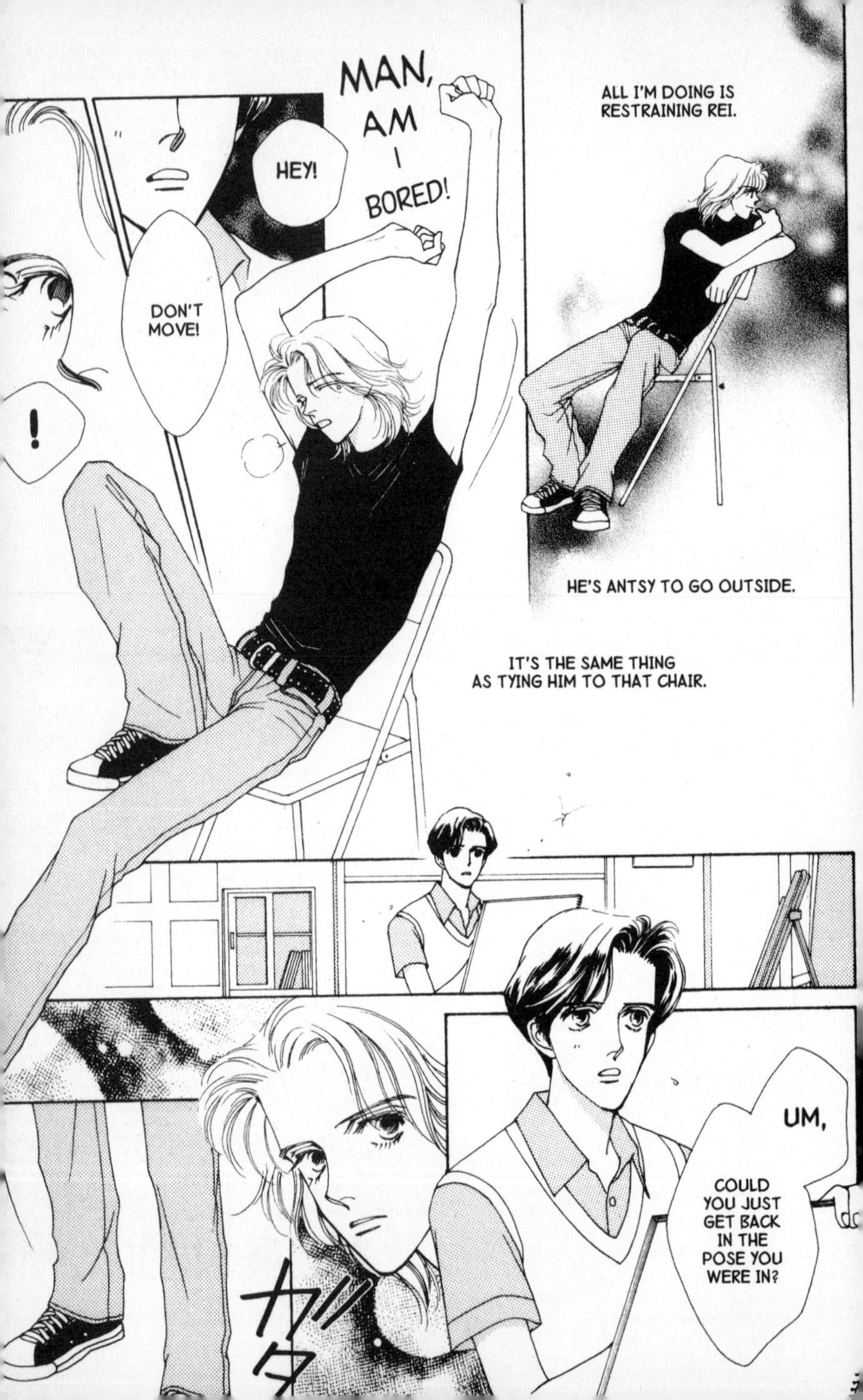
ALL I'M DOING IS RESTRAINING REI.
HE'S ANTSY TO GO OUTSIDE.
MAN, AM I BORED!
HEY!
DON'T MOVE!
!
IT'S THE SAME THING AS TYING HIM TO THAT CHAIR.
UM,
COULD YOU JUST GET BACK IN THE POSE YOU WERE IN?
ガタ

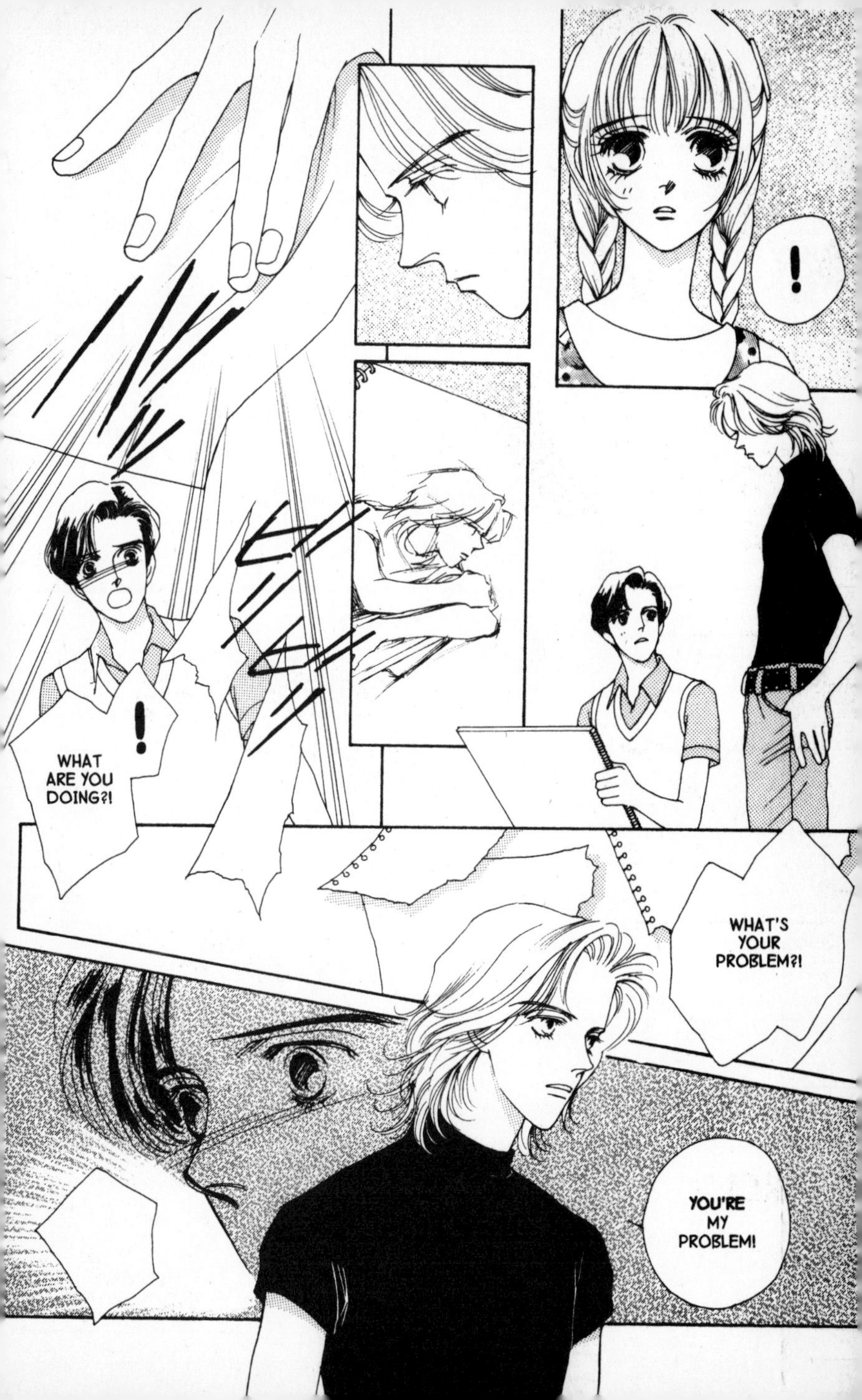
!
!
WHAT ARE YOU DOING?!
WHAT'S YOUR PROBLEM?!
YOU'RE MY PROBLEM!

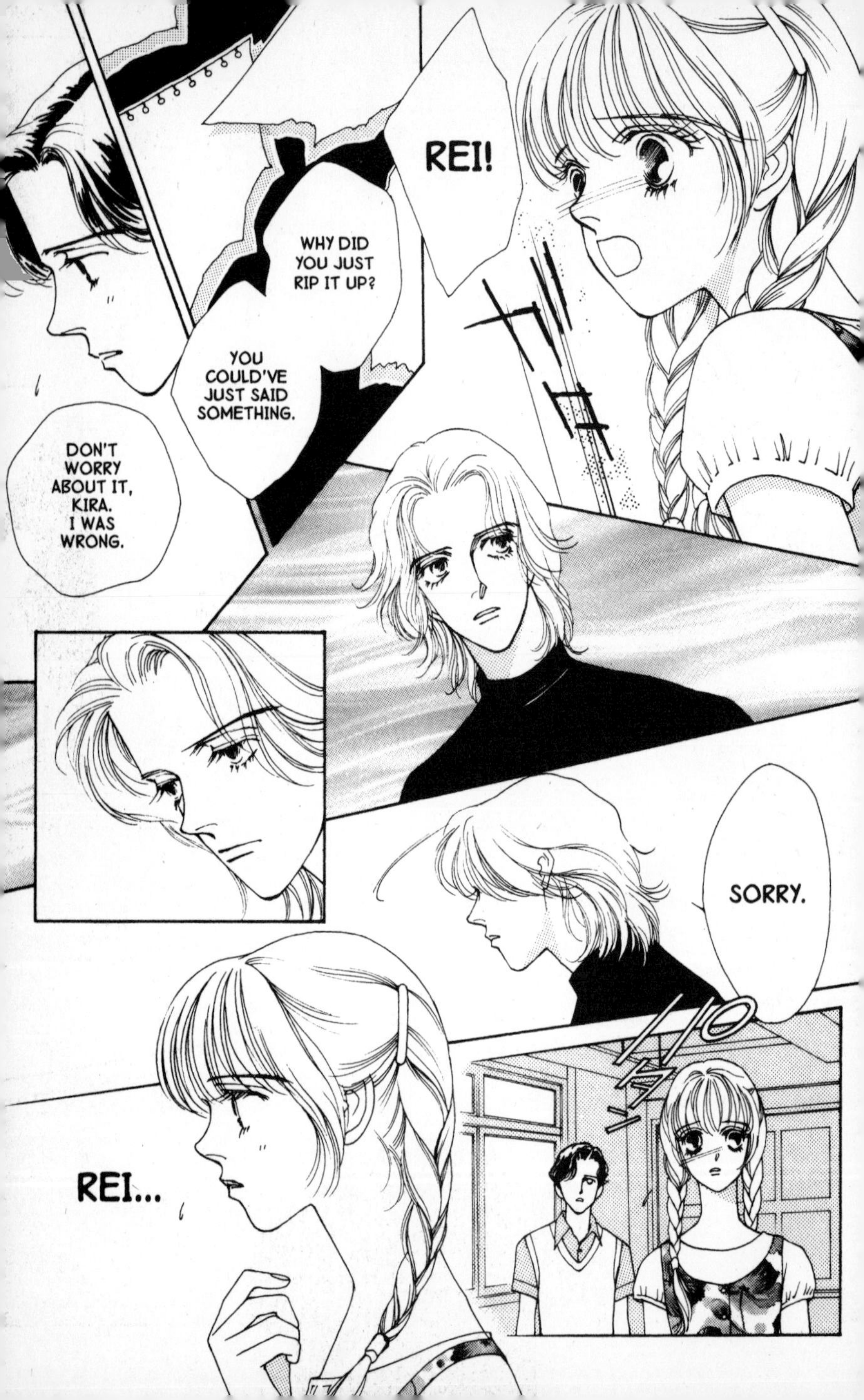
REI!
WHY DID YOU JUST RIP IT UP?
YOU COULD'VE JUST SAID SOMETHING.
DON'T WORRY ABOUT IT, KIRA. I WAS WRONG.
SORRY.
REI...

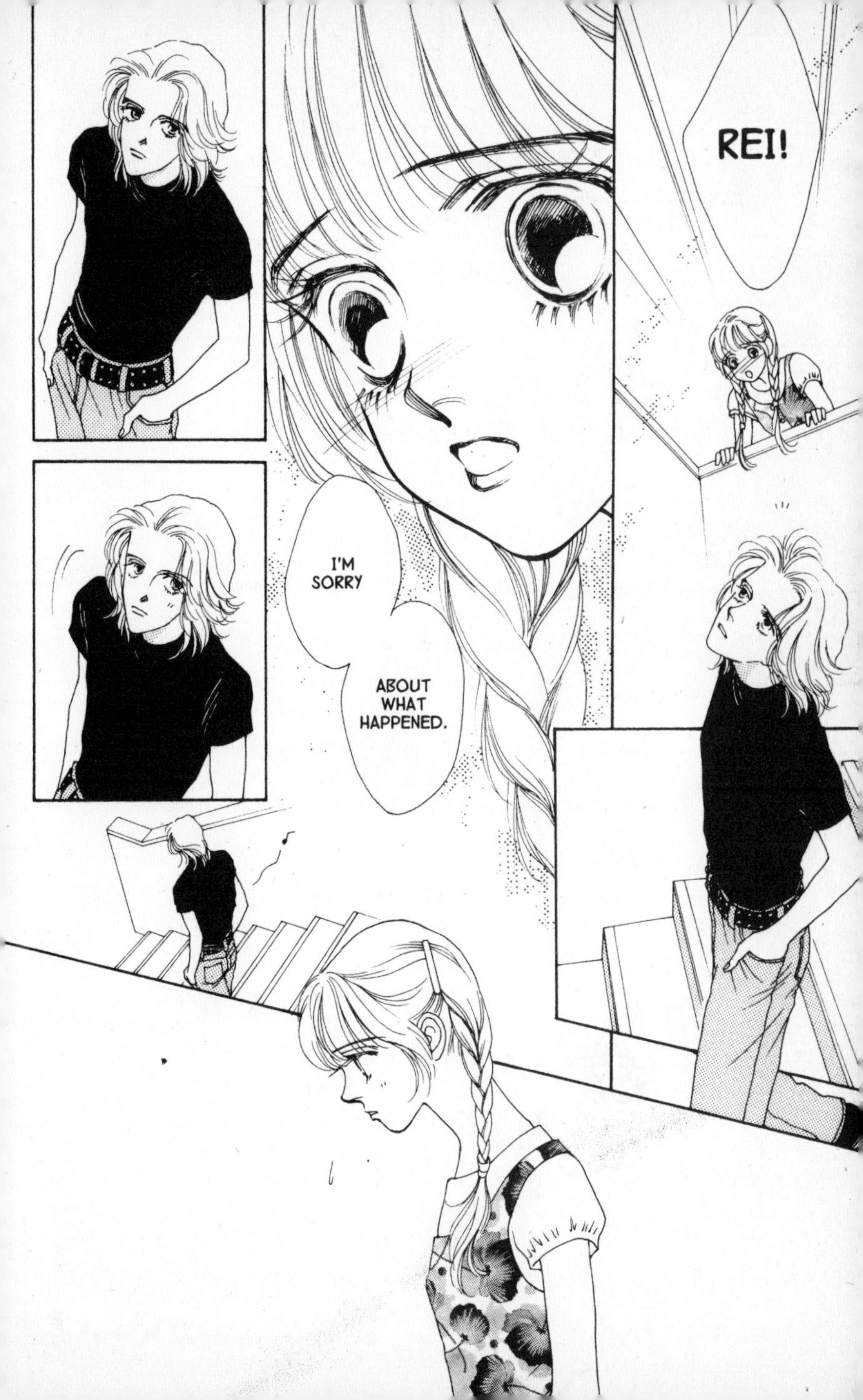
REI!
I'M SORRY
ABOUT WHAT HAPPENED.

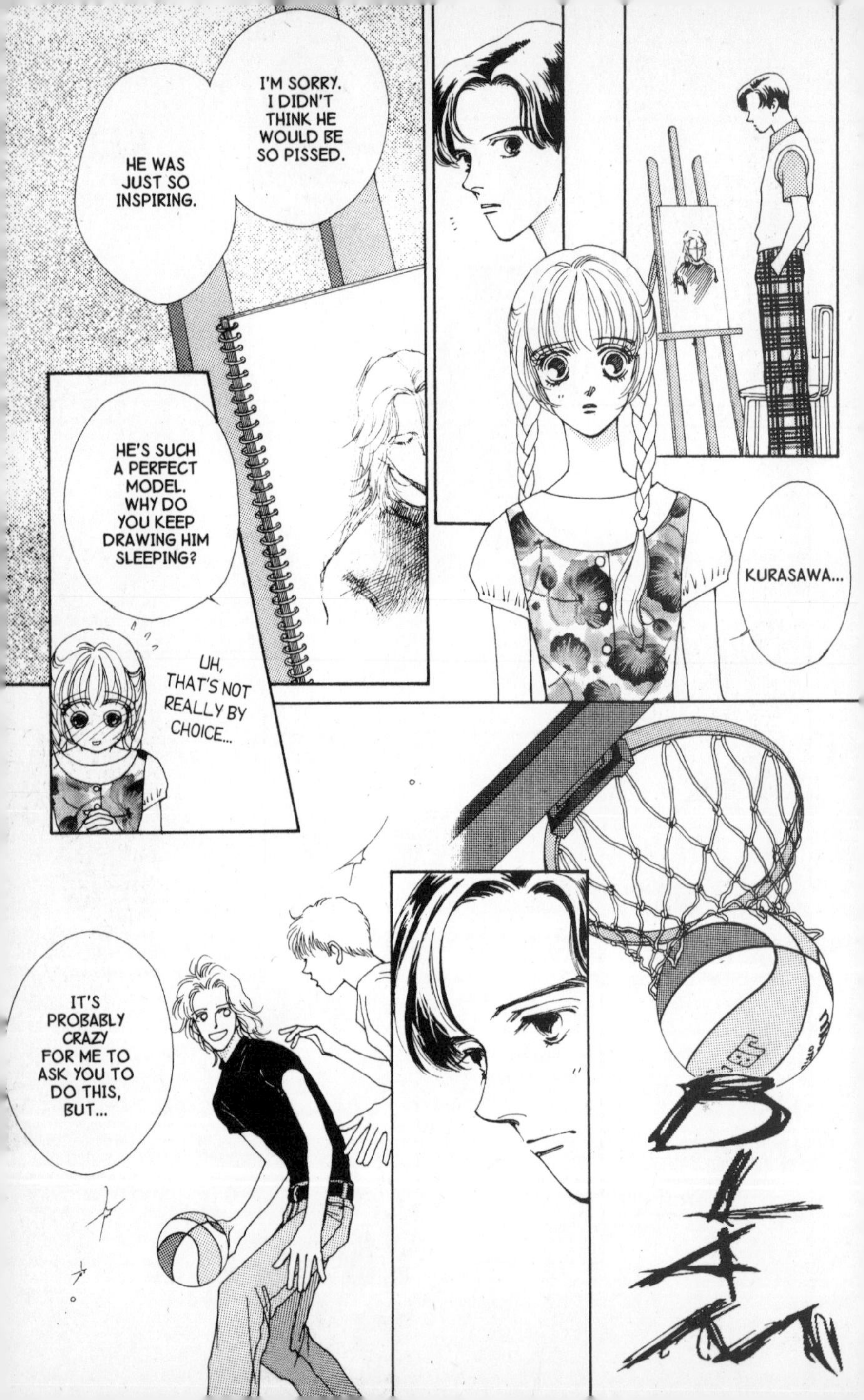
KURASAWA...
I'M SORRY. I DIDN'T THINK HE WOULD BE SO PISSED.
HE WAS JUST SO INSPIRING.
HE'S SUCH A PERFECT MODEL. WHY DO YOU KEEP DRAWING HIM SLEEPING?
UH, THAT'S NOT REALLY BY CHOICE...
IT'S PROBABLY CRAZY FOR ME TO ASK YOU TO DO THIS, BUT...

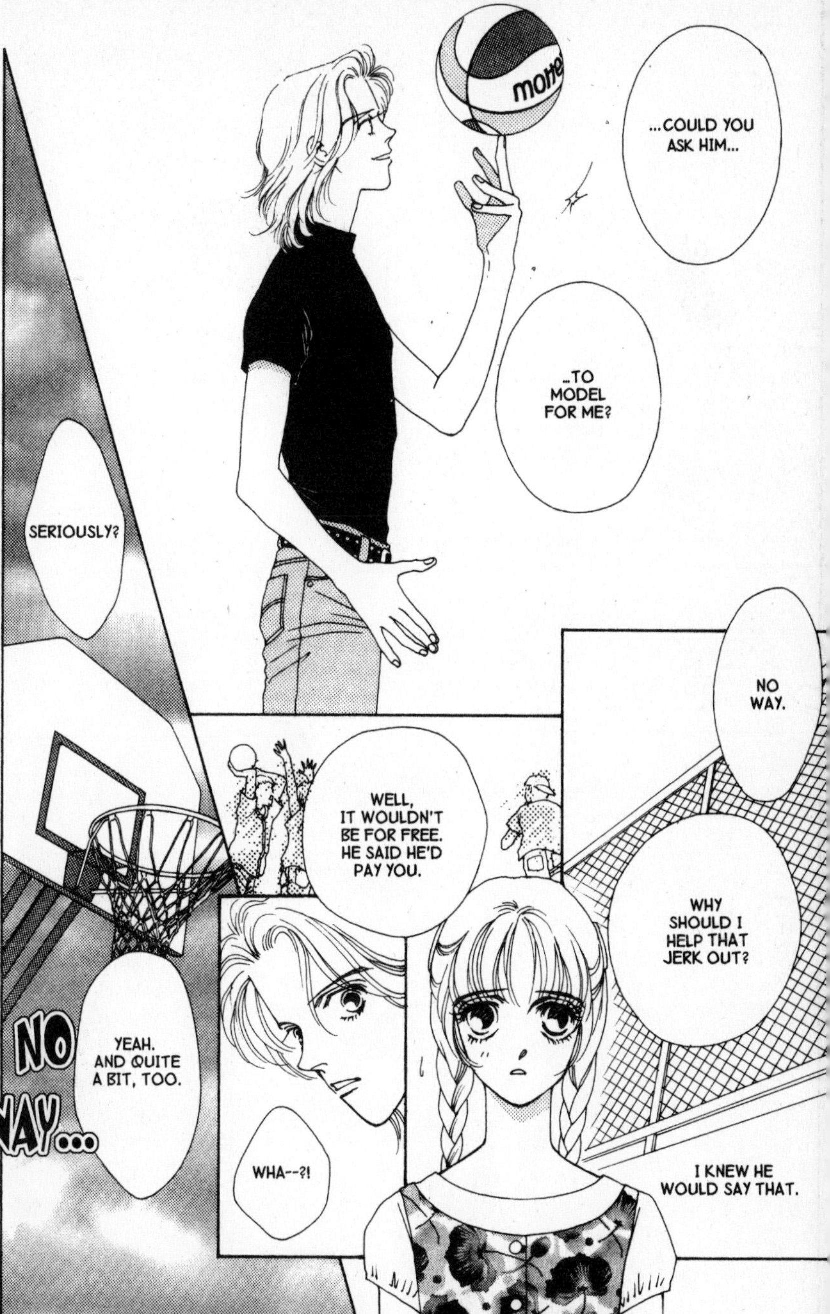
...COULD YOU ASK HIM...
...TO MODEL FOR ME?
SERIOUSLY?
NO WAY.
WHY SHOULD I HELP THAT JERK OUT?
I KNEW HE WOULD SAY THAT.
WELL, IT WOULDN'T BE FOR FREE. HE SAID HE'D PAY YOU.
WHA--?!
YEAH. AND QUITE A BIT, TOO.
NO WAY...

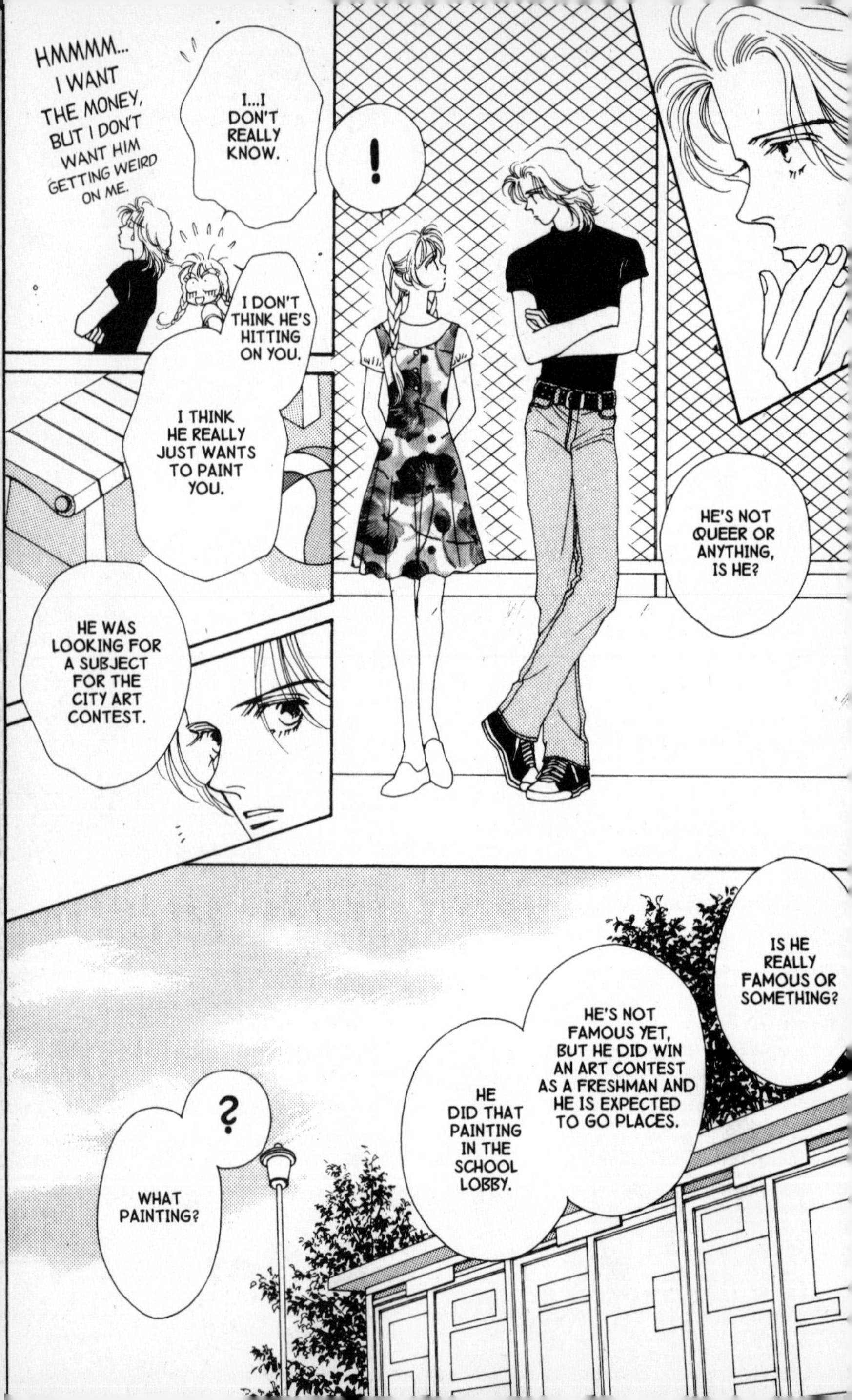
HE'S NOT QUEER OR ANYTHING, IS HE?
!
I...I DON'T REALLY KNOW.
HMMMM... I WANT THE MONEY, BUT I DON'T WANT HIM GETTING WEIRD ON ME.
I DON'T THINK HE'S HITTING ON YOU.
I THINK HE REALLY JUST WANTS TO PAINT YOU.
HE WAS LOOKING FOR A SUBJECT FOR THE CITY ART CONTEST.
IS HE REALLY FAMOUS OR SOMETHING?
HE'S NOT FAMOUS YET, BUT HE DID WIN AN ART CONTEST AS A FRESHMAN AND HE IS EXPECTED TO GO PLACES.
HE DID THAT PAINTING IN THE SCHOOL LOBBY.
?
WHAT PAINTING?

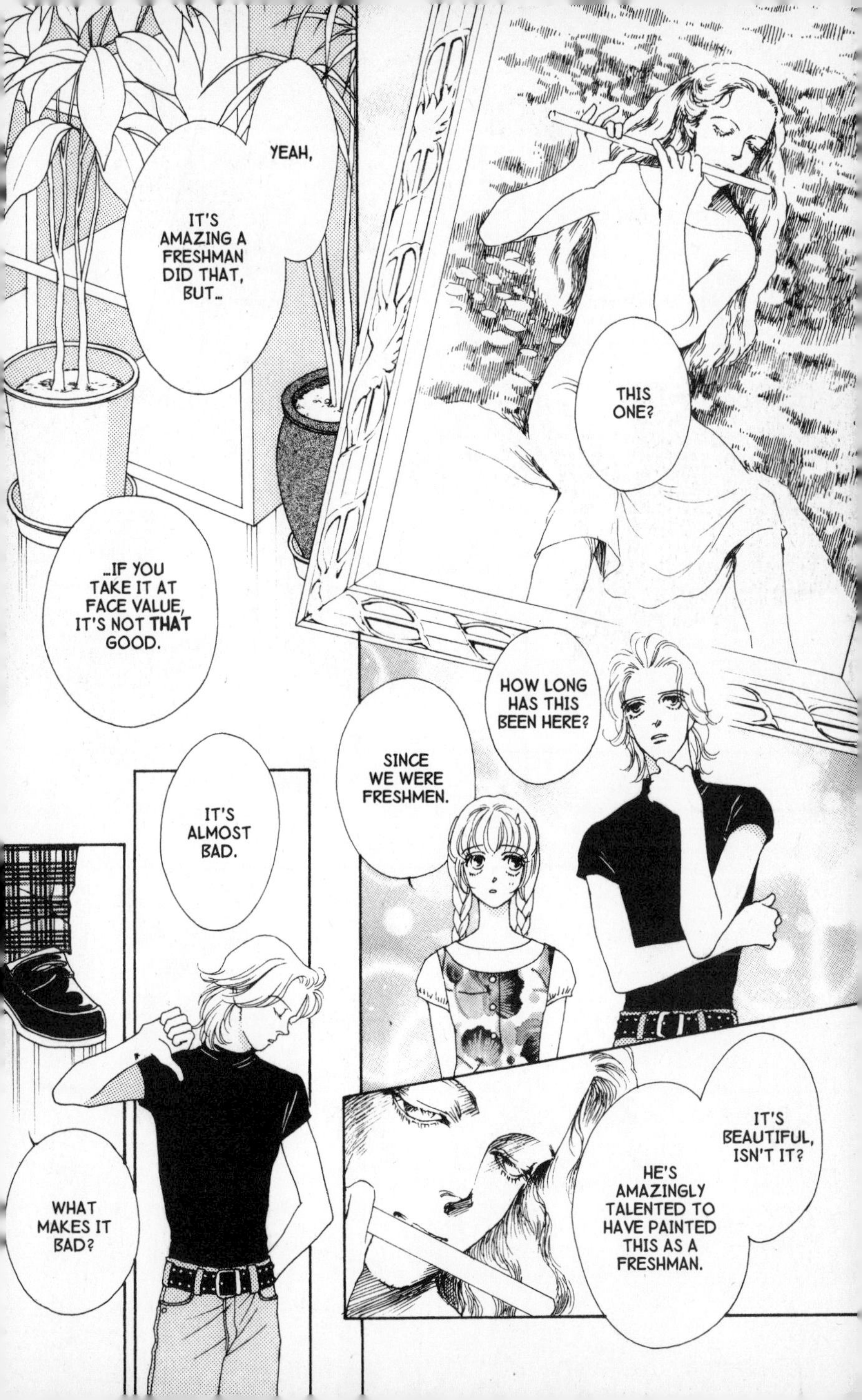
THIS ONE?
HOW LONG HAS THIS BEEN HERE?
SINCE WE WERE FRESHMEN.
IT'S BEAUTIFUL, ISN'T IT?
HE'S AMAZINGLY TALENTED TO HAVE PAINTED THIS AS A FRESHMAN.
YEAH,
IT'S AMAZING A FRESHMAN DID THAT, BUT...
...IF YOU TAKE IT AT FACE VALUE, IT'S NOT THAT GOOD.
IT'S ALMOST BAD.
WHAT MAKES IT BAD?

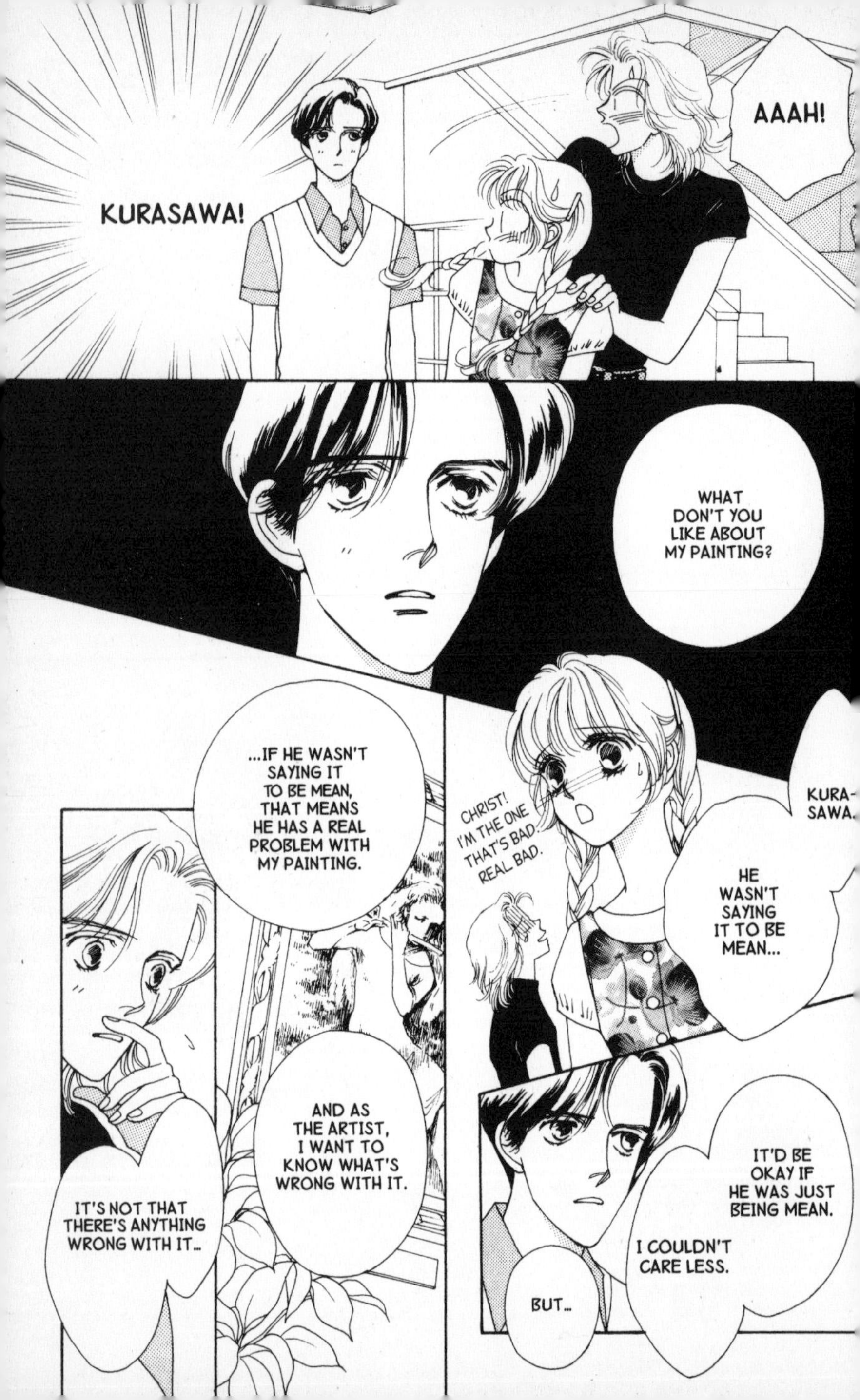
AAAH!
KURASAWA!
WHAT DON'T YOU LIKE ABOUT MY PAINTING?
KURA-SAWA.
HE WASN'T SAYING IT TO BE MEAN...
CHRIST! I'M THE ONE THAT'S BAD. REAL BAD.
IT'D BE OKAY IF HE WAS JUST BEING MEAN.
I COULDN'T CARE LESS.
BUT...
...IF HE WASN'T SAYING IT TO BE MEAN, THAT MEANS HE HAS A REAL PROBLEM WITH MY PAINTING.
AND AS THE ARTIST, I WANT TO KNOW WHAT'S WRONG WITH IT.
IT'S NOT THAT THERE'S ANYTHING WRONG WITH IT...

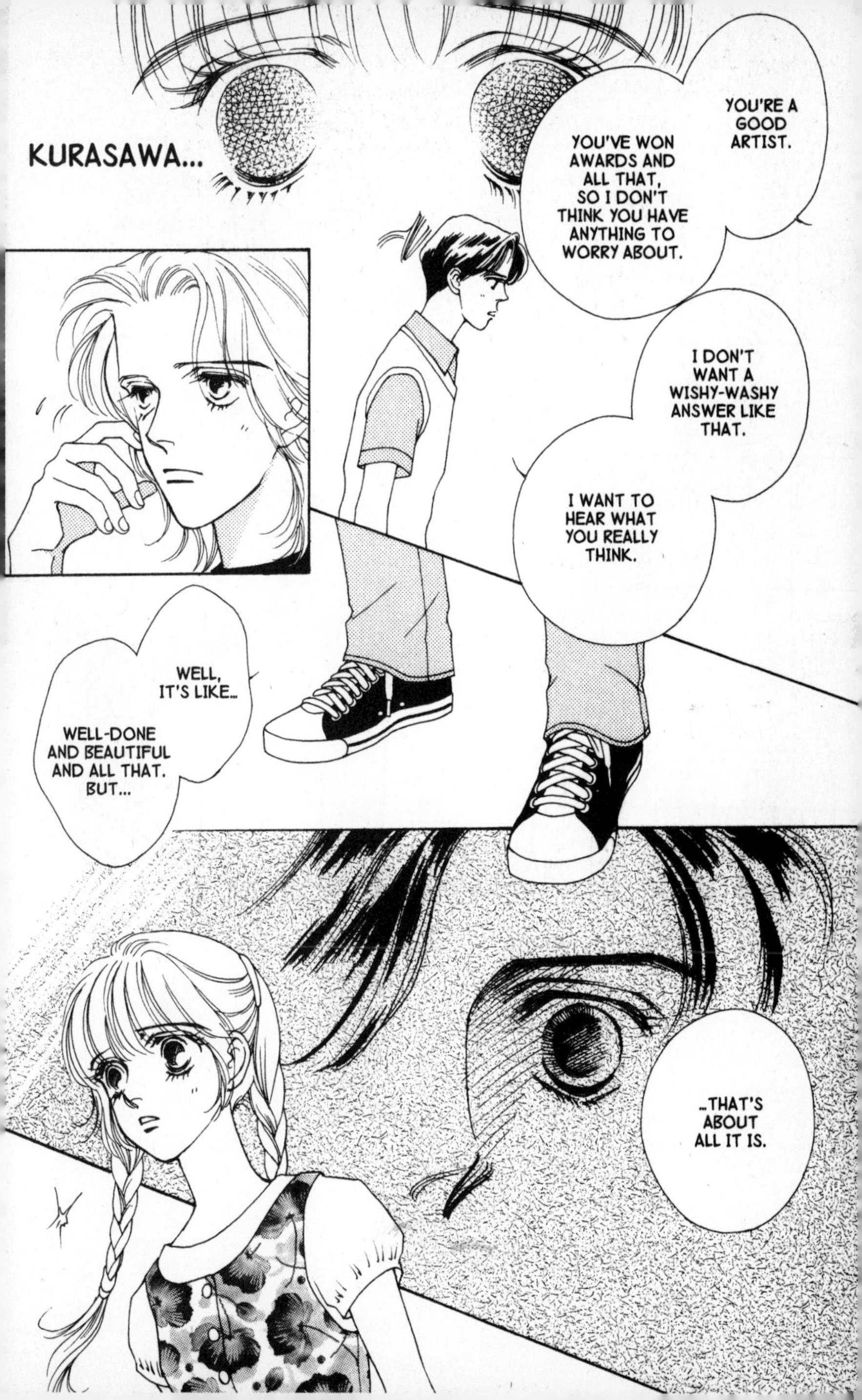
KURASAWA...
YOU'RE A GOOD ARTIST.
YOU'VE WON AWARDS AND ALL THAT, SO I DON'T THINK YOU HAVE ANYTHING TO WORRY ABOUT.
I DON'T WANT A WISHY-WASHY ANSWER LIKE THAT.
I WANT TO HEAR WHAT YOU REALLY THINK.
WELL, IT'S LIKE...
WELL-DONE AND BEAUTIFUL AND ALL THAT. BUT...
...THAT'S ABOUT ALL IT IS.

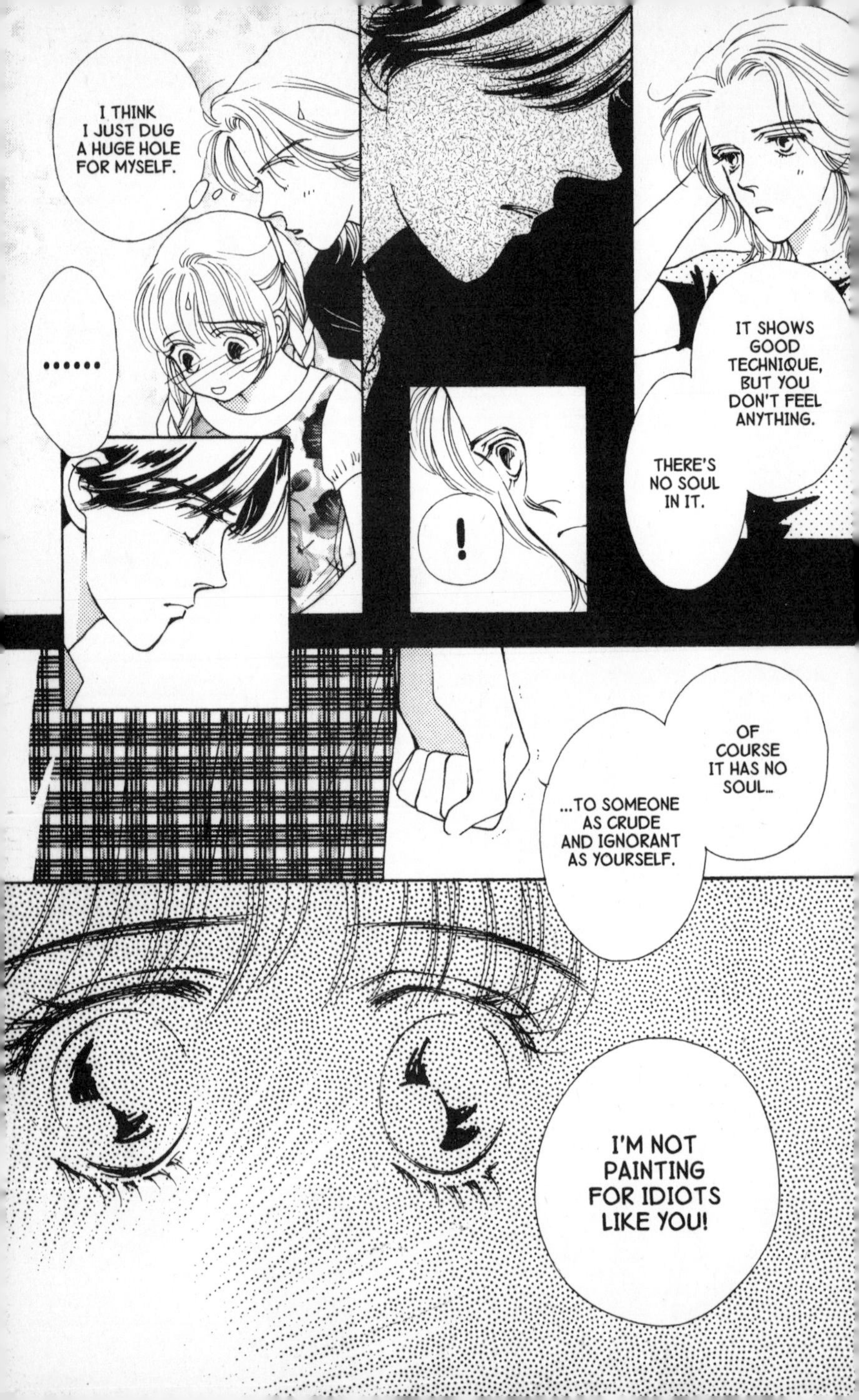
IT SHOWS GOOD TECHNIQUE, BUT YOU DON'T FEEL ANYTHING.
THERE'S NO SOUL IN IT.
!
I THINK I JUST DUG A HUGE HOLE FOR MYSELF.
......
OF COURSE IT HAS NO SOUL...
...TO SOMEONE AS CRUDE AND IGNORANT AS YOURSELF.
I'M NOT PAINTING FOR IDIOTS LIKE YOU!

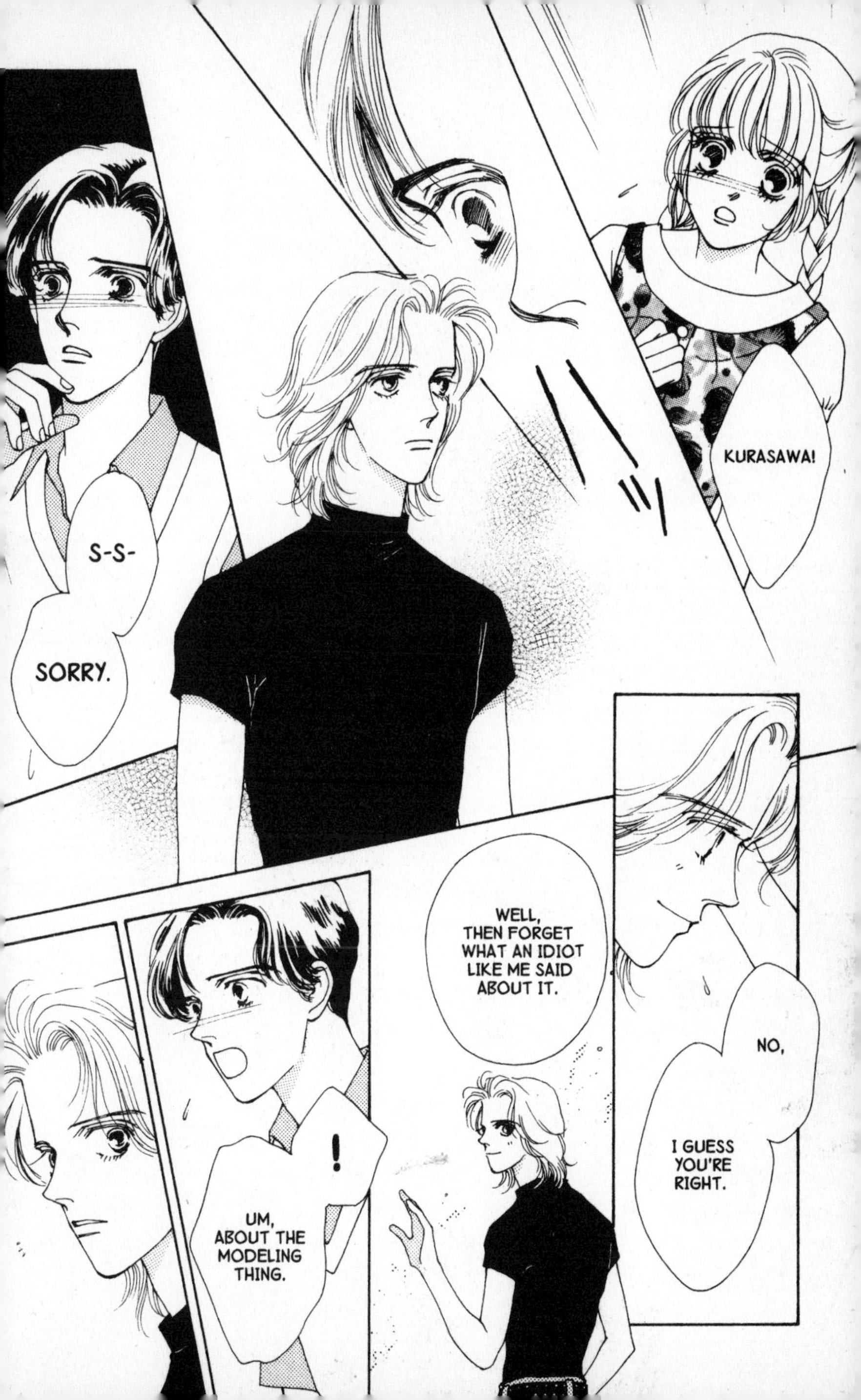
KURASAWA!
S-S-
SORRY.
NO,
I GUESS YOU'RE RIGHT.
WELL, THEN FORGET WHAT AN IDIOT LIKE ME SAID ABOUT IT.
!
UM, ABOUT THE MODELING THING.

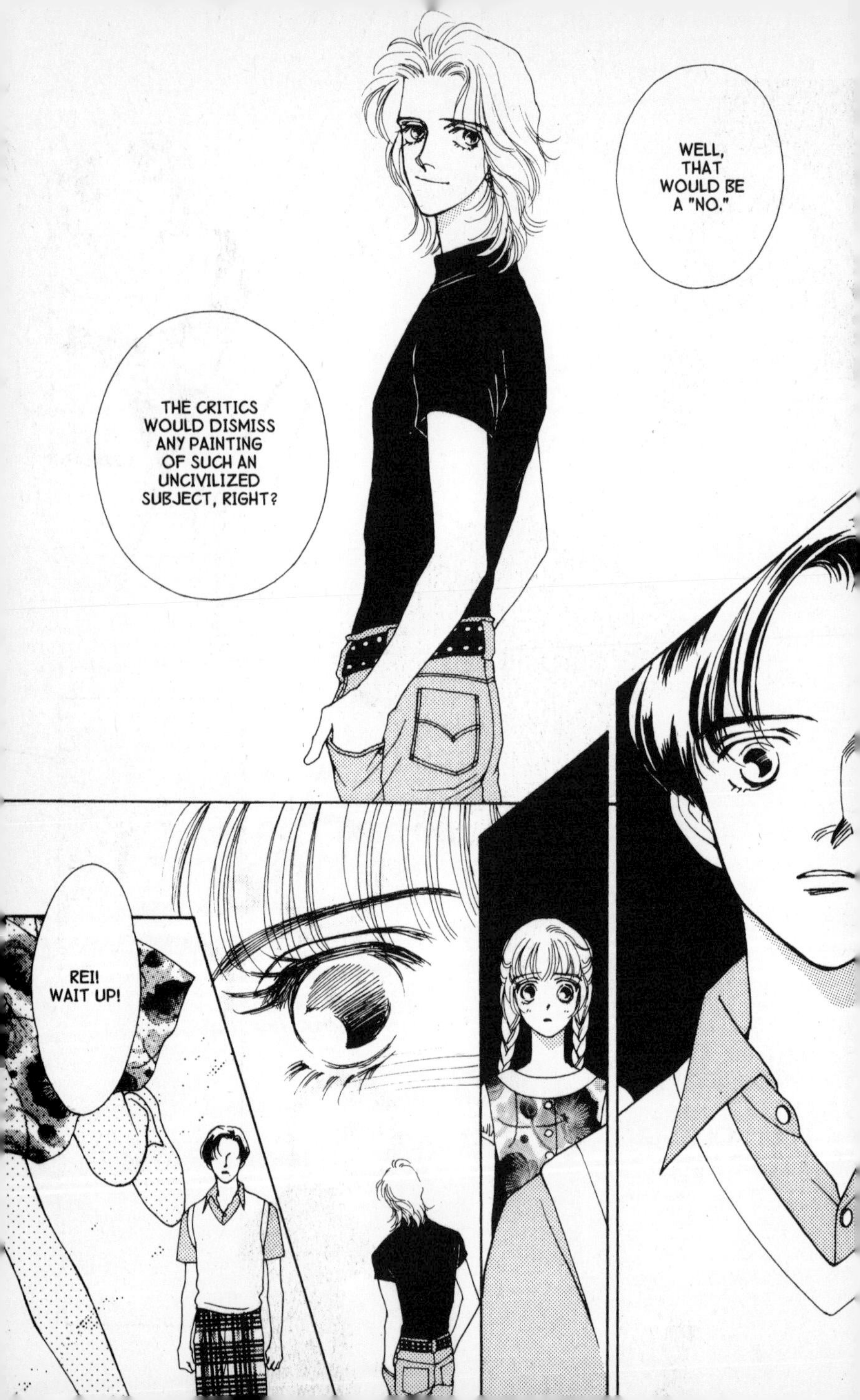
WELL, THAT WOULD BE A "NO."
THE CRITICS WOULD DISMISS ANY PAINTING OF SUCH AN UNCIVILIZED SUBJECT, RIGHT?
REI! WAIT UP!

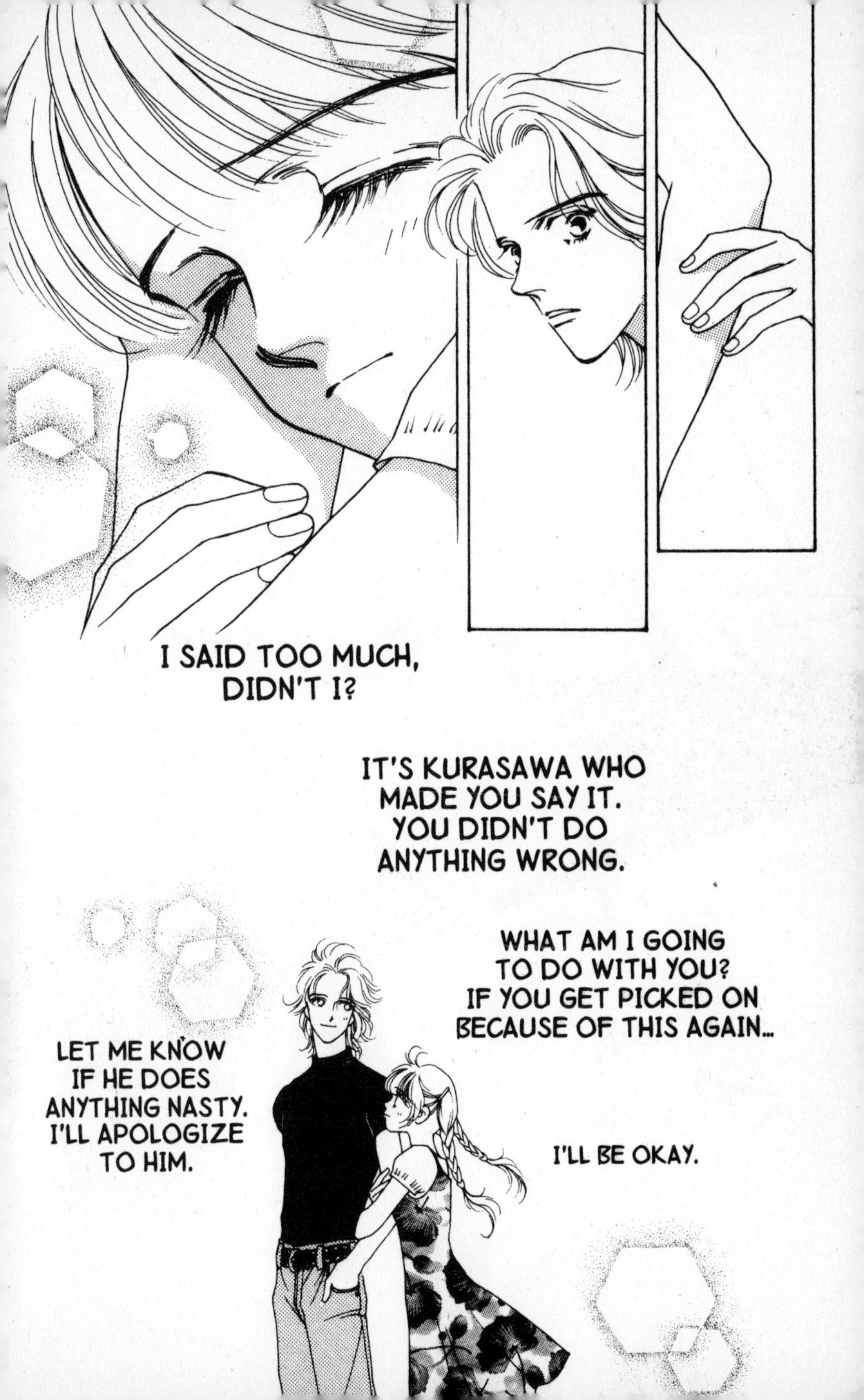
I SAID TOO MUCH, DIDN'T I?
IT'S KURASAWA WHO MADE YOU SAY IT. YOU DIDN'T DO ANYTHING WRONG.
WHAT AM I GOING TO DO WITH YOU? IF YOU GET PICKED ON BECAUSE OF THIS AGAIN...
I'LL BE OKAY.
LET ME KNOW IF HE DOES ANYTHING NASTY. I'LL APOLOGIZE TO HIM.

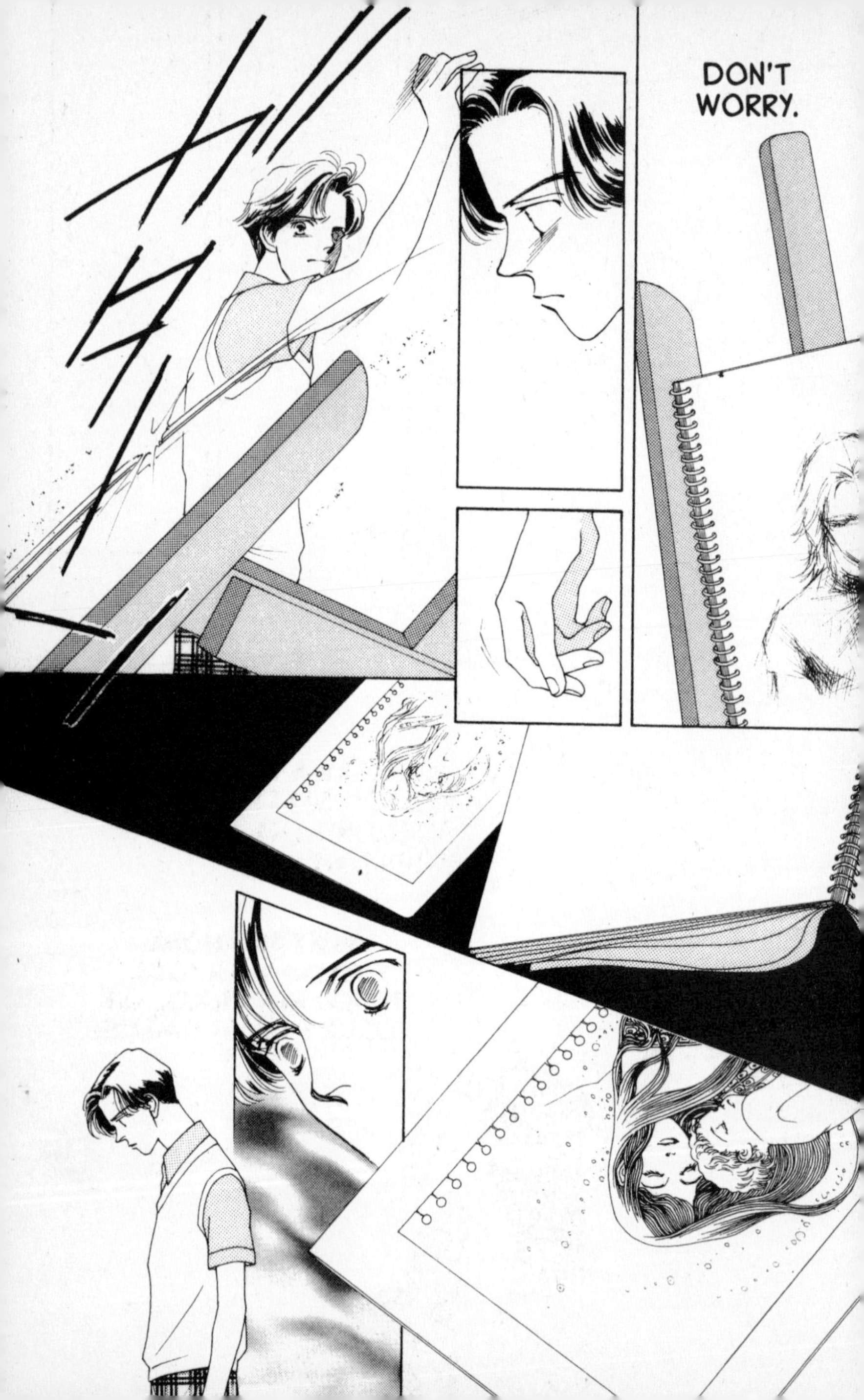
DON'T WORRY.

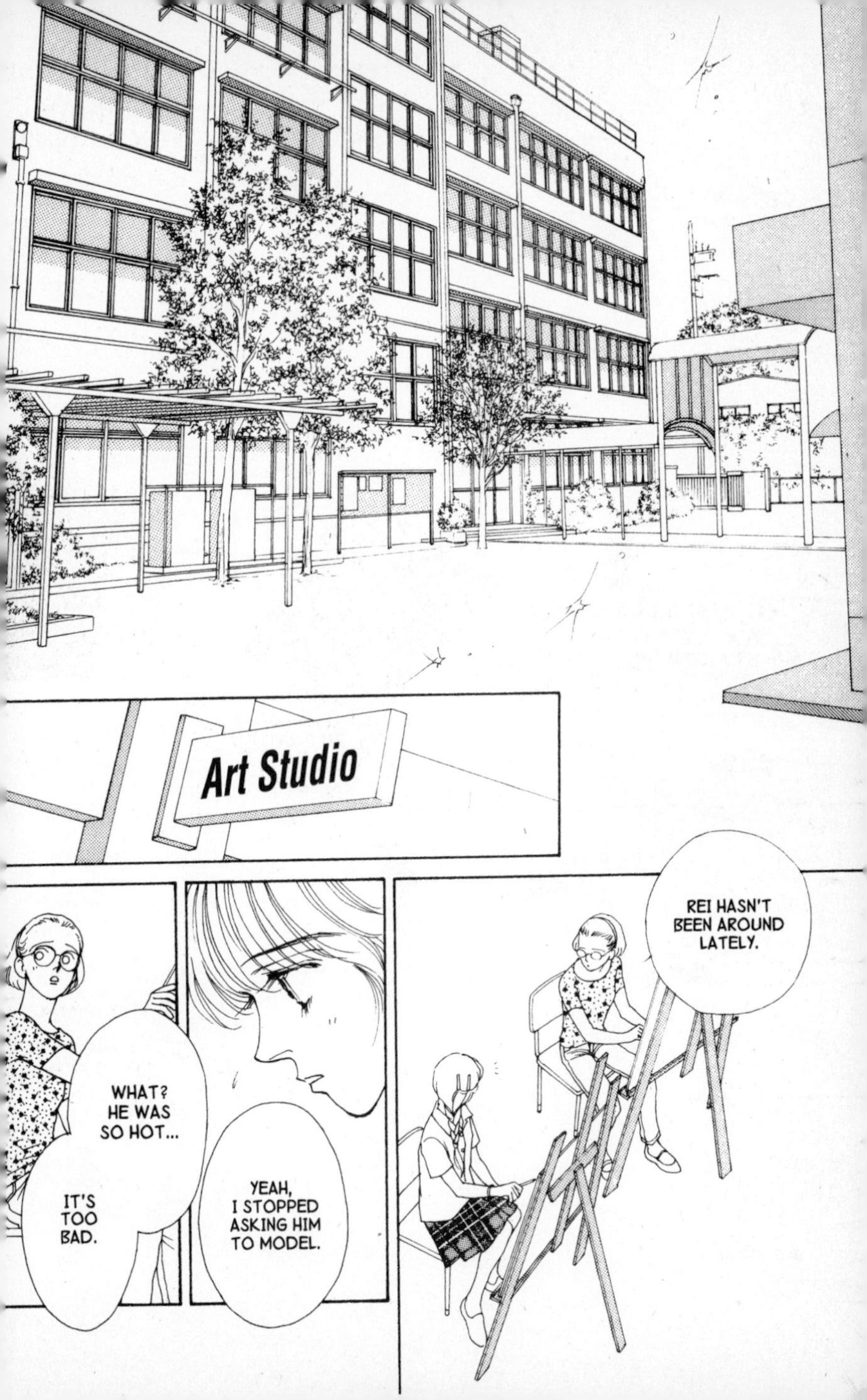

Art Studio
REI HASN'T BEEN AROUND LATELY.
YEAH, I STOPPED ASKING HIM TO MODEL.
WHAT? HE WAS SO HOT...
IT'S TOO BAD.

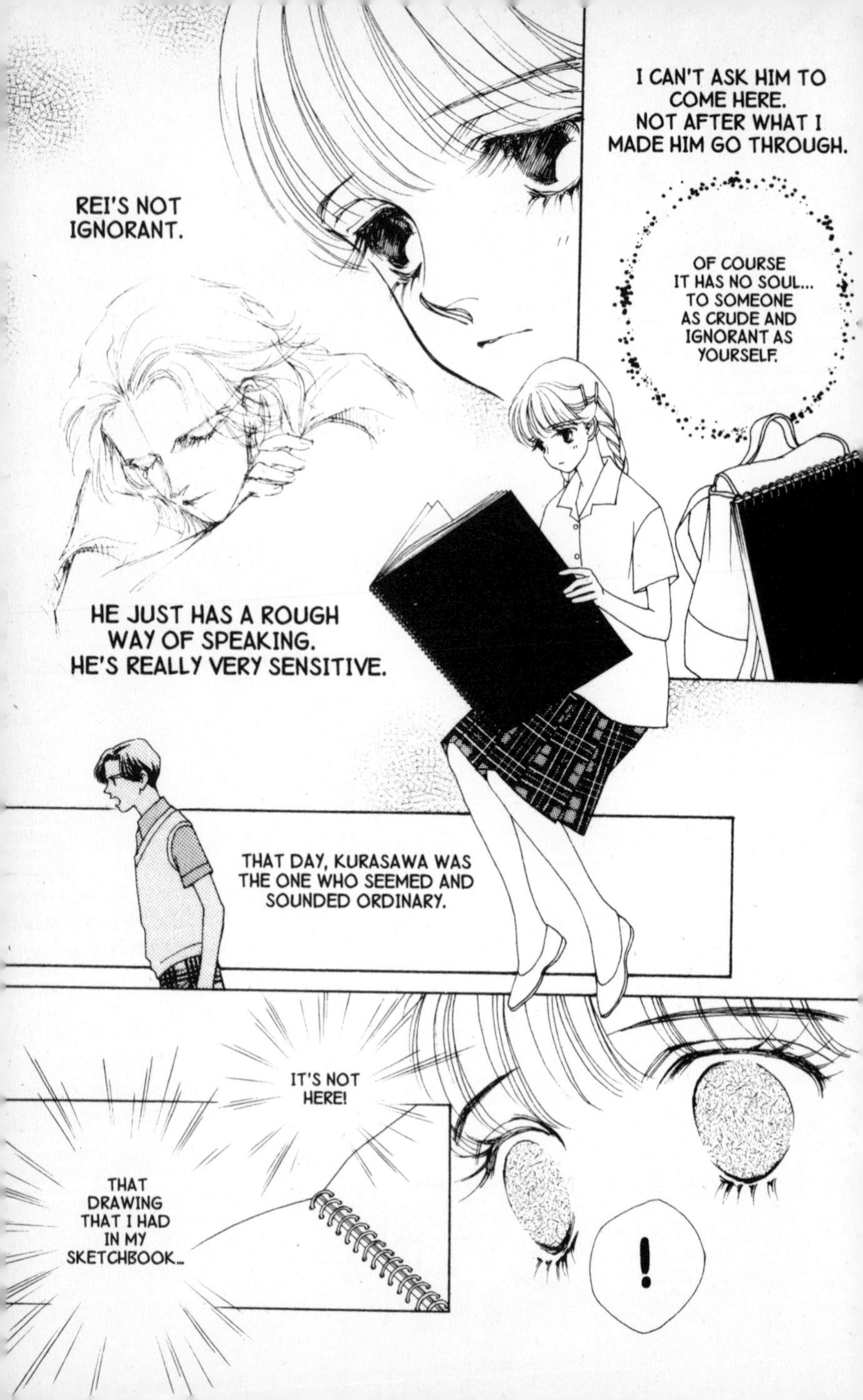
I CAN'T ASK HIM TO COME HERE. NOT AFTER WHAT I MADE HIM GO THROUGH.
OF COURSE IT HAS NO SOUL... TO SOMEONE AS CRUDE AND IGNORANT AS YOURSELF.
REI'S NOT IGNORANT.
HE JUST HAS A ROUGH WAY OF SPEAKING. HE'S REALLY VERY SENSITIVE.
THAT DAY, KURASAWA WAS THE ONE WHO SEEMED AND SOUNDED ORDINARY.
!
IT'S NOT HERE!
THAT DRAWING THAT I HAD IN MY SKETCHBOOK...

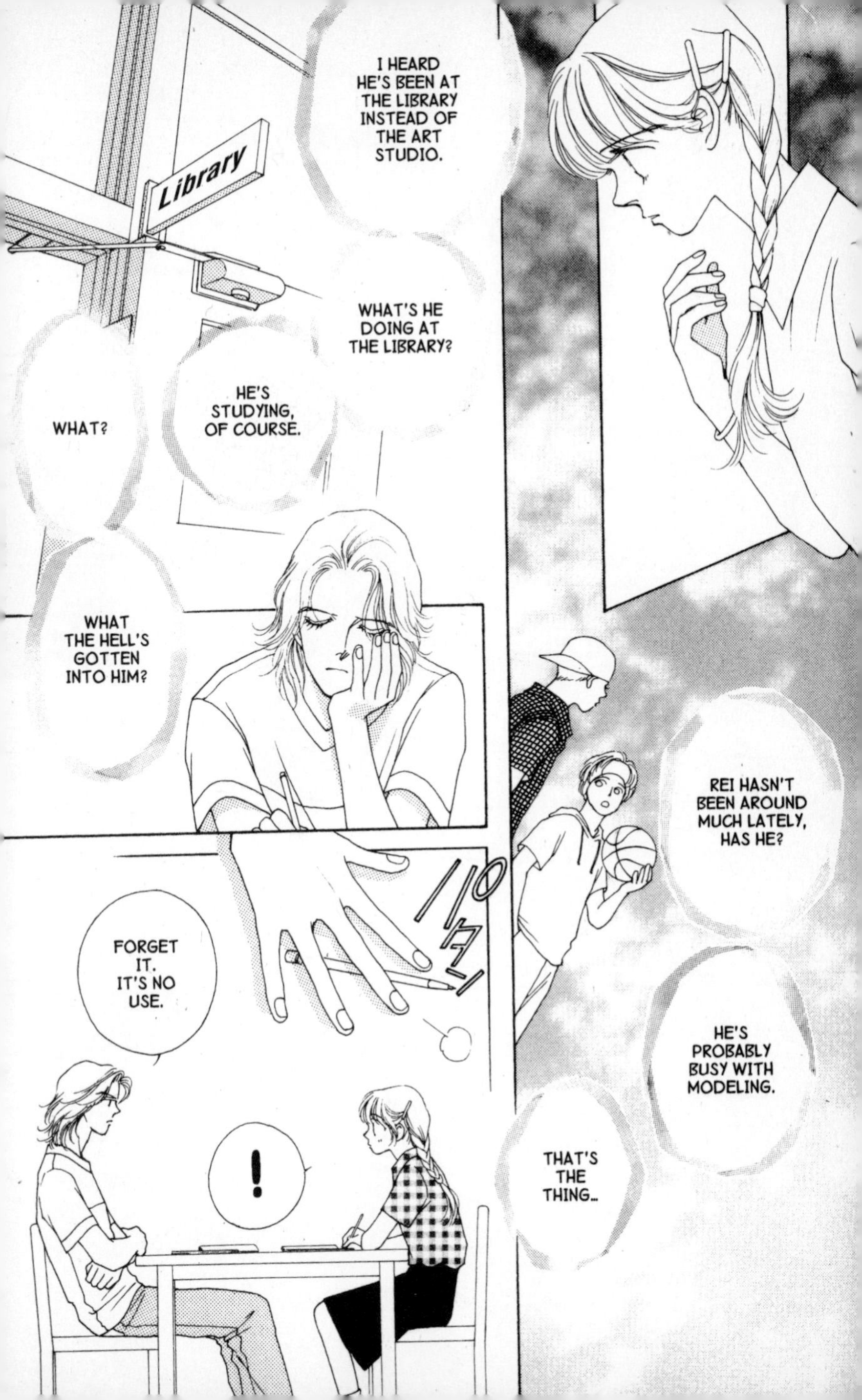
REI HASN'T BEEN AROUND MUCH LATELY, HAS HE?
HE'S PROBABLY BUSY WITH MODELING.
THAT'S THE THING...
Library
I HEARD HE'S BEEN AT THE LIBRARY INSTEAD OF THE ART STUDIO.
WHAT'S HE DOING AT THE LIBRARY?
HE'S STUDYING, OF COURSE.
WHAT?
WHAT THE HELL'S GOTTEN INTO HIM?
FORGET IT. IT'S NO USE.
!

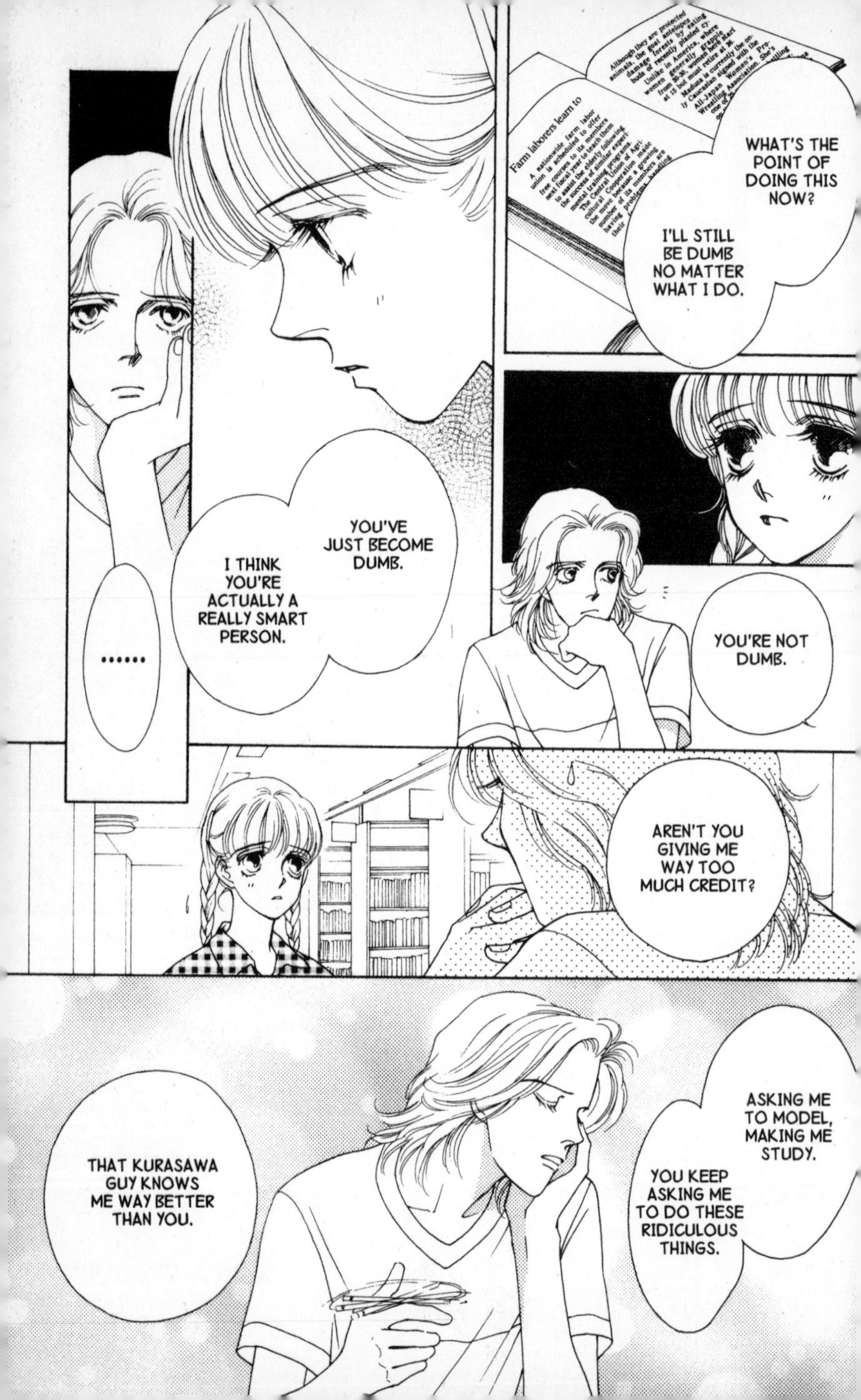
Farm laborers learn to
WHAT'S THE POINT OF DOING THIS NOW?
I'LL STILL BE DUMB NO MATTER WHAT I DO.
YOU'RE NOT DUMB.
YOU'VE JUST BECOME DUMB.
I THINK YOU'RE ACTUALLY A REALLY SMART PERSON.
......
AREN'T YOU GIVING ME WAY TOO MUCH CREDIT?
ASKING ME TO MODEL, MAKING ME STUDY.
YOU KEEP ASKING ME TO DO THESE RIDICULOUS THINGS.
THAT KURASAWA GUY KNOWS ME WAY BETTER THAN YOU.

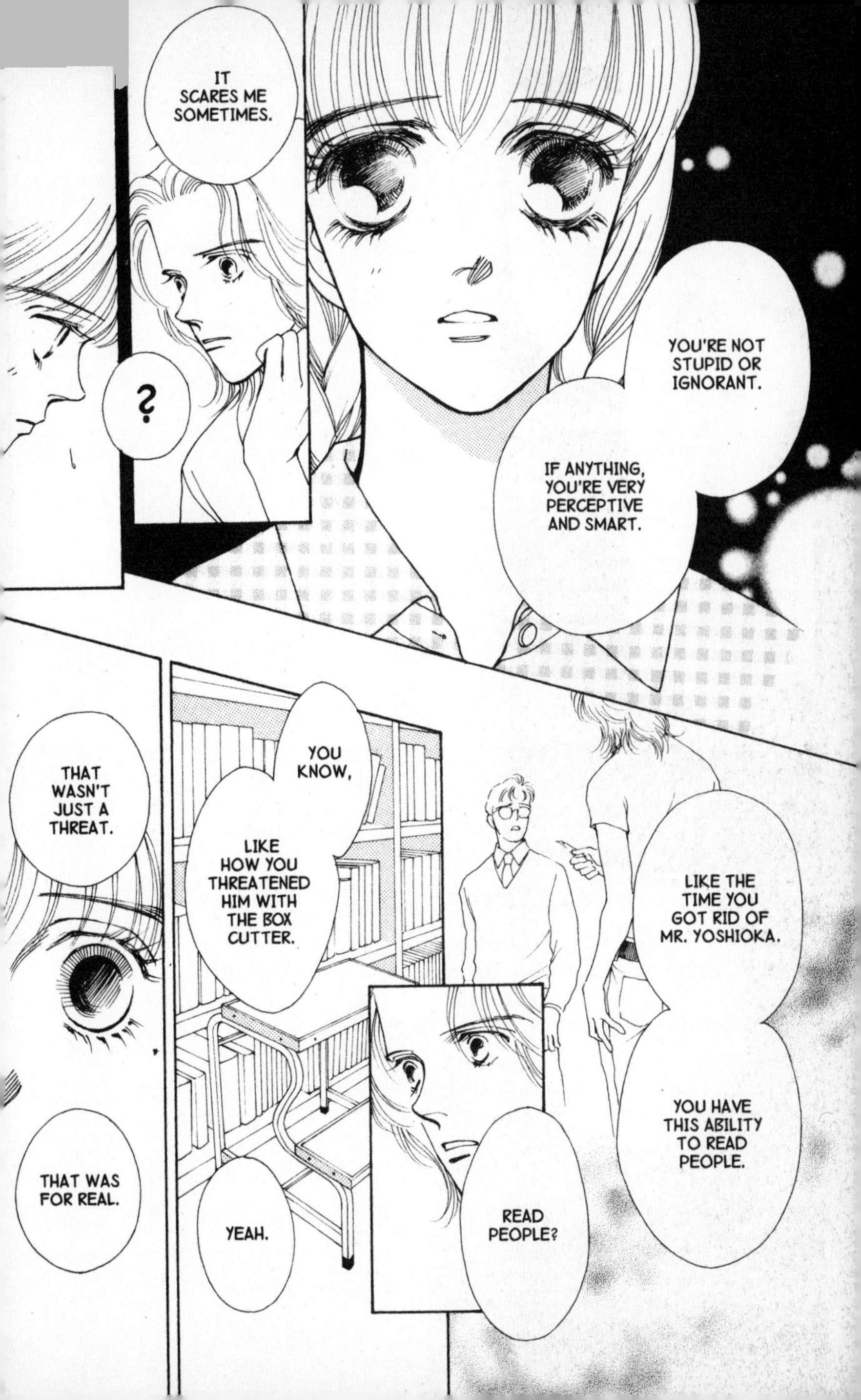
YOU'RE NOT STUPID OR IGNORANT.
IF ANYTHING, YOU'RE VERY PERCEPTIVE AND SMART.
IT SCARES ME SOMETIMES.
?
LIKE THE TIME YOU GOT RID OF MR. YOSHIOKA.
YOU HAVE THIS ABILITY TO READ PEOPLE.
READ PEOPLE?
YOU KNOW,
LIKE HOW YOU THREATENED HIM WITH THE BOX CUTTER.
YEAH.
THAT WASN'T JUST A THREAT.
THAT WAS FOR REAL.

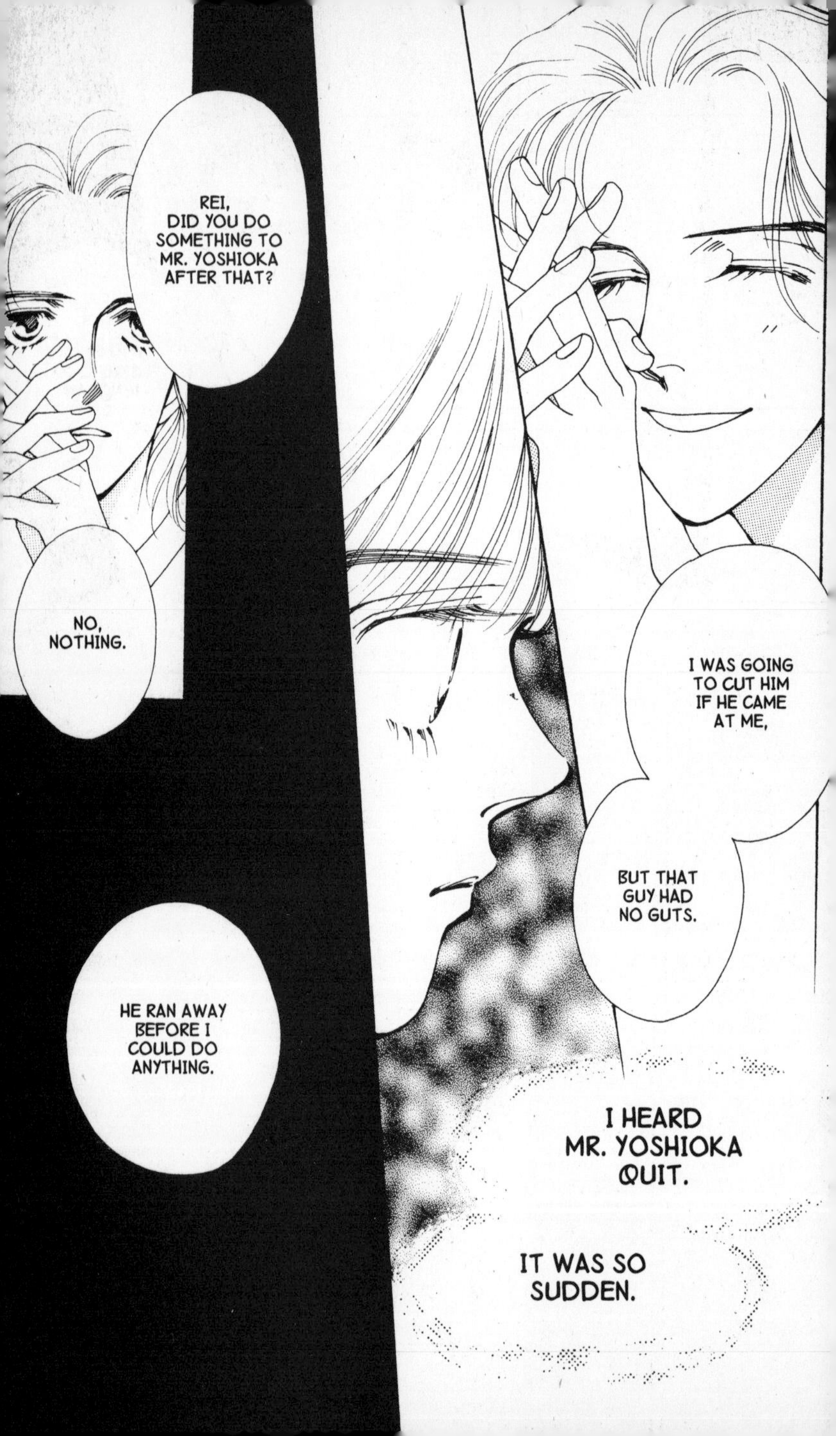
I WAS GOING TO CUT HIM IF HE CAME AT ME,
BUT THAT GUY HAD NO GUTS.
I HEARD MR. YOSHIOKA QUIT.
IT WAS SO SUDDEN.
REI, DID YOU DO SOMETHING TO MR. YOSHIOKA AFTER THAT?
NO, NOTHING.
HE RAN AWAY BEFORE I COULD DO ANYTHING.

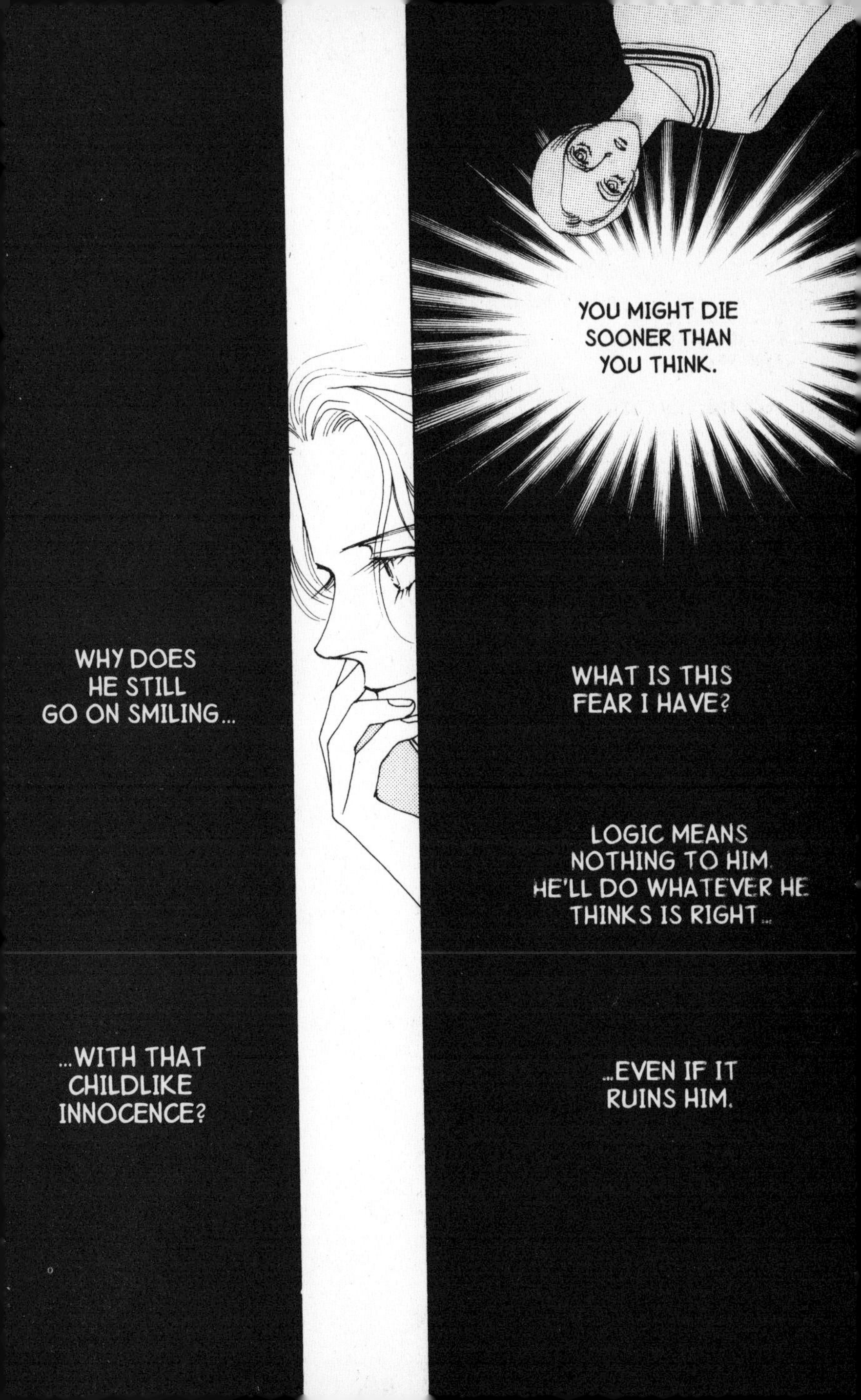
YOU MIGHT DIE SOONER THAN YOU THINK.
WHAT IS THIS FEAR I HAVE?
LOGIC MEANS NOTHING TO HIM. HE'LL DO WHATEVER HE THINKS IS RIGHT...
WHY DOES HE STILL GO ON SMILING...
...EVEN IF IT RUINS HIM.
...WITH THAT CHILDLIKE INNOCENCE?

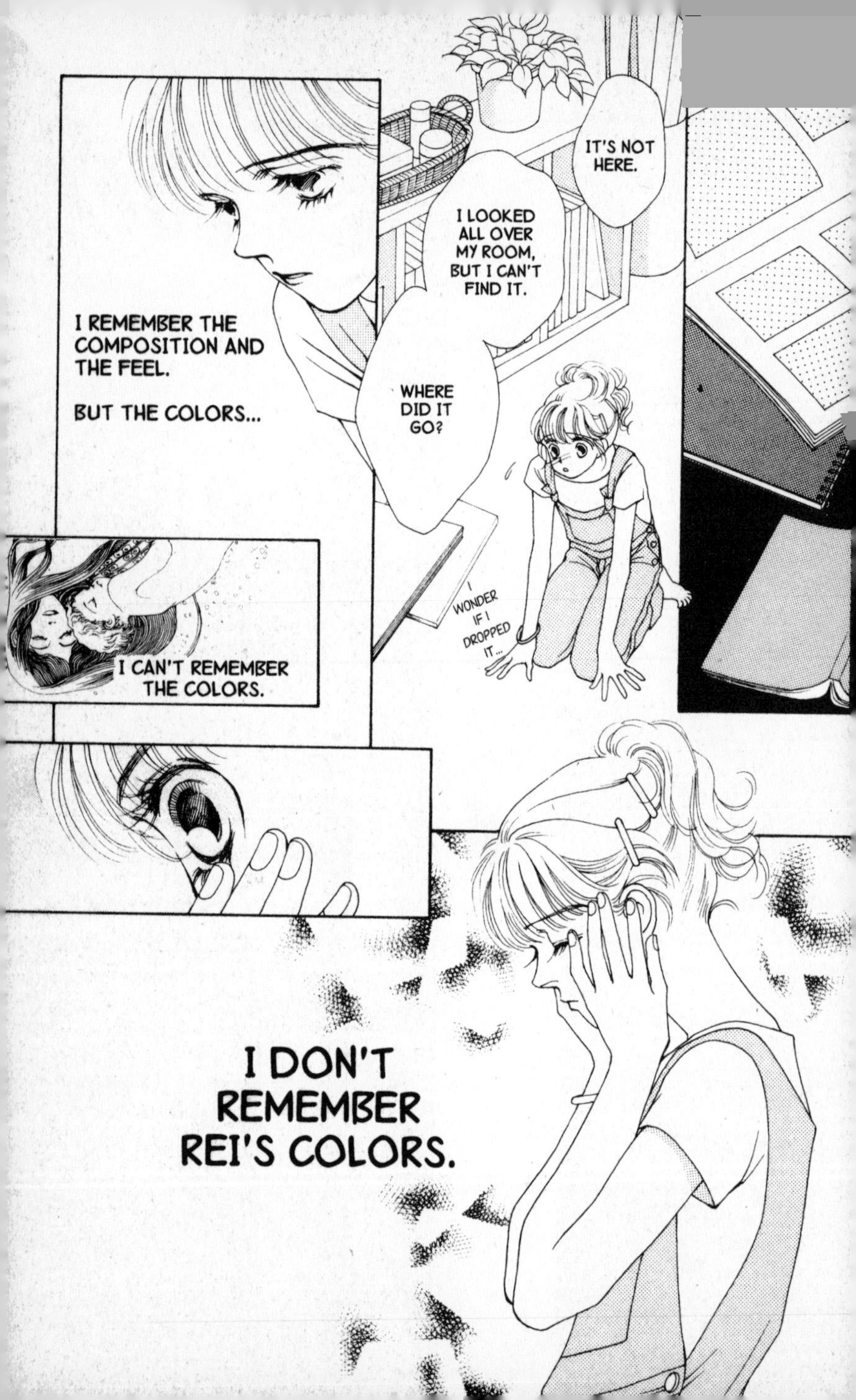
IT'S NOT HERE.
I LOOKED ALL OVER MY ROOM, BUT I CAN'T FIND IT.
WHERE DID IT GO?
I WONDER IF I DROPPED IT...
I REMEMBER THE COMPOSITION AND THE FEEL.
BUT THE COLORS...
I CAN'T REMEMBER THE COLORS.
I DON'T REMEMBER REI'S COLORS.

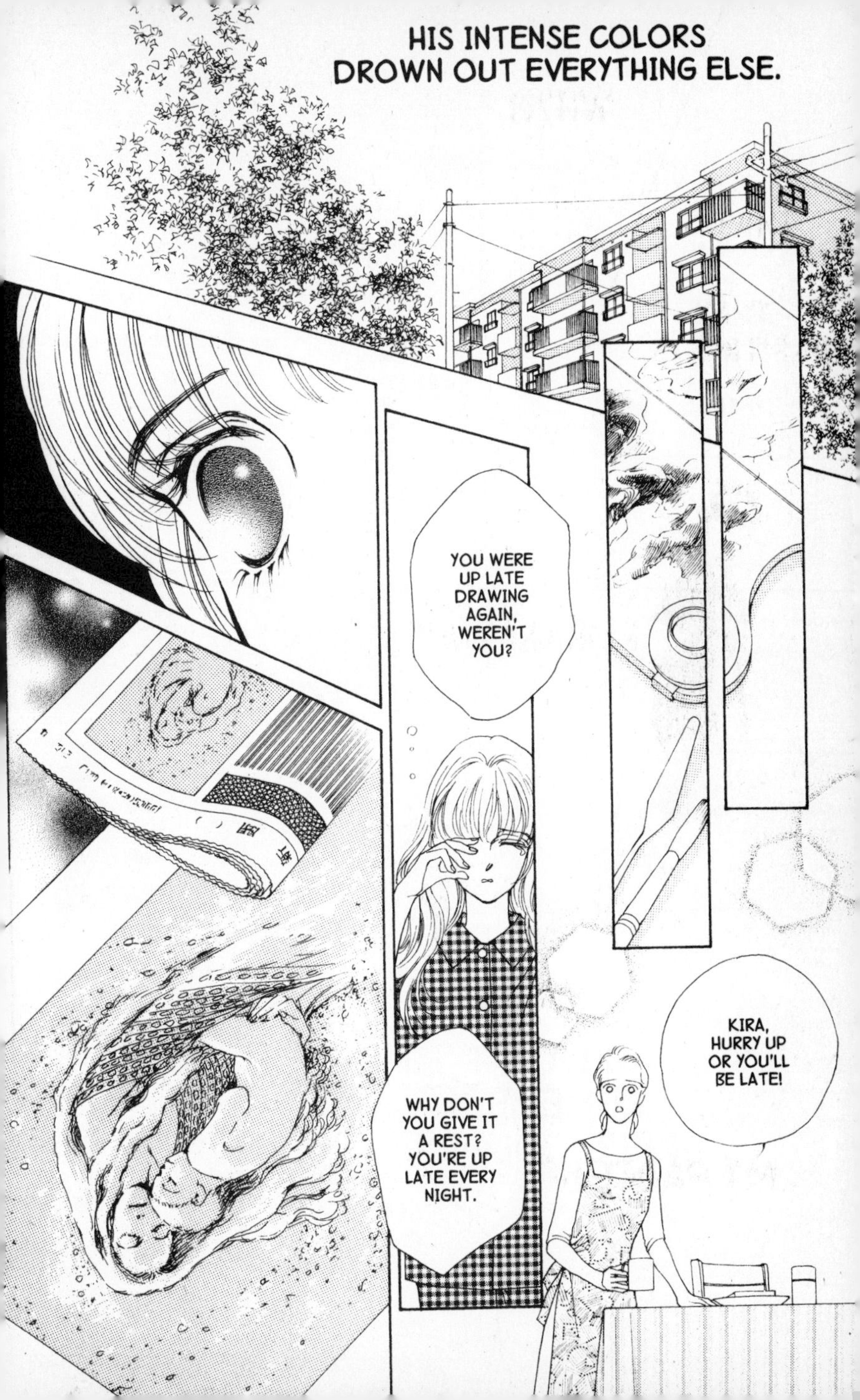
HIS INTENSE COLORS DROWN OUT EVERYTHING ELSE.
KIRA, HURRY UP OR YOU'LL BE LATE!
YOU WERE UP LATE DRAWING AGAIN, WEREN'T YOU?
WHY DON'T YOU GIVE IT A REST? YOU'RE UP LATE EVERY NIGHT.

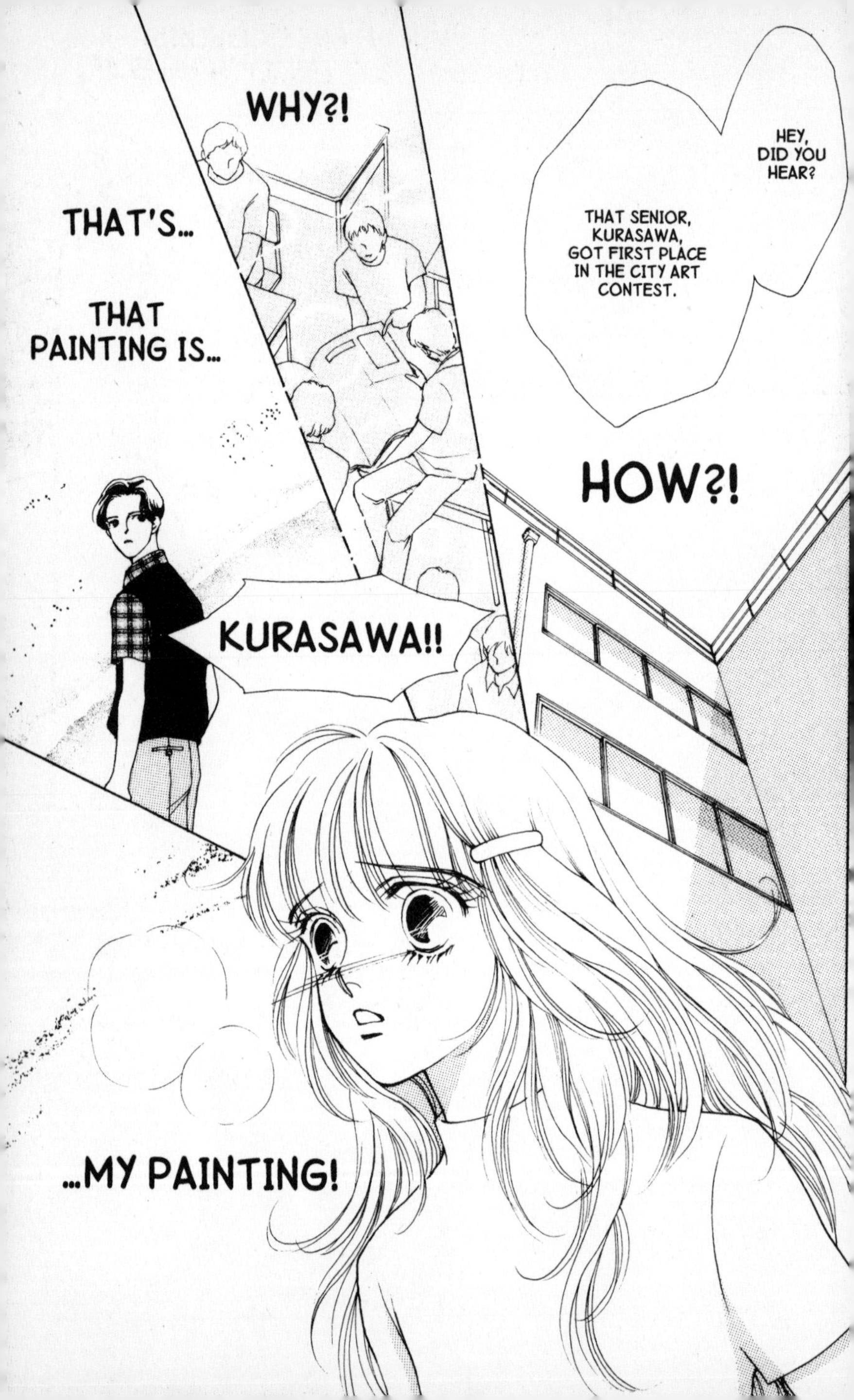
HEY, DID YOU HEAR?
THAT SENIOR, KURASAWA, GOT FIRST PLACE IN THE CITY ART CONTEST.
HOW?!
WHY?!
THAT'S...
THAT PAINTING IS...
KURASAWA!!
...MY PAINTING!

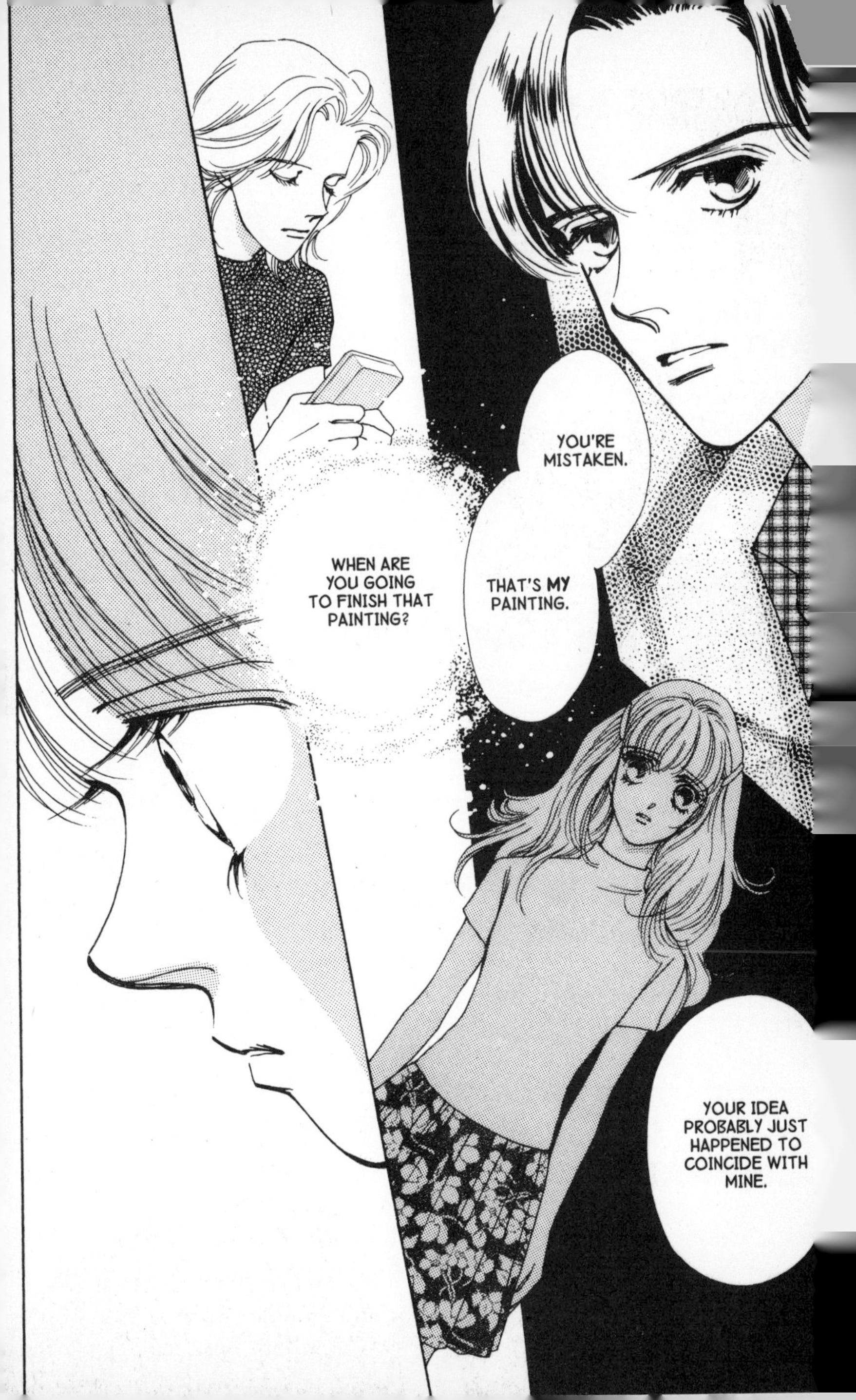
YOU'RE MISTAKEN.
THAT'S MY PAINTING.
WHEN ARE YOU GOING TO FINISH THAT PAINTING?
YOUR IDEA PROBABLY JUST HAPPENED TO COINCIDE WITH MINE.

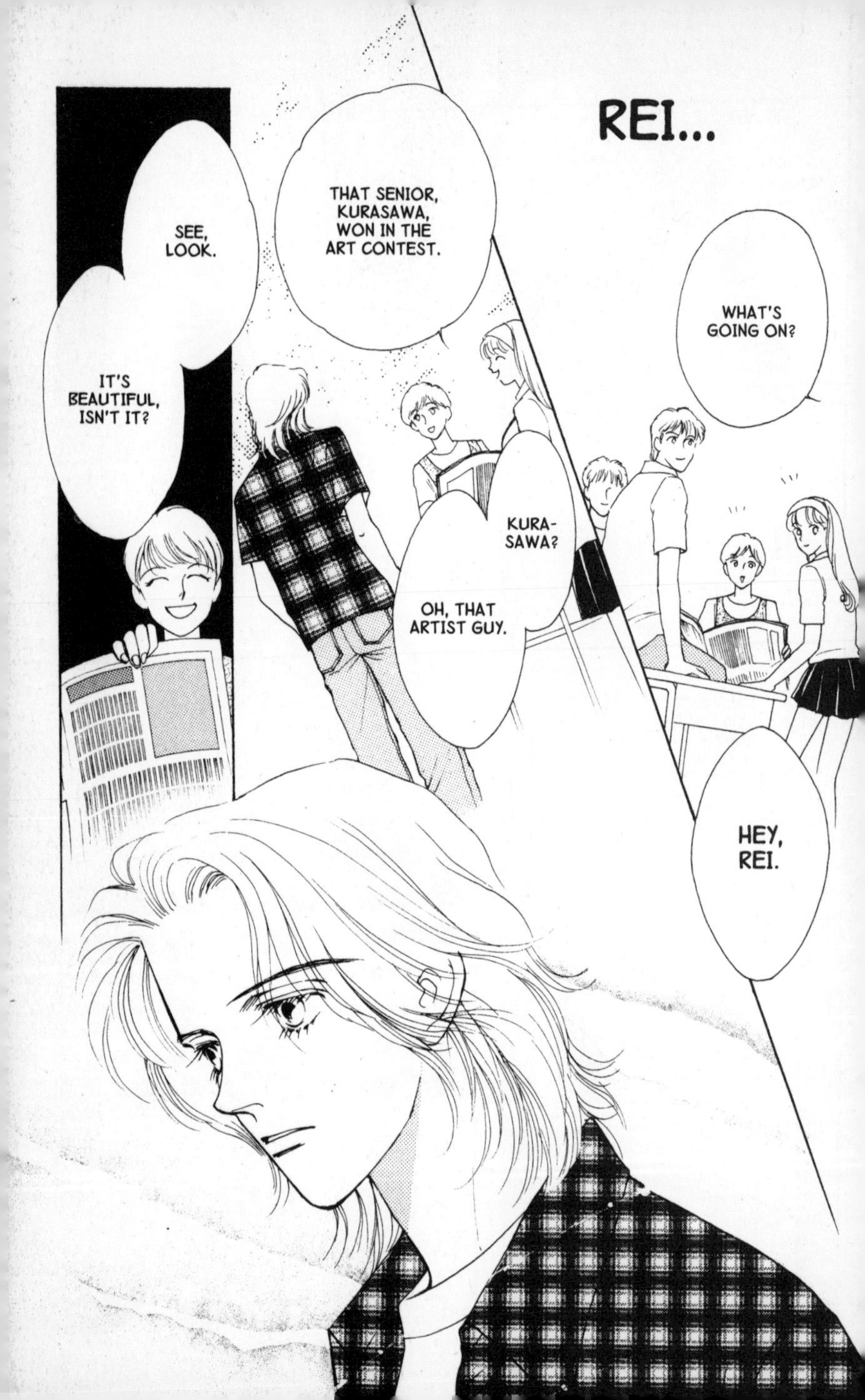
REI...
WHAT'S GOING ON?
HEY, REI.
THAT SENIOR, KURASAWA, WON IN THE ART CONTEST.
SEE, LOOK.
IT'S BEAUTIFUL, ISN'T IT?
KURA-SAWA?
OH, THAT ARTIST GUY.

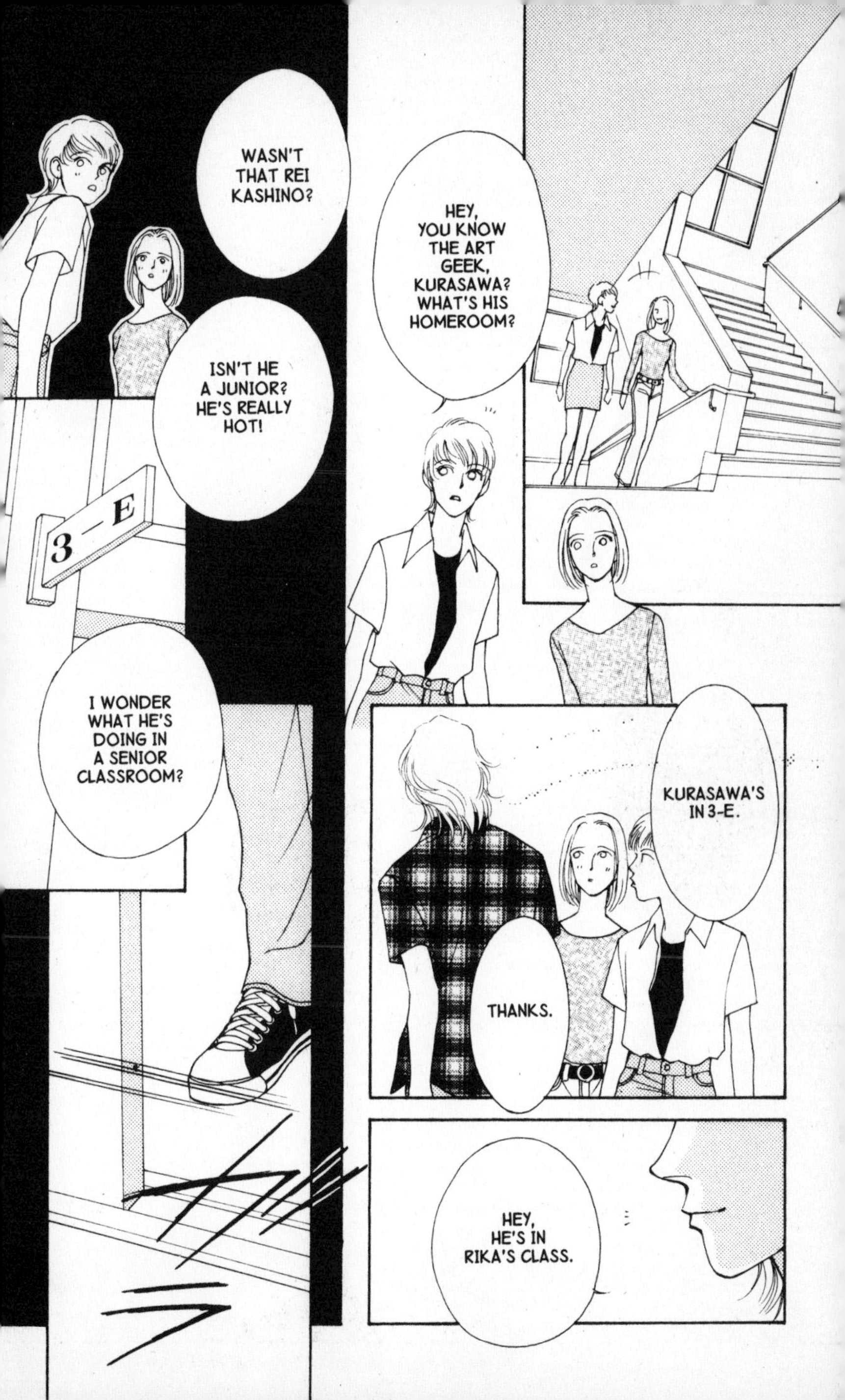
HEY, YOU KNOW THE ART GEEK, KURASAWA? WHAT'S HIS HOMEROOM?
KURASAWA'S IN 3-E.
THANKS.
HEY, HE'S IN RIKA'S CLASS.
WASN'T THAT REI KASHINO?
ISN'T HE A JUNIOR? HE'S REALLY HOT!
3-E
I WONDER WHAT HE'S DOING IN A SENIOR CLASSROOM?

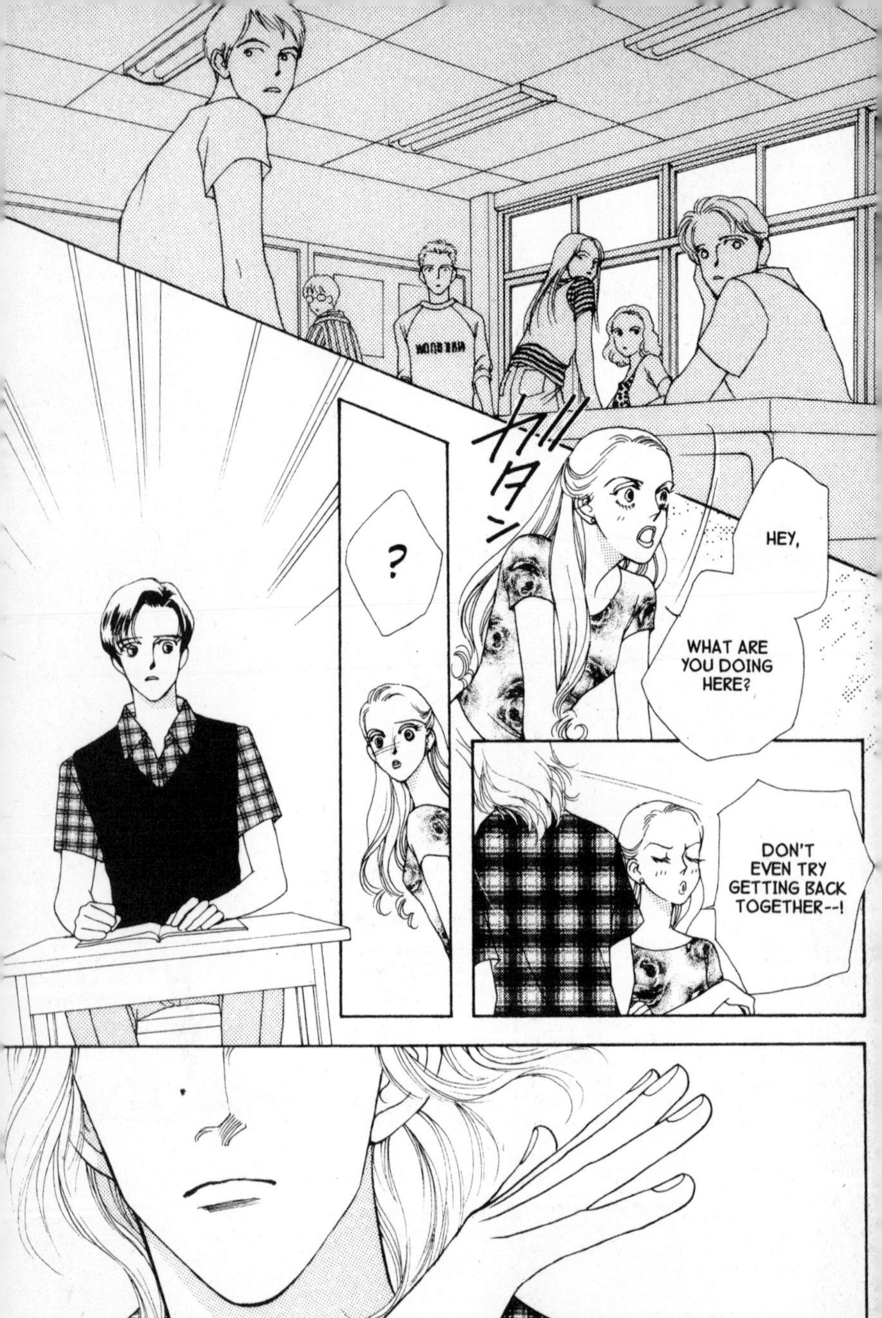
ガタン
HEY,
WHAT ARE YOU DOING HERE?
DON'T EVEN TRY GETTING BACK TOGETHER--!
?

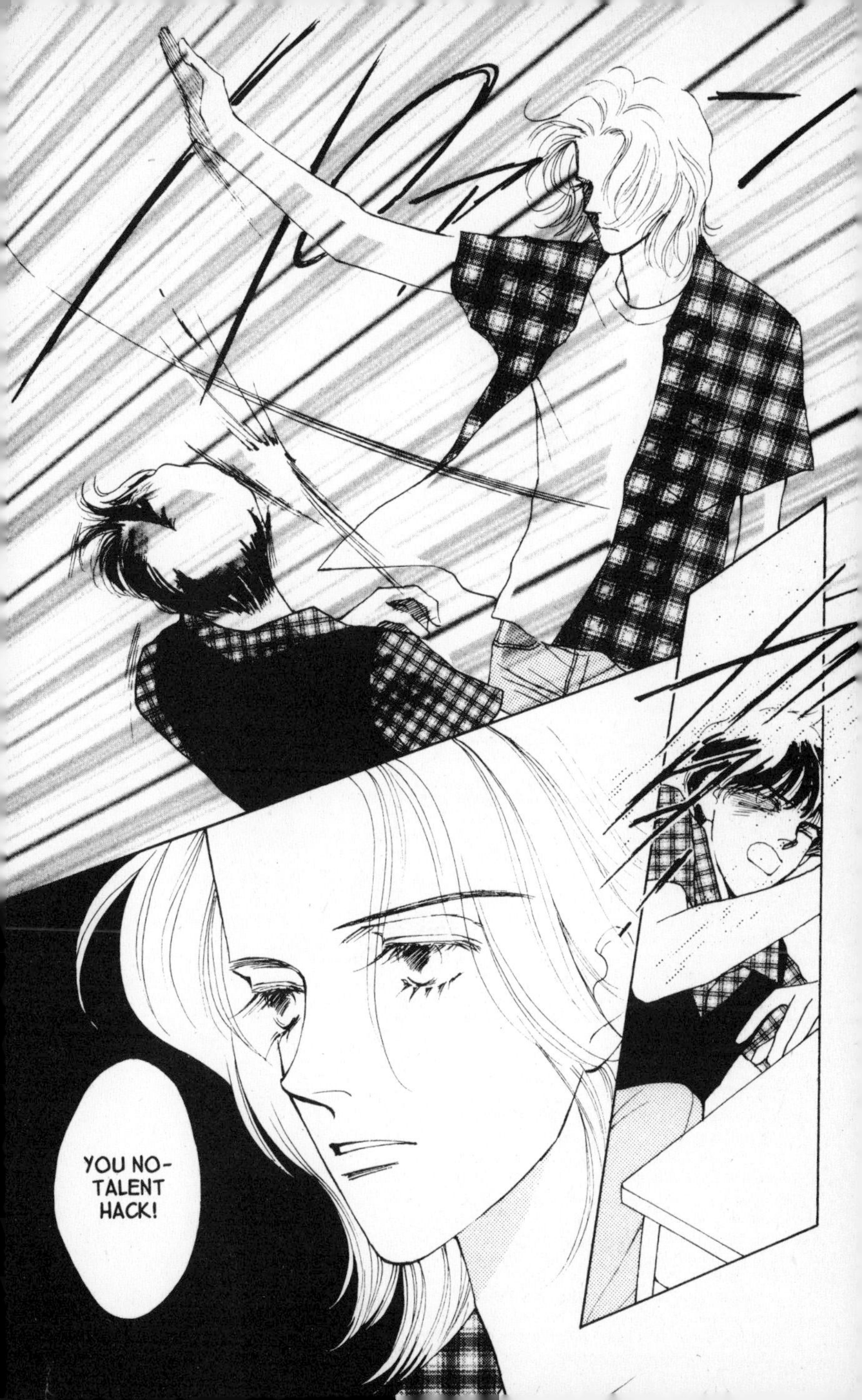
YOU NO-TALENT HACK!

MARS

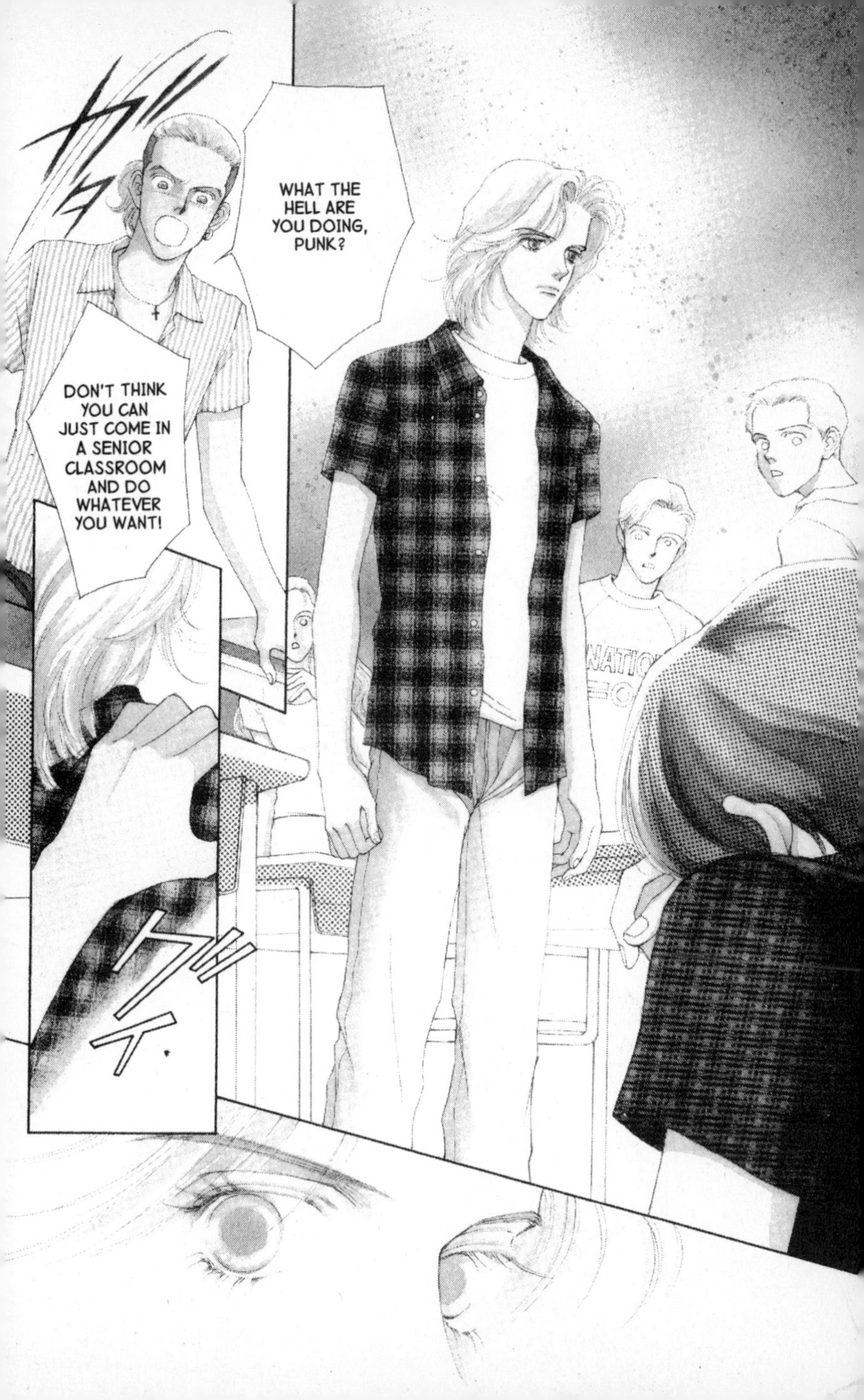
WHAT THE HELL ARE YOU DOING, PUNK?
DON'T THINK YOU CAN JUST COME IN A SENIOR CLASSROOM AND DO WHATEVER YOU WANT!

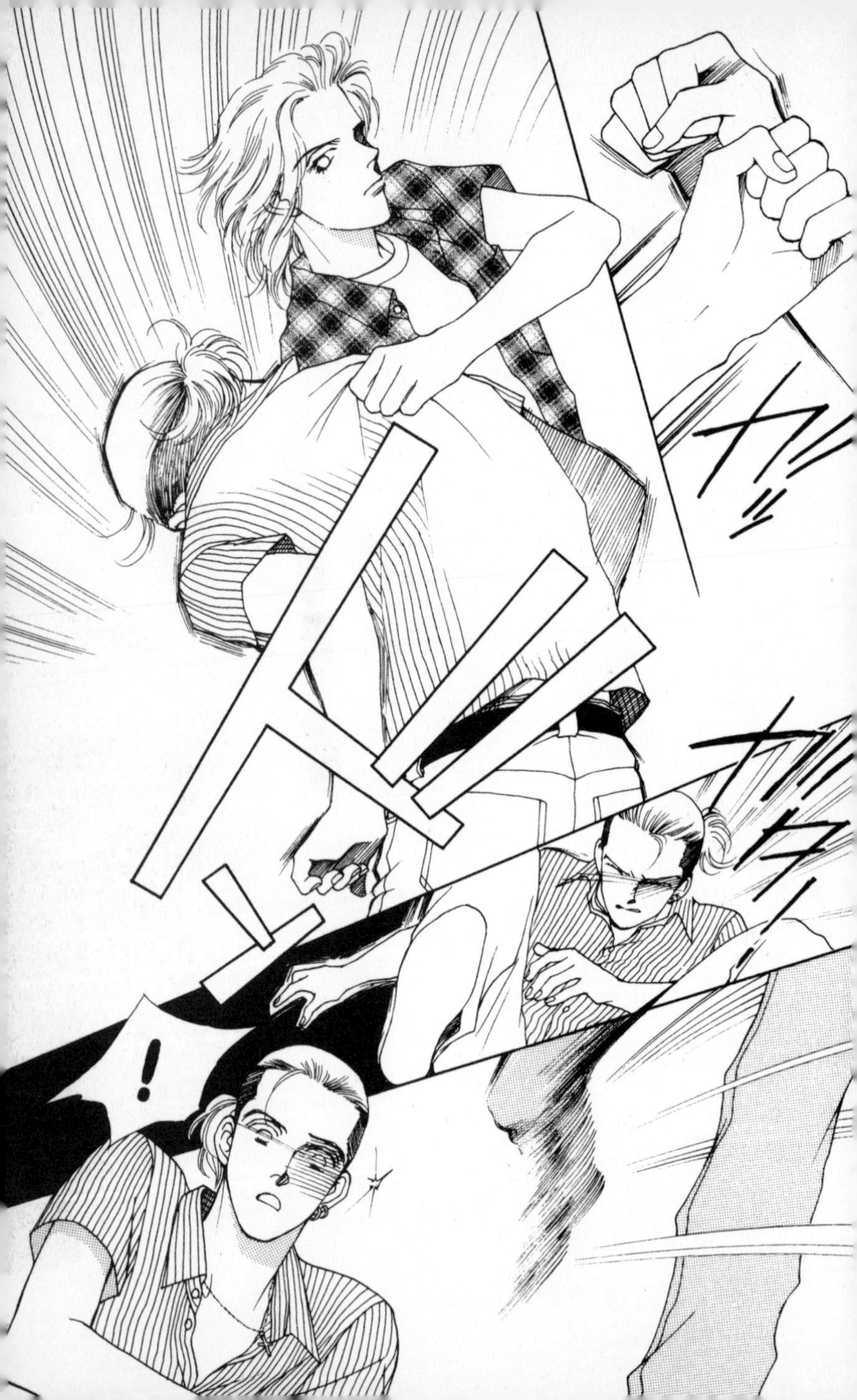
ズッ
ガタ!
!

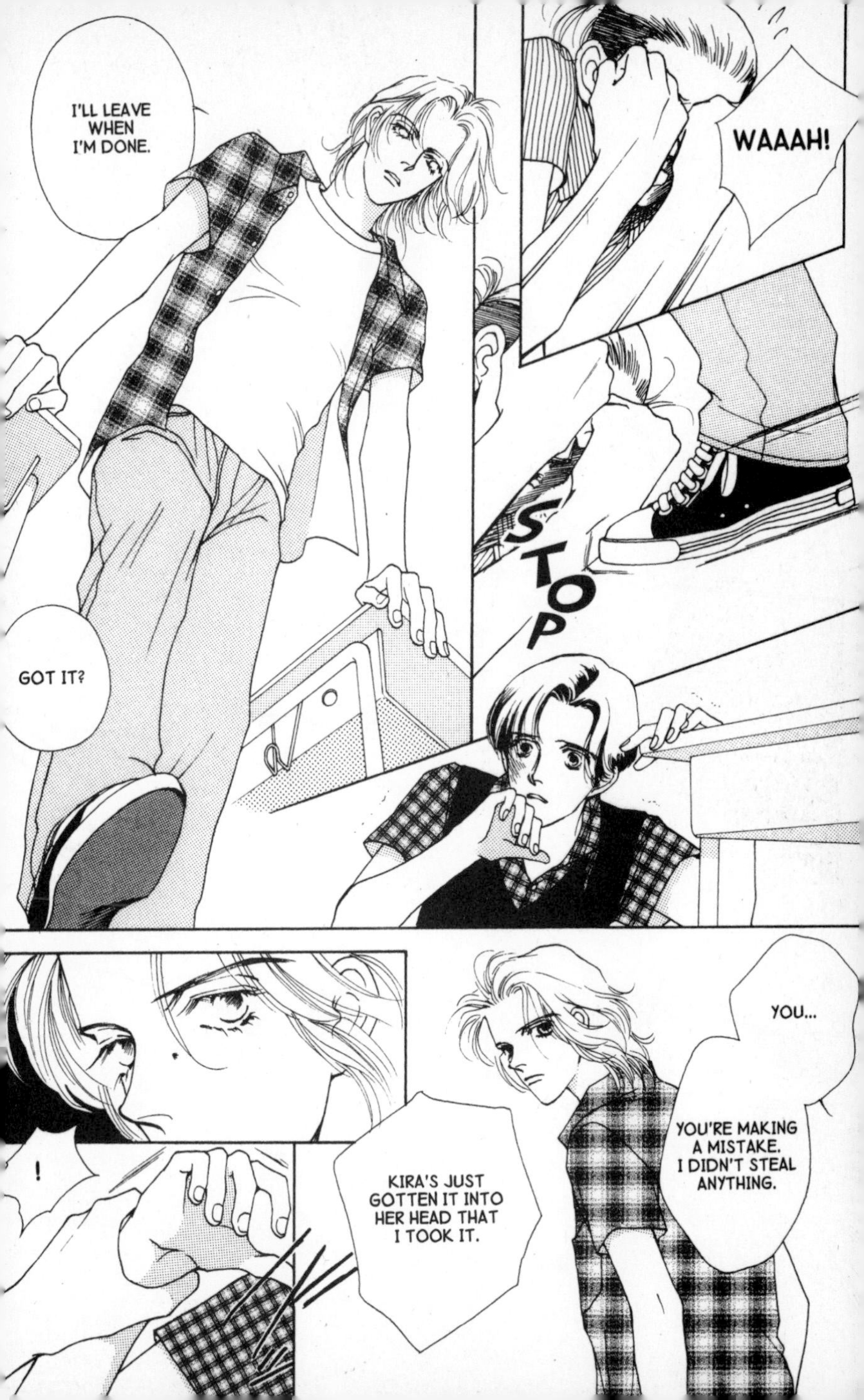
WAAAH!
STOP
I'LL LEAVE WHEN I'M DONE.
GOT IT?
YOU...
YOU'RE MAKING A MISTAKE. I DIDN'T STEAL ANYTHING.
KIRA'S JUST GOTTEN IT INTO HER HEAD THAT I TOOK IT.
!

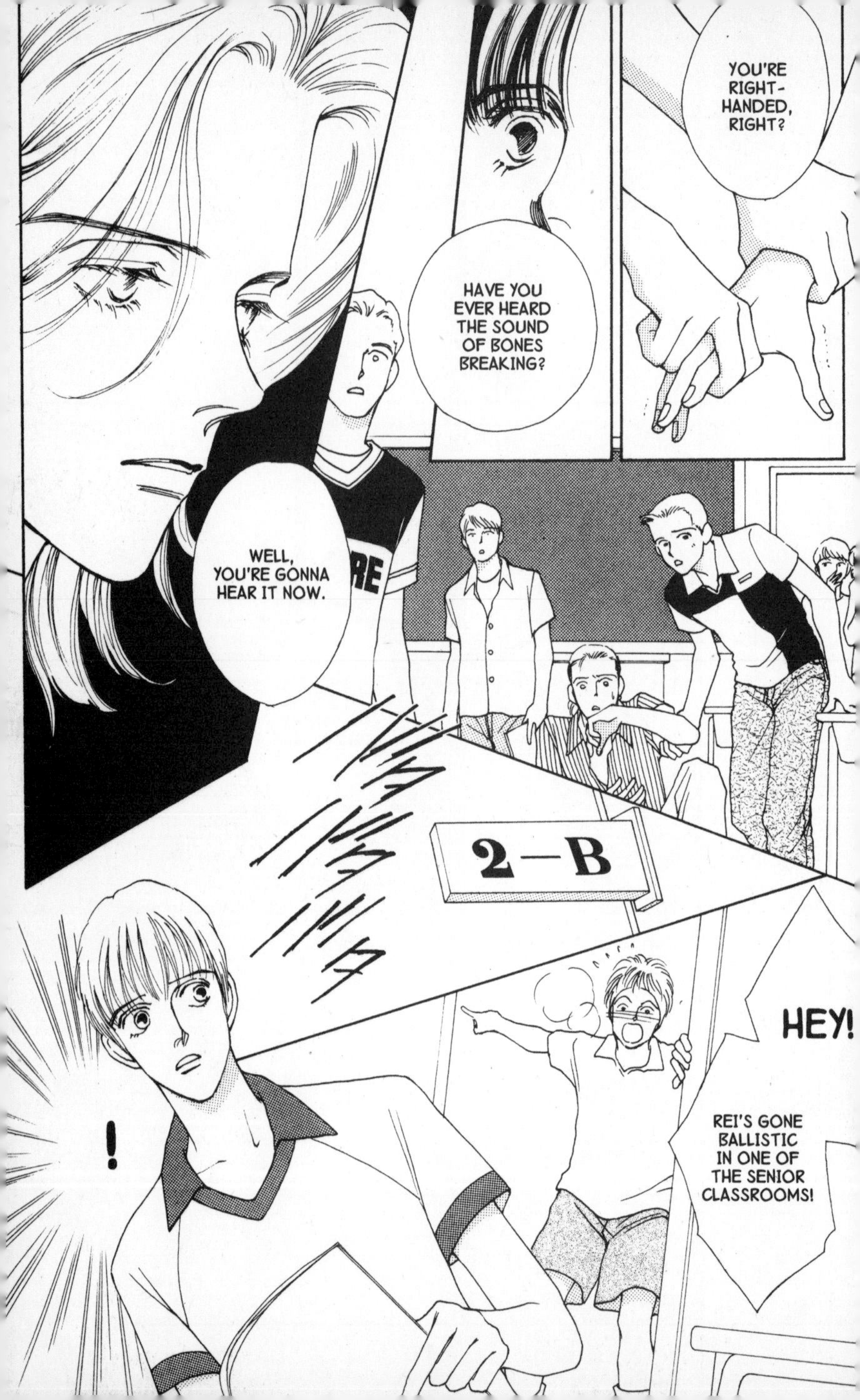
YOU'RE RIGHT-HANDED, RIGHT?
HAVE YOU EVER HEARD THE SOUND OF BONES BREAKING?
WELL, YOU'RE GONNA HEAR IT NOW.
2—B
HEY!
REI'S GONE BALLISTIC IN ONE OF THE SENIOR CLASSROOMS!
!

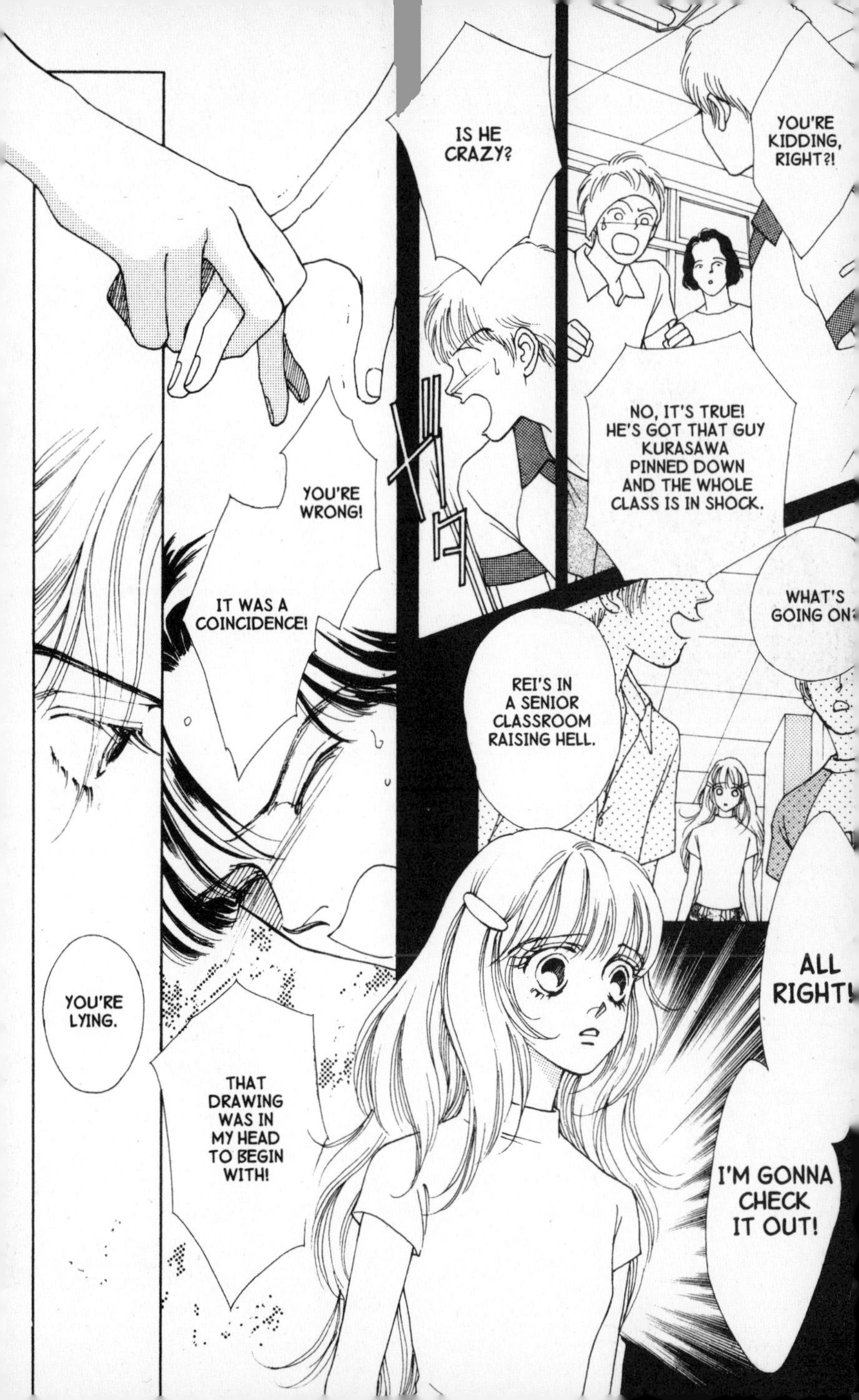
YOU'RE KIDDING, RIGHT?!
NO, IT'S TRUE! HE'S GOT THAT GUY KURASAWA PINNED DOWN AND THE WHOLE CLASS IS IN SHOCK.
IS HE CRAZY?
WHAT'S GOING ON
REI'S IN A SENIOR CLASSROOM RAISING HELL.
ALL RIGHT!
I'M GONNA CHECK IT OUT!
YOU'RE WRONG!
IT WAS A COINCIDENCE!
THAT DRAWING WAS IN MY HEAD TO BEGIN WITH!
YOU'RE LYING.

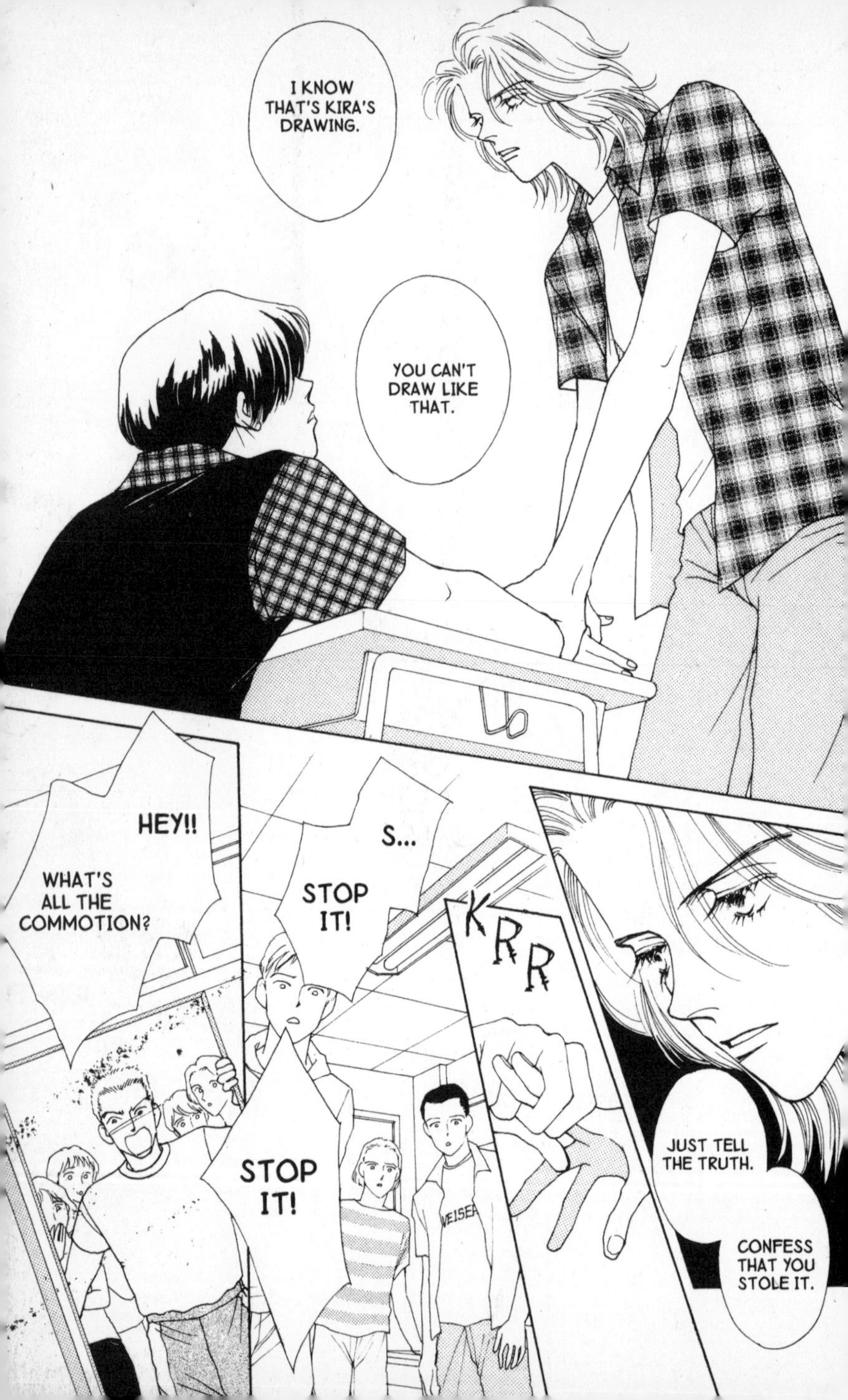
I KNOW THAT'S KIRA'S DRAWING.
YOU CAN'T DRAW LIKE THAT.
KRR
JUST TELL THE TRUTH.
CONFESS THAT YOU STOLE IT.
S... STOP IT!
HEY!! WHAT'S ALL THE COMMOTION?
STOP IT!

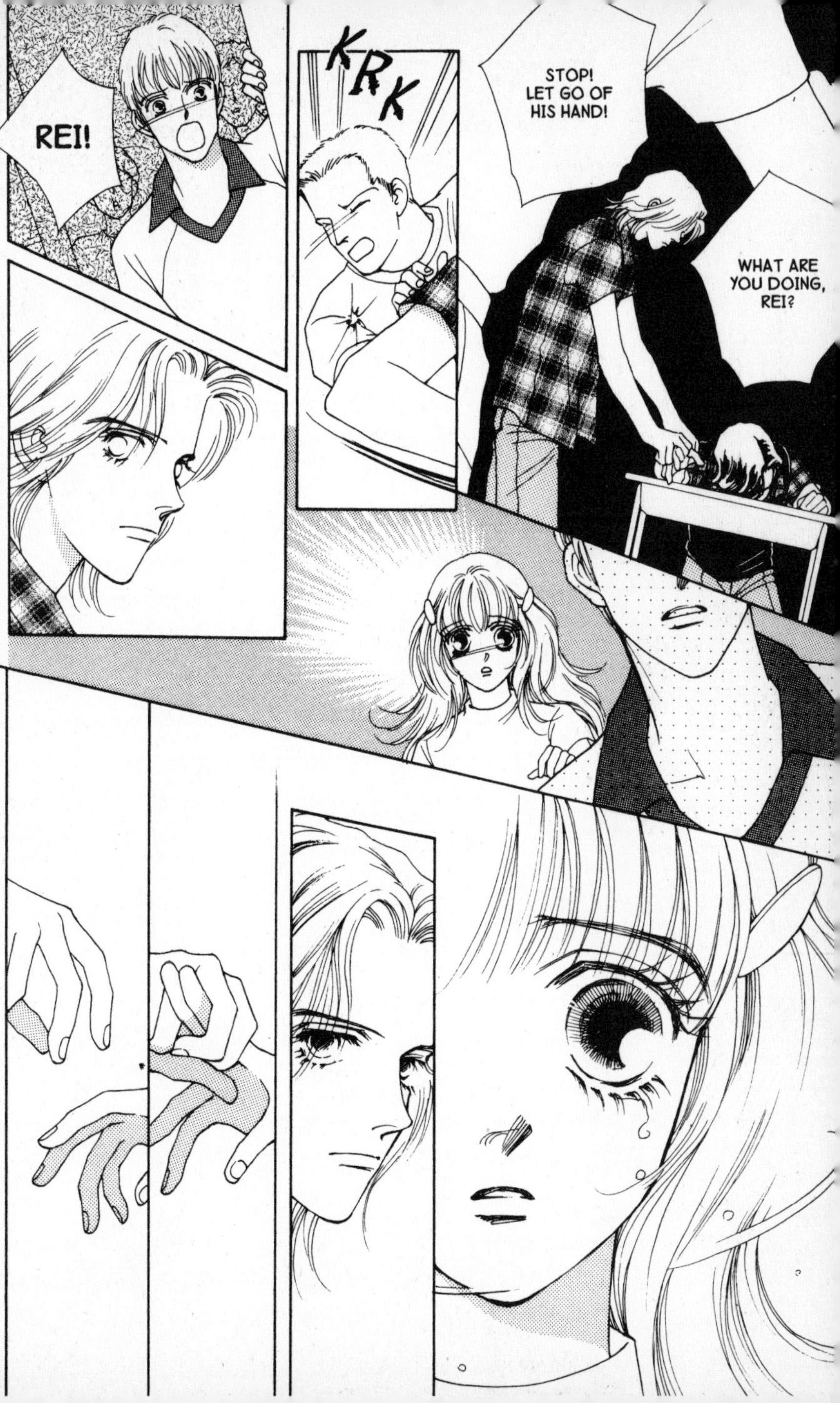
STOP! LET GO OF HIS HAND!
WHAT ARE YOU DOING, REI?
KRK
REI!

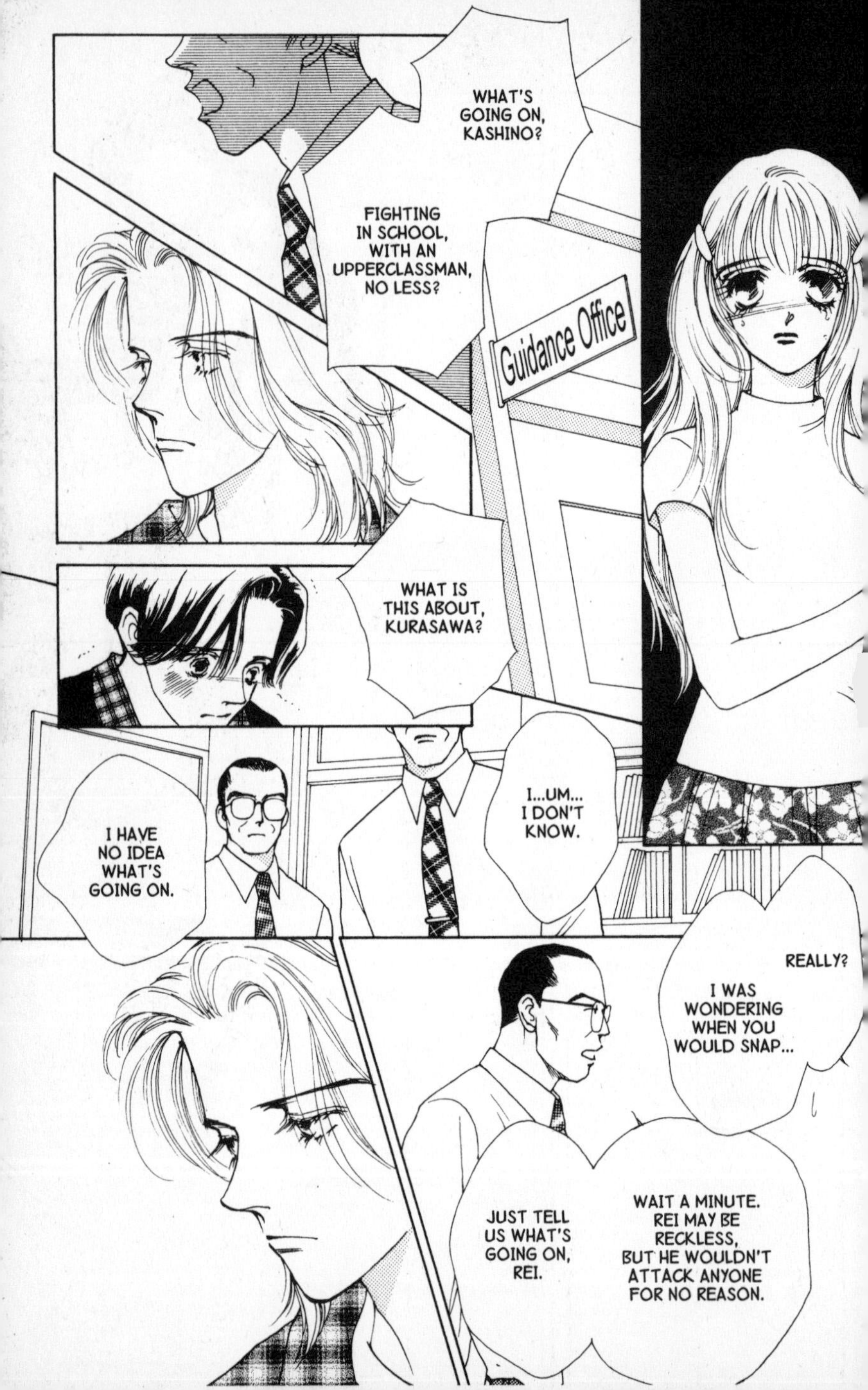
WHAT'S GOING ON, KASHINO?
Guidance Office
FIGHTING IN SCHOOL, WITH AN UPPERCLASSMAN, NO LESS?
WHAT IS THIS ABOUT, KURASAWA?
I...UM... I DON'T KNOW.
I HAVE NO IDEA WHAT'S GOING ON.
REALLY?
I WAS WONDERING WHEN YOU WOULD SNAP...
WAIT A MINUTE. REI MAY BE RECKLESS, BUT HE WOULDN'T ATTACK ANYONE FOR NO REASON.
JUST TELL US WHAT'S GOING ON, REI.

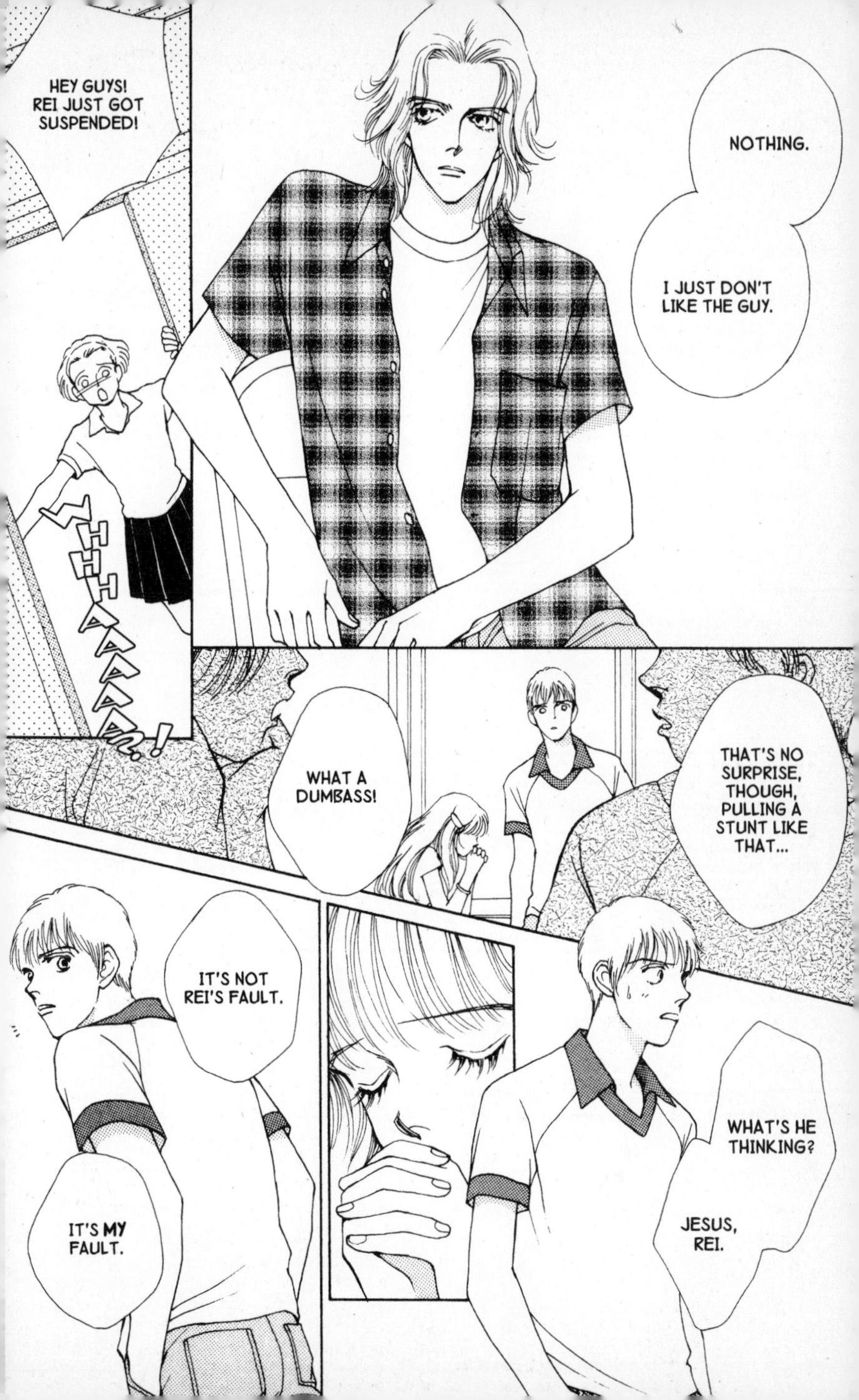
NOTHING.
I JUST DON'T LIKE THE GUY.
HEY GUYS! REI JUST GOT SUSPENDED!
WHHHAAAAAA!
THAT'S NO SURPRISE, THOUGH, PULLING A STUNT LIKE THAT...
WHAT A DUMBASS!
WHAT'S HE THINKING?
JESUS, REI.
IT'S NOT REI'S FAULT.
IT'S **MY** FAULT.

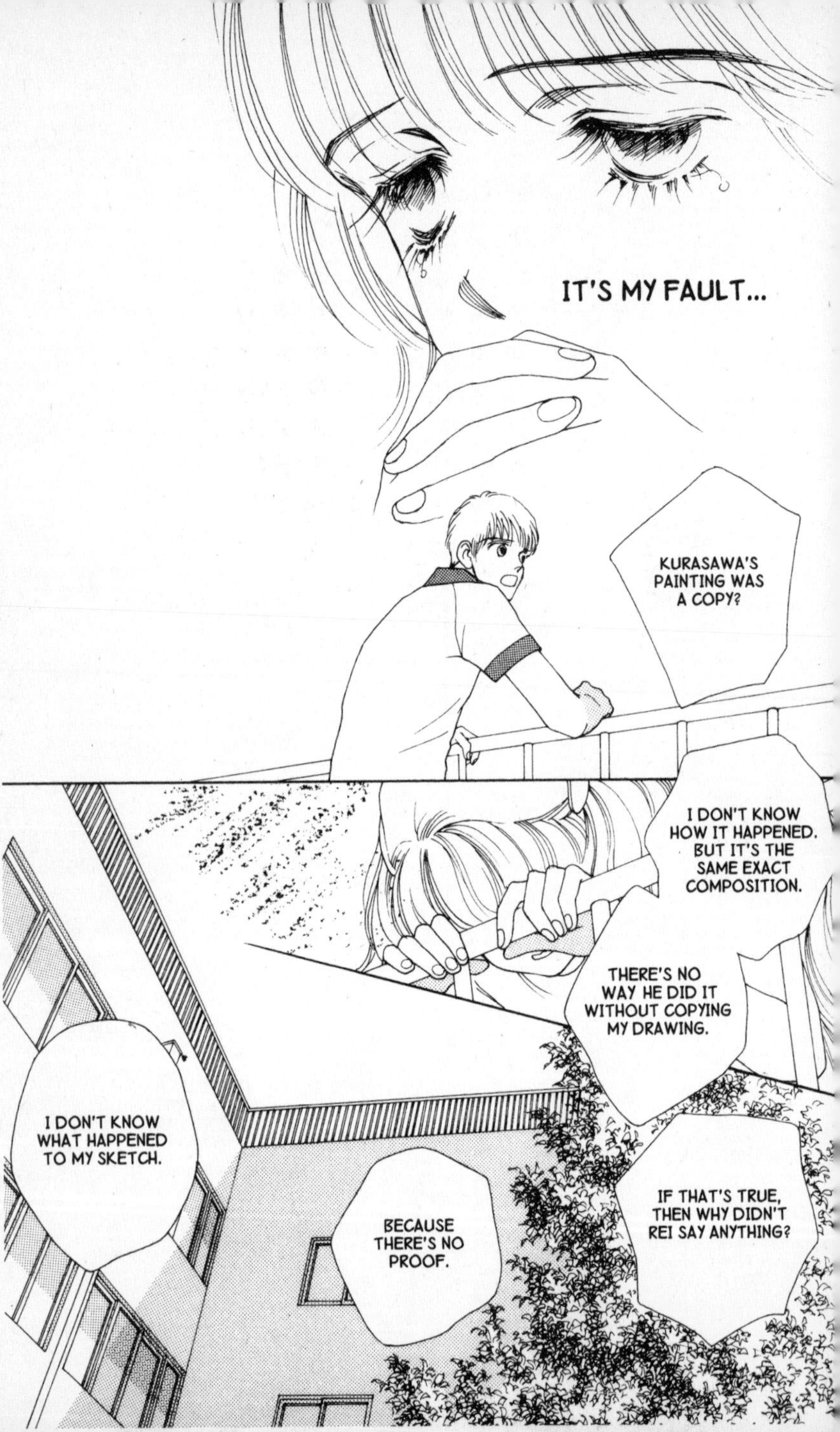
IT'S MY FAULT...
KURASAWA'S PAINTING WAS A COPY?
I DON'T KNOW HOW IT HAPPENED. BUT IT'S THE SAME EXACT COMPOSITION.
THERE'S NO WAY HE DID IT WITHOUT COPYING MY DRAWING.
IF THAT'S TRUE, THEN WHY DIDN'T REI SAY ANYTHING?
BECAUSE THERE'S NO PROOF.
I DON'T KNOW WHAT HAPPENED TO MY SKETCH.

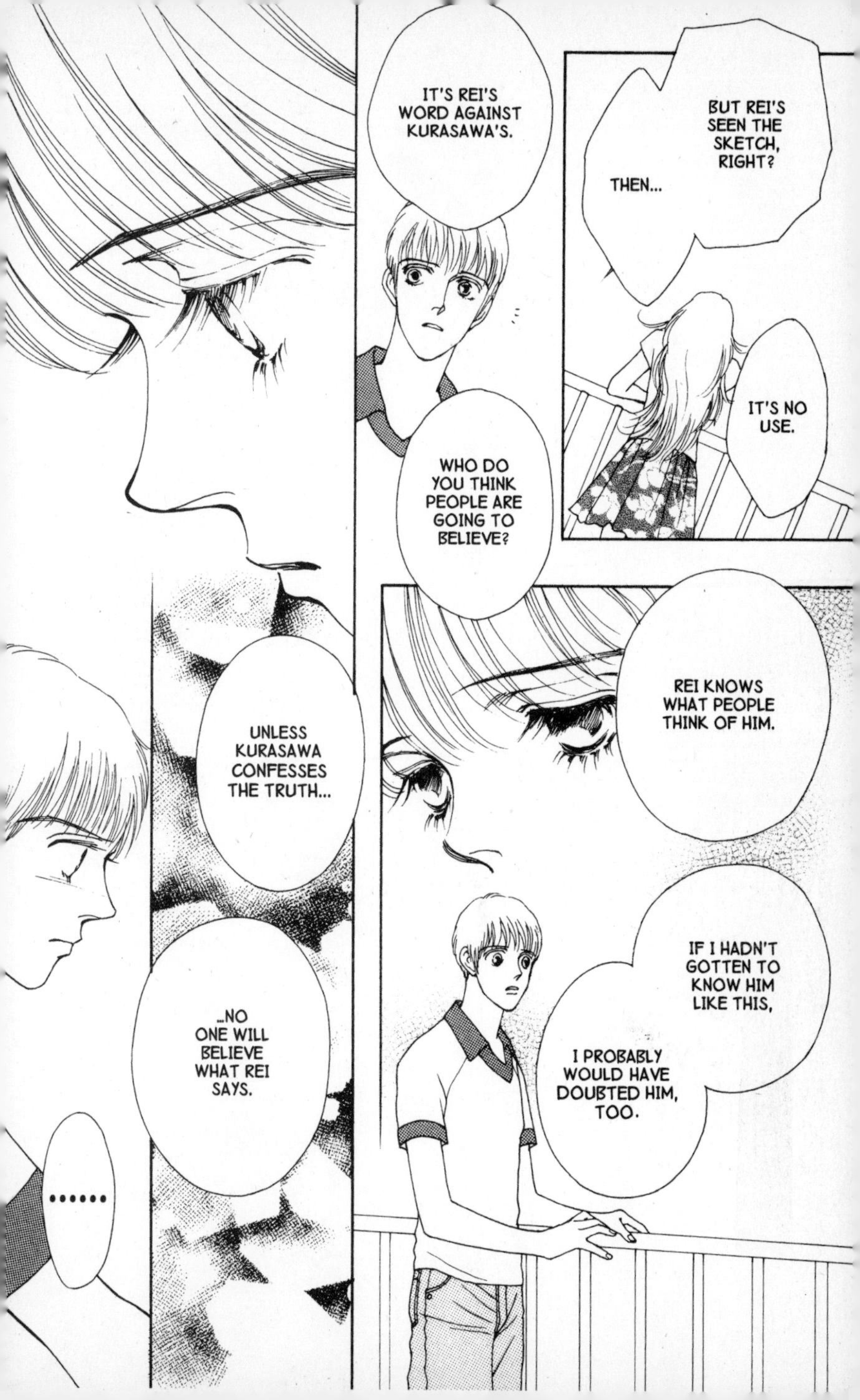
BUT REI'S SEEN THE SKETCH, RIGHT?
THEN...
IT'S NO USE.
IT'S REI'S WORD AGAINST KURASAWA'S.
WHO DO YOU THINK PEOPLE ARE GOING TO BELIEVE?
REI KNOWS WHAT PEOPLE THINK OF HIM.
IF I HADN'T GOTTEN TO KNOW HIM LIKE THIS,
I PROBABLY WOULD HAVE DOUBTED HIM, TOO.
UNLESS KURASAWA CONFESSES THE TRUTH...
...NO ONE WILL BELIEVE WHAT REI SAYS.
......

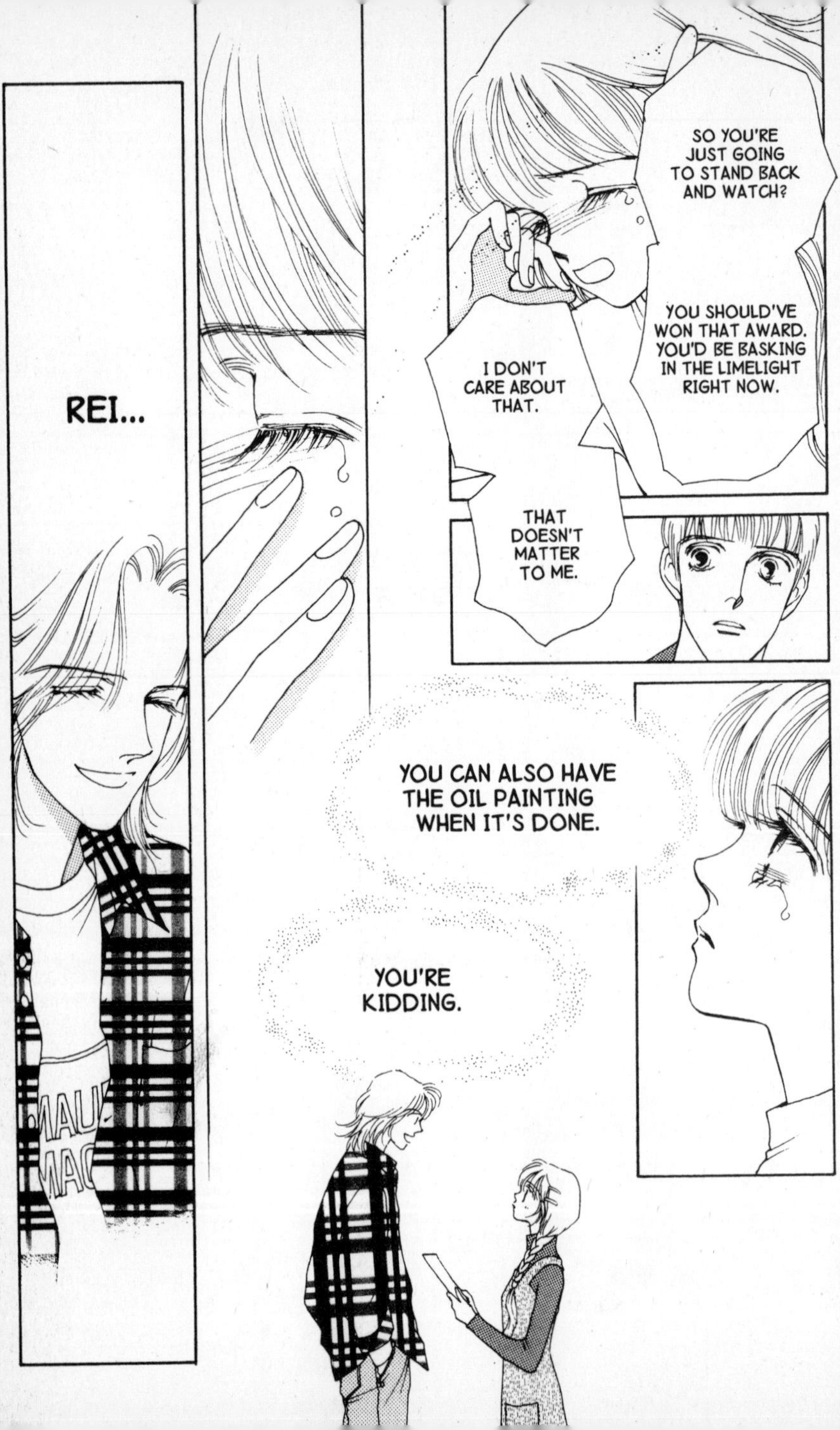
SO YOU'RE JUST GOING TO STAND BACK AND WATCH?
YOU SHOULD'VE WON THAT AWARD. YOU'D BE BASKING IN THE LIMELIGHT RIGHT NOW.
I DON'T CARE ABOUT THAT.
THAT DOESN'T MATTER TO ME.
YOU CAN ALSO HAVE THE OIL PAINTING WHEN IT'S DONE.
YOU'RE KIDDING.
REI...

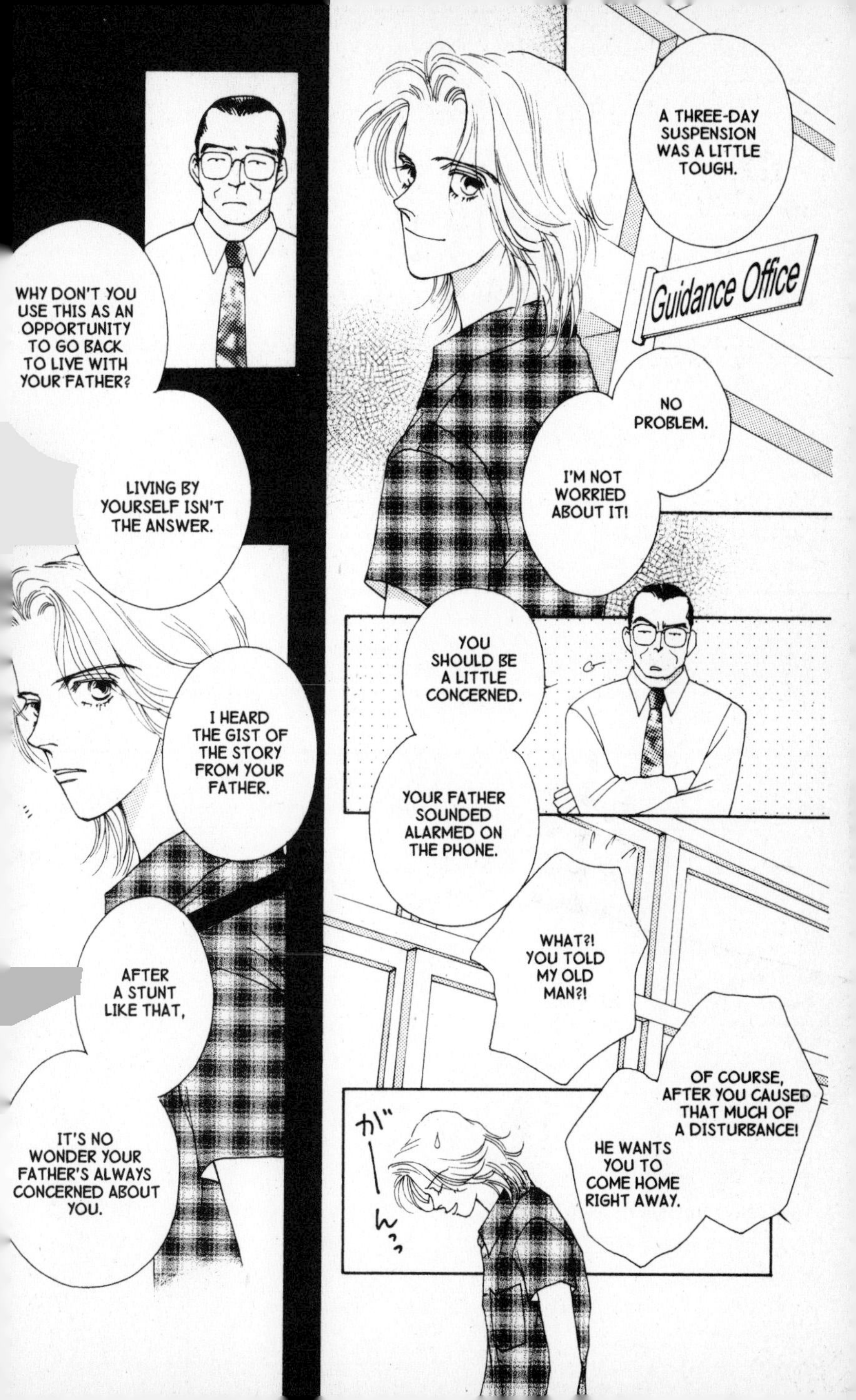
A THREE-DAY SUSPENSION WAS A LITTLE TOUGH.
Guidance Office
NO PROBLEM.
I'M NOT WORRIED ABOUT IT!
YOU SHOULD BE A LITTLE CONCERNED.
YOUR FATHER SOUNDED ALARMED ON THE PHONE.
WHAT?! YOU TOLD MY OLD MAN?!
OF COURSE, AFTER YOU CAUSED THAT MUCH OF A DISTURBANCE!
HE WANTS YOU TO COME HOME RIGHT AWAY.
ガーんっ
WHY DON'T YOU USE THIS AS AN OPPORTUNITY TO GO BACK TO LIVE WITH YOUR FATHER?
LIVING BY YOURSELF ISN'T THE ANSWER.
I HEARD THE GIST OF THE STORY FROM YOUR FATHER.
AFTER A STUNT LIKE THAT,
IT'S NO WONDER YOUR FATHER'S ALWAYS CONCERNED ABOUT YOU.

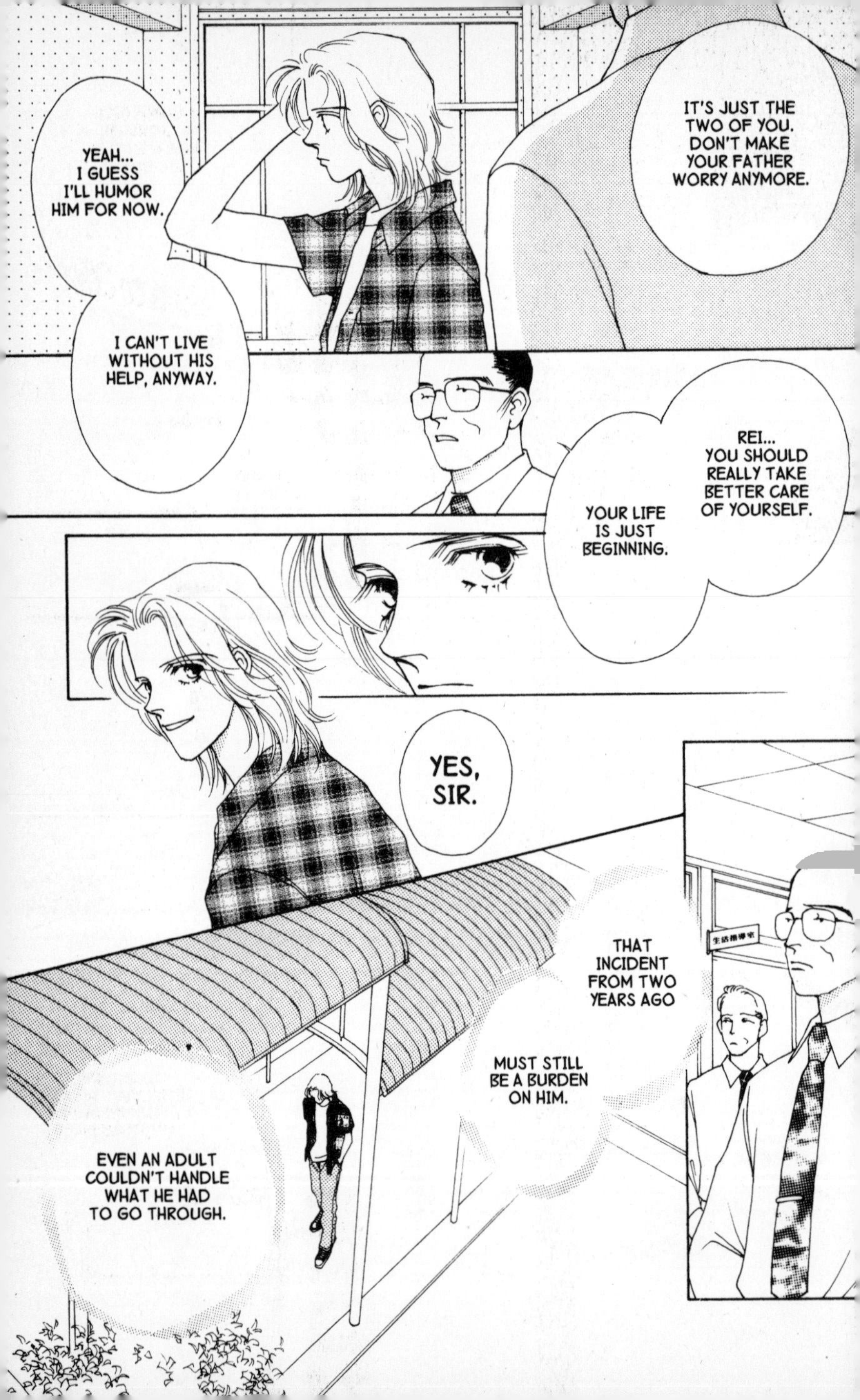
IT'S JUST THE TWO OF YOU. DON'T MAKE YOUR FATHER WORRY ANYMORE.
YEAH... I GUESS I'LL HUMOR HIM FOR NOW.
I CAN'T LIVE WITHOUT HIS HELP, ANYWAY.
REI... YOU SHOULD REALLY TAKE BETTER CARE OF YOURSELF.
YOUR LIFE IS JUST BEGINNING.
YES, SIR.
THAT INCIDENT FROM TWO YEARS AGO
MUST STILL BE A BURDEN ON HIM.
EVEN AN ADULT COULDN'T HANDLE WHAT HE HAD TO GO THROUGH.

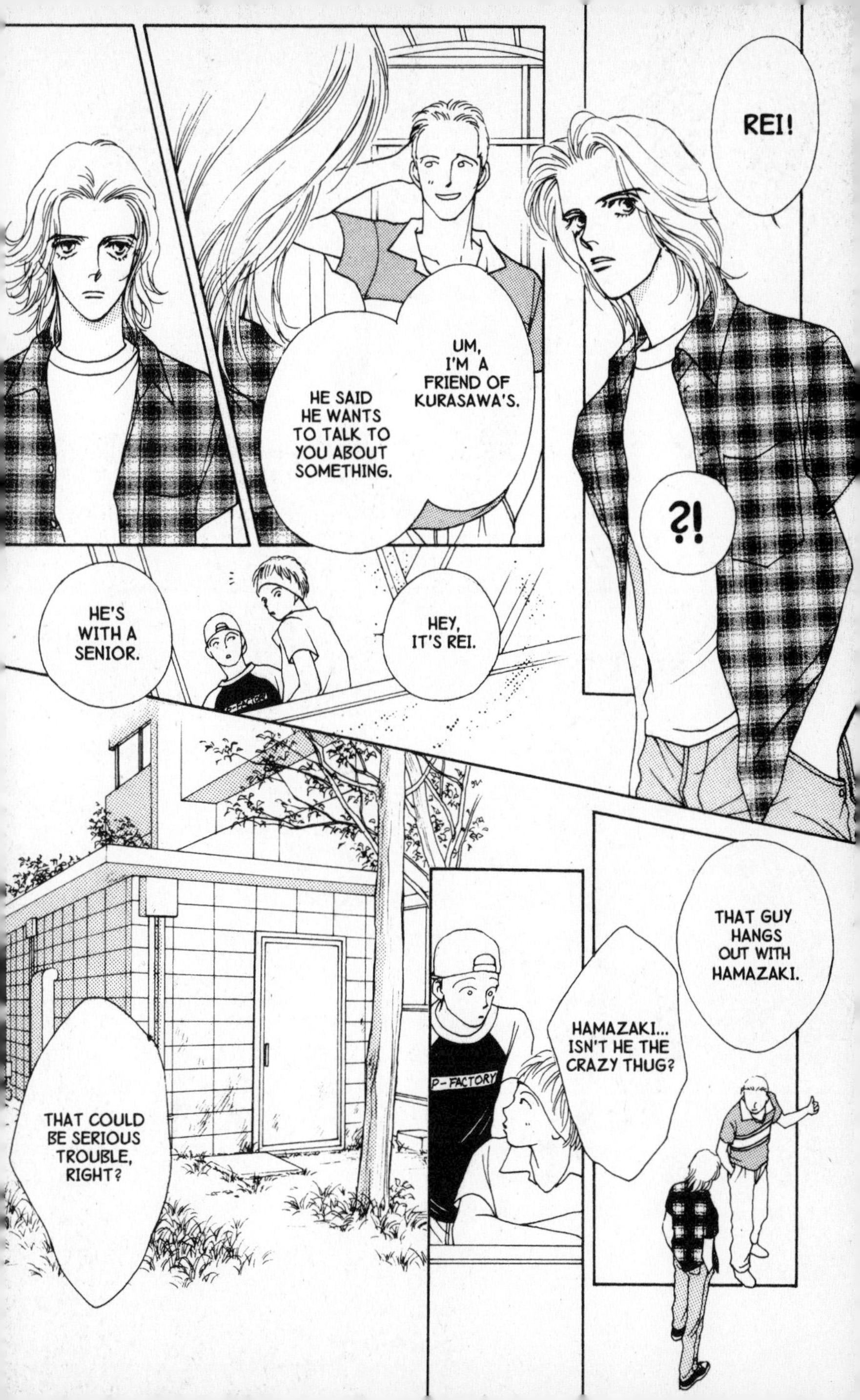
REI!
?!
UM, I'M A FRIEND OF KURASAWA'S.
HE SAID HE WANTS TO TALK TO YOU ABOUT SOMETHING.
HEY, IT'S REI.
HE'S WITH A SENIOR.
THAT GUY HANGS OUT WITH HAMAZAKI.
HAMAZAKI... ISN'T HE THE CRAZY THUG?
THAT COULD BE SERIOUS TROUBLE, RIGHT?

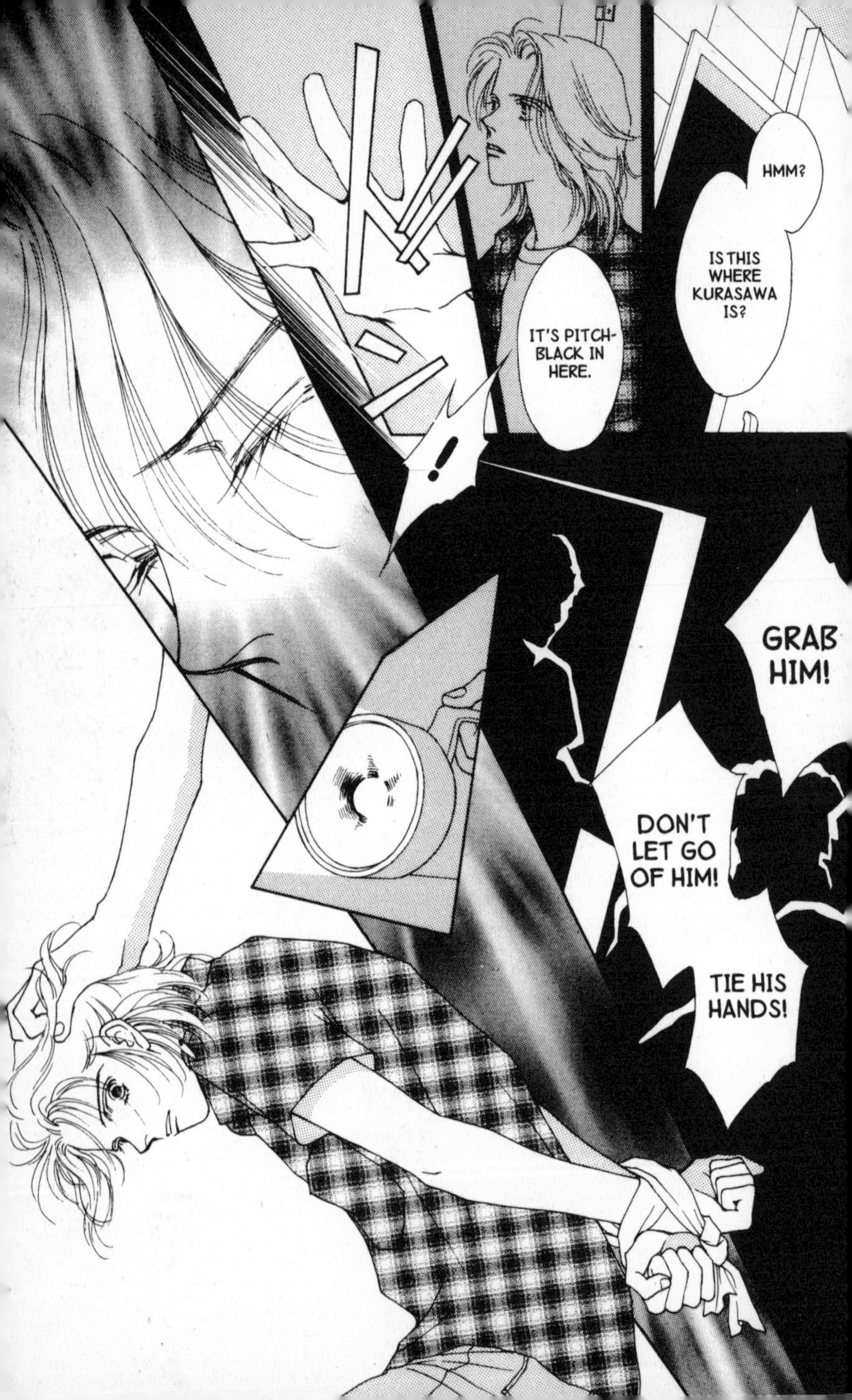

HMM?
IS THIS WHERE KURASAWA IS?
IT'S PITCH-BLACK IN HERE.
!
GRAB HIM!
DON'T LET GO OF HIM!
TIE HIS HANDS!

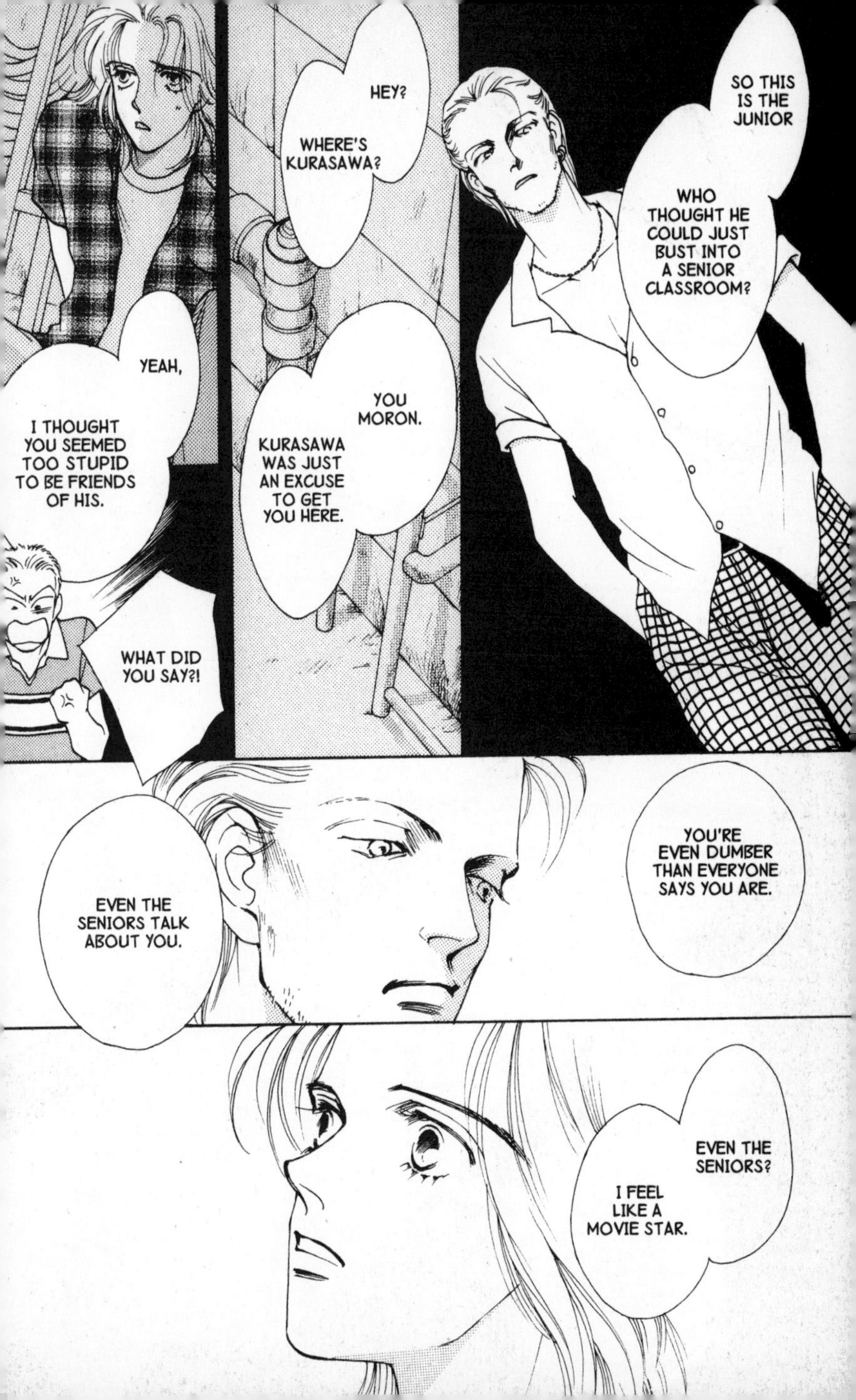
SO THIS IS THE JUNIOR
WHO THOUGHT HE COULD JUST BUST INTO A SENIOR CLASSROOM?
HEY?
WHERE'S KURASAWA?
YOU MORON.
KURASAWA WAS JUST AN EXCUSE TO GET YOU HERE.
YEAH,
I THOUGHT YOU SEEMED TOO STUPID TO BE FRIENDS OF HIS.
WHAT DID YOU SAY?!
YOU'RE EVEN DUMBER THAN EVERYONE SAYS YOU ARE.
EVEN THE SENIORS TALK ABOUT YOU.
EVEN THE SENIORS?
I FEEL LIKE A MOVIE STAR.

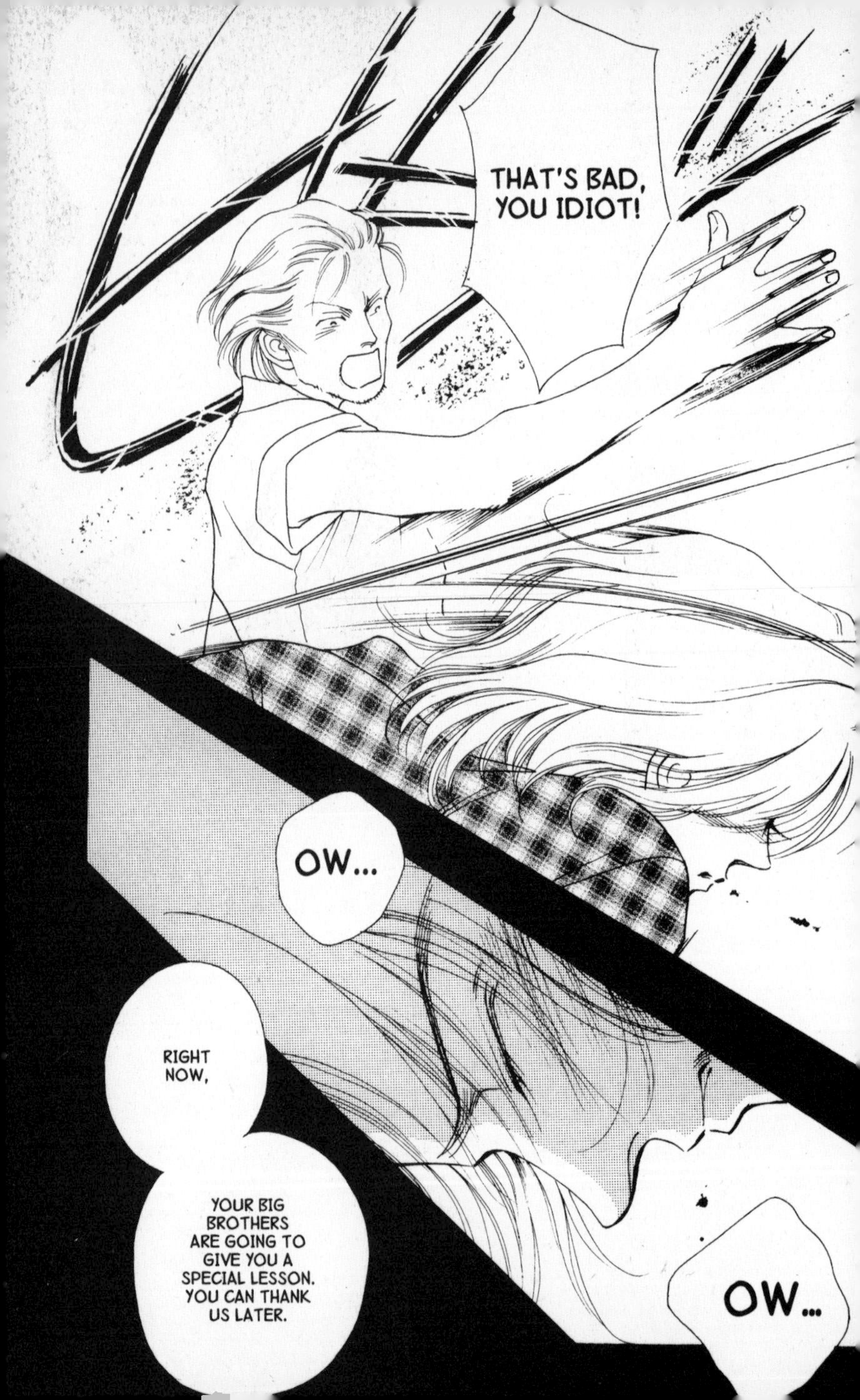
THAT'S BAD, YOU IDIOT!
OW...
OW...
RIGHT NOW,
YOUR BIG BROTHERS ARE GOING TO GIVE YOU A SPECIAL LESSON. YOU CAN THANK US LATER.

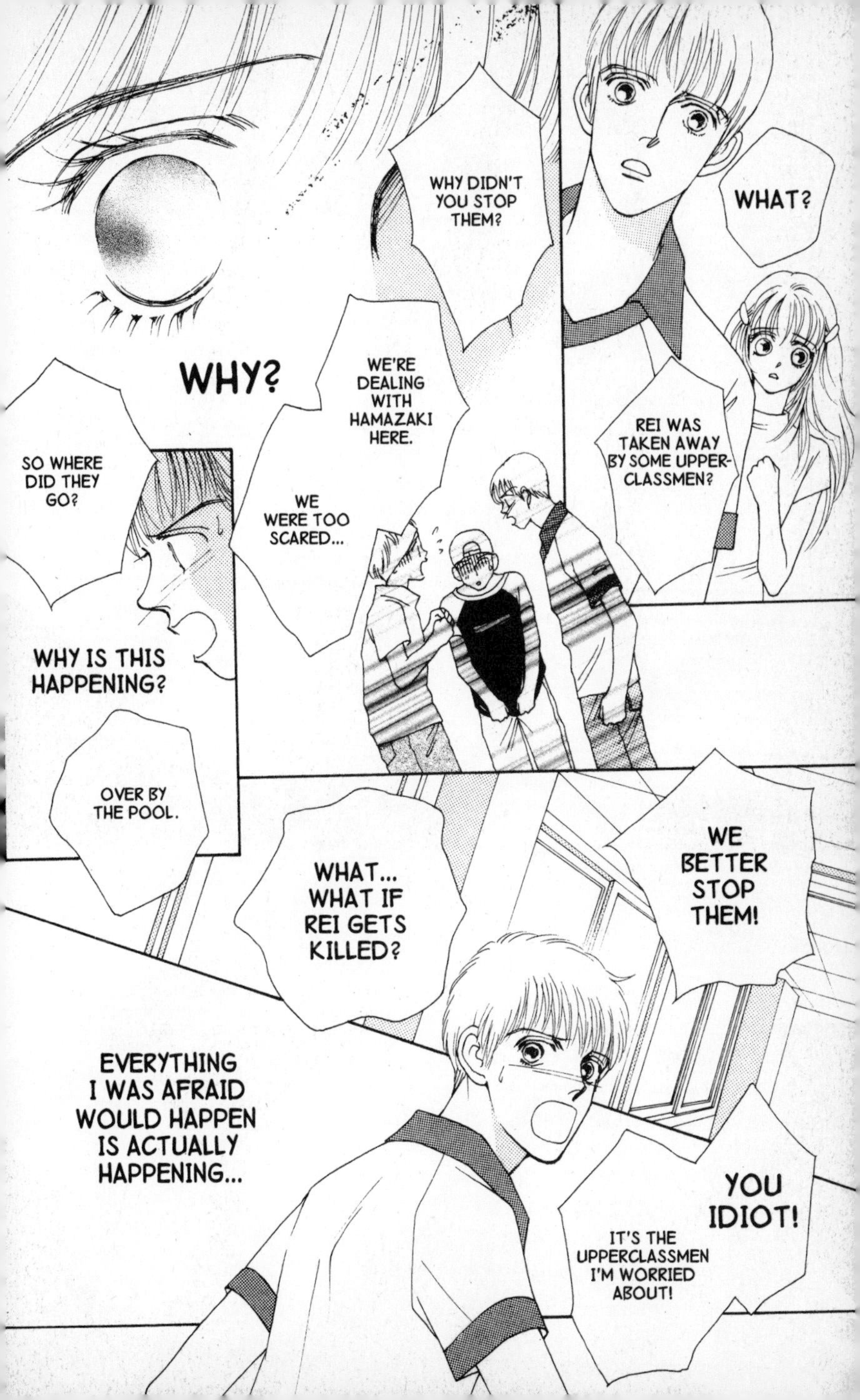
WHAT?
REI WAS TAKEN AWAY BY SOME UPPER-CLASSMEN?
WHY DIDN'T YOU STOP THEM?
WE'RE DEALING WITH HAMAZAKI HERE.
WE WERE TOO SCARED...
WHY?
SO WHERE DID THEY GO?
OVER BY THE POOL.
WHY IS THIS HAPPENING?
WE BETTER STOP THEM!
WHAT... WHAT IF REI GETS KILLED?
YOU IDIOT!
IT'S THE UPPERCLASSMEN I'M WORRIED ABOUT!
EVERYTHING I WAS AFRAID WOULD HAPPEN IS ACTUALLY HAPPENING...

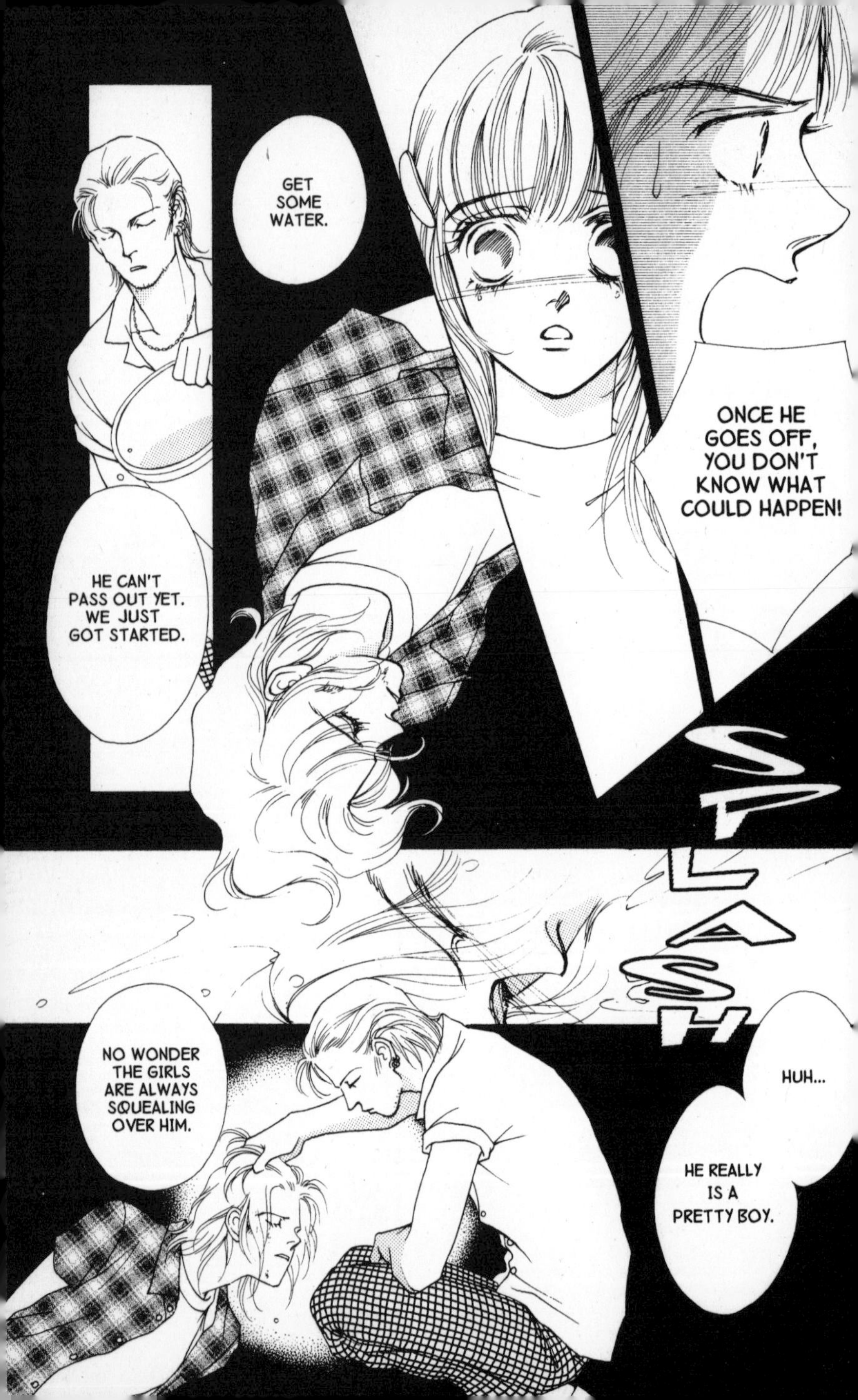
ONCE HE GOES OFF, YOU DON'T KNOW WHAT COULD HAPPEN!
GET SOME WATER.
HE CAN'T PASS OUT YET. WE JUST GOT STARTED.
SPLASH
HUH...
HE REALLY IS A PRETTY BOY.
NO WONDER THE GIRLS ARE ALWAYS SQUEALING OVER HIM.

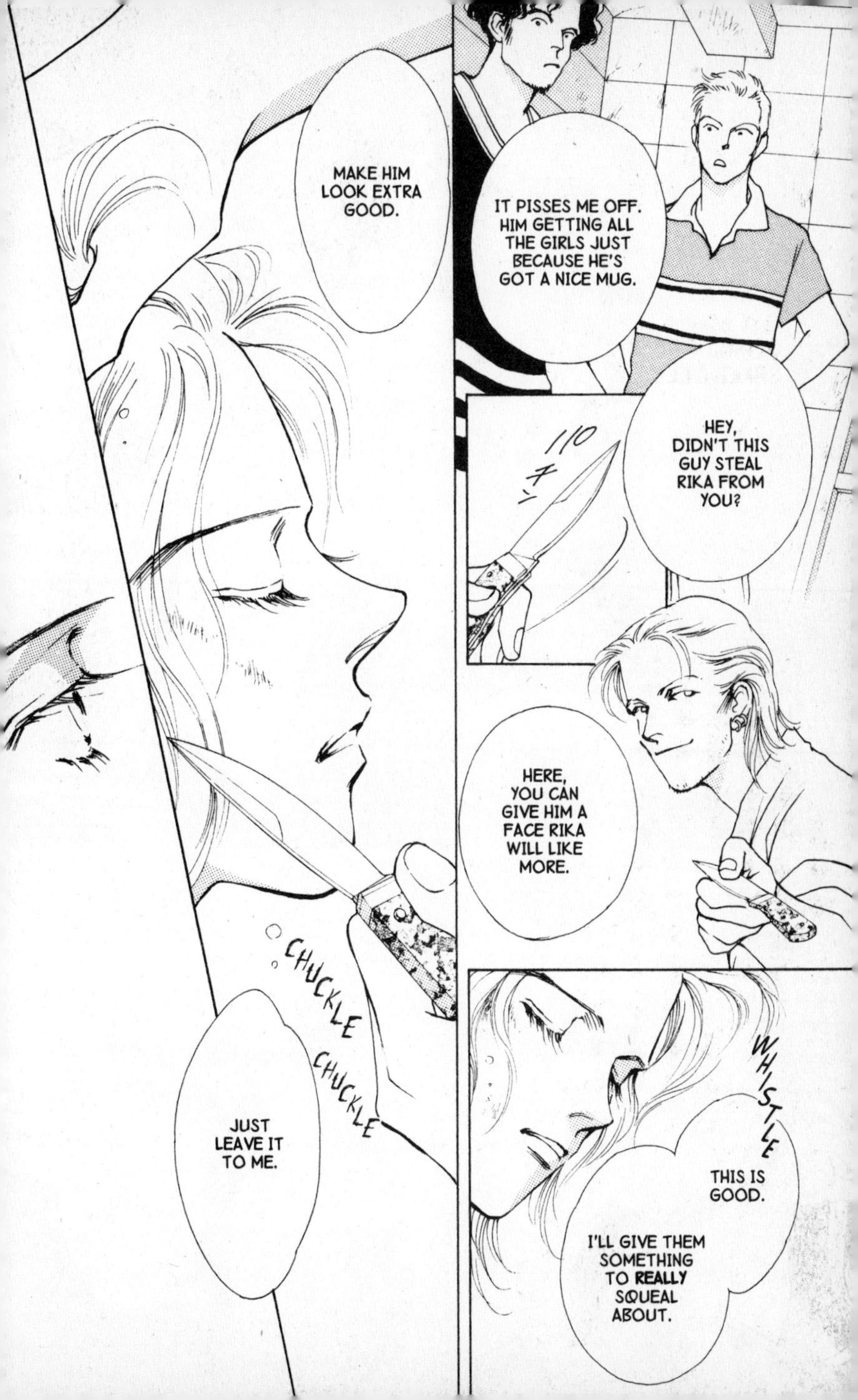

IT PISSES ME OFF. HIM GETTING ALL THE GIRLS JUST BECAUSE HE'S GOT A NICE MUG.
HEY, DIDN'T THIS GUY STEAL RIKA FROM YOU?
HERE, YOU CAN GIVE HIM A FACE RIKA WILL LIKE MORE.
WHISTLE
THIS IS GOOD.
I'LL GIVE THEM SOMETHING TO **REALLY** SQUEAL ABOUT.
MAKE HIM LOOK EXTRA GOOD.
CHUCKLE
CHUCKLE
JUST LEAVE IT TO ME.

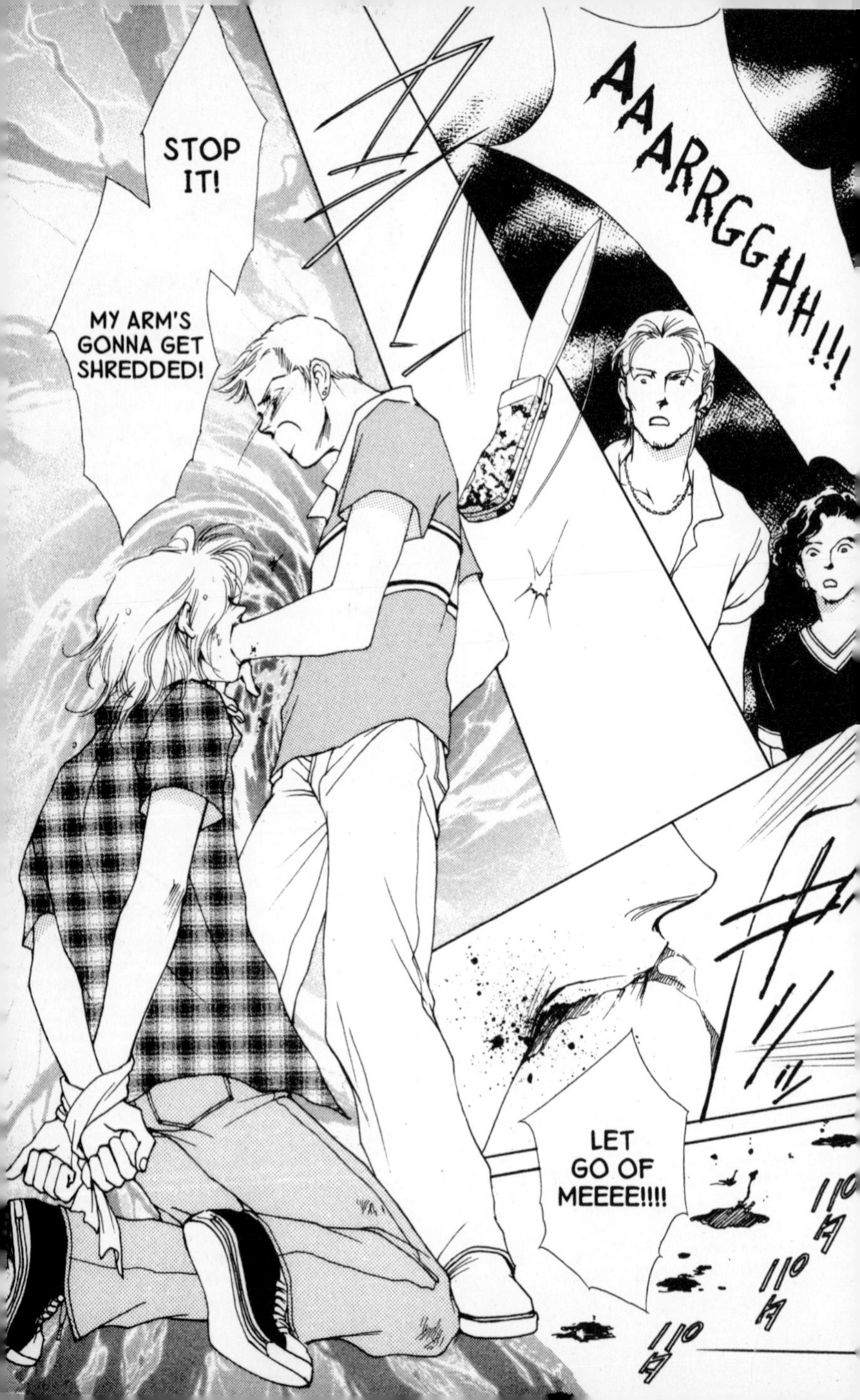
AAARRGGHH!!!
LET GO OF MEEEE!!!!
STOP IT!
MY ARM'S GONNA GET SHREDDED!

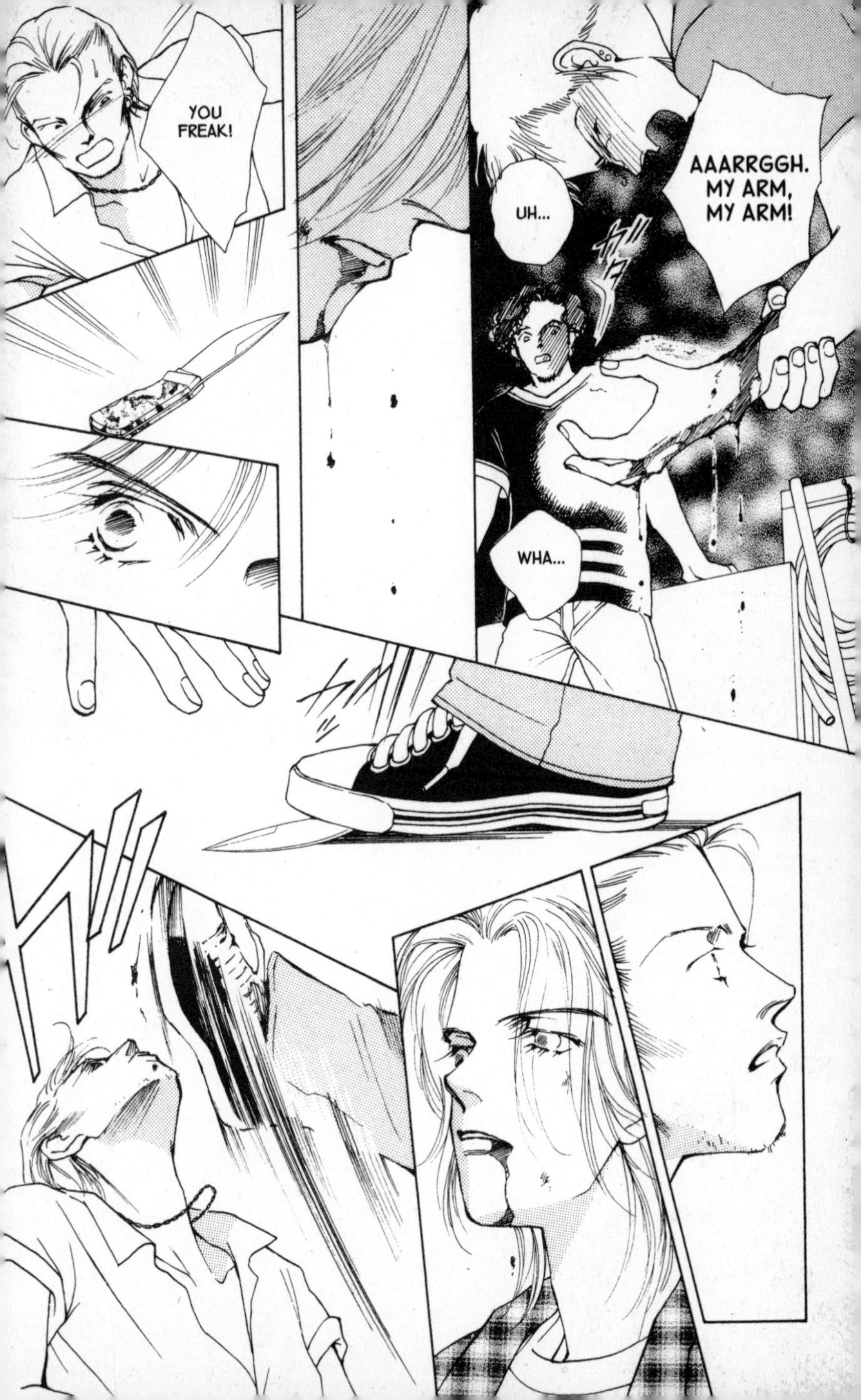
AAARRGGH. MY ARM, MY ARM!
UH...
WHA...
YOU FREAK!

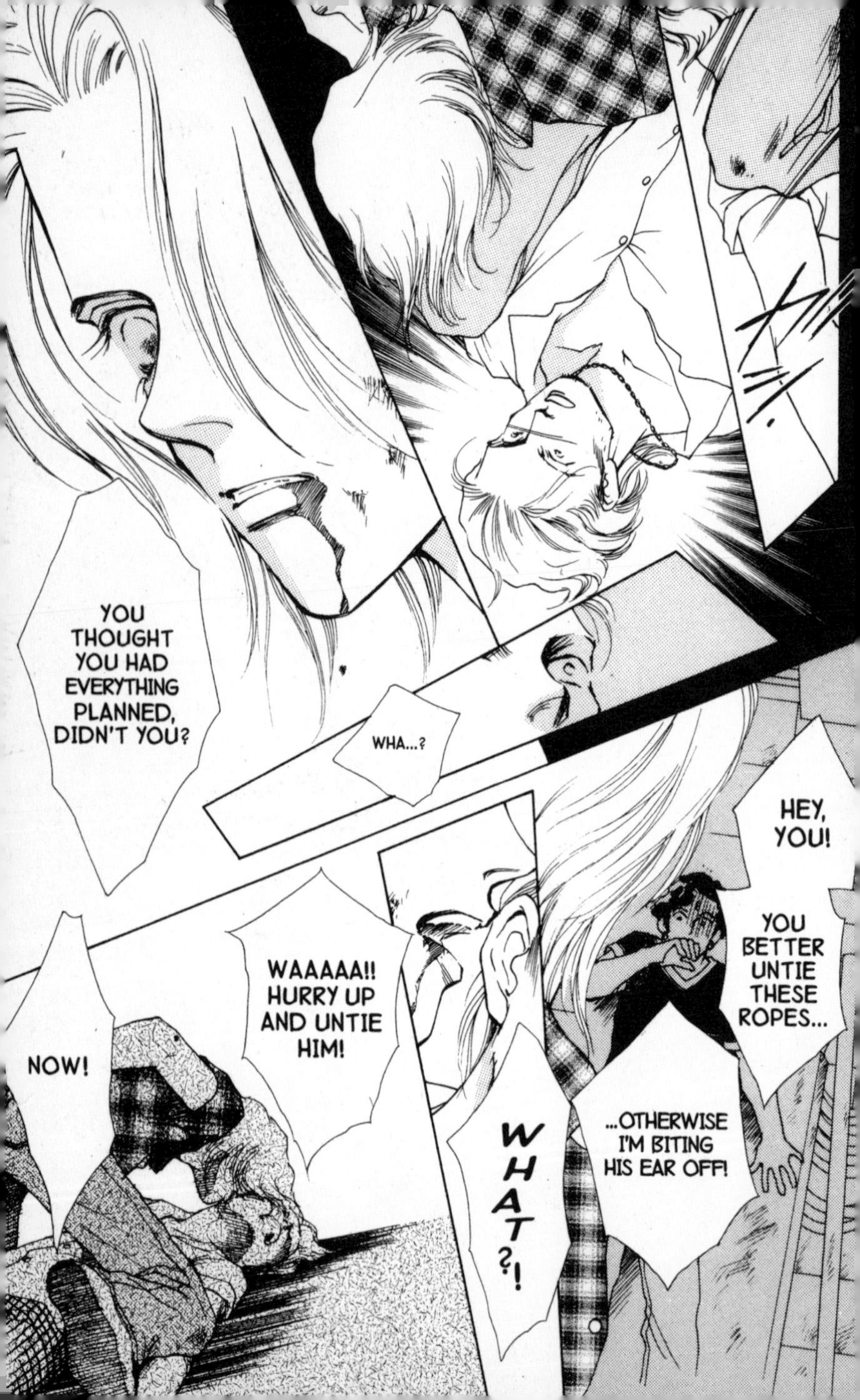
YOU THOUGHT YOU HAD EVERYTHING PLANNED, DIDN'T YOU?
WHA...?
HEY, YOU!
YOU BETTER UNTIE THESE ROPES...
...OTHERWISE I'M BITING HIS EAR OFF!
WHAT?!
WAAAAA!! HURRY UP AND UNTIE HIM!
NOW!

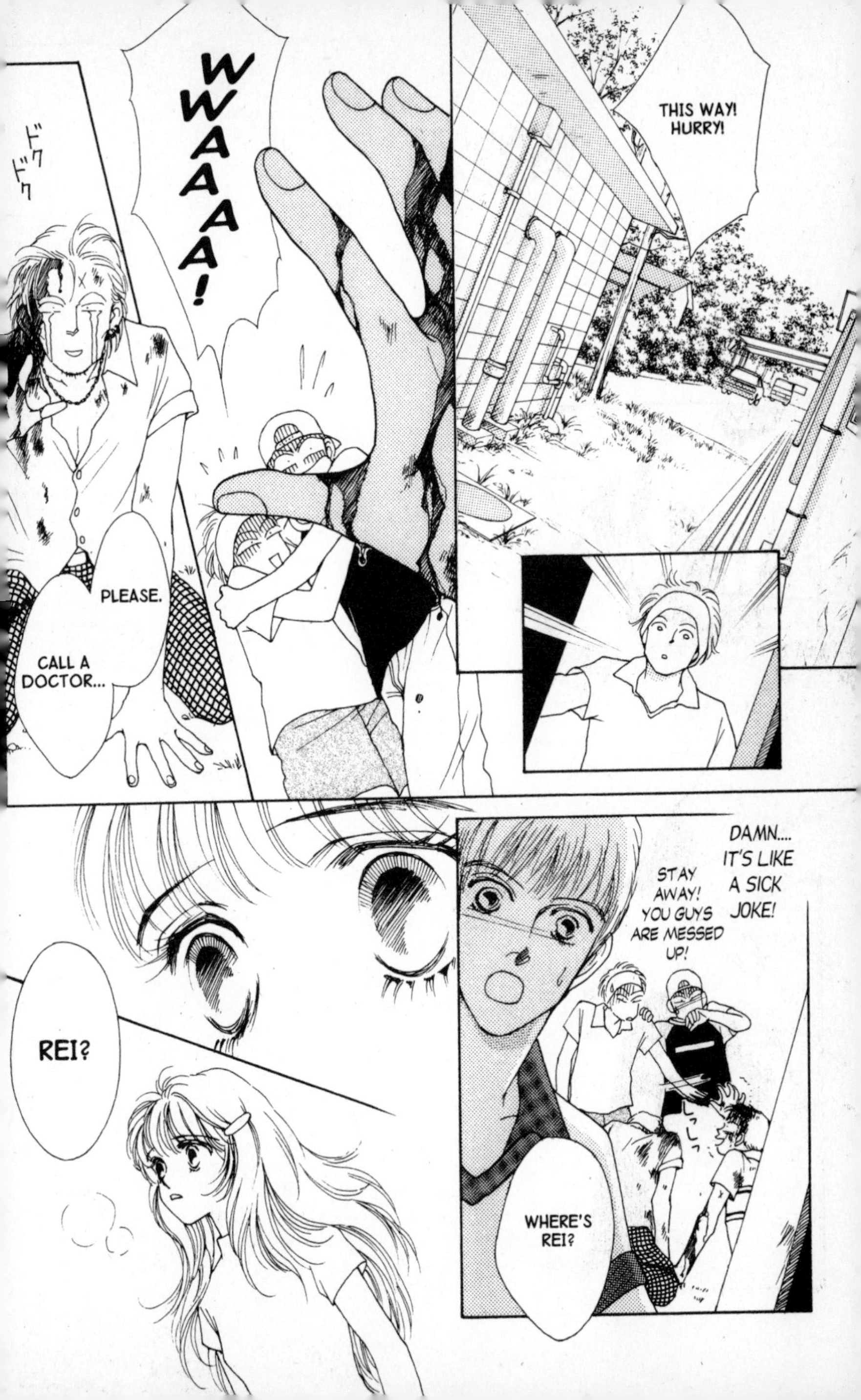
THIS WAY! HURRY!
WWAAAAA!
ドクドク
PLEASE.
CALL A DOCTOR...
DAMN.... IT'S LIKE A SICK JOKE!
STAY AWAY! YOU GUYS ARE MESSED UP!
WHERE'S REI?
REI?

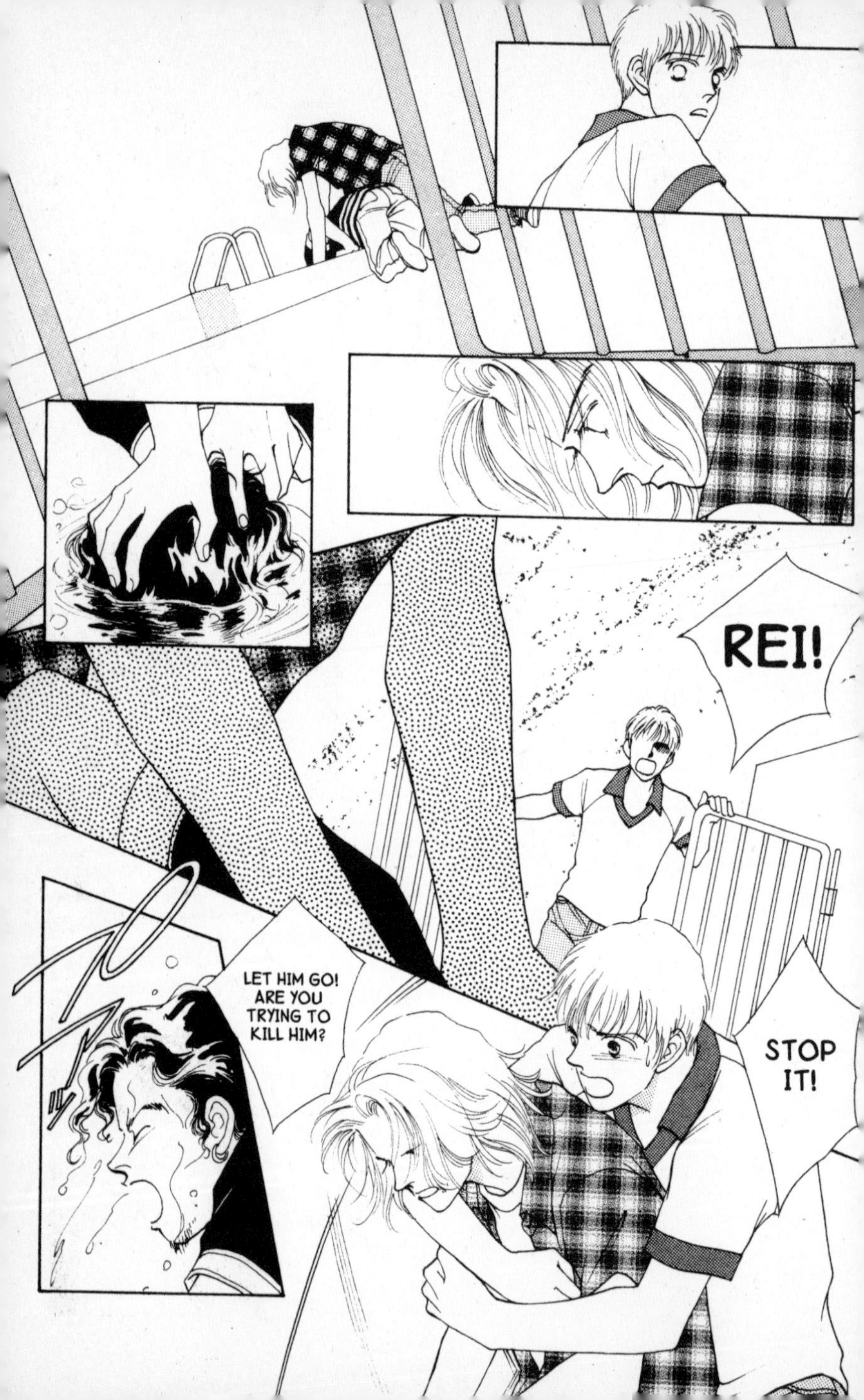
REI!
STOP IT!
LET HIM GO! ARE YOU TRYING TO KILL HIM?

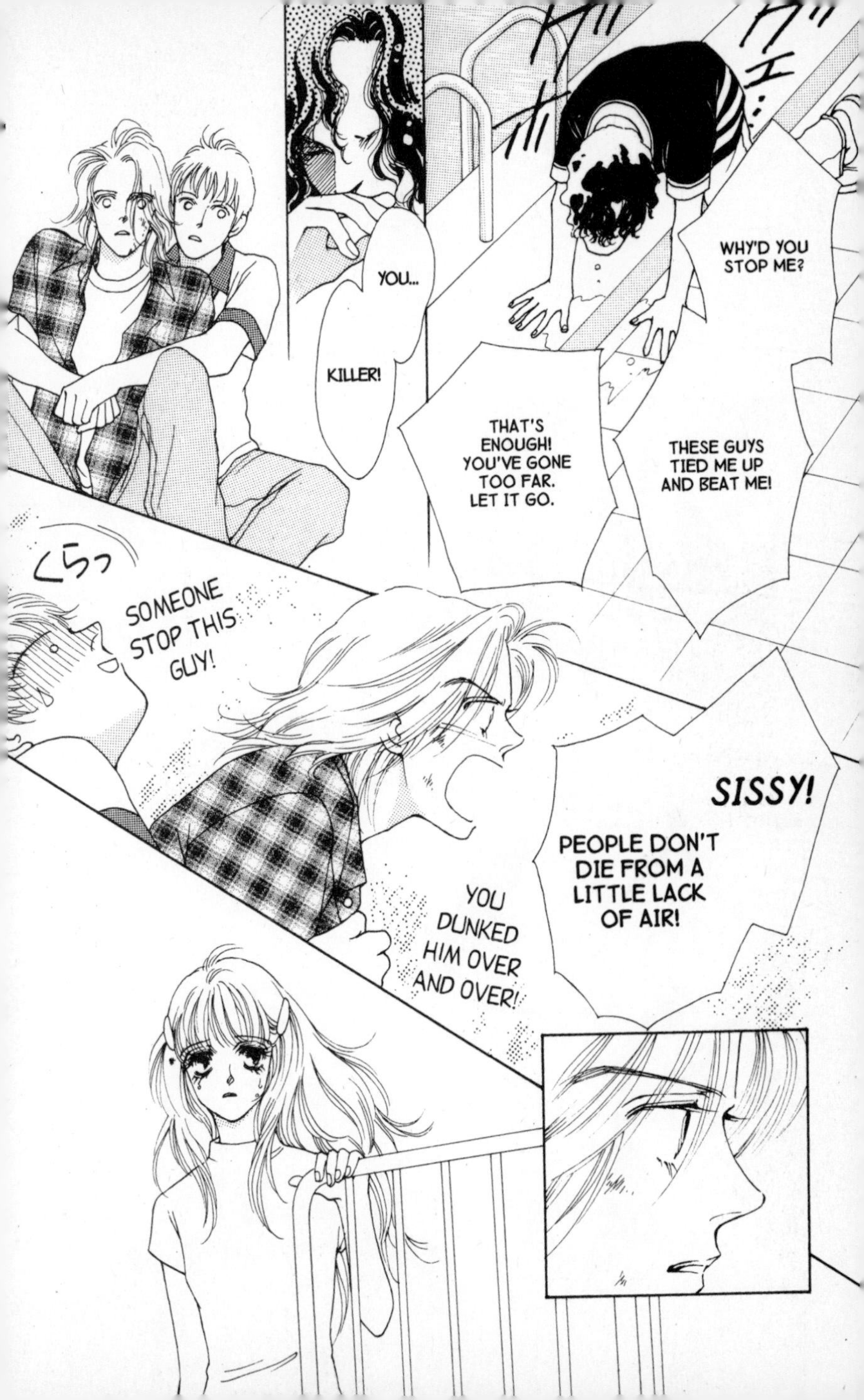
WHY'D YOU STOP ME?
THESE GUYS TIED ME UP AND BEAT ME!
THAT'S ENOUGH! YOU'VE GONE TOO FAR. LET IT GO.
YOU...
KILLER!
SISSY!
PEOPLE DON'T DIE FROM A LITTLE LACK OF AIR!
YOU DUNKED HIM OVER AND OVER!
SOMEONE STOP THIS GUY!
くらっ

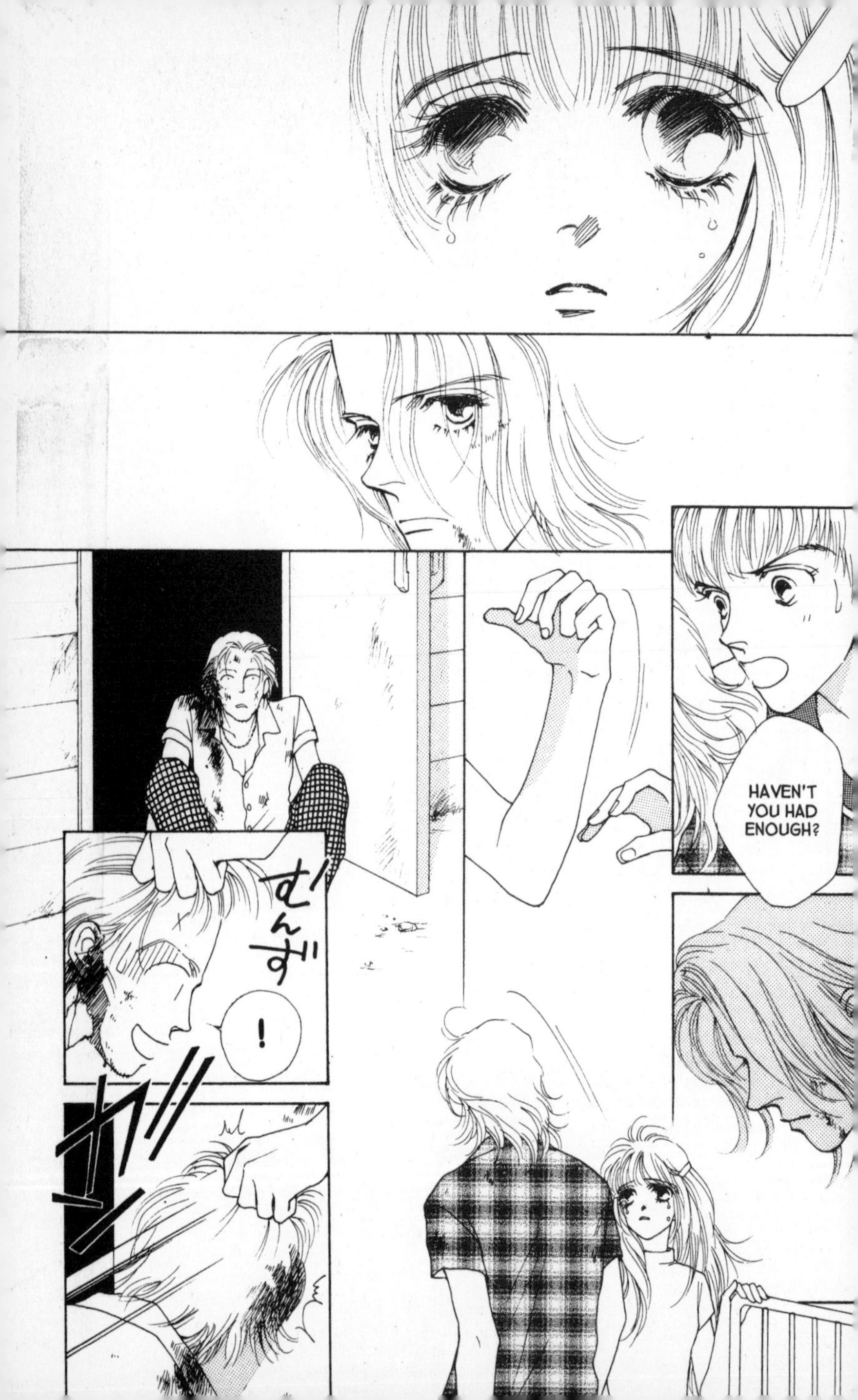
HAVEN'T YOU HAD ENOUGH?
むんず
!

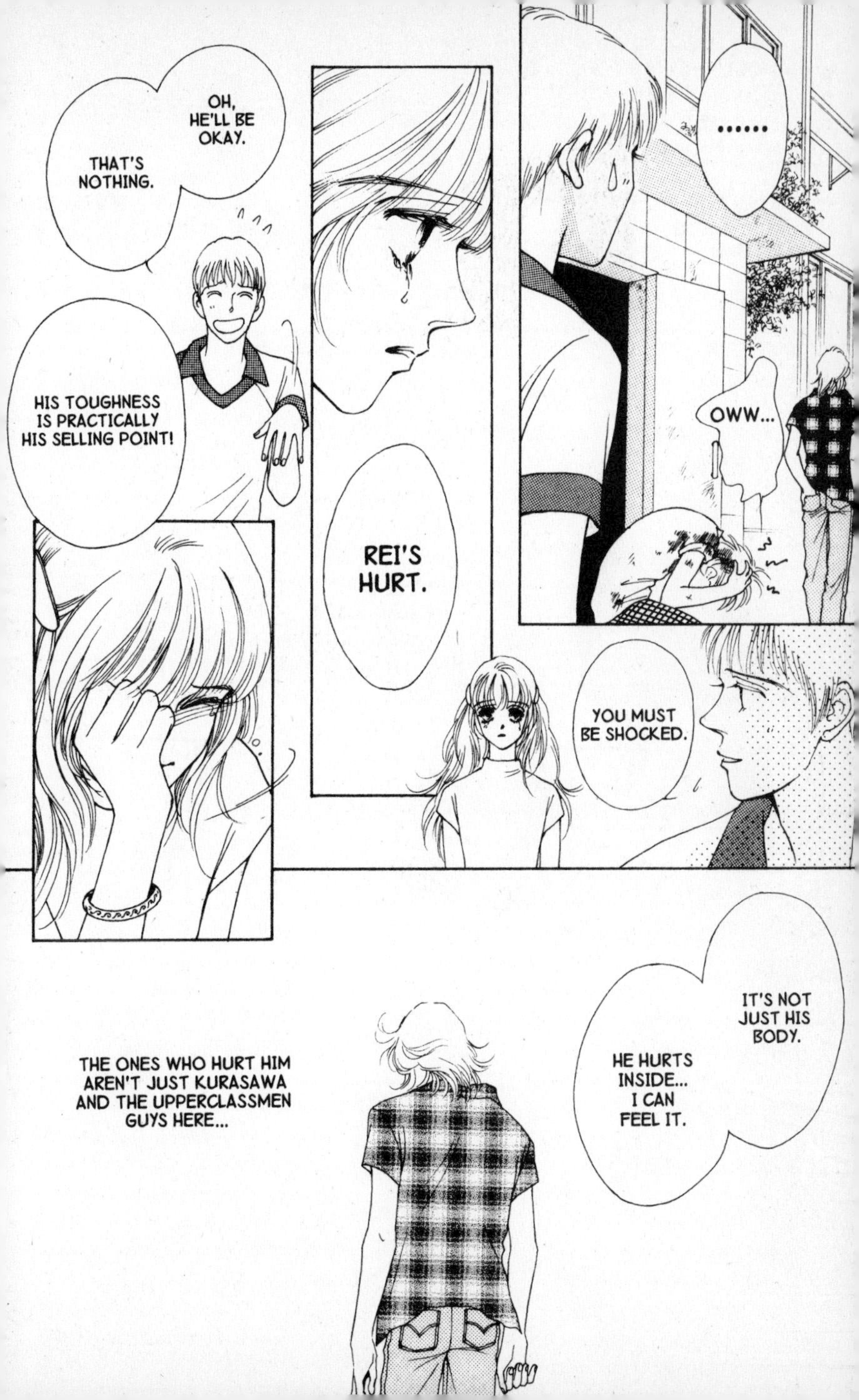

......
OWW...
REI'S HURT.
OH, HE'LL BE OKAY.
THAT'S NOTHING.
HIS TOUGHNESS IS PRACTICALLY HIS SELLING POINT!
YOU MUST BE SHOCKED.
IT'S NOT JUST HIS BODY.
HE HURTS INSIDE... I CAN FEEL IT.
THE ONES WHO HURT HIM AREN'T JUST KURASAWA AND THE UPPERCLASSMEN GUYS HERE...

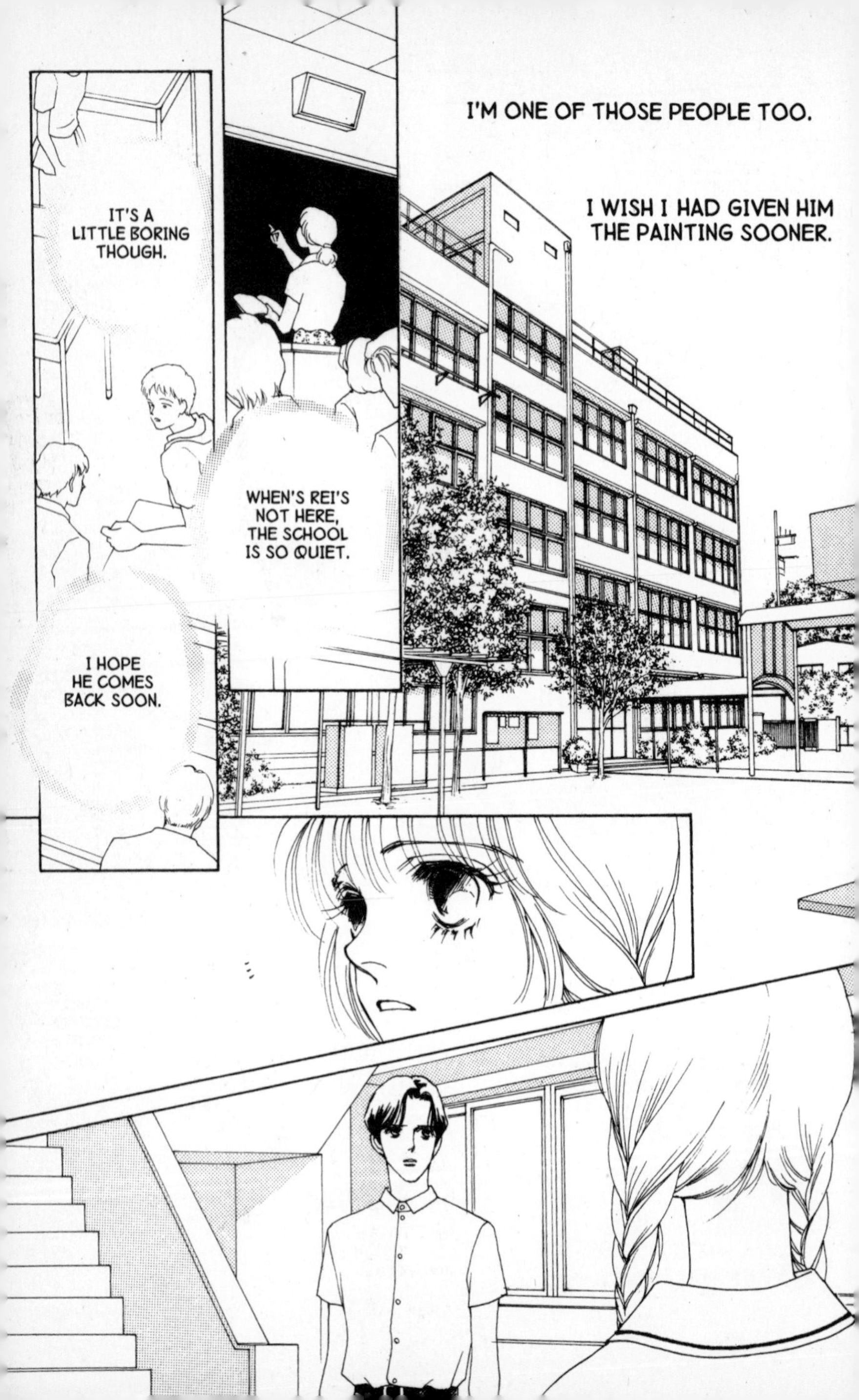
I'M ONE OF THOSE PEOPLE TOO.
I WISH I HAD GIVEN HIM THE PAINTING SOONER.
WHEN'S REI'S NOT HERE, THE SCHOOL IS SO QUIET.
IT'S A LITTLE BORING THOUGH.
I HOPE HE COMES BACK SOON.
...

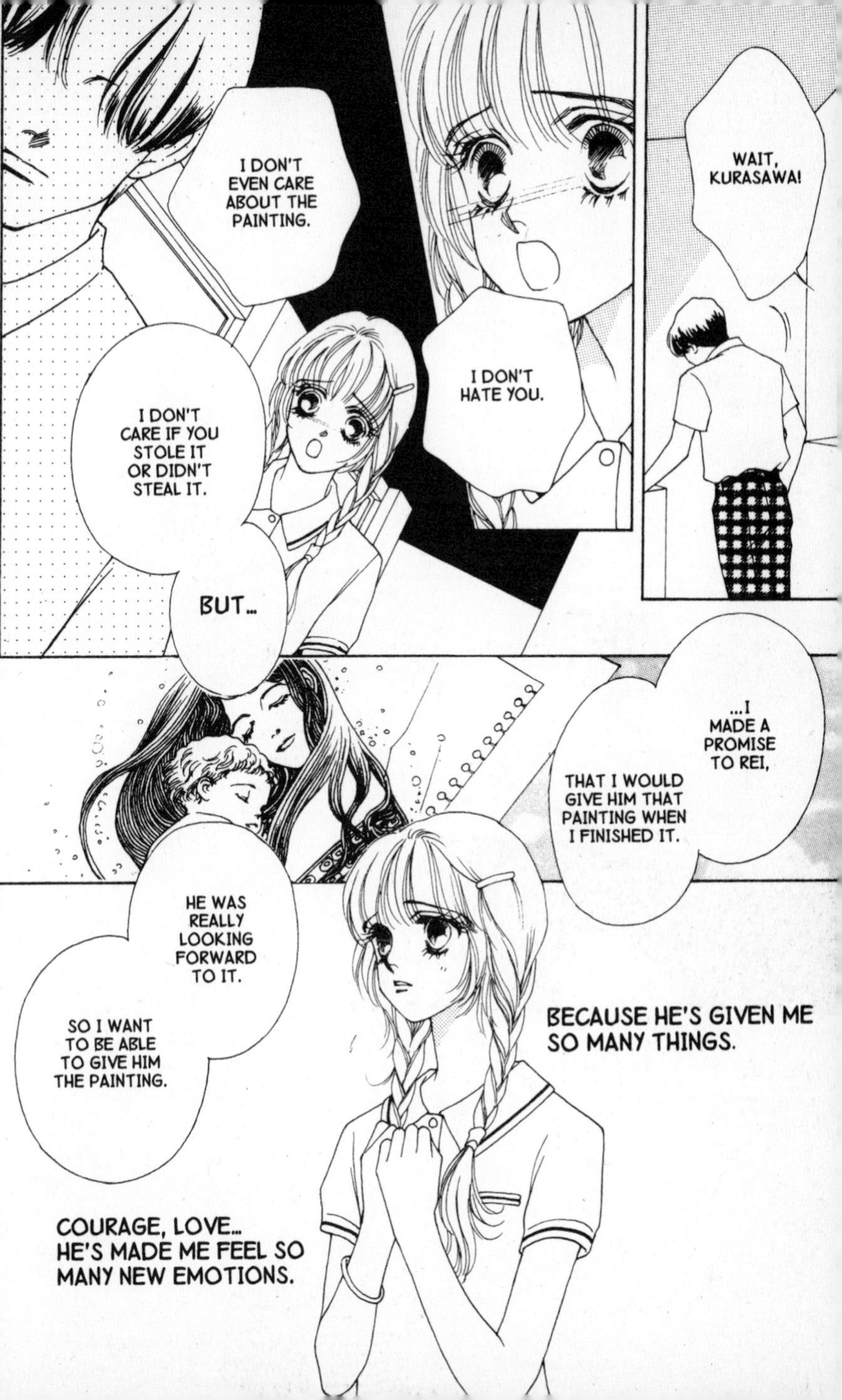
WAIT, KURASAWA!
I DON'T HATE YOU.
I DON'T EVEN CARE ABOUT THE PAINTING.
I DON'T CARE IF YOU STOLE IT OR DIDN'T STEAL IT.
BUT...
...I MADE A PROMISE TO REI,
THAT I WOULD GIVE HIM THAT PAINTING WHEN I FINISHED IT.
HE WAS REALLY LOOKING FORWARD TO IT.
SO I WANT TO BE ABLE TO GIVE HIM THE PAINTING.
BECAUSE HE'S GIVEN ME SO MANY THINGS.
COURAGE, LOVE... HE'S MADE ME FEEL SO MANY NEW EMOTIONS.

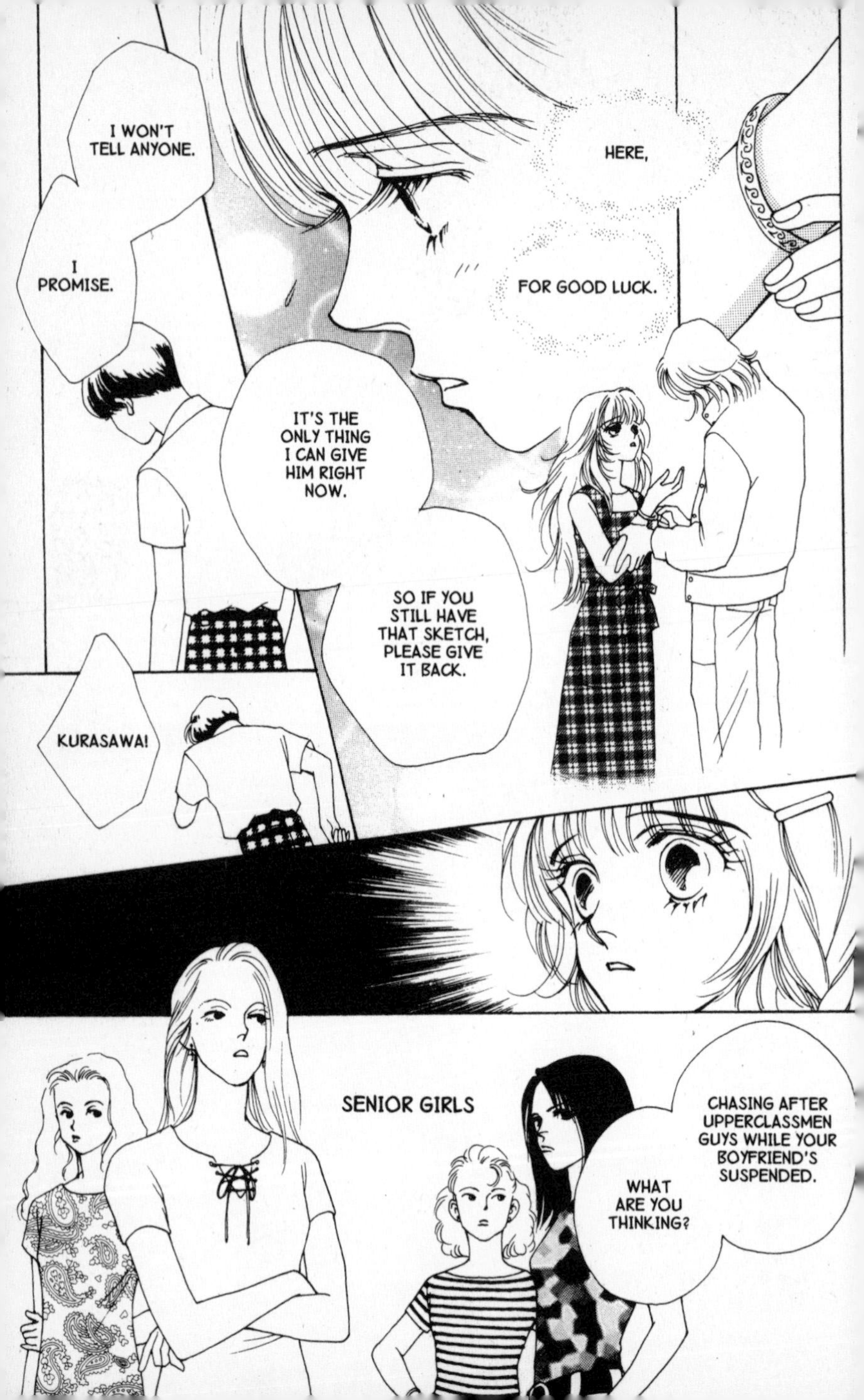
HERE,
FOR GOOD LUCK.
I WON'T TELL ANYONE.
I PROMISE.
IT'S THE ONLY THING I CAN GIVE HIM RIGHT NOW.
SO IF YOU STILL HAVE THAT SKETCH, PLEASE GIVE IT BACK.
KURASAWA!
CHASING AFTER UPPERCLASSMEN GUYS WHILE YOUR BOYFRIEND'S SUSPENDED.
WHAT ARE YOU THINKING?
SENIOR GIRLS

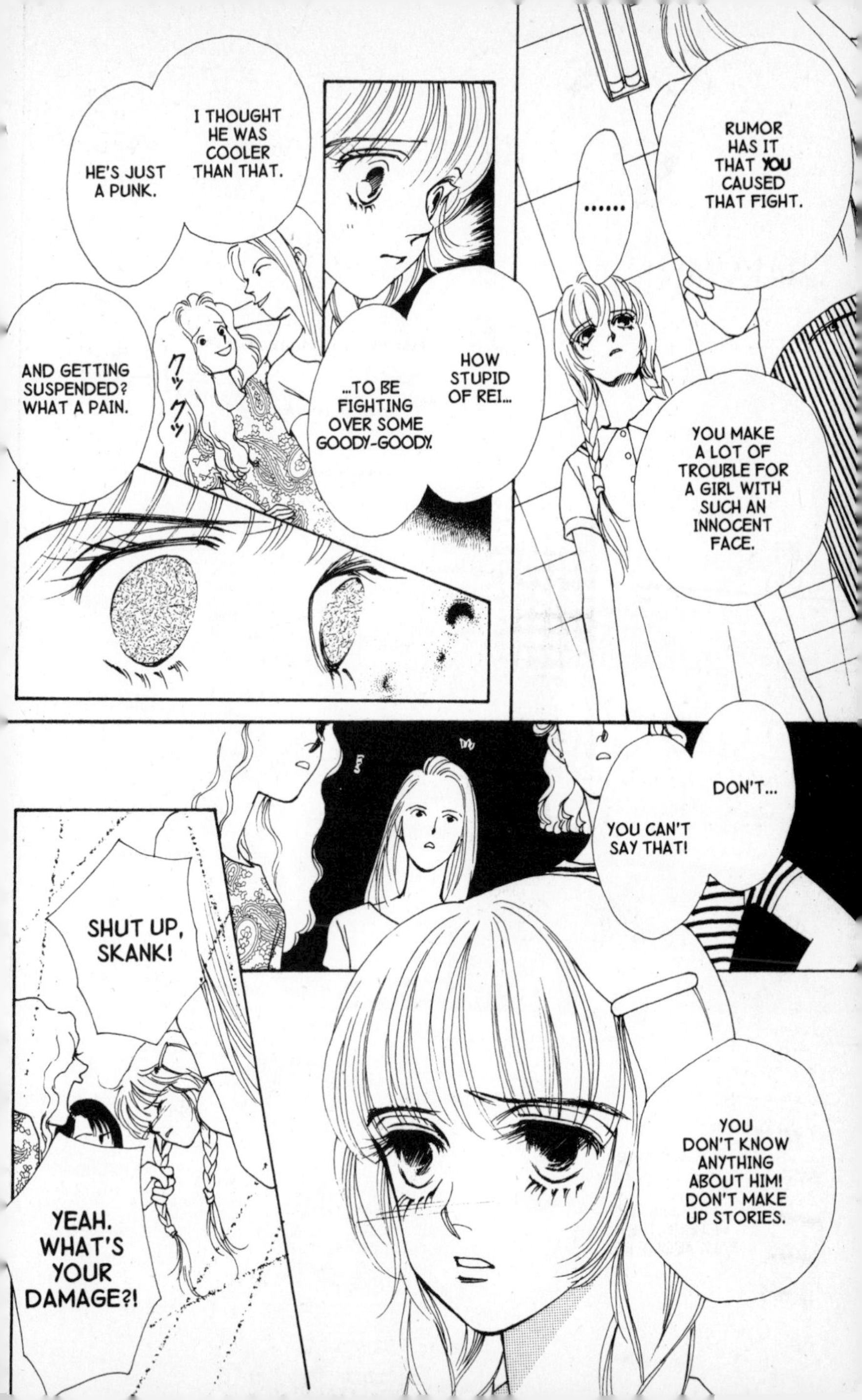
RUMOR HAS IT THAT YOU CAUSED THAT FIGHT.
......
YOU MAKE A LOT OF TROUBLE FOR A GIRL WITH SUCH AN INNOCENT FACE.
HOW STUPID OF REI...
...TO BE FIGHTING OVER SOME GOODY-GOODY.
I THOUGHT HE WAS COOLER THAN THAT.
HE'S JUST A PUNK.
クックッ
AND GETTING SUSPENDED? WHAT A PAIN.
DON'T...
YOU CAN'T SAY THAT!
YOU DON'T KNOW ANYTHING ABOUT HIM! DON'T MAKE UP STORIES.
SHUT UP, SKANK!
YEAH. WHAT'S YOUR DAMAGE?!

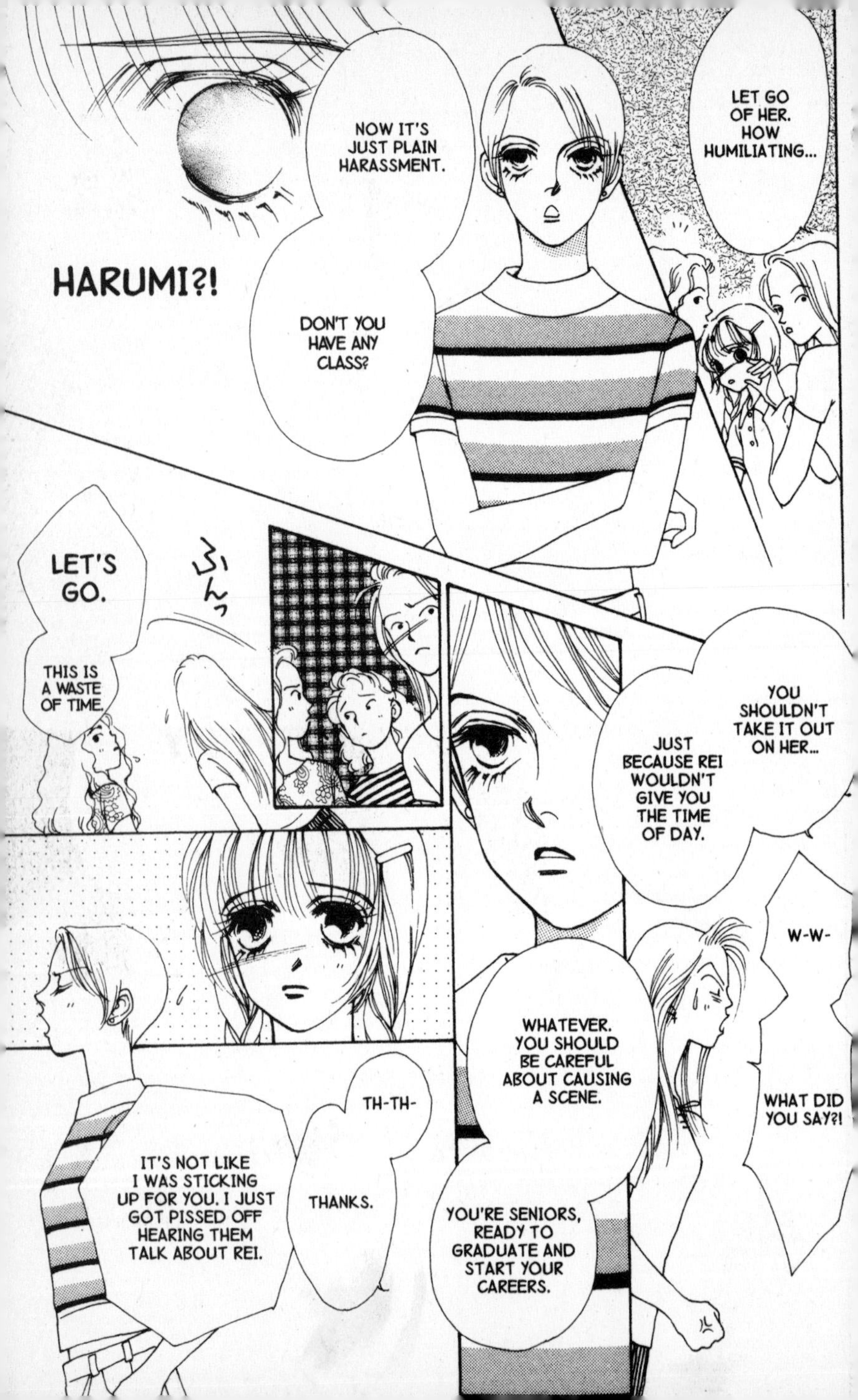
LET GO OF HER. HOW HUMILIATING...
NOW IT'S JUST PLAIN HARASSMENT.
DON'T YOU HAVE ANY CLASS?
HARUMI?!
YOU SHOULDN'T TAKE IT OUT ON HER...
JUST BECAUSE REI WOULDN'T GIVE YOU THE TIME OF DAY.
W-W-
WHAT DID YOU SAY?!
WHATEVER. YOU SHOULD BE CAREFUL ABOUT CAUSING A SCENE.
YOU'RE SENIORS, READY TO GRADUATE AND START YOUR CAREERS.
ふんっ
LET'S GO.
THIS IS A WASTE OF TIME.
TH-TH-
THANKS.
IT'S NOT LIKE I WAS STICKING UP FOR YOU. I JUST GOT PISSED OFF HEARING THEM TALK ABOUT REI.

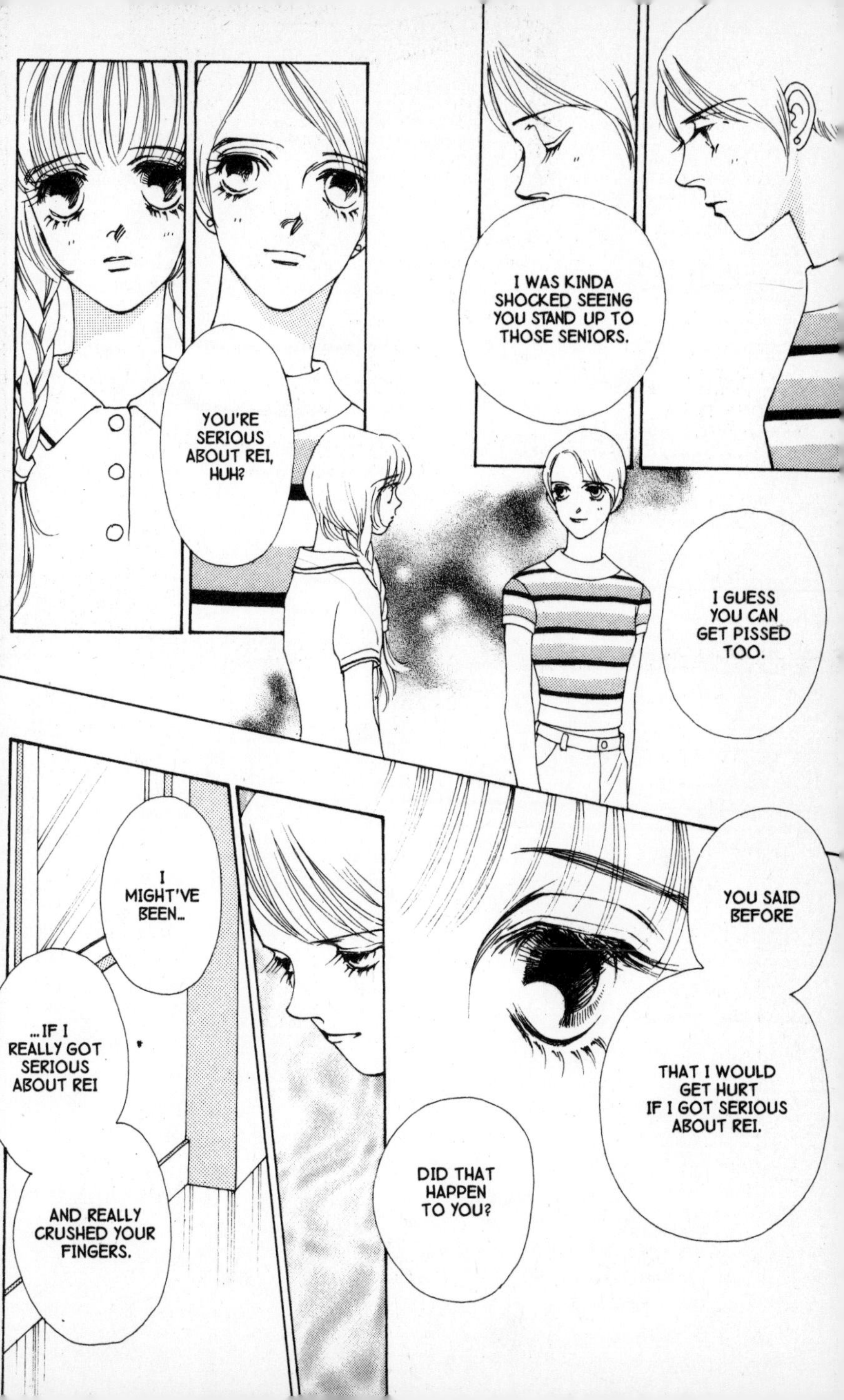
I WAS KINDA SHOCKED SEEING YOU STAND UP TO THOSE SENIORS.
I GUESS YOU CAN GET PISSED TOO.
YOU'RE SERIOUS ABOUT REI, HUH?
YOU SAID BEFORE
THAT I WOULD GET HURT IF I GOT SERIOUS ABOUT REI.
DID THAT HAPPEN TO YOU?
I MIGHT'VE BEEN...
...IF I REALLY GOT SERIOUS ABOUT REI
AND REALLY CRUSHED YOUR FINGERS.

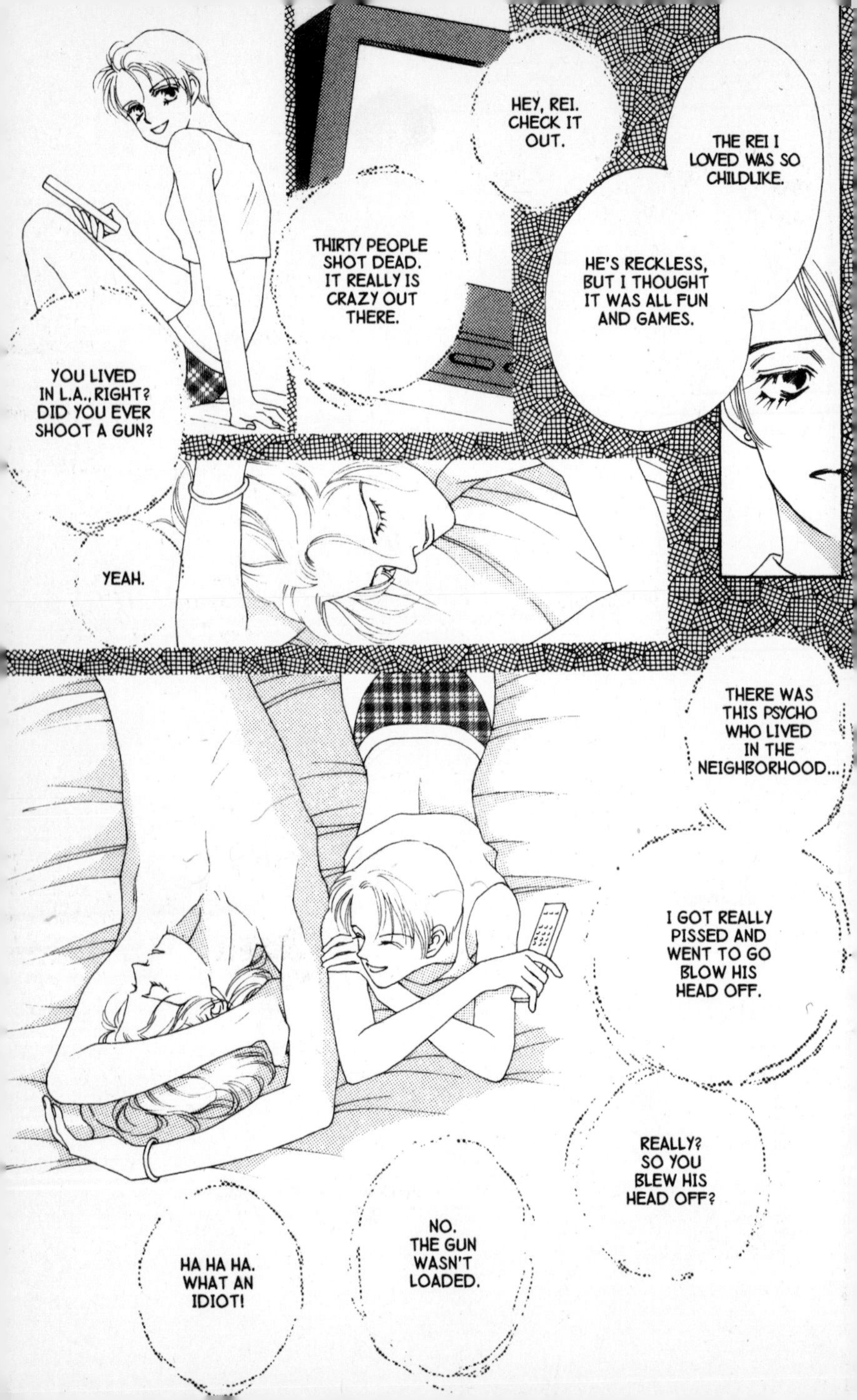
THE REI I LOVED WAS SO CHILDLIKE.
HE'S RECKLESS, BUT I THOUGHT IT WAS ALL FUN AND GAMES.
HEY, REI. CHECK IT OUT.
THIRTY PEOPLE SHOT DEAD. IT REALLY IS CRAZY OUT THERE.
YOU LIVED IN L.A., RIGHT? DID YOU EVER SHOOT A GUN?
YEAH.
THERE WAS THIS PSYCHO WHO LIVED IN THE NEIGHBORHOOD...
I GOT REALLY PISSED AND WENT TO GO BLOW HIS HEAD OFF.
REALLY? SO YOU BLEW HIS HEAD OFF?
NO. THE GUN WASN'T LOADED.
HA HA HA. WHAT AN IDIOT!

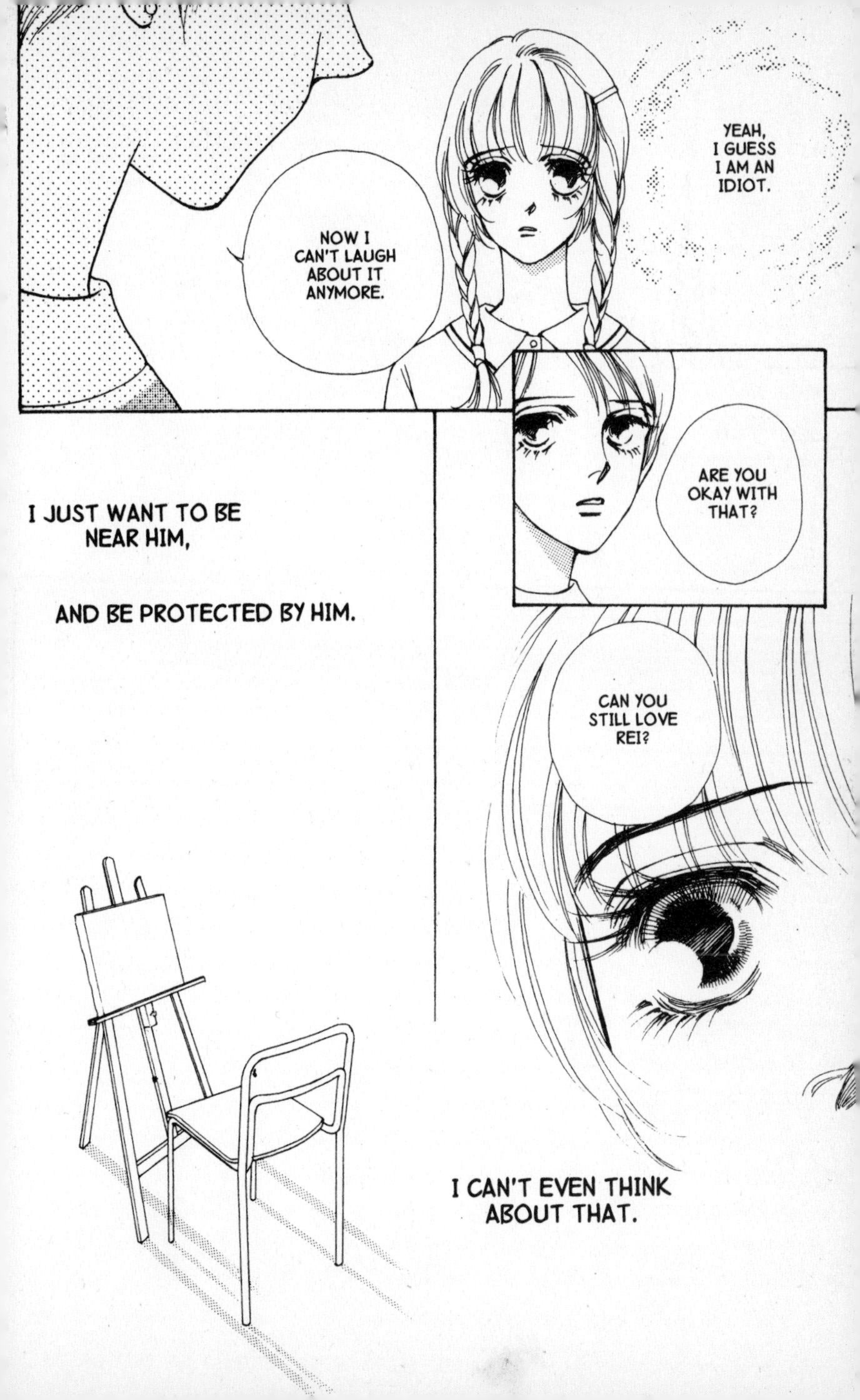
YEAH, I GUESS I AM AN IDIOT.
NOW I CAN'T LAUGH ABOUT IT ANYMORE.
ARE YOU OKAY WITH THAT?
CAN YOU STILL LOVE REI?
I CAN'T EVEN THINK ABOUT THAT.
I JUST WANT TO BE NEAR HIM,
AND BE PROTECTED BY HIM.

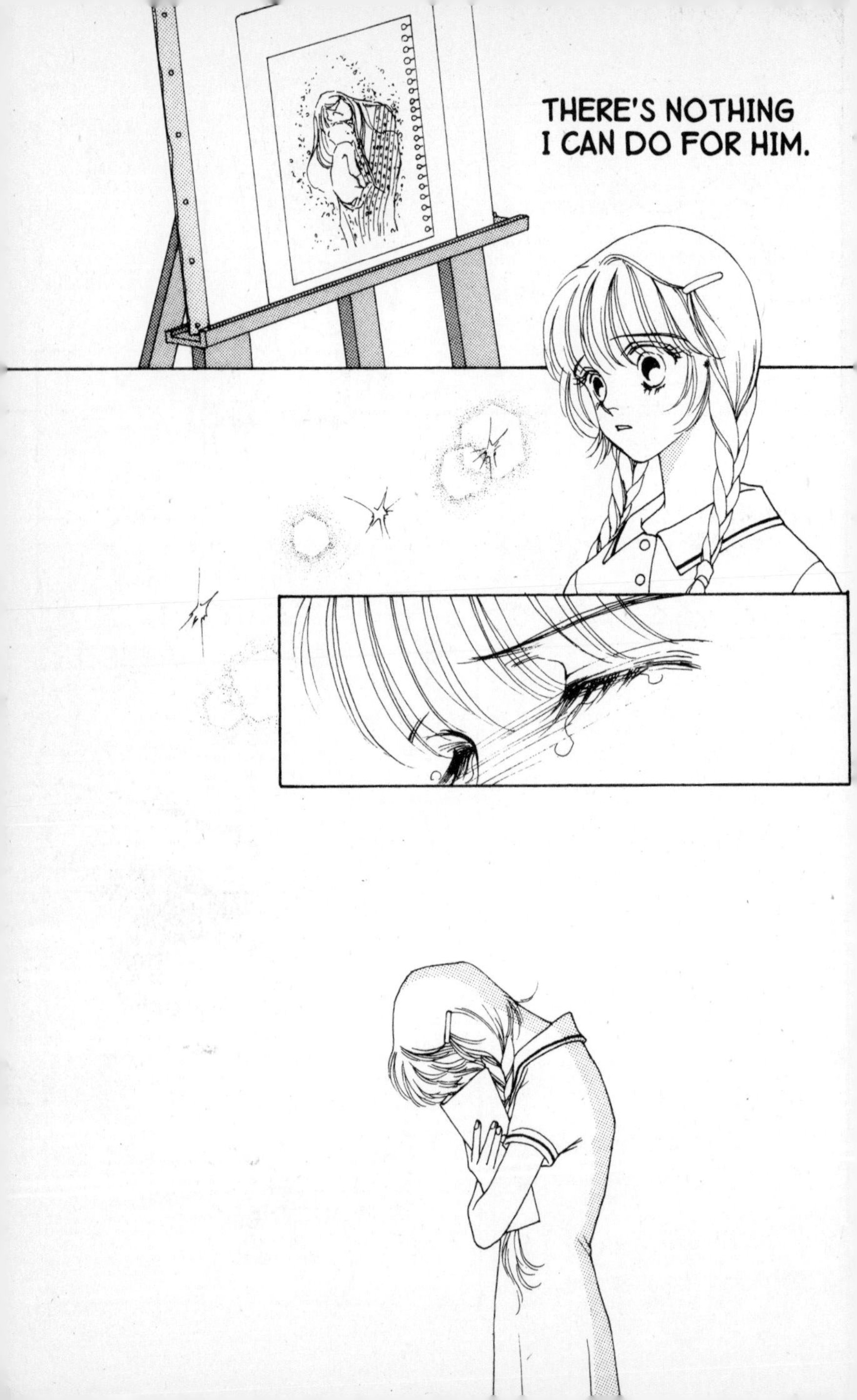
THERE'S NOTHING I CAN DO FOR HIM.

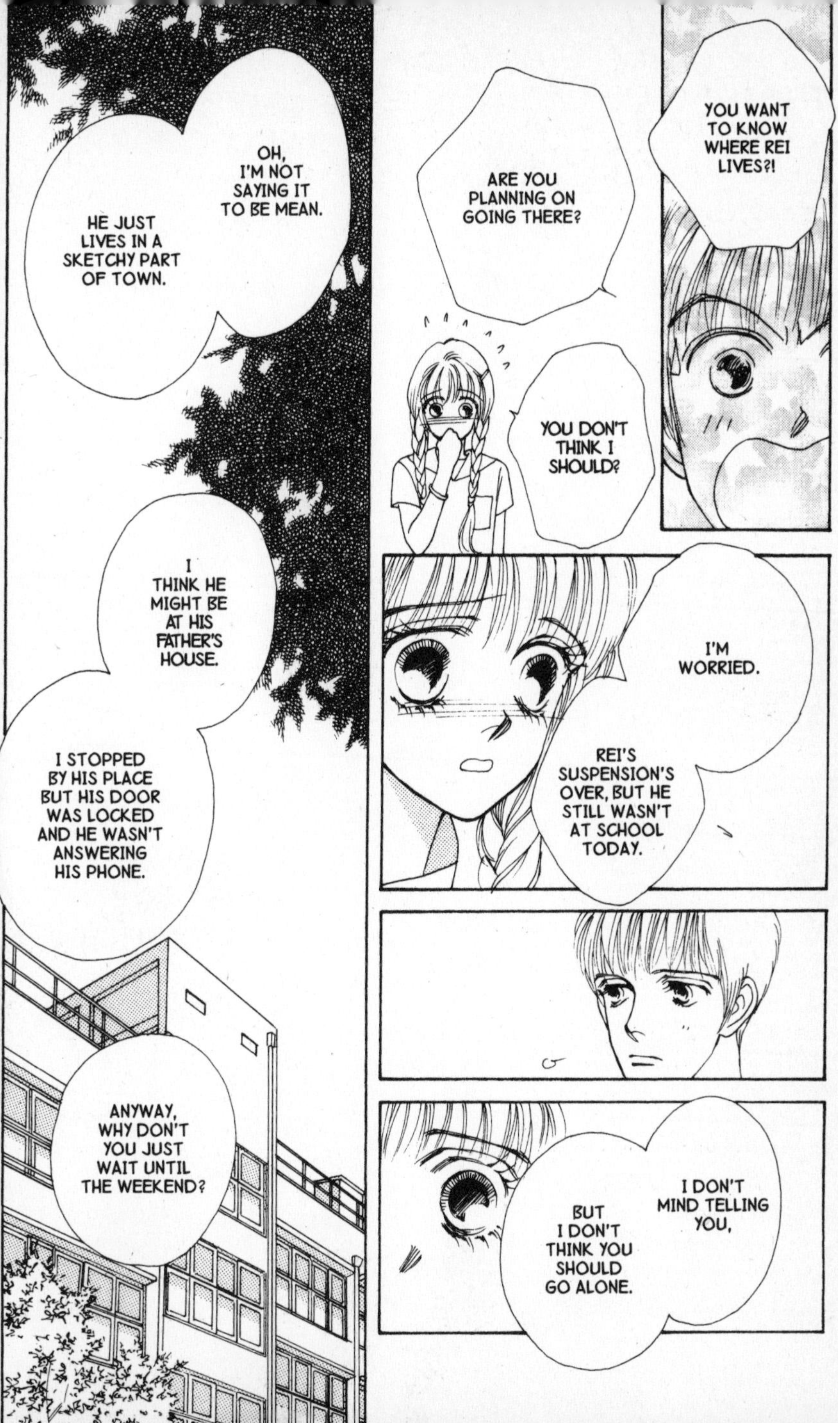
YOU WANT TO KNOW WHERE REI LIVES?!
ARE YOU PLANNING ON GOING THERE?
YOU DON'T THINK I SHOULD?
I'M WORRIED.
REI'S SUSPENSION'S OVER, BUT HE STILL WASN'T AT SCHOOL TODAY.
I DON'T MIND TELLING YOU,
BUT I DON'T THINK YOU SHOULD GO ALONE.
OH, I'M NOT SAYING IT TO BE MEAN.
HE JUST LIVES IN A SKETCHY PART OF TOWN.
I THINK HE MIGHT BE AT HIS FATHER'S HOUSE.
I STOPPED BY HIS PLACE BUT HIS DOOR WAS LOCKED AND HE WASN'T ANSWERING HIS PHONE.
ANYWAY, WHY DON'T YOU JUST WAIT UNTIL THE WEEKEND?

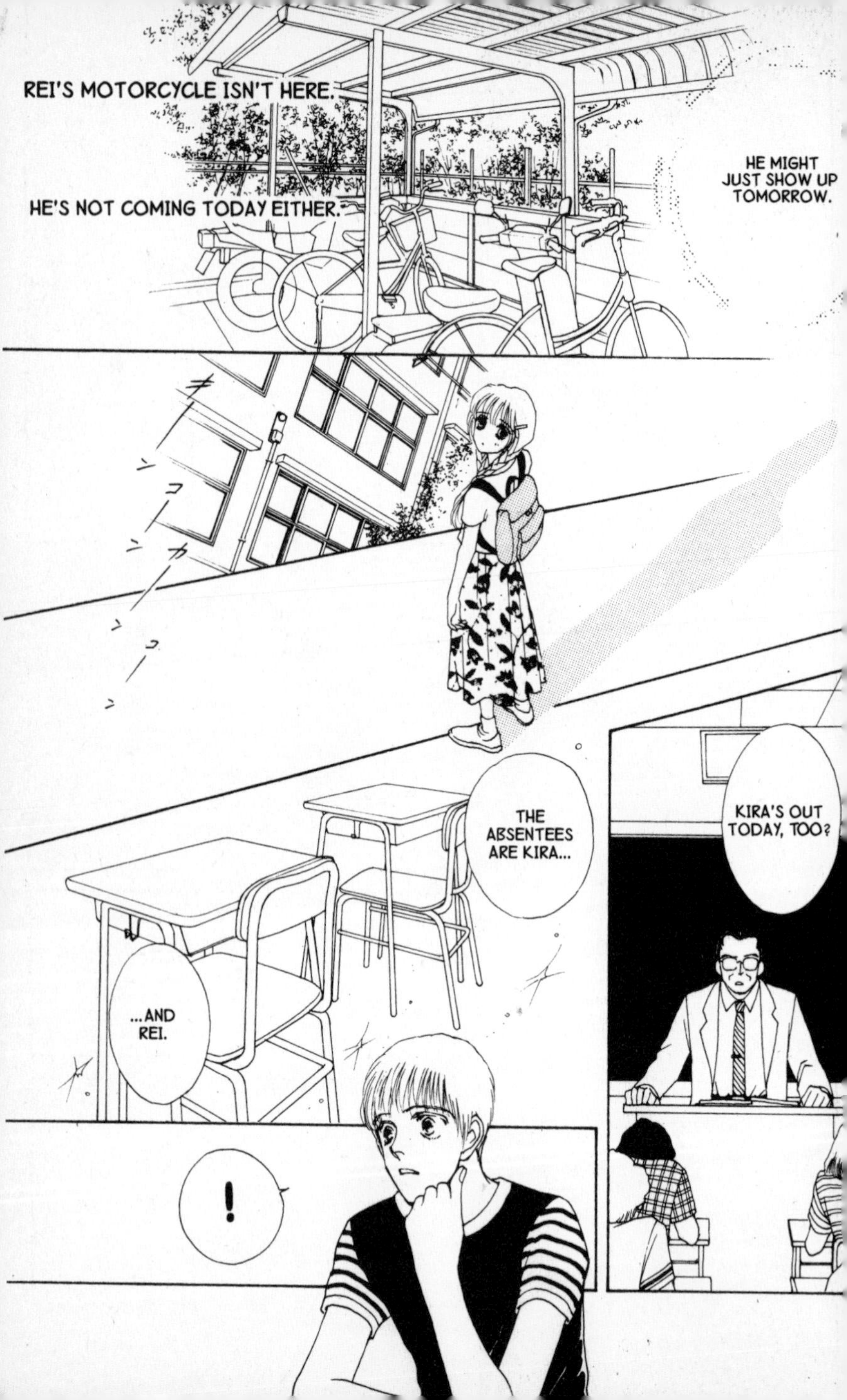
REI'S MOTORCYCLE ISN'T HERE.
HE'S NOT COMING TODAY EITHER.
HE MIGHT JUST SHOW UP TOMORROW.
キーンコーンカーンコーン
KIRA'S OUT TODAY, TOO?
THE ABSENTEES ARE KIRA...
...AND REI.
!

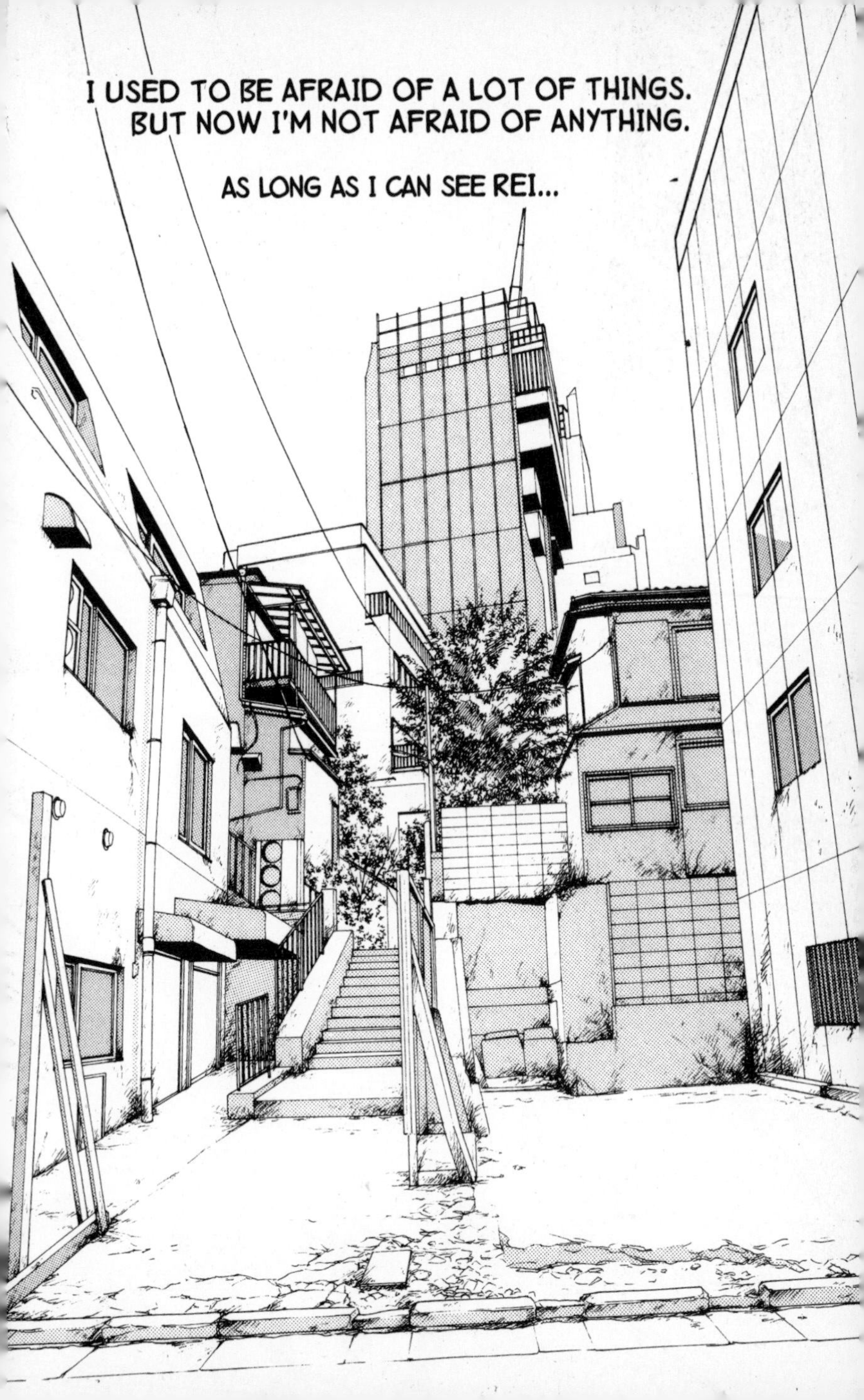
I USED TO BE AFRAID OF A LOT OF THINGS.
BUT NOW I'M NOT AFRAID OF ANYTHING.
AS LONG AS I CAN SEE REI...

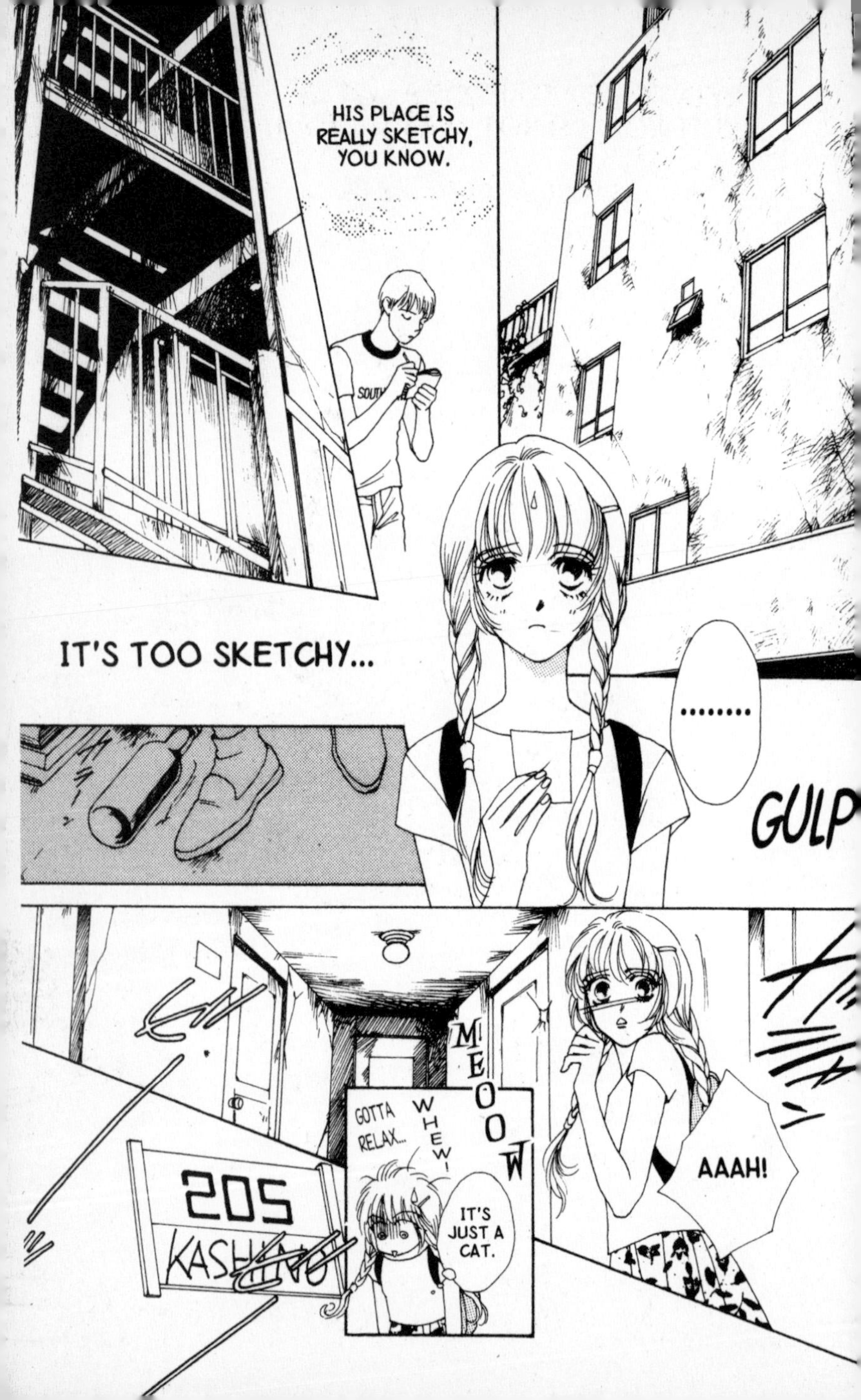

....
GULP
HIS PLACE IS REALLY SKETCHY, YOU KNOW.
IT'S TOO SKETCHY...
AAAH!
MEOOOW
205
WHEW!
GOTTA RELAX...
IT'S JUST A CAT.

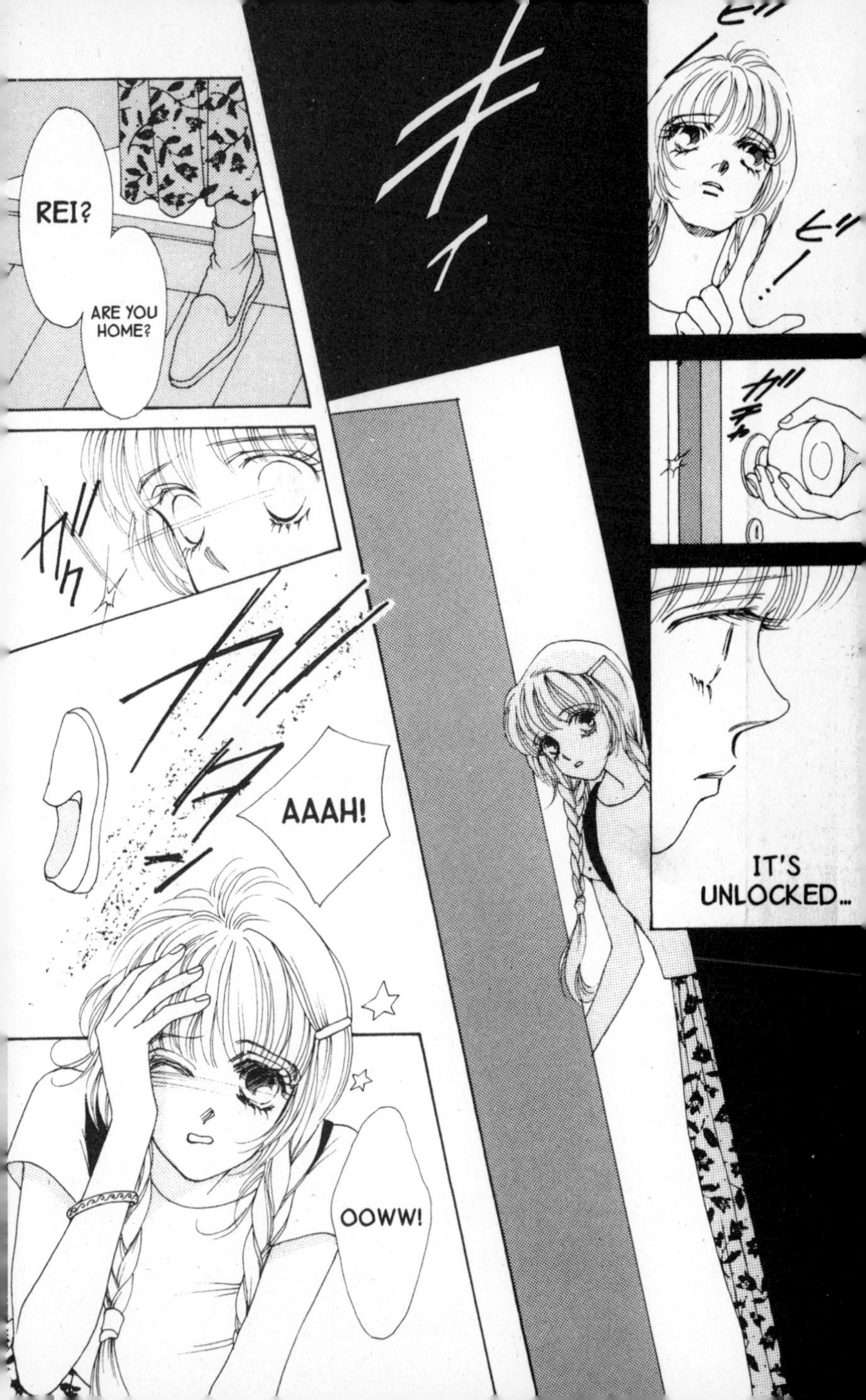
IT'S UNLOCKED...
REI?
ARE YOU HOME?
AAAH!
OOWW!

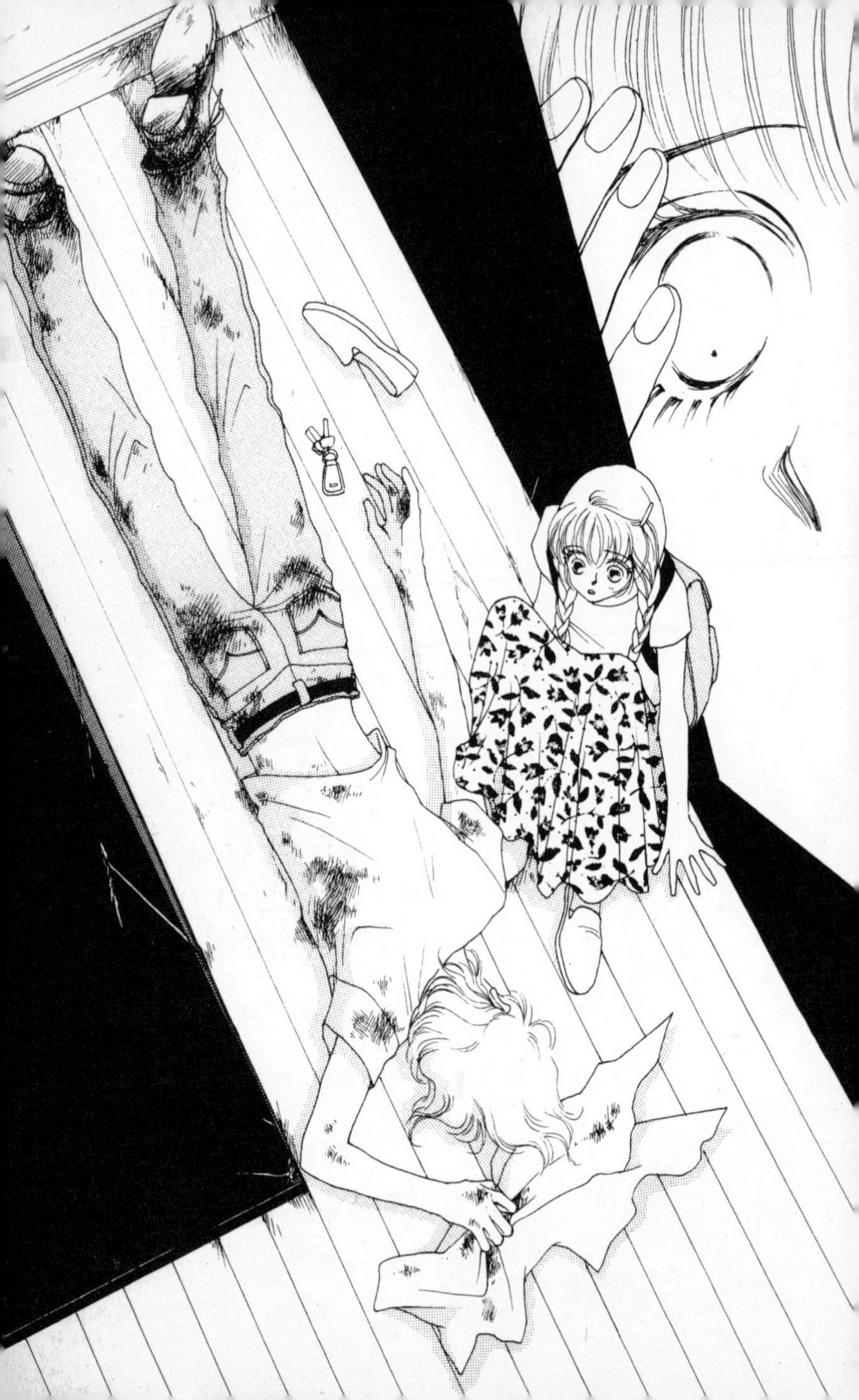

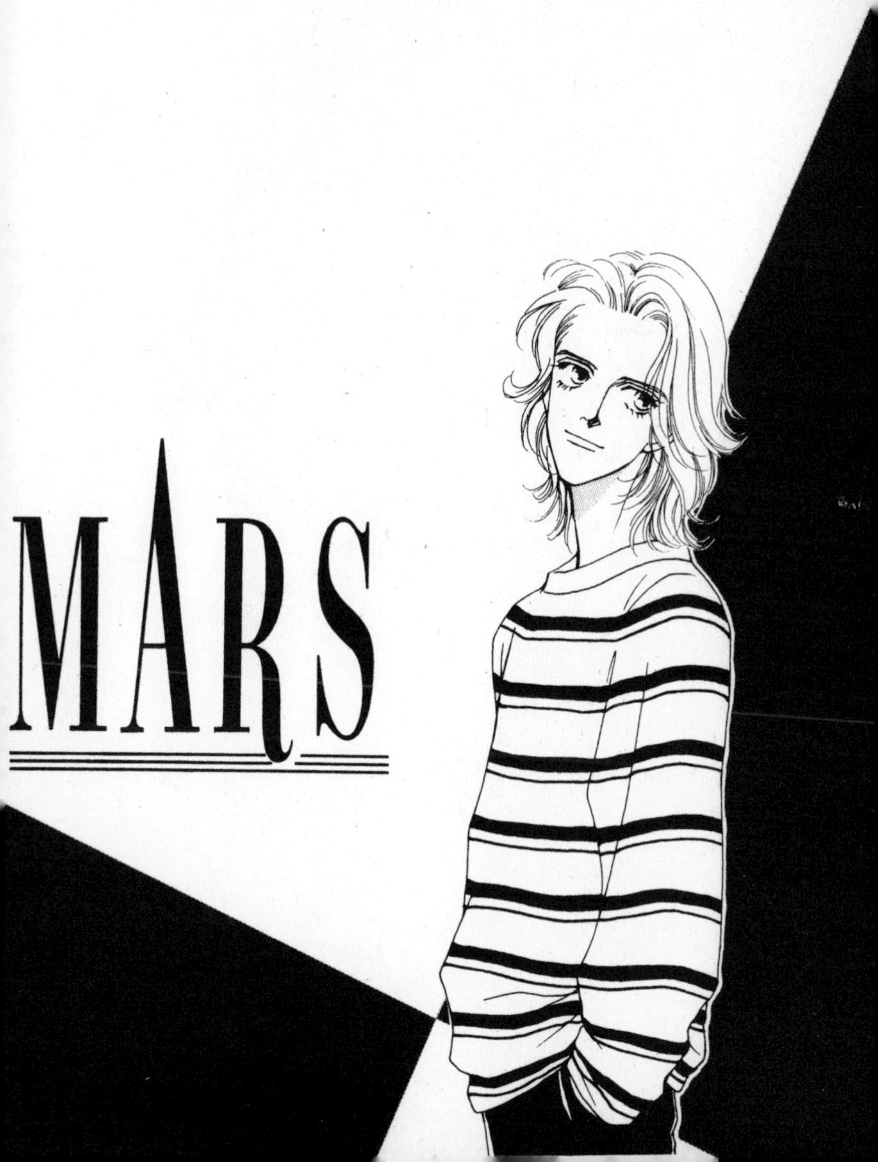
MARS

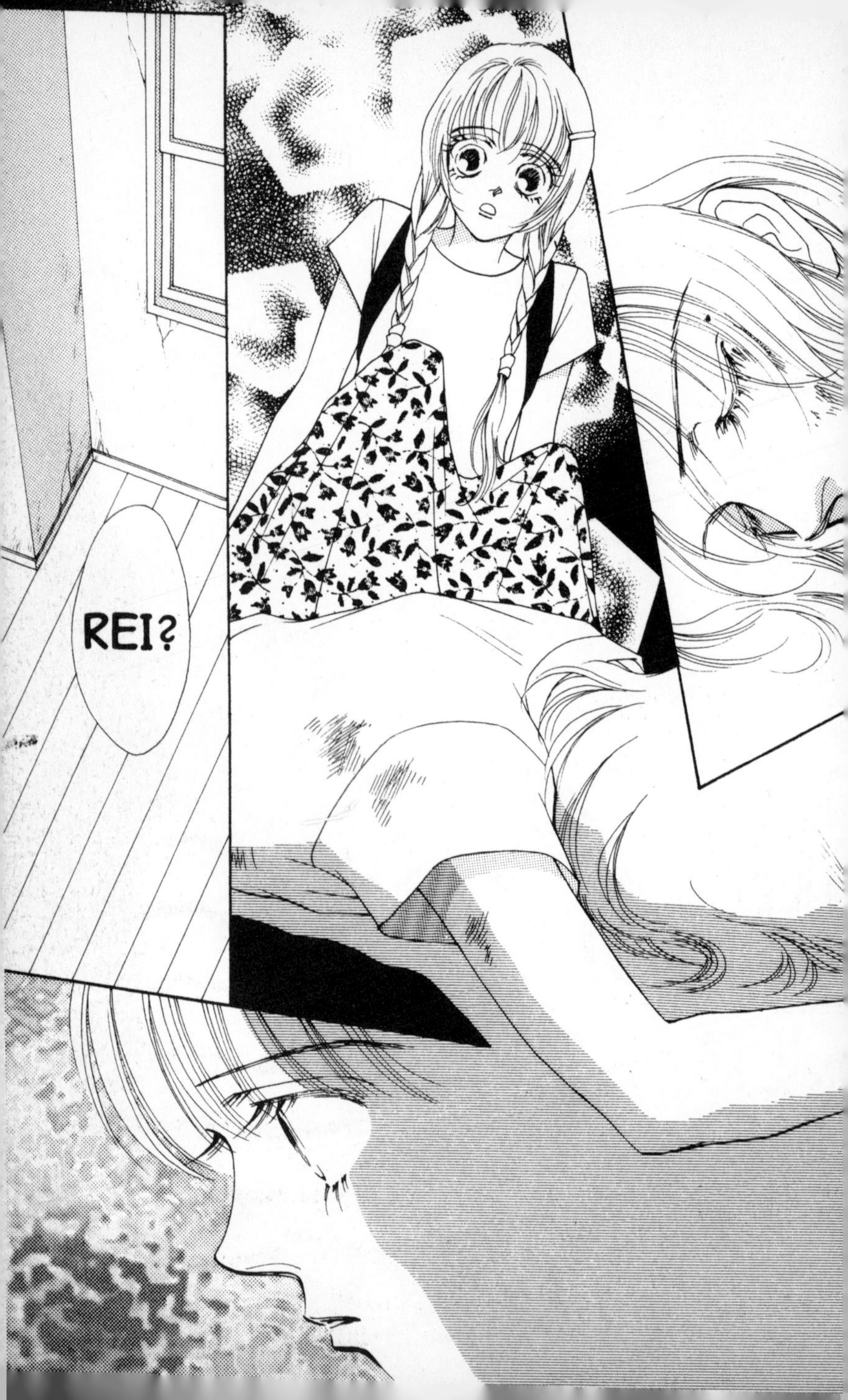
REI?

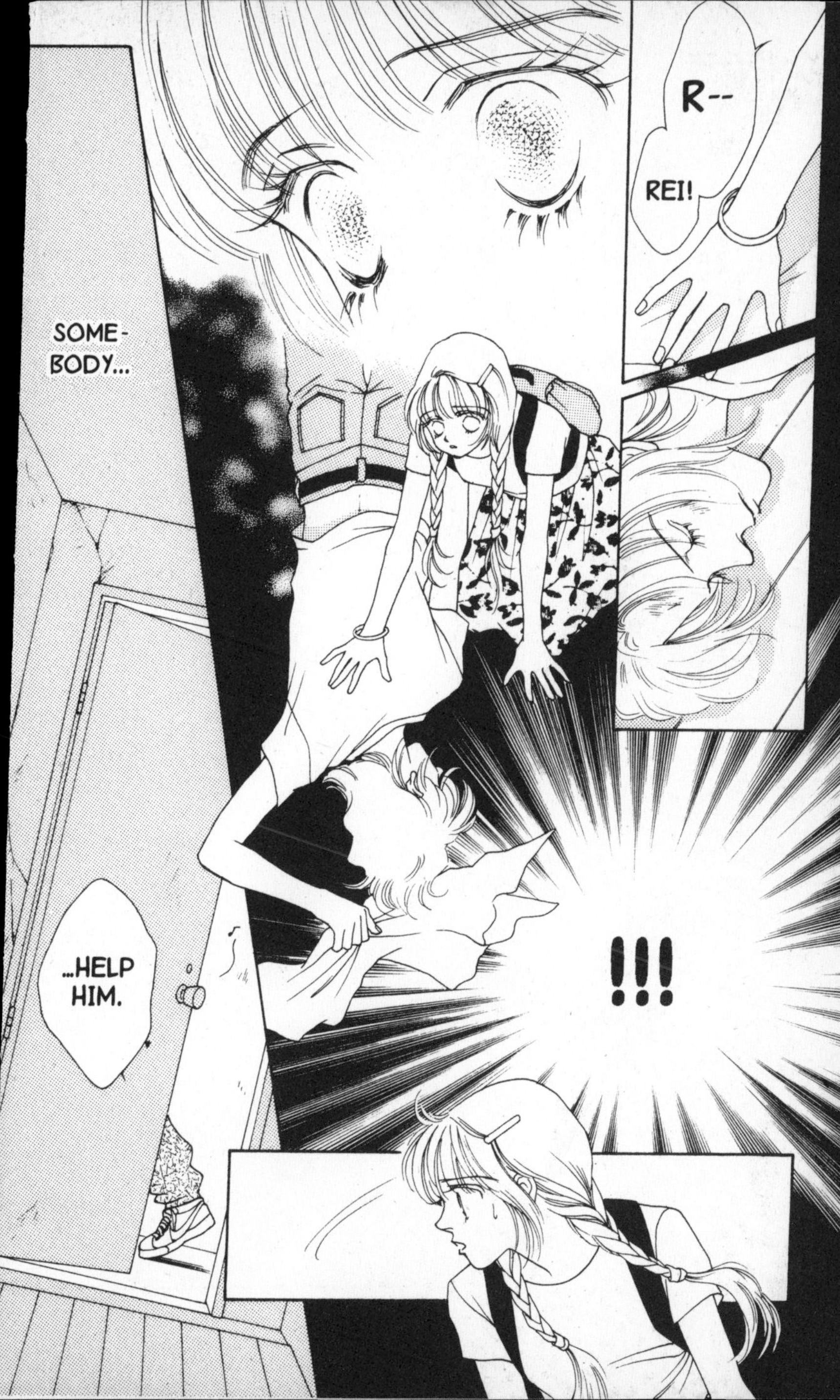
R--
REI!
SOME-BODY...
...HELP HIM.
!!!

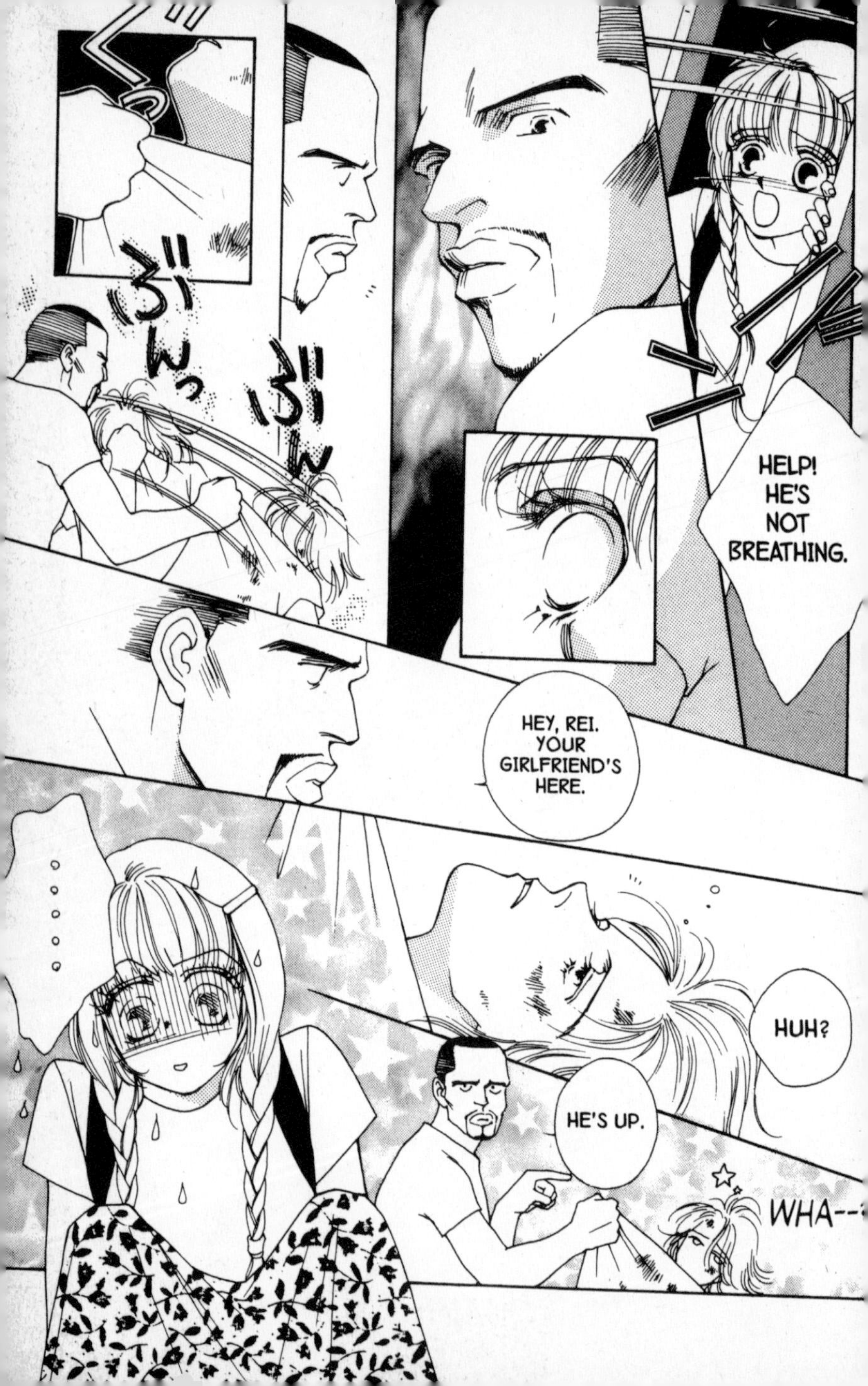
HELP! HE'S NOT BREATHING.
HEY, REI. YOUR GIRLFRIEND'S HERE.
HUH?
HE'S UP.
WHA--

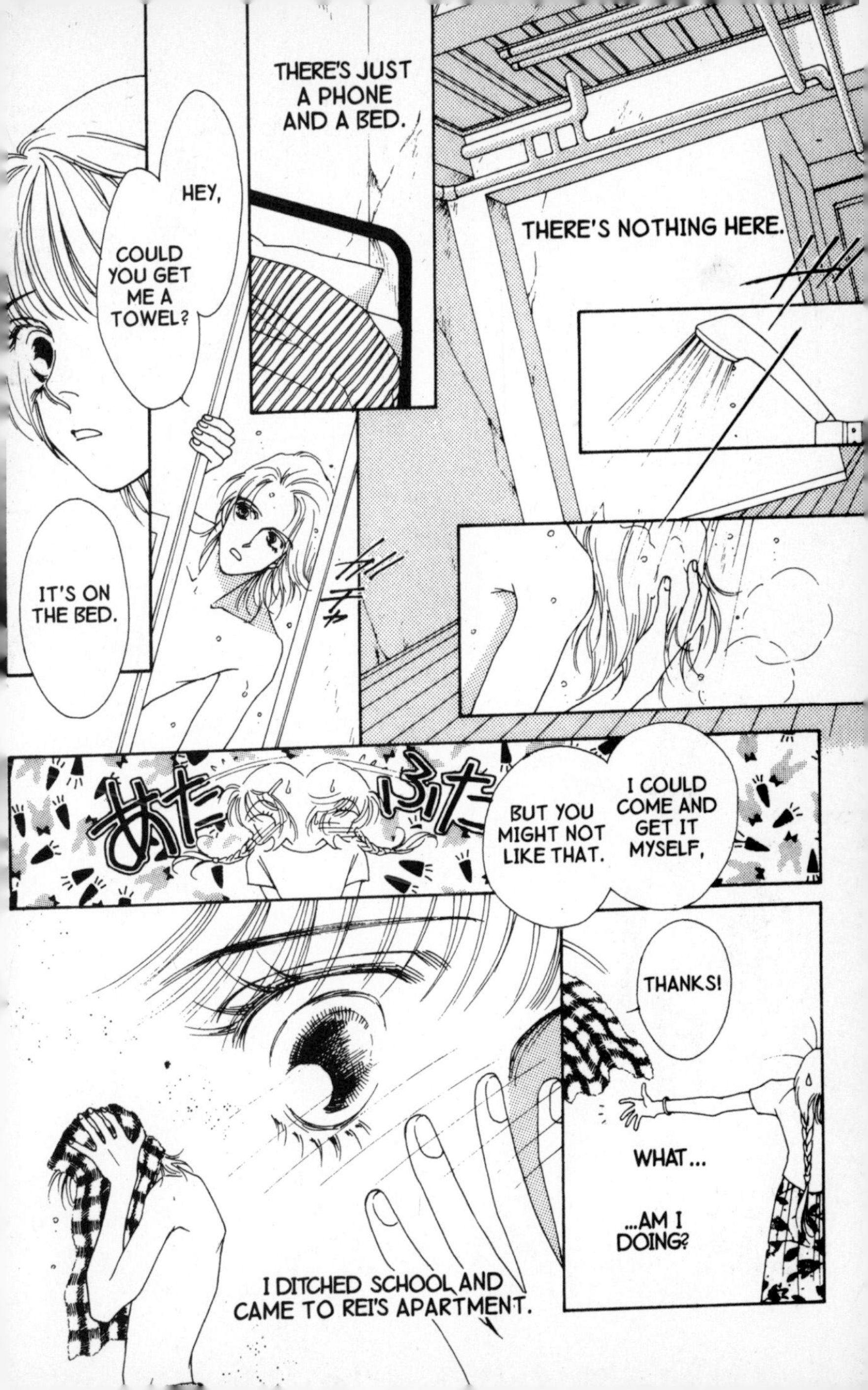
THERE'S NOTHING HERE.
THERE'S JUST A PHONE AND A BED.
HEY,
COULD YOU GET ME A TOWEL?
IT'S ON THE BED.
I COULD COME AND GET IT MYSELF,
BUT YOU MIGHT NOT LIKE THAT.
あたふた
THANKS!
WHAT...
...AM I DOING?
I DITCHED SCHOOL AND CAME TO REI'S APARTMENT.

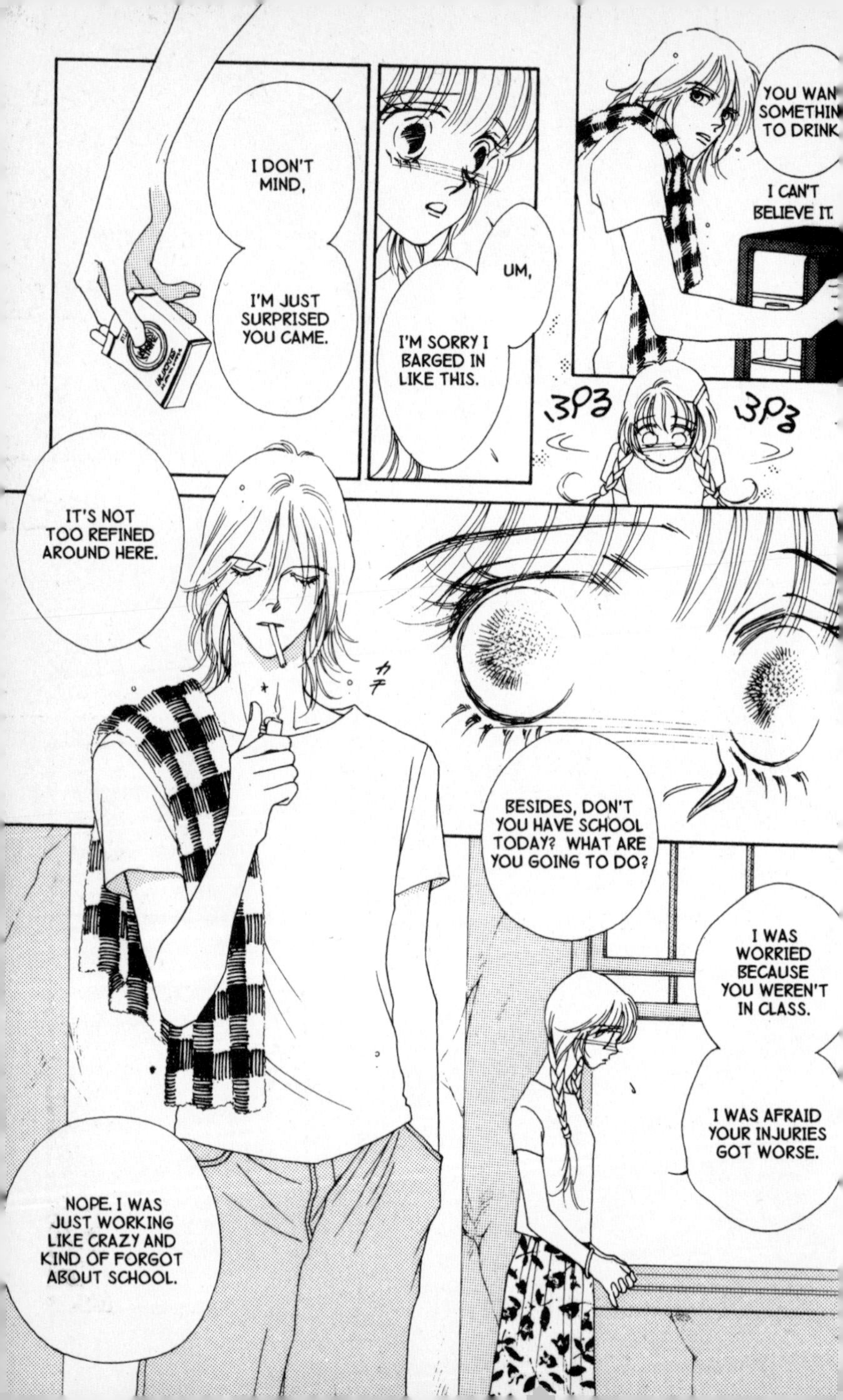
YOU WAN SOMETHIN TO DRINK
I CAN'T BELIEVE IT.
UM,
I'M SORRY I BARGED IN LIKE THIS.
I DON'T MIND,
I'M JUST SURPRISED YOU CAME.
BESIDES, DON'T YOU HAVE SCHOOL TODAY? WHAT ARE YOU GOING TO DO?
I WAS WORRIED BECAUSE YOU WEREN'T IN CLASS.
I WAS AFRAID YOUR INJURIES GOT WORSE.
IT'S NOT TOO REFINED AROUND HERE.
NOPE. I WAS JUST WORKING LIKE CRAZY AND KIND OF FORGOT ABOUT SCHOOL.

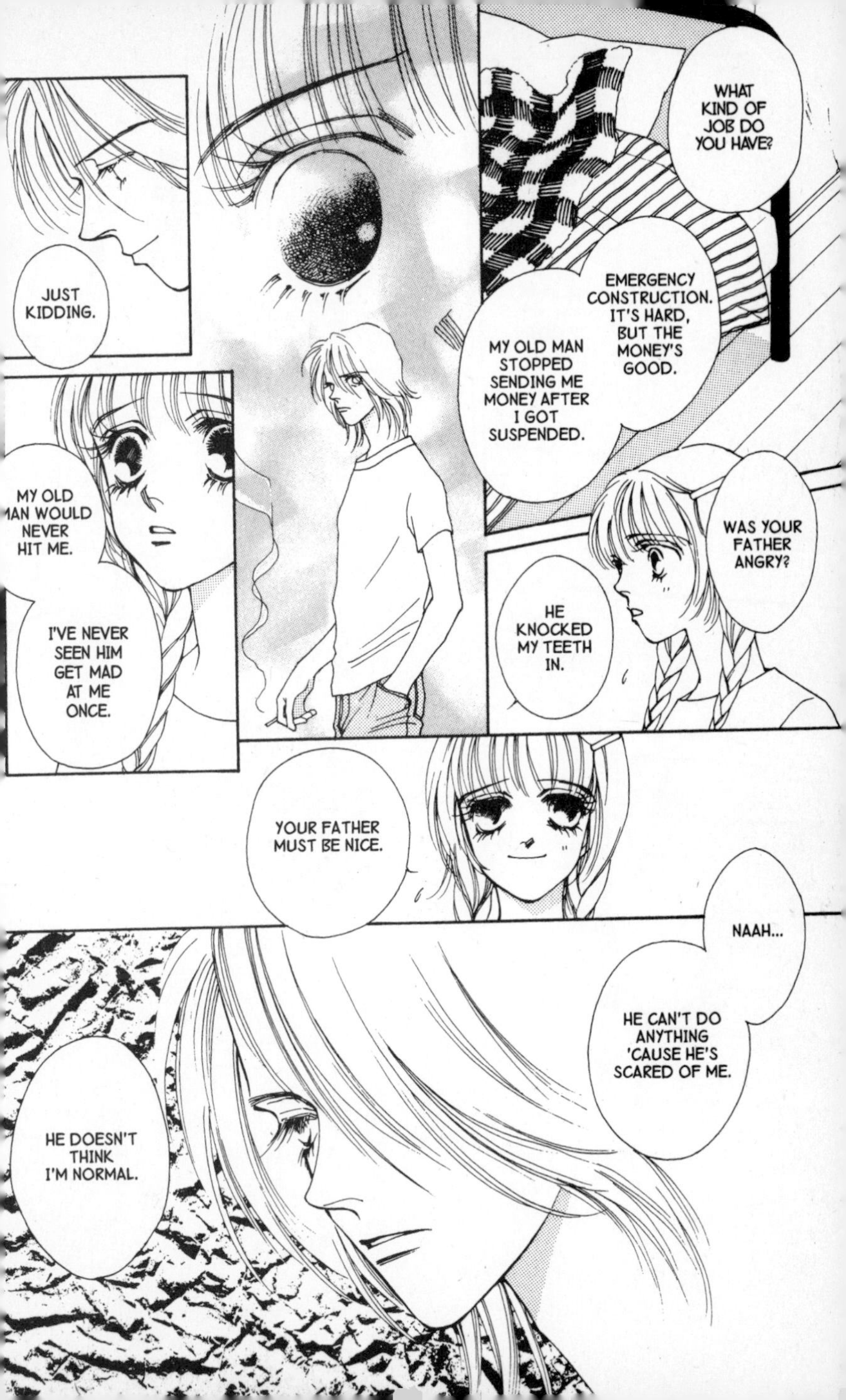
WHAT KIND OF JOB DO YOU HAVE?
EMERGENCY CONSTRUCTION. IT'S HARD, BUT THE MONEY'S GOOD.
MY OLD MAN STOPPED SENDING ME MONEY AFTER I GOT SUSPENDED.
WAS YOUR FATHER ANGRY?
HE KNOCKED MY TEETH IN.
JUST KIDDING.
MY OLD MAN WOULD NEVER HIT ME.
I'VE NEVER SEEN HIM GET MAD AT ME ONCE.
YOUR FATHER MUST BE NICE.
NAAH...
HE CAN'T DO ANYTHING 'CAUSE HE'S SCARED OF ME.
HE DOESN'T THINK I'M NORMAL.

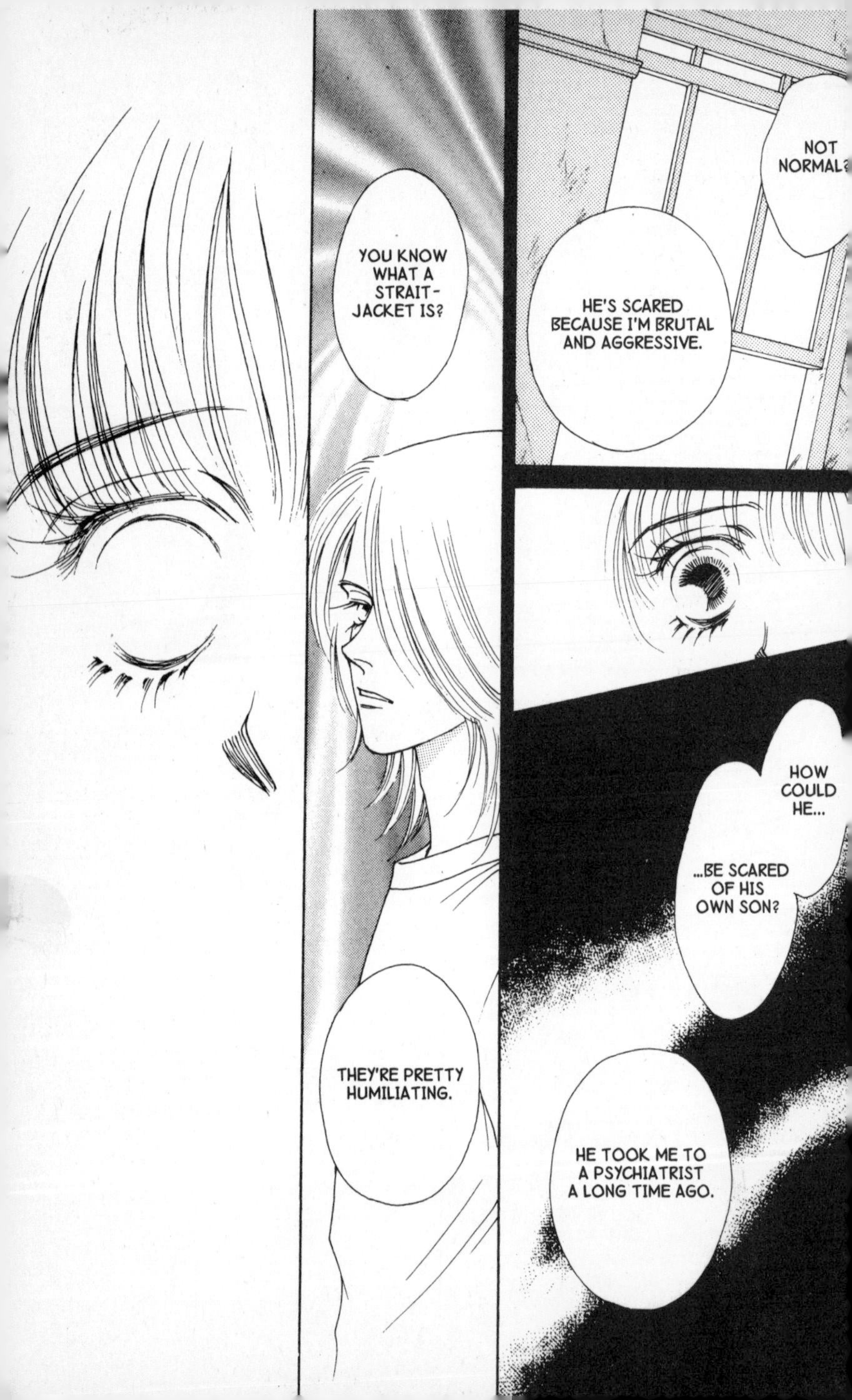
NOT NORMAL?
HE'S SCARED BECAUSE I'M BRUTAL AND AGGRESSIVE.
HOW COULD HE...
...BE SCARED OF HIS OWN SON?
HE TOOK ME TO A PSYCHIATRIST A LONG TIME AGO.
YOU KNOW WHAT A STRAIT-JACKET IS?
THEY'RE PRETTY HUMILIATING.

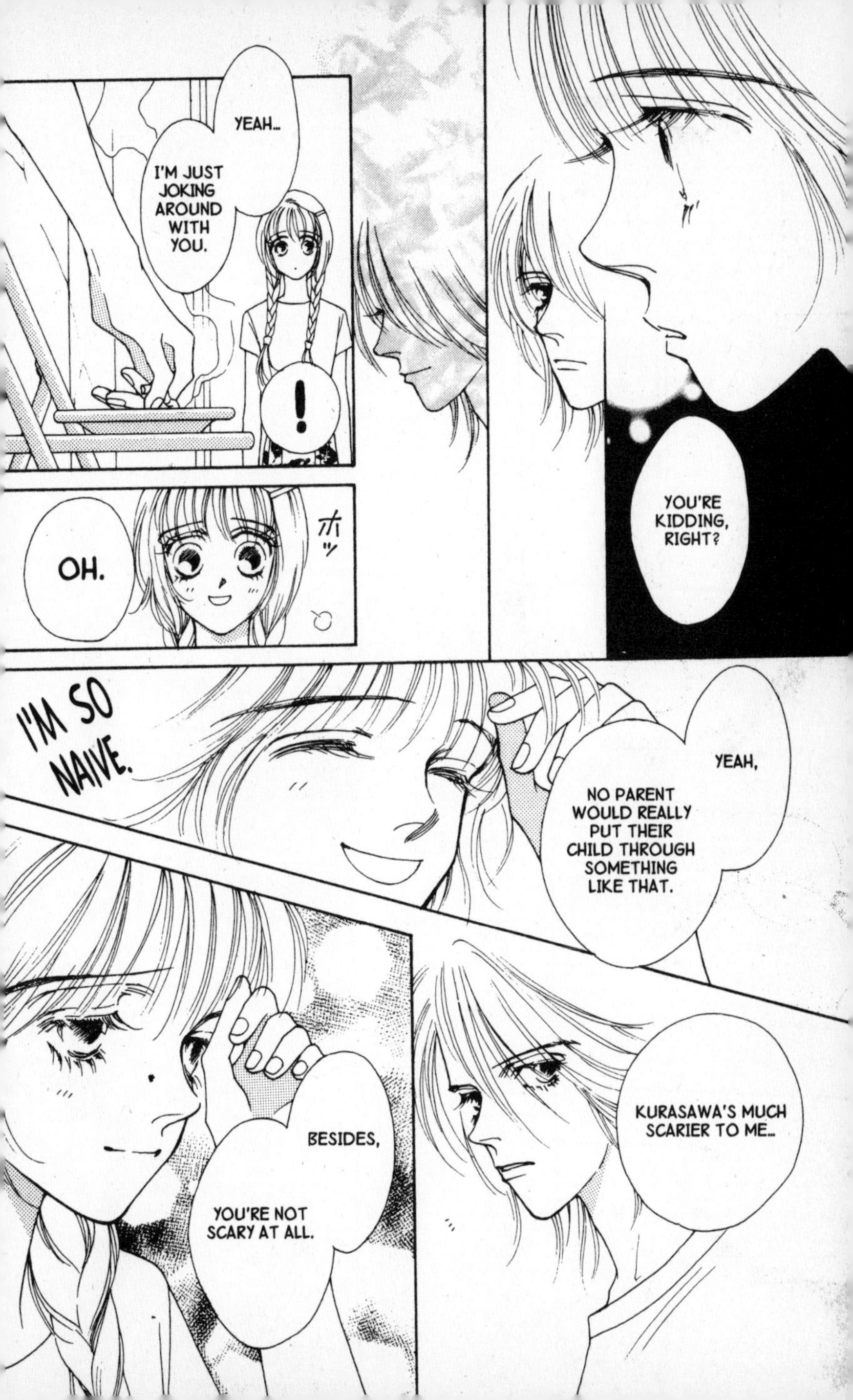
YOU'RE KIDDING, RIGHT?
YEAH...
I'M JUST JOKING AROUND WITH YOU.
!
ホッ
OH.
YEAH,
NO PARENT WOULD REALLY PUT THEIR CHILD THROUGH SOMETHING LIKE THAT.
I'M SO NAIVE.
KURASAWA'S MUCH SCARIER TO ME..
BESIDES,
YOU'RE NOT SCARY AT ALL.

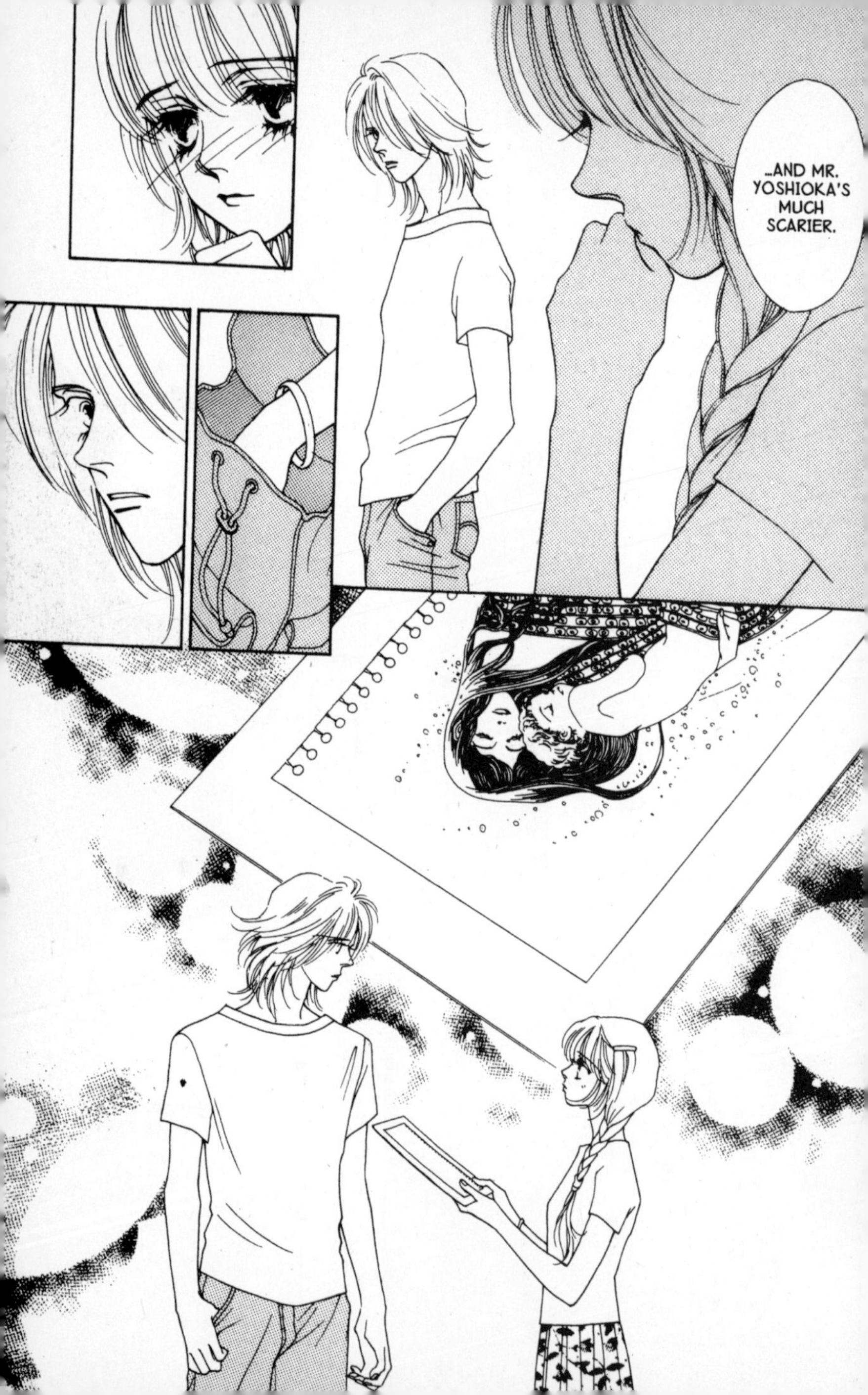
...AND MR. YOSHIOKA'S MUCH SCARIER.

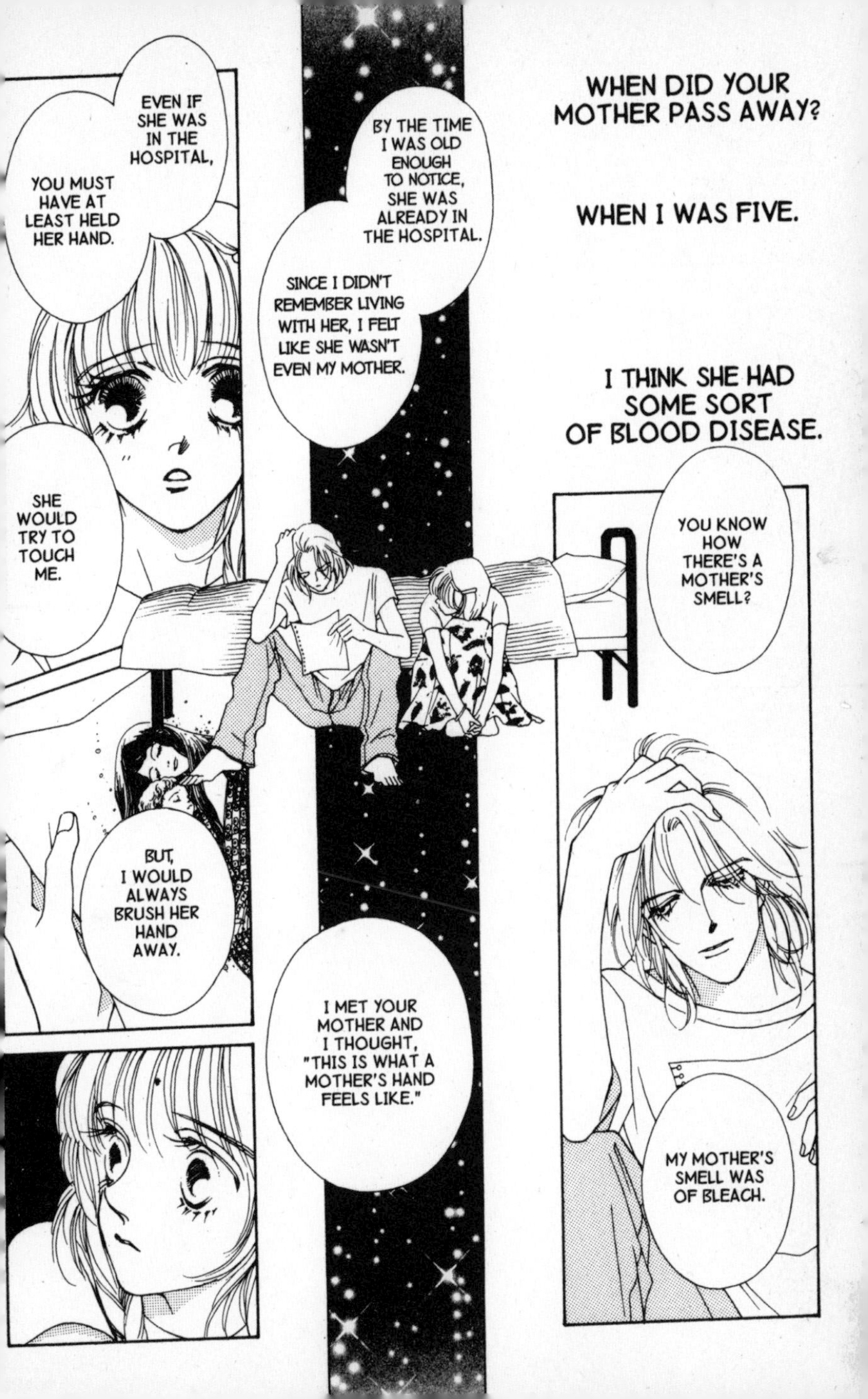
WHEN DID YOUR MOTHER PASS AWAY?
WHEN I WAS FIVE.
I THINK SHE HAD SOME SORT OF BLOOD DISEASE.
YOU KNOW HOW THERE'S A MOTHER'S SMELL?
MY MOTHER'S SMELL WAS OF BLEACH.
BY THE TIME I WAS OLD ENOUGH TO NOTICE, SHE WAS ALREADY IN THE HOSPITAL.
SINCE I DIDN'T REMEMBER LIVING WITH HER, I FELT LIKE SHE WASN'T EVEN MY MOTHER.
EVEN IF SHE WAS IN THE HOSPITAL,
YOU MUST HAVE AT LEAST HELD HER HAND.
SHE WOULD TRY TO TOUCH ME.
BUT, I WOULD ALWAYS BRUSH HER HAND AWAY.
I MET YOUR MOTHER AND I THOUGHT, "THIS IS WHAT A MOTHER'S HAND FEELS LIKE."

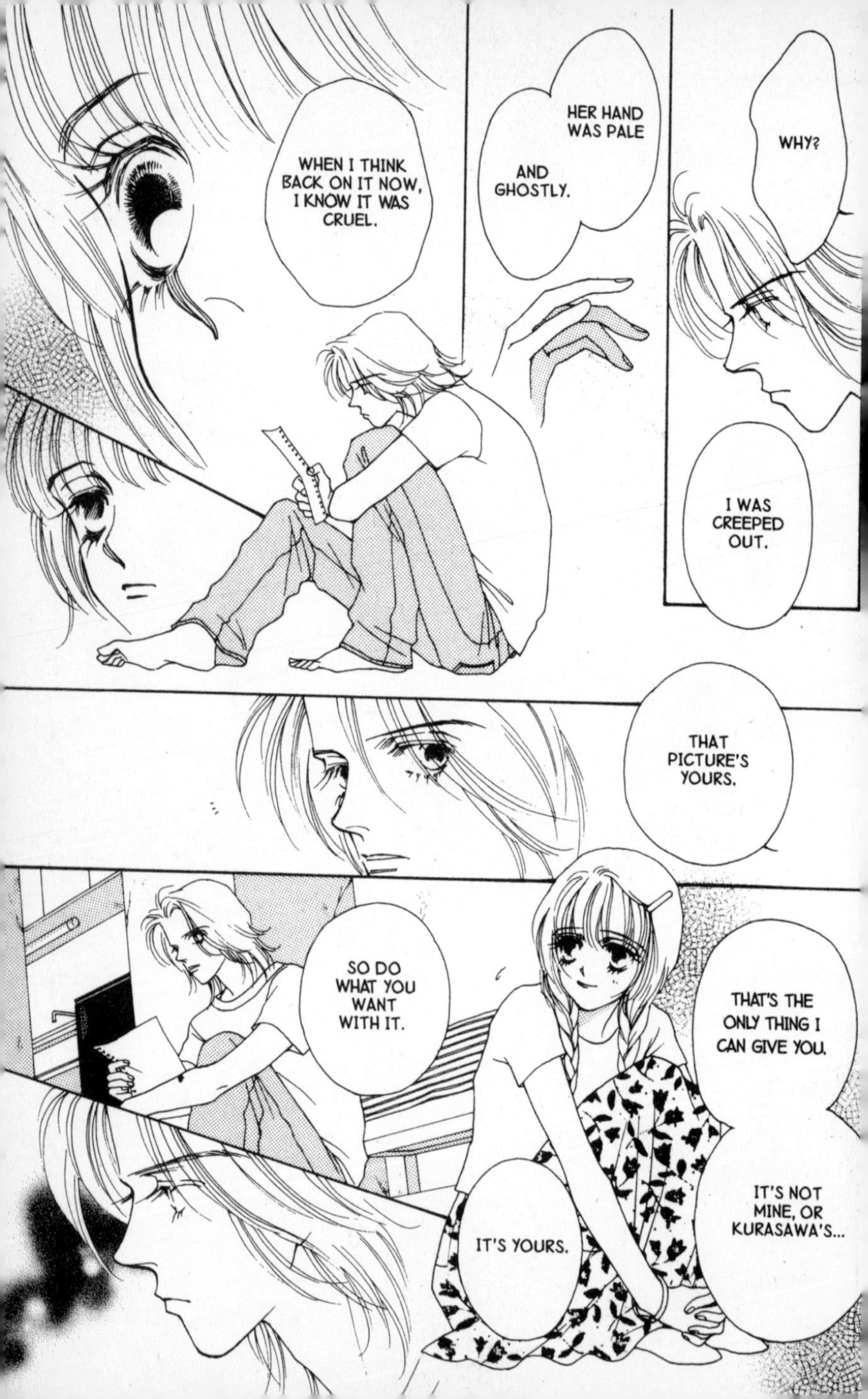
WHY?
I WAS CREEPED OUT.
HER HAND WAS PALE
AND GHOSTLY.
WHEN I THINK BACK ON IT NOW, I KNOW IT WAS CRUEL.
THAT PICTURE'S YOURS.
THAT'S THE ONLY THING I CAN GIVE YOU.
IT'S NOT MINE, OR KURASAWA'S...
IT'S YOURS.
SO DO WHAT YOU WANT WITH IT.

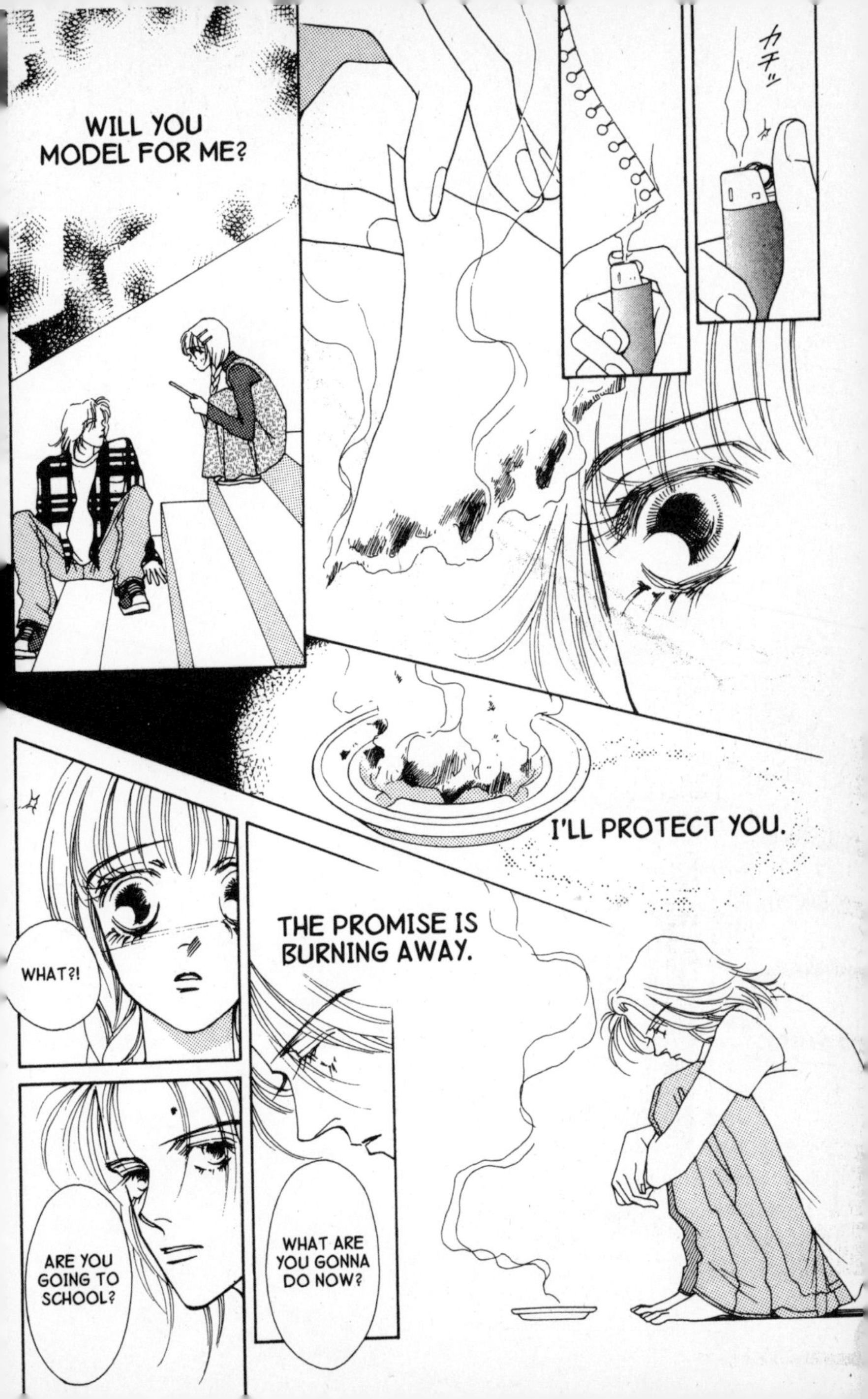
カチッ
WILL YOU MODEL FOR ME?
I'LL PROTECT YOU.
THE PROMISE IS BURNING AWAY.
WHAT?!
WHAT ARE YOU GONNA DO NOW?
ARE YOU GOING TO SCHOOL?

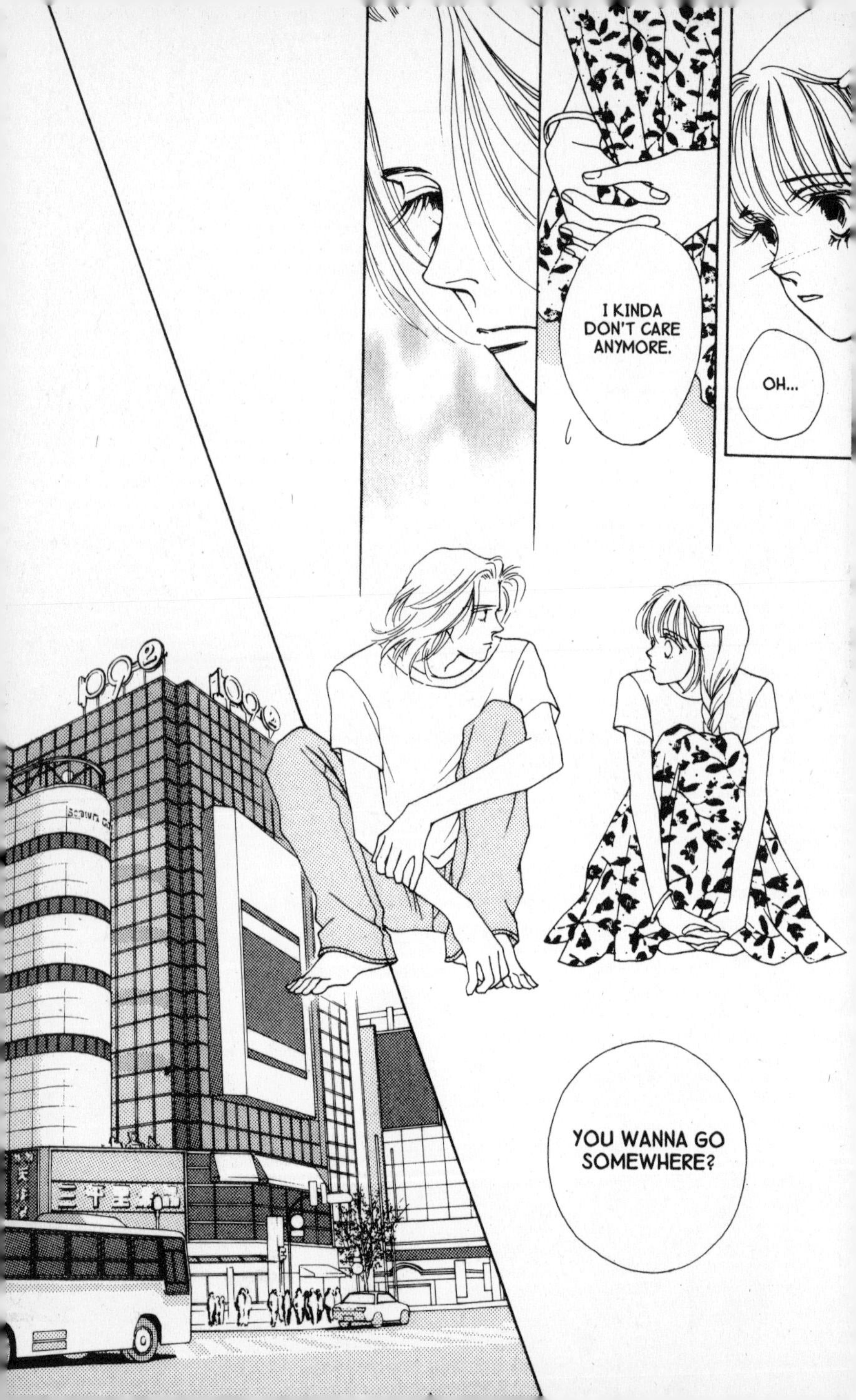
OH...
I KINDA DON'T CARE ANYMORE.
YOU WANNA GO SOMEWHERE?

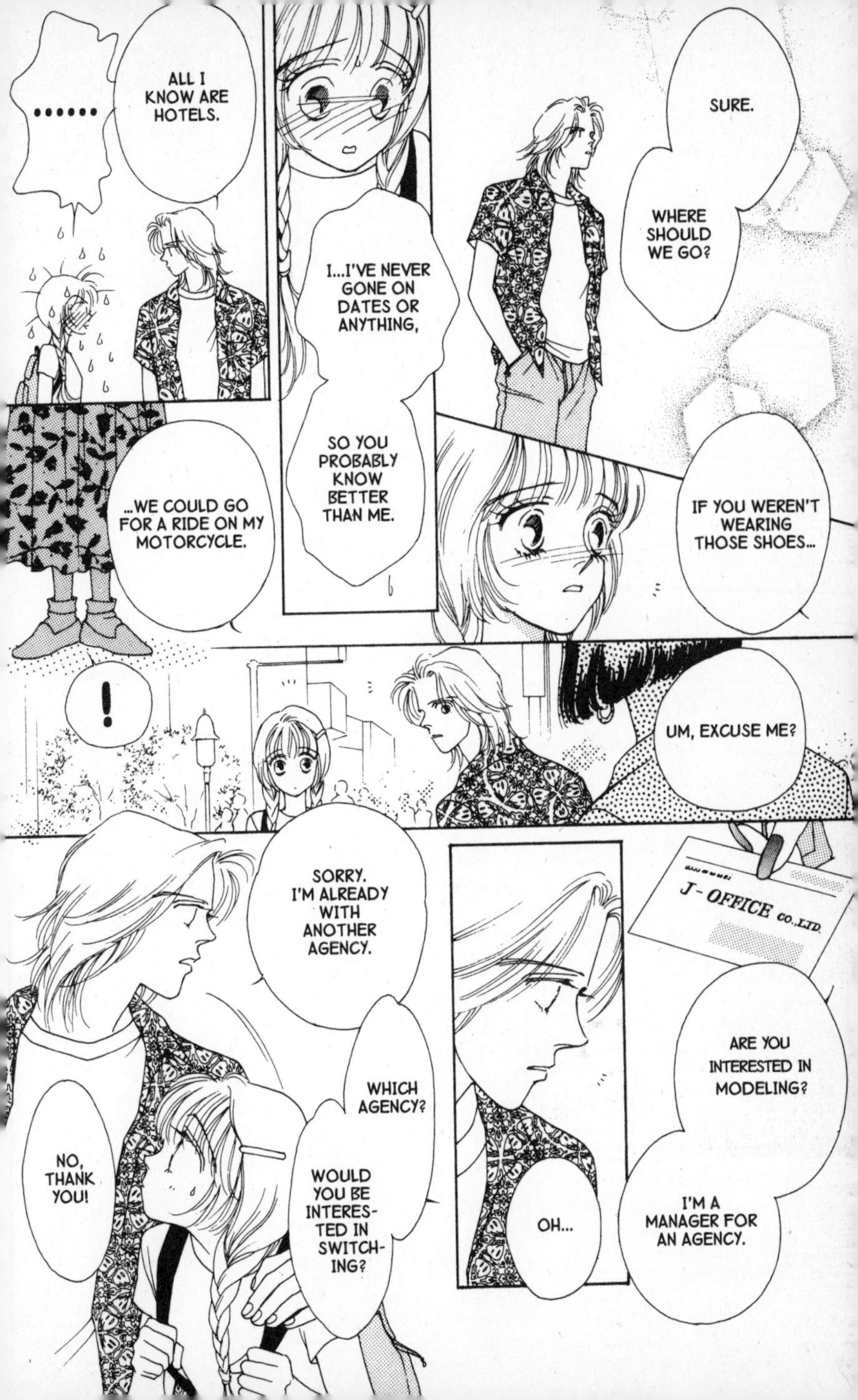
SURE.
WHERE SHOULD WE GO?
I...I'VE NEVER GONE ON DATES OR ANYTHING,
SO YOU PROBABLY KNOW BETTER THAN ME.
ALL I KNOW ARE HOTELS.
......
IF YOU WEREN'T WEARING THOSE SHOES...
...WE COULD GO FOR A RIDE ON MY MOTORCYCLE.
UM, EXCUSE ME?
!
J-OFFICE CO.,LTD.
ARE YOU INTERESTED IN MODELING?
I'M A MANAGER FOR AN AGENCY.
OH...
SORRY. I'M ALREADY WITH ANOTHER AGENCY.
WHICH AGENCY?
WOULD YOU BE INTERESTED IN SWITCHING?
NO, THANK YOU!

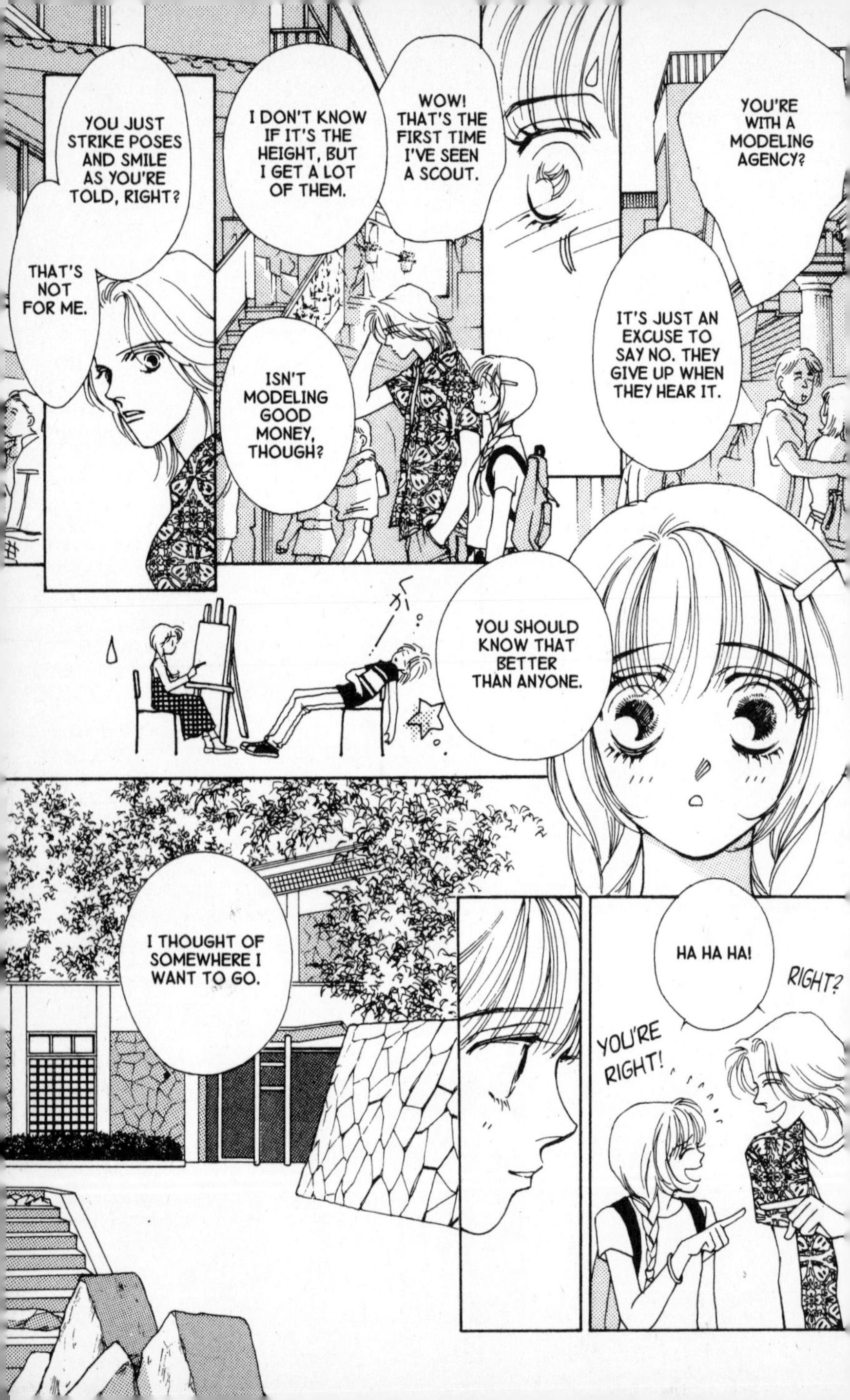
YOU'RE WITH A MODELING AGENCY?
IT'S JUST AN EXCUSE TO SAY NO. THEY GIVE UP WHEN THEY HEAR IT.
WOW! THAT'S THE FIRST TIME I'VE SEEN A SCOUT.
I DON'T KNOW IF IT'S THE HEIGHT, BUT I GET A LOT OF THEM.
ISN'T MODELING GOOD MONEY, THOUGH?
YOU JUST STRIKE POSES AND SMILE AS YOU'RE TOLD, RIGHT?
THAT'S NOT FOR ME.
YOU SHOULD KNOW THAT BETTER THAN ANYONE.
HA HA HA!
RIGHT?
YOU'RE RIGHT!
I THOUGHT OF SOMEWHERE I WANT TO GO.

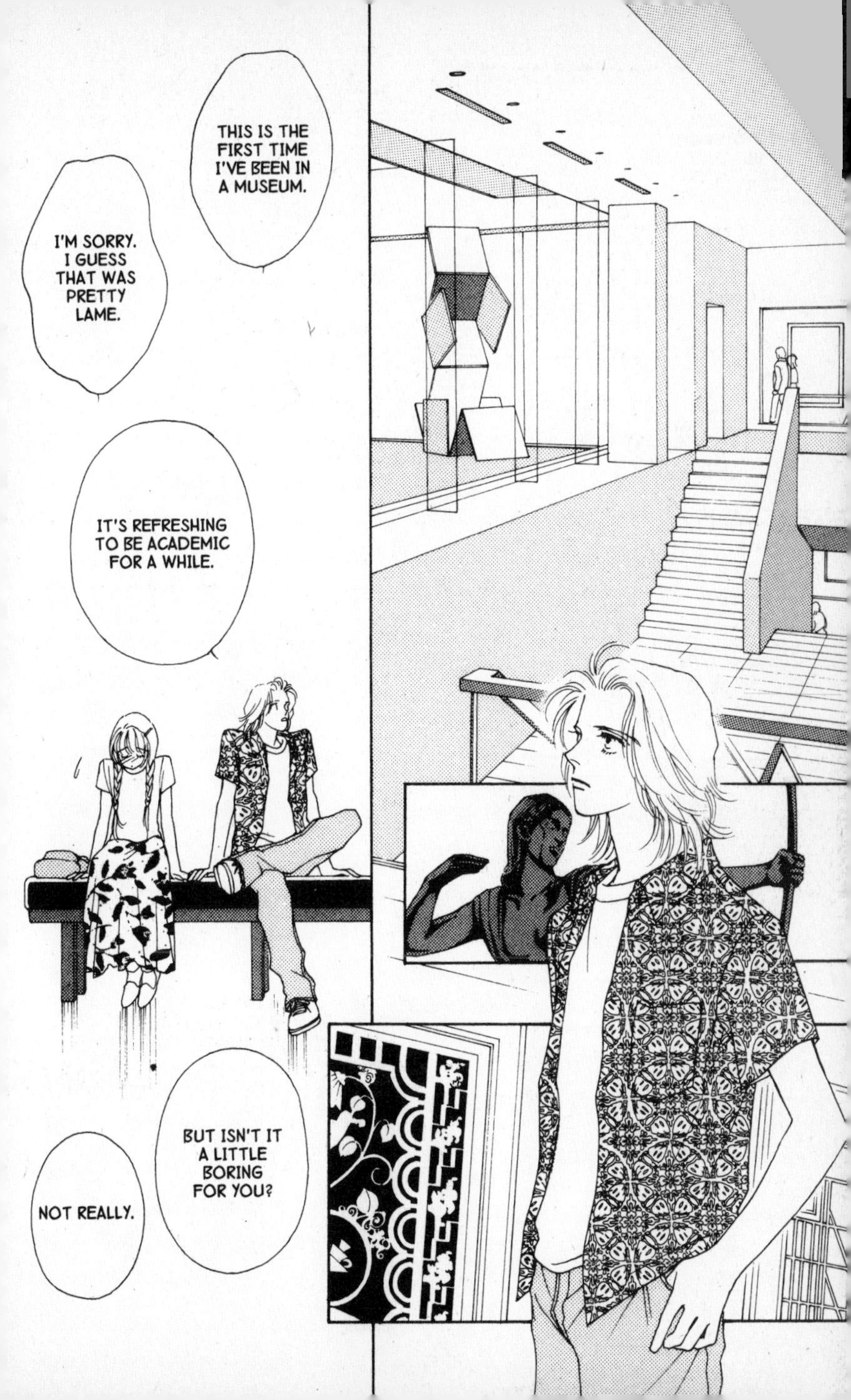
THIS IS THE FIRST TIME I'VE BEEN IN A MUSEUM.
I'M SORRY. I GUESS THAT WAS PRETTY LAME.
IT'S REFRESHING TO BE ACADEMIC FOR A WHILE.
BUT ISN'T IT A LITTLE BORING FOR YOU?
NOT REALLY.

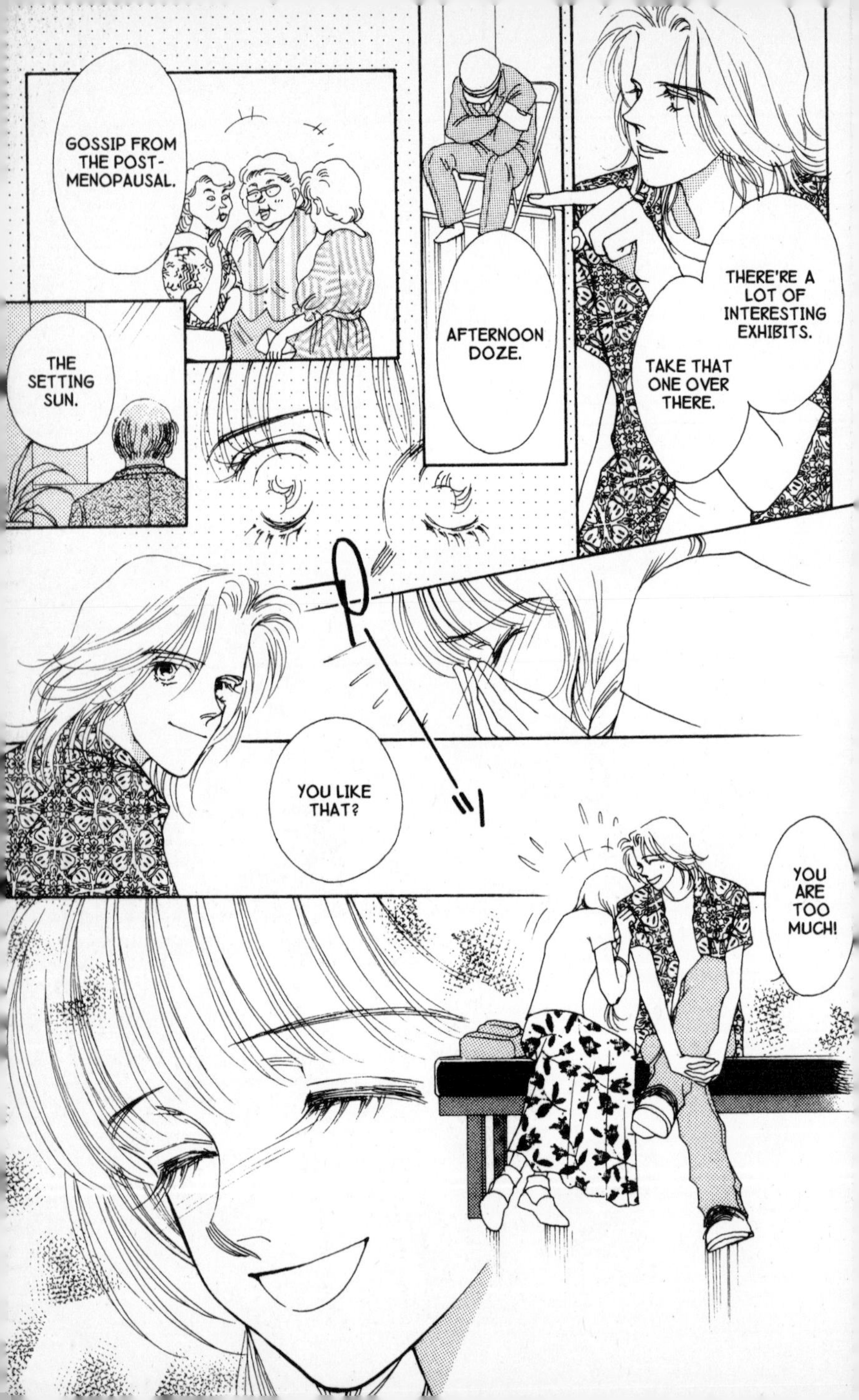
THERE'RE A LOT OF INTERESTING EXHIBITS.
TAKE THAT ONE OVER THERE.
AFTERNOON DOZE.
GOSSIP FROM THE POST-MENOPAUSAL.
THE SETTING SUN.
YOU LIKE THAT?
YOU ARE TOO MUCH!

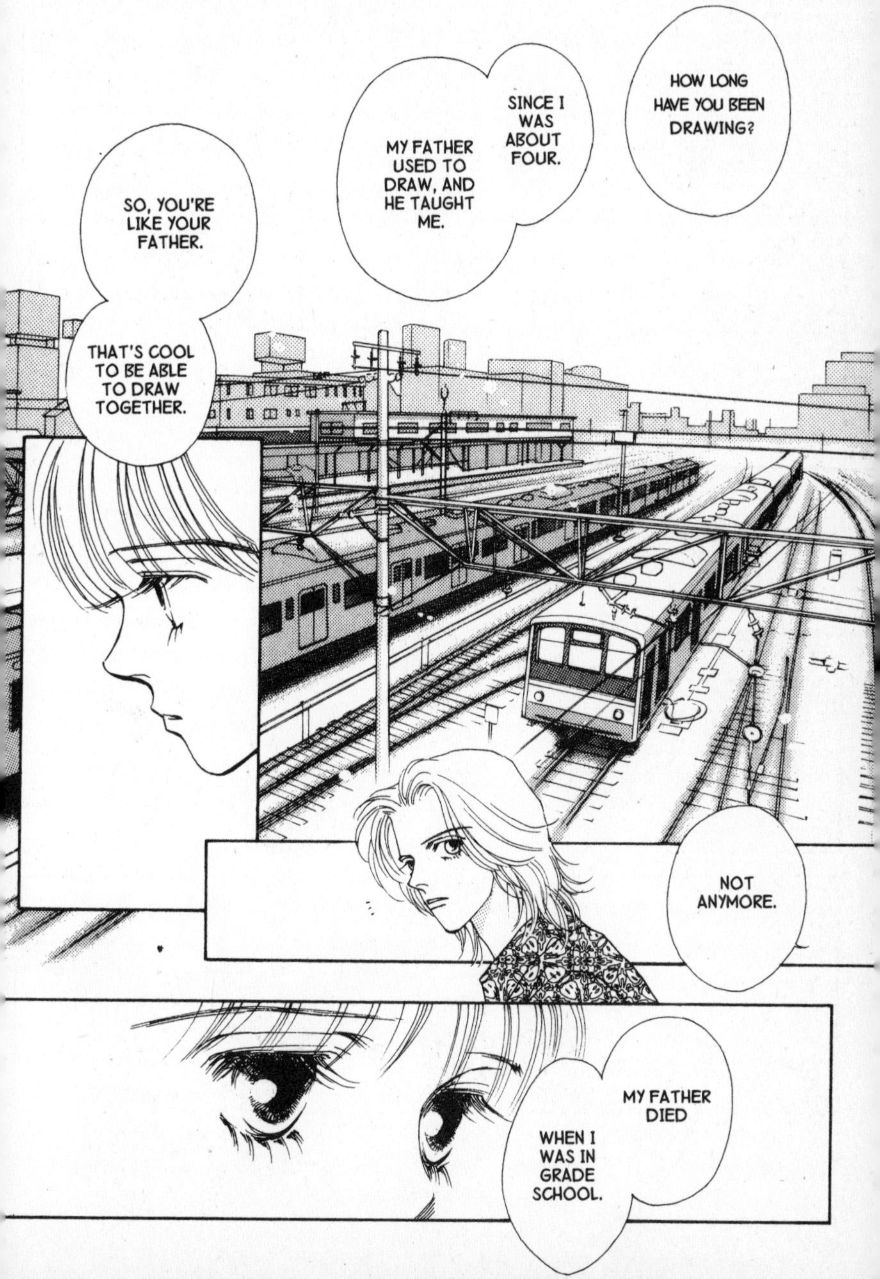
HOW LONG HAVE YOU BEEN DRAWING?
SINCE I WAS ABOUT FOUR.
MY FATHER USED TO DRAW, AND HE TAUGHT ME.
SO, YOU'RE LIKE YOUR FATHER.
THAT'S COOL TO BE ABLE TO DRAW TOGETHER.
NOT ANYMORE.
MY FATHER DIED
WHEN I WAS IN GRADE SCHOOL.

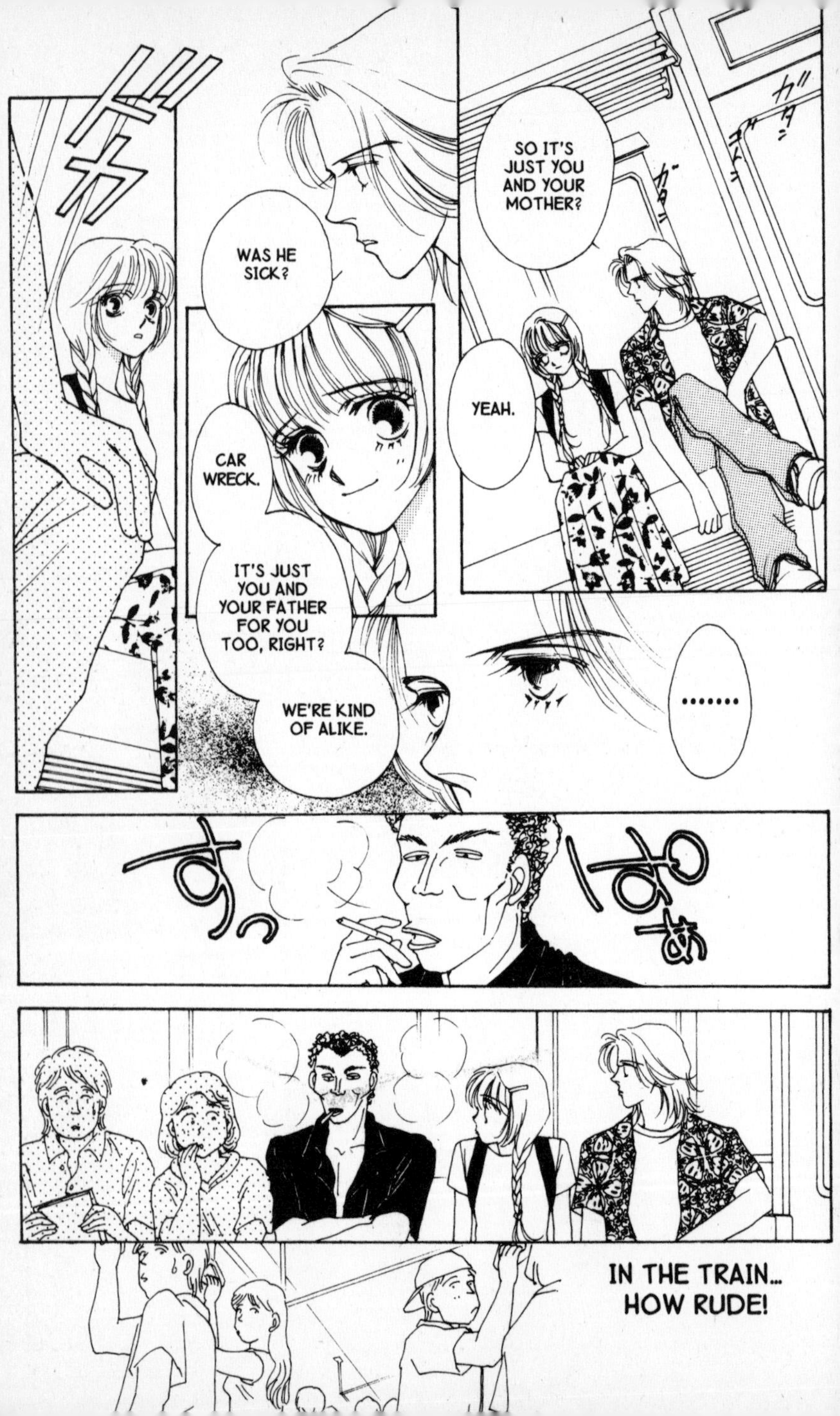
SO IT'S JUST YOU AND YOUR MOTHER?
YEAH.
WAS HE SICK?
CAR WRECK.
IT'S JUST YOU AND YOUR FATHER FOR YOU TOO, RIGHT?
WE'RE KIND OF ALIKE.
....
すっ
IN THE TRAIN... HOW RUDE!

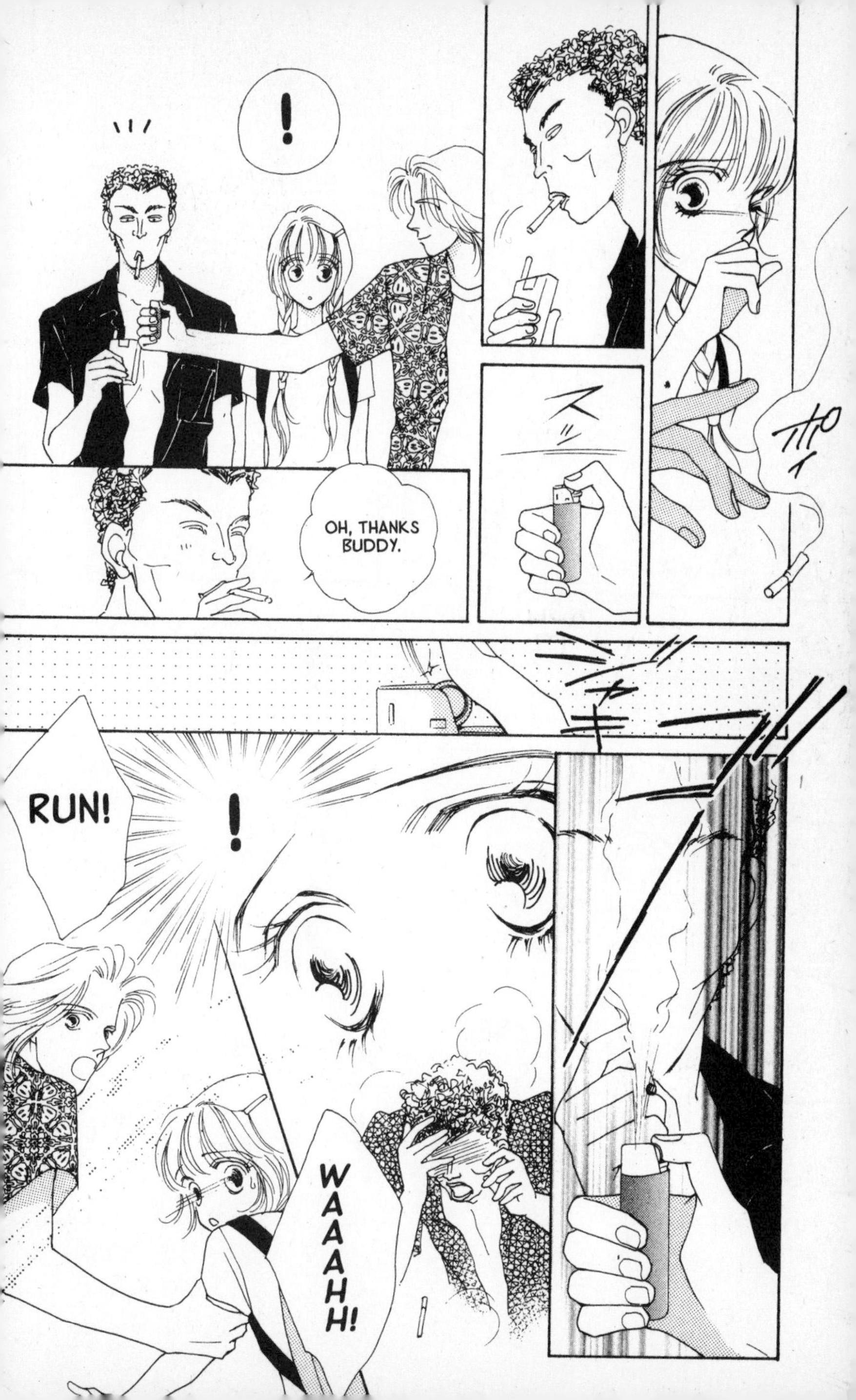

スッ
!
OH, THANKS BUDDY.
!
RUN!
WAAAAHH!

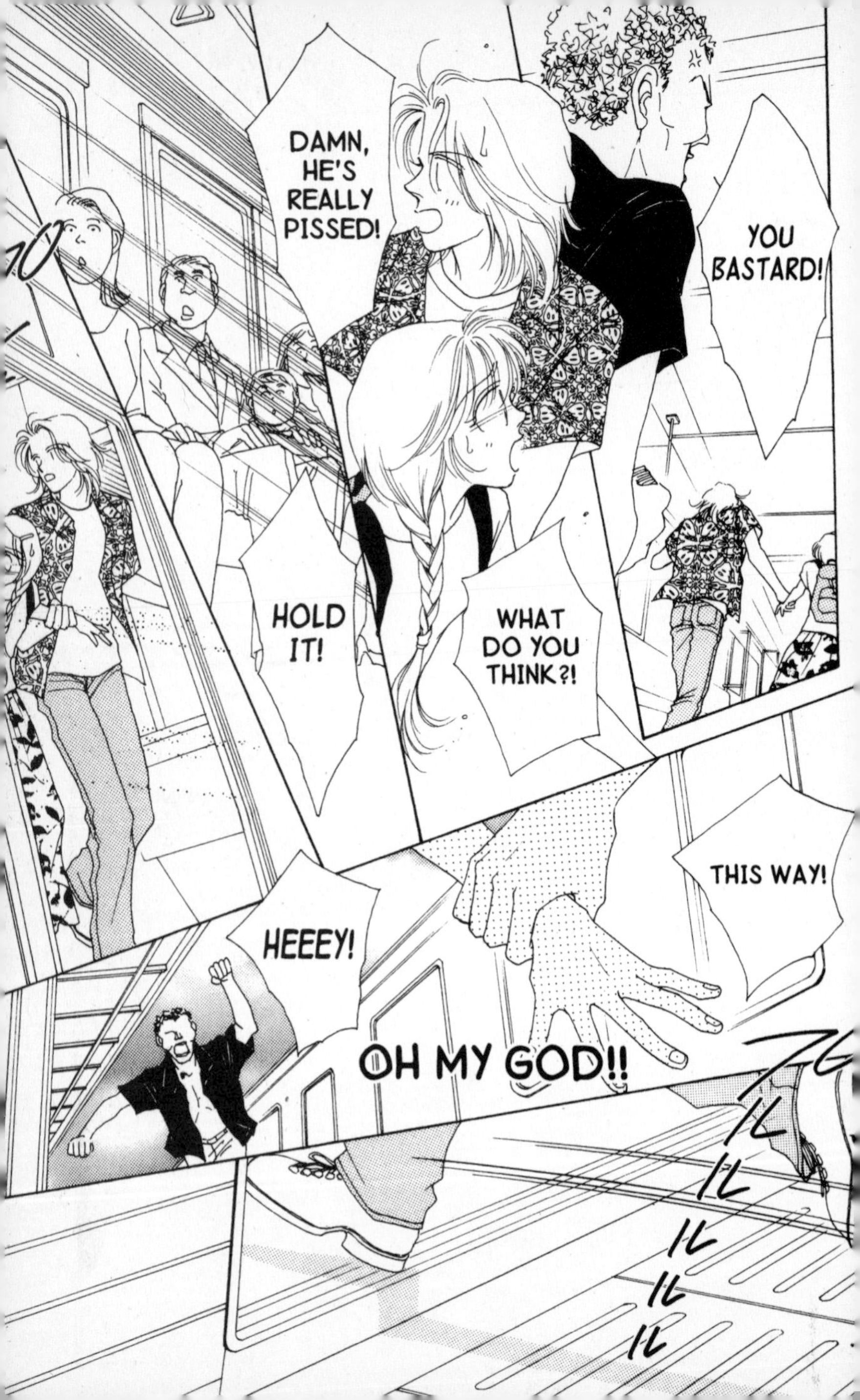
YOU BASTARD!
DAMN, HE'S REALLY PISSED!
WHAT DO YOU THINK?!
HOLD IT!
THIS WAY!
HEEEY!
OH MY GOD!!

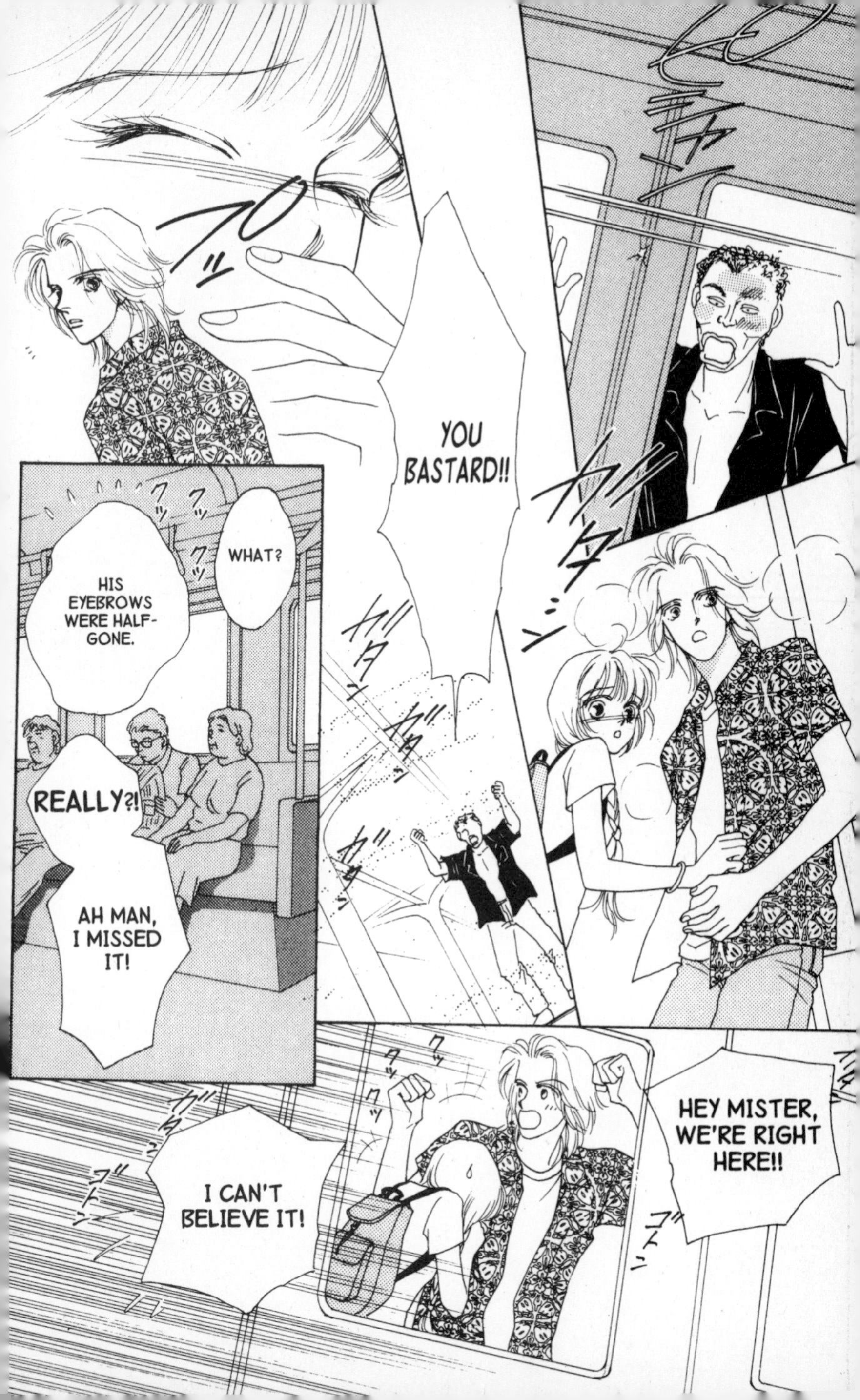
YOU BASTARD!!
WHAT?
HIS EYEBROWS WERE HALF-GONE.
REALLY?!
AH MAN, I MISSED IT!
HEY MISTER, WE'RE RIGHT HERE!!
I CAN'T BELIEVE IT!

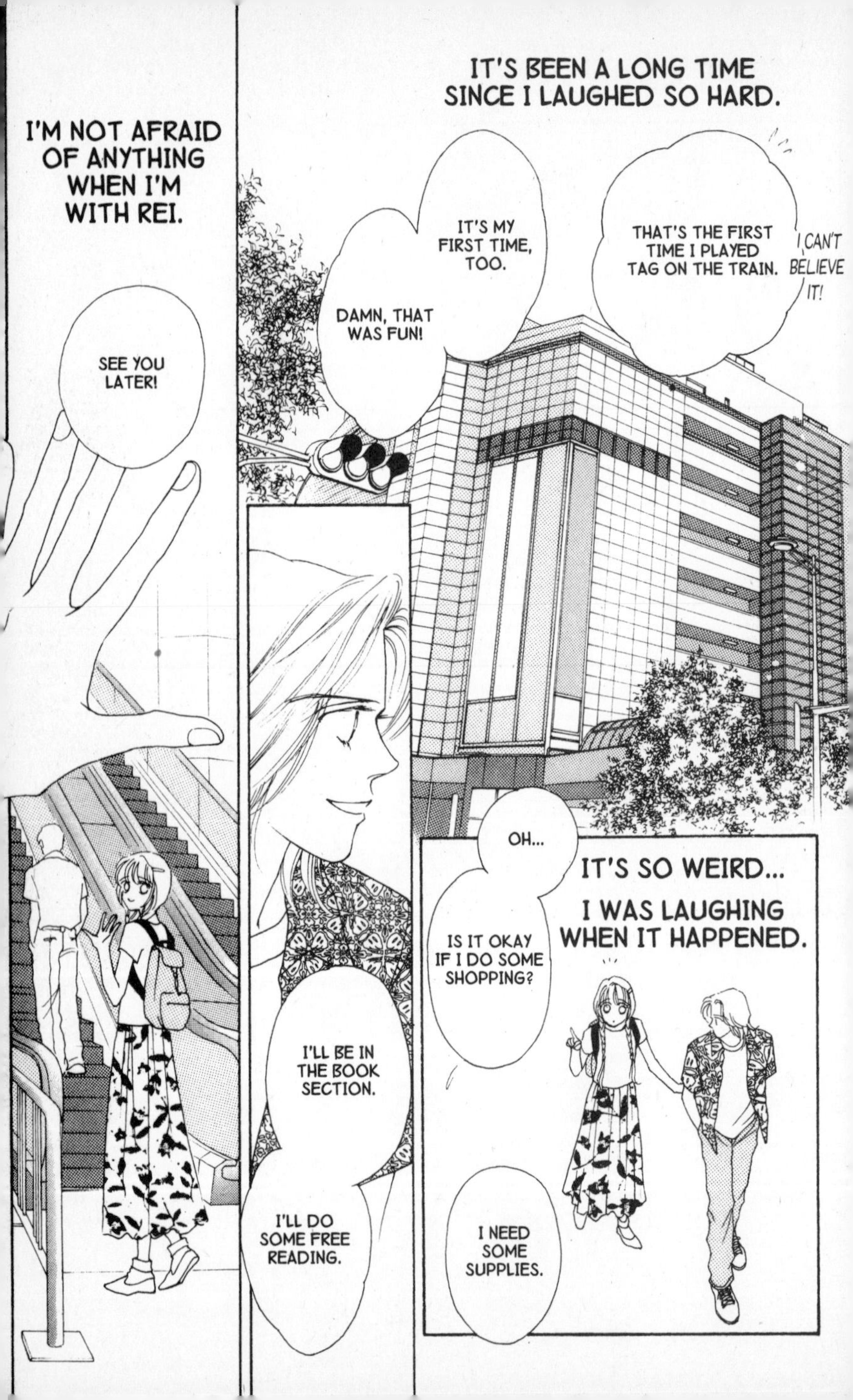
IT'S BEEN A LONG TIME SINCE I LAUGHED SO HARD.
I CAN'T BELIEVE IT!
THAT'S THE FIRST TIME I PLAYED TAG ON THE TRAIN.
IT'S MY FIRST TIME, TOO.
DAMN, THAT WAS FUN!
IT'S SO WEIRD... I WAS LAUGHING WHEN IT HAPPENED.
OH...
IS IT OKAY IF I DO SOME SHOPPING?
I NEED SOME SUPPLIES.
I'LL BE IN THE BOOK SECTION.
I'LL DO SOME FREE READING.
I'M NOT AFRAID OF ANYTHING WHEN I'M WITH REI.
SEE YOU LATER!

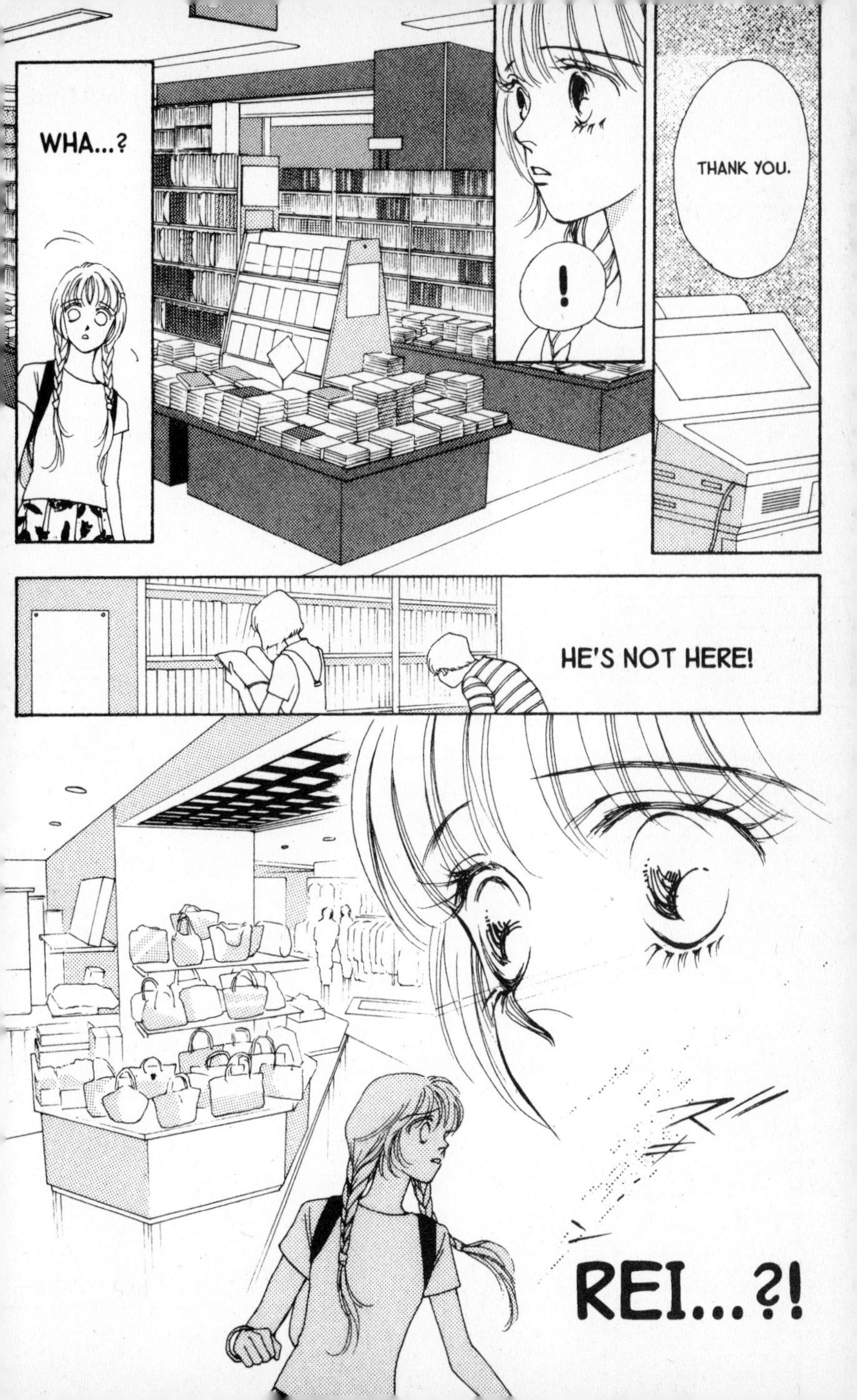
THANK YOU.
!
WHA...?
HE'S NOT HERE!
REI...?!

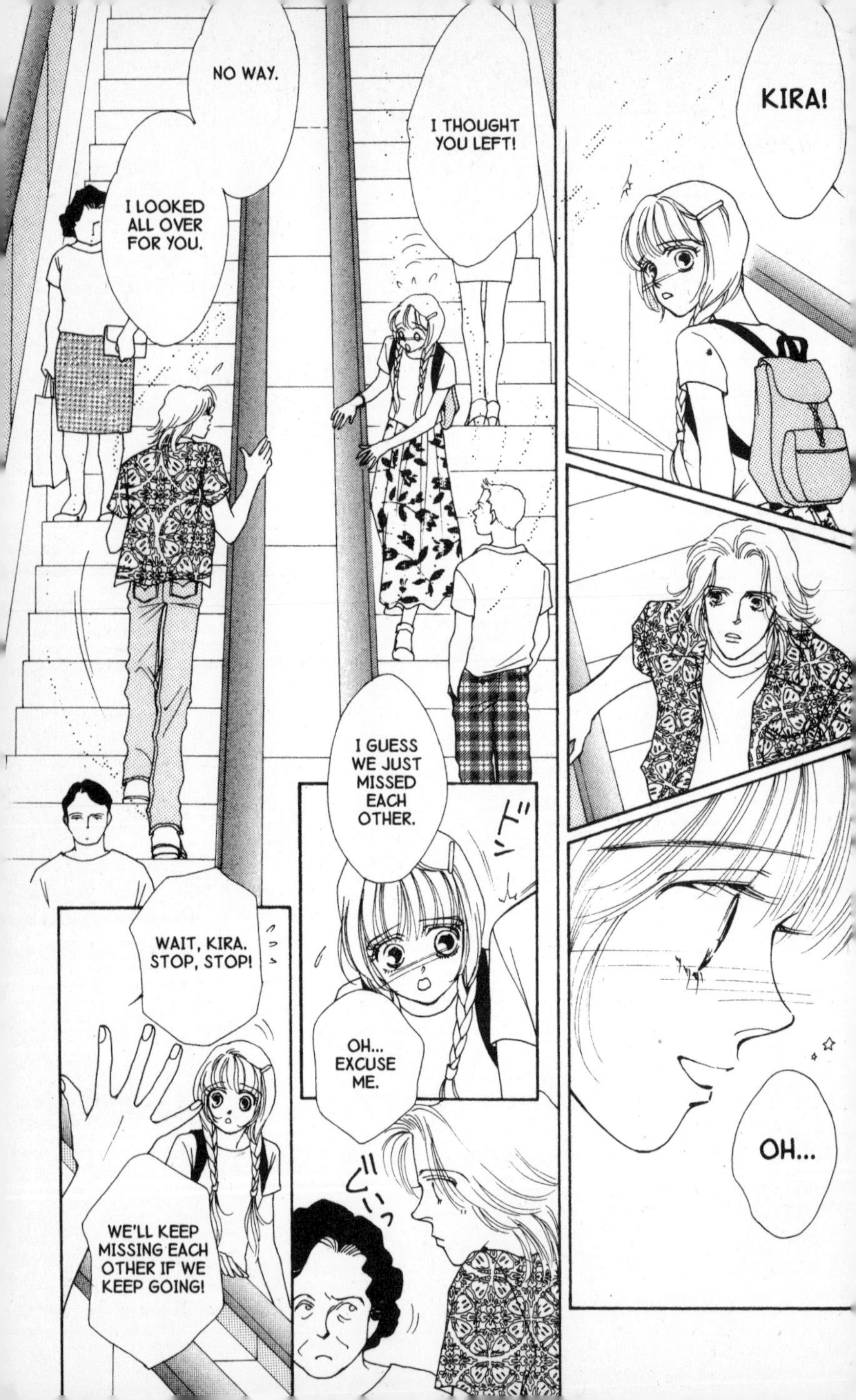
KIRA!
OH...
I THOUGHT YOU LEFT!
NO WAY.
I LOOKED ALL OVER FOR YOU.
I GUESS WE JUST MISSED EACH OTHER.
ドン
OH... EXCUSE ME.
じーっ
WAIT, KIRA. STOP, STOP!
WE'LL KEEP MISSING EACH OTHER IF WE KEEP GOING!

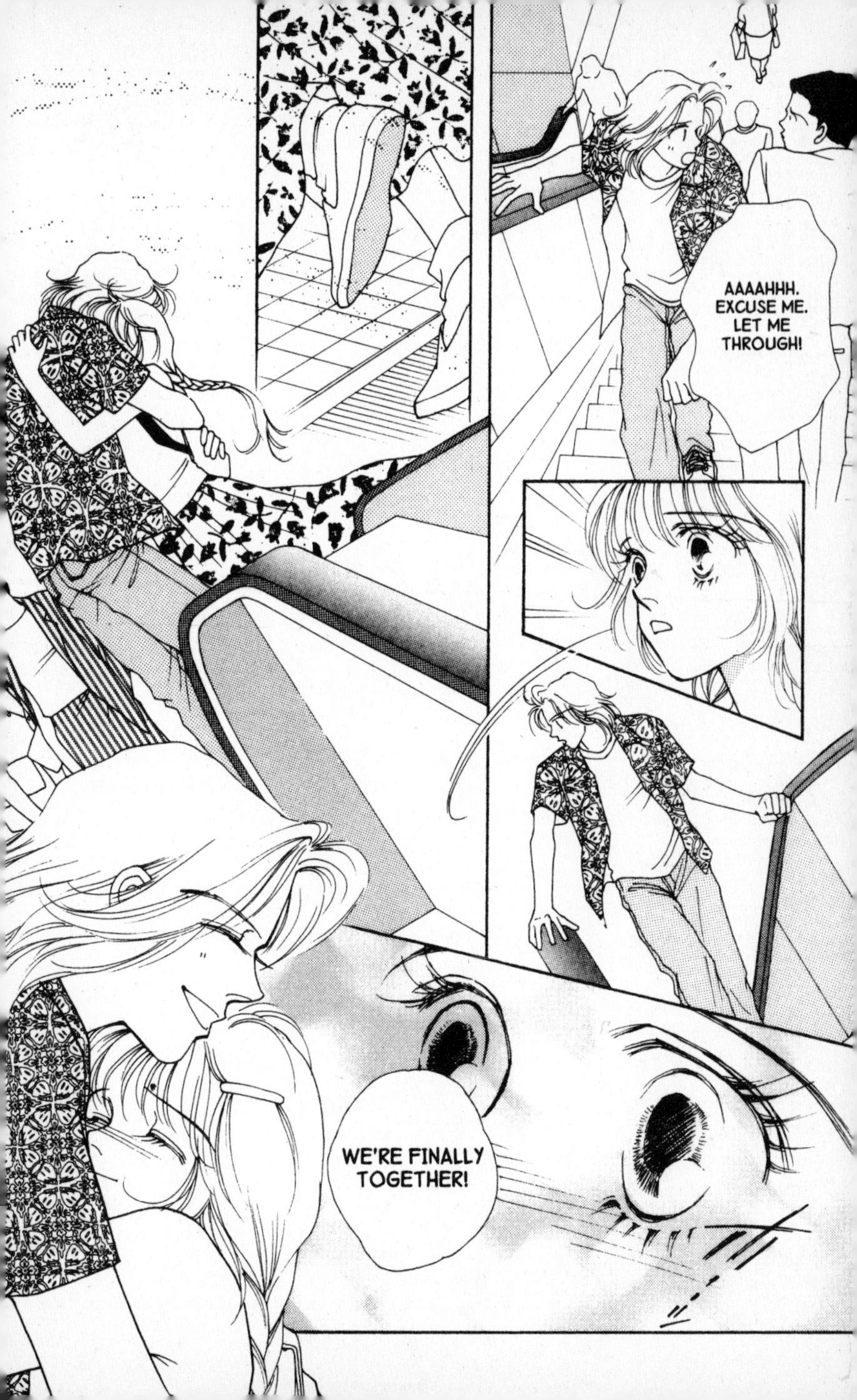
AAAAHHH. EXCUSE ME. LET ME THROUGH!
WE'RE FINALLY TOGETHER!

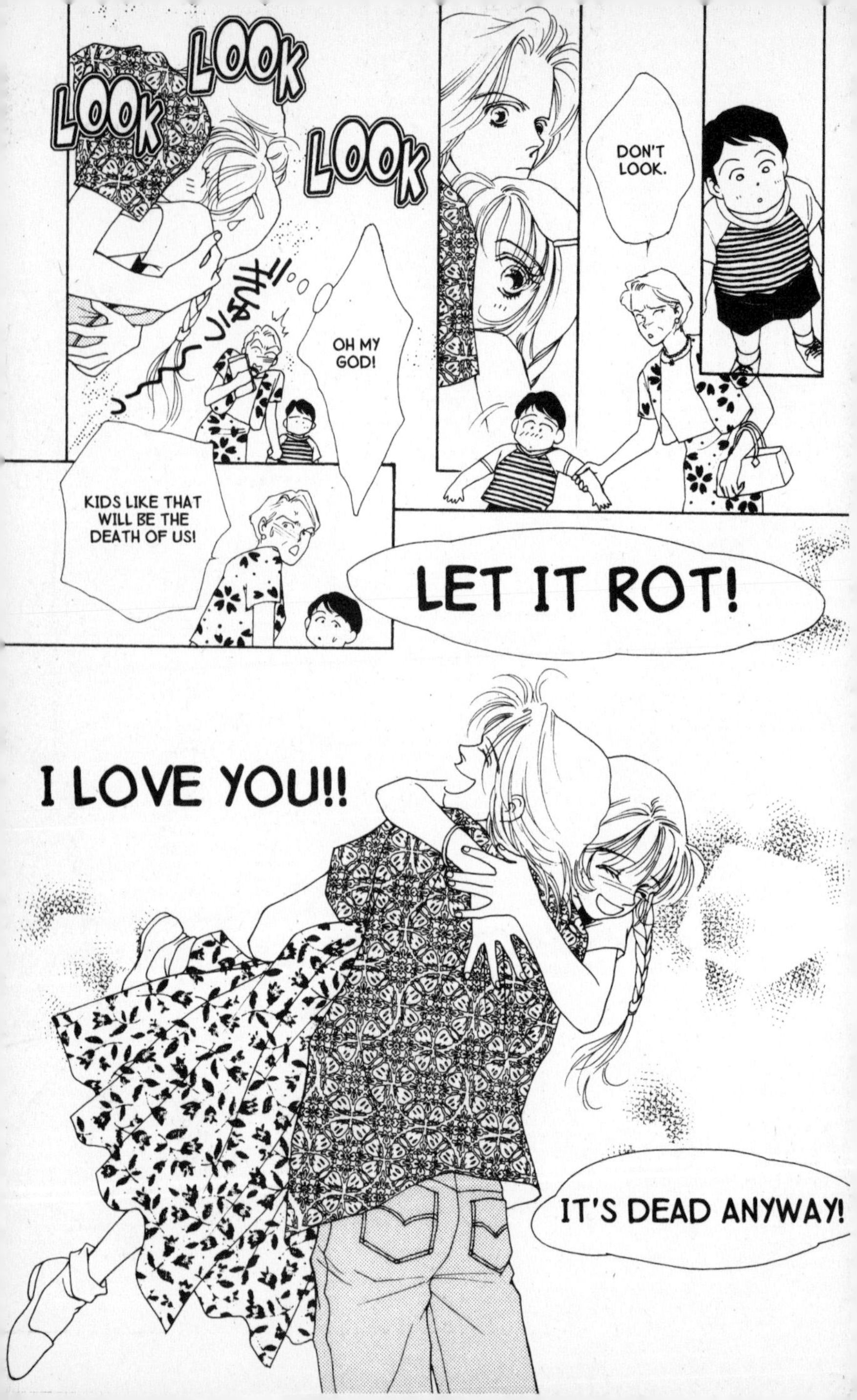
DON'T LOOK.
LOOK
LOOK
LOOK
OH MY GOD!
LET IT ROT!
KIDS LIKE THAT WILL BE THE DEATH OF US!
I LOVE YOU!!
IT'S DEAD ANYWAY!

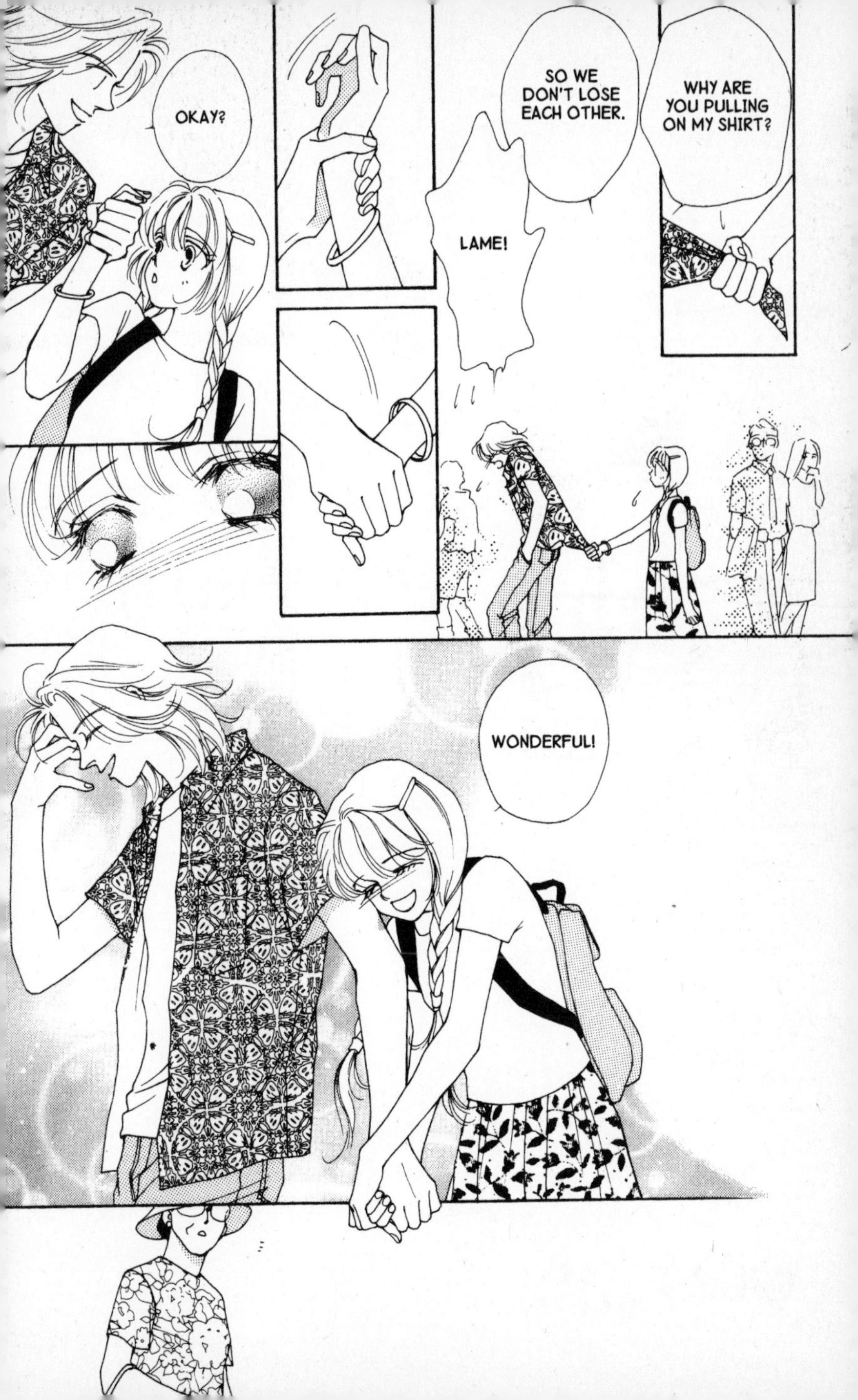
WHY ARE YOU PULLING ON MY SHIRT?
SO WE DON'T LOSE EACH OTHER.
LAME!
OKAY?
WONDERFUL!

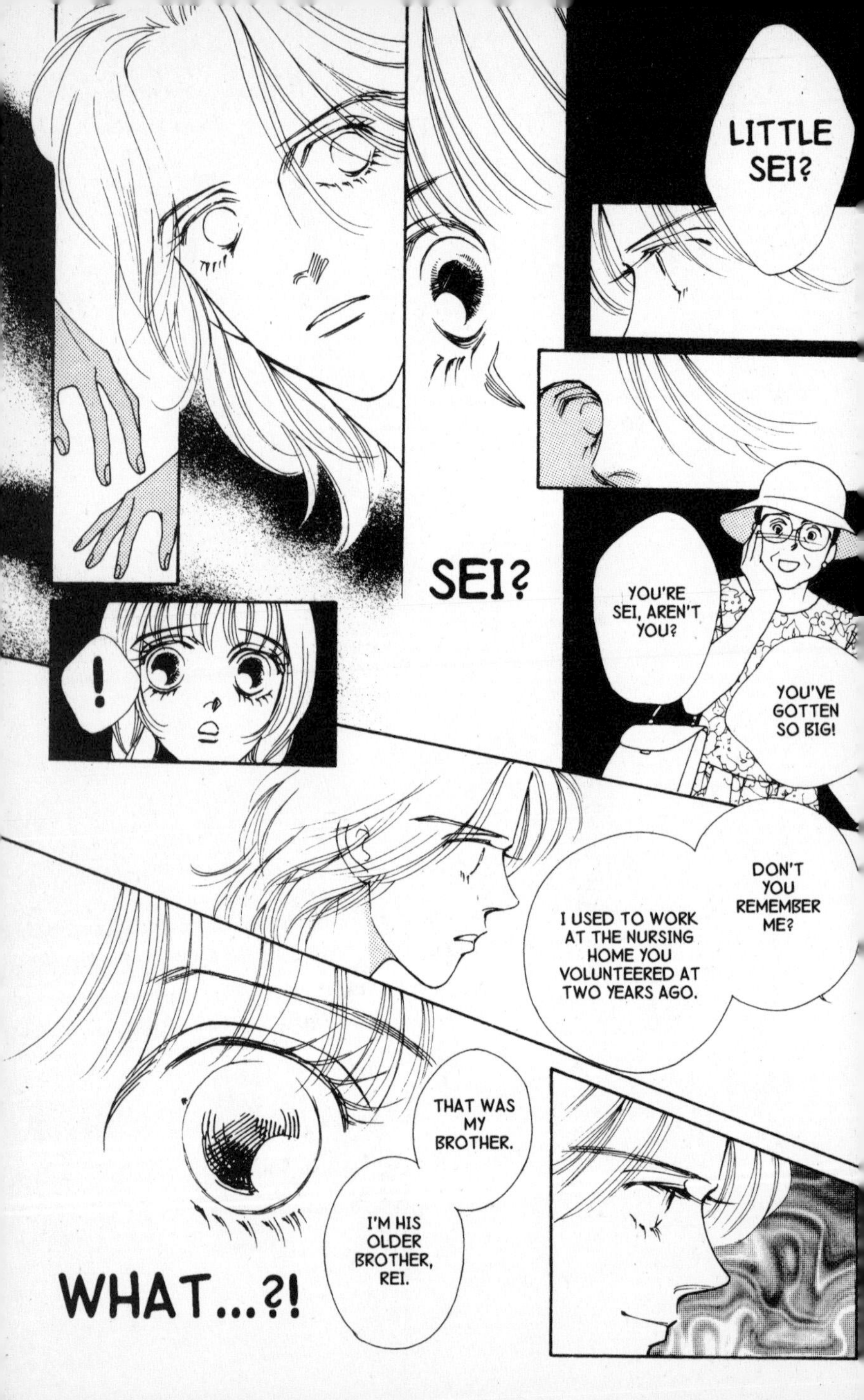

LITTLE SEI?
SEI?
YOU'RE SEI, AREN'T YOU?
YOU'VE GOTTEN SO BIG!
!
DON'T YOU REMEMBER ME?
I USED TO WORK AT THE NURSING HOME YOU VOLUNTEERED AT TWO YEARS AGO.
THAT WAS MY BROTHER.
I'M HIS OLDER BROTHER, REI.
WHAT...?!

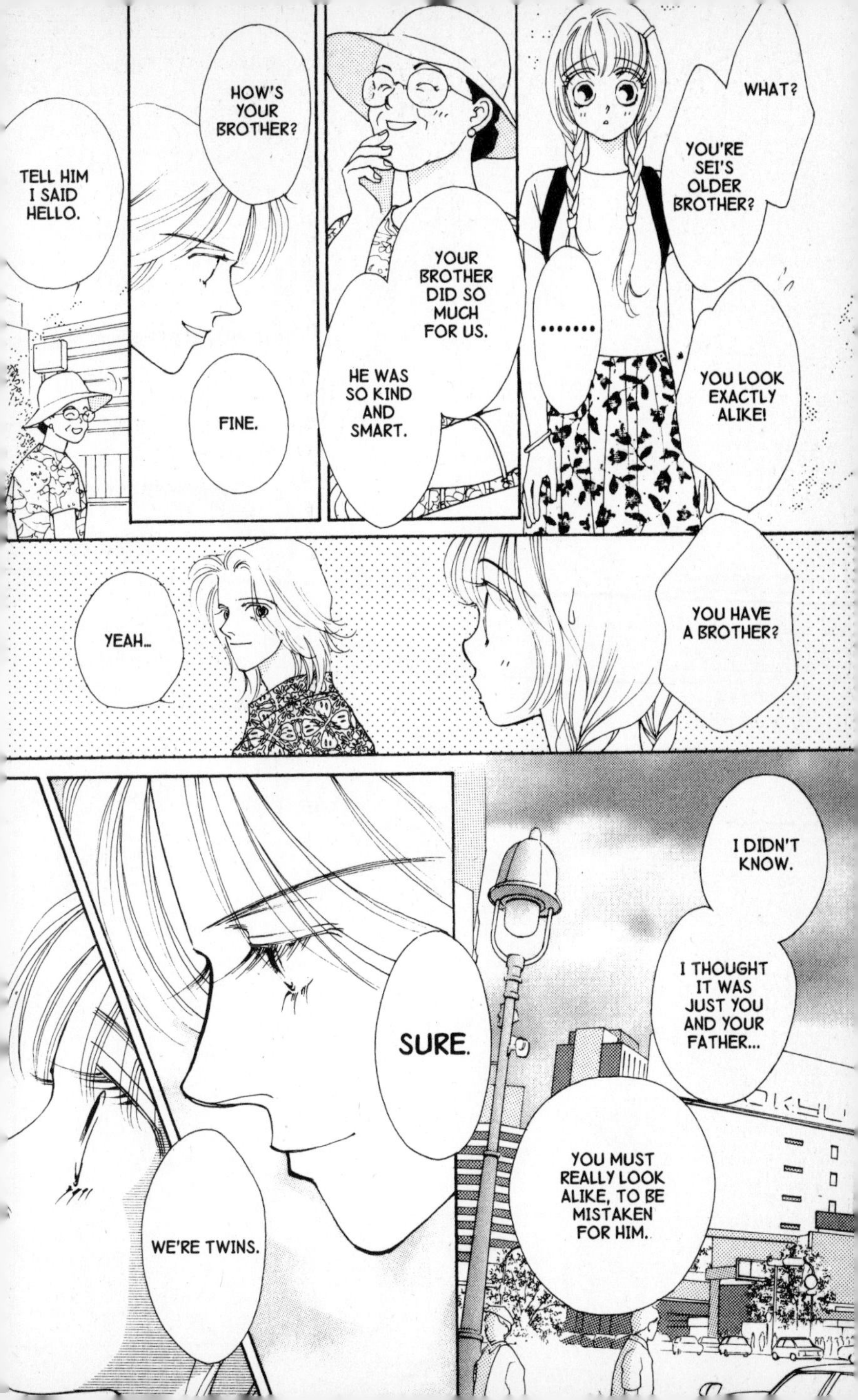

WHAT?
YOU'RE SEI'S OLDER BROTHER?
YOU LOOK EXACTLY ALIKE!
....
YOUR BROTHER DID SO MUCH FOR US.
HE WAS SO KIND AND SMART.
HOW'S YOUR BROTHER?
FINE.
TELL HIM I SAID HELLO.
YOU HAVE A BROTHER?
YEAH...
I DIDN'T KNOW.
I THOUGHT IT WAS JUST YOU AND YOUR FATHER...
YOU MUST REALLY LOOK ALIKE, TO BE MISTAKEN FOR HIM.
SURE.
WE'RE TWINS.

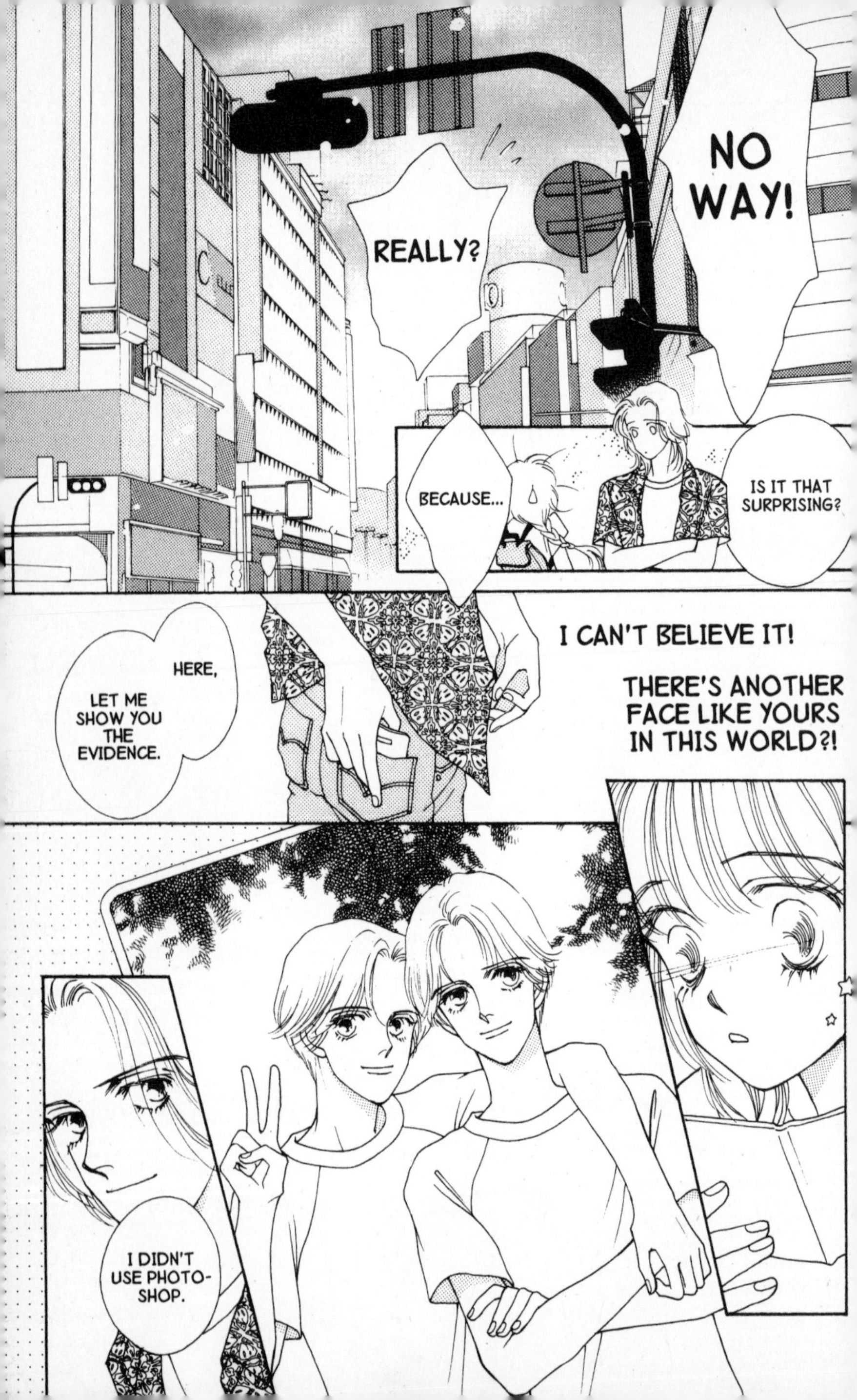
NO WAY!
REALLY?
IS IT THAT SURPRISING?
BECAUSE...
I CAN'T BELIEVE IT!
THERE'S ANOTHER FACE LIKE YOURS IN THIS WORLD?!
HERE, LET ME SHOW YOU THE EVIDENCE.
I DIDN'T USE PHOTO-SHOP.

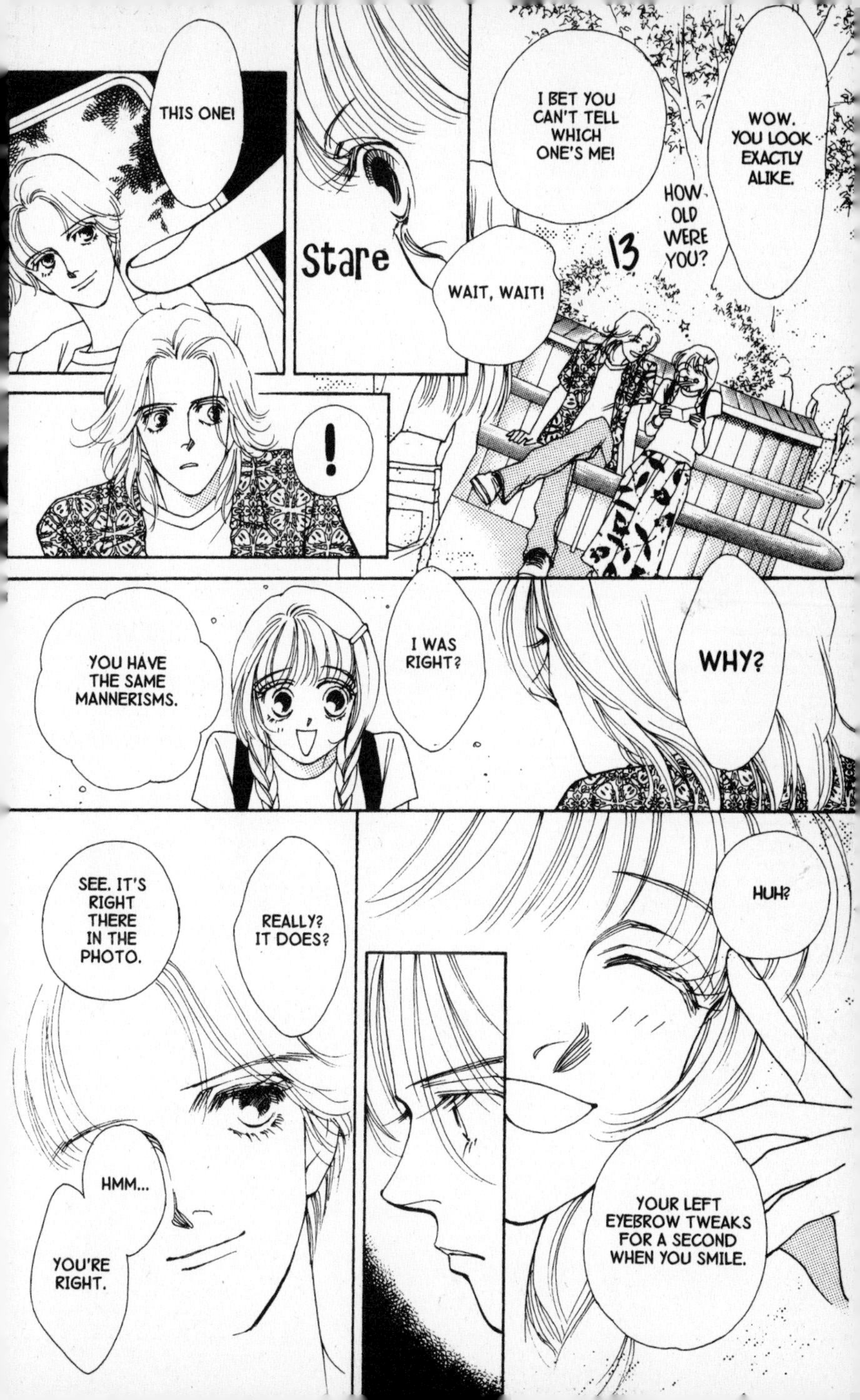
WOW. YOU LOOK EXACTLY ALIKE.
HOW OLD WERE YOU?
13
I BET YOU CAN'T TELL WHICH ONE'S ME!
WAIT, WAIT!
Stare
THIS ONE!
!
WHY?
I WAS RIGHT?
YOU HAVE THE SAME MANNERISMS.
HUH?
YOUR LEFT EYEBROW TWEAKS FOR A SECOND WHEN YOU SMILE.
REALLY? IT DOES?
SEE. IT'S RIGHT THERE IN THE PHOTO.
HMM...
YOU'RE RIGHT.

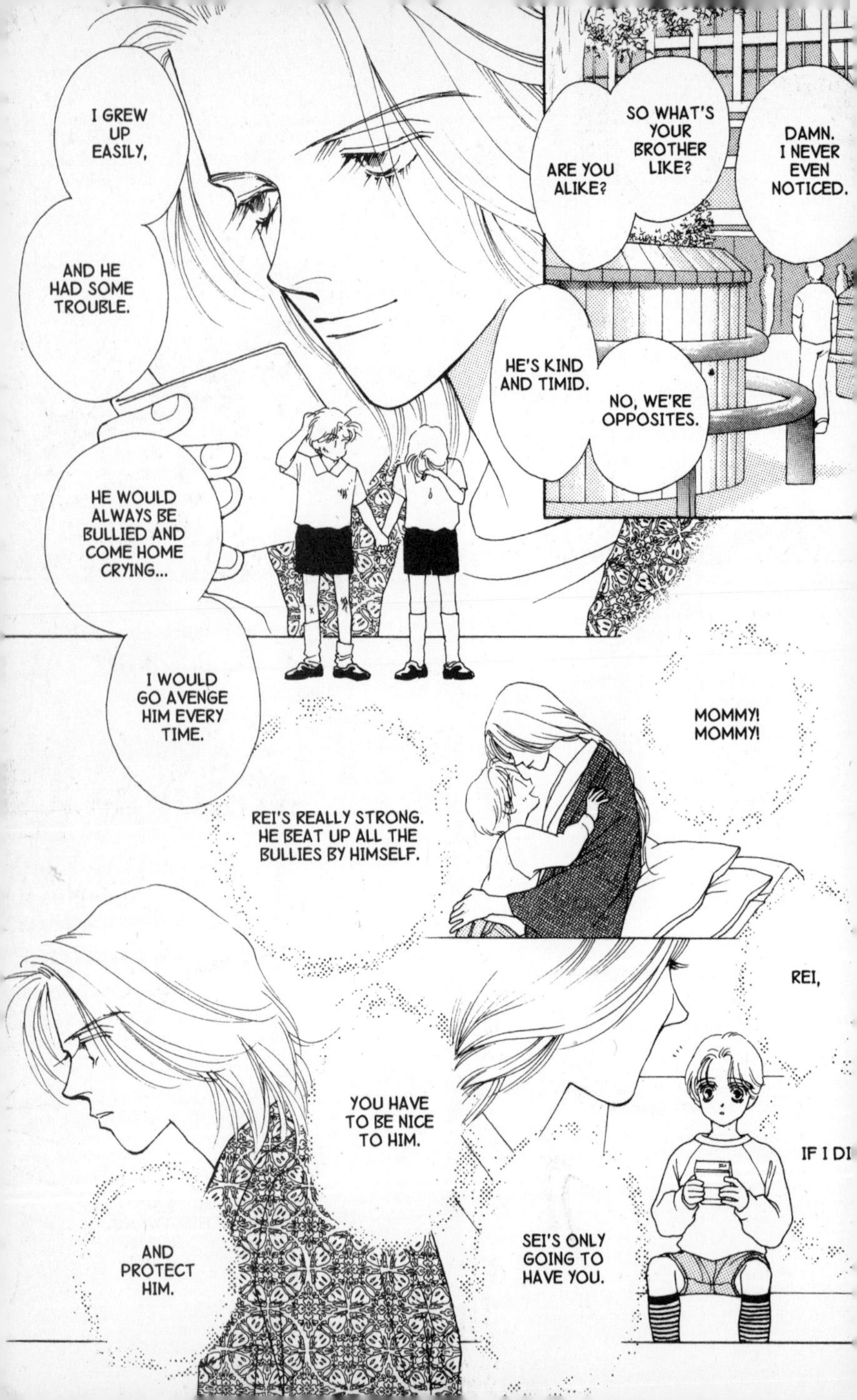
DAMN. I NEVER EVEN NOTICED.
SO WHAT'S YOUR BROTHER LIKE?
ARE YOU ALIKE?
NO, WE'RE OPPOSITES.
HE'S KIND AND TIMID.
I GREW UP EASILY,
AND HE HAD SOME TROUBLE.
HE WOULD ALWAYS BE BULLIED AND COME HOME CRYING...
I WOULD GO AVENGE HIM EVERY TIME.
MOMMY! MOMMY!
REI'S REALLY STRONG. HE BEAT UP ALL THE BULLIES BY HIMSELF.
REI,
IF I DI
SEI'S ONLY GOING TO HAVE YOU.
YOU HAVE TO BE NICE TO HIM.
AND PROTECT HIM.

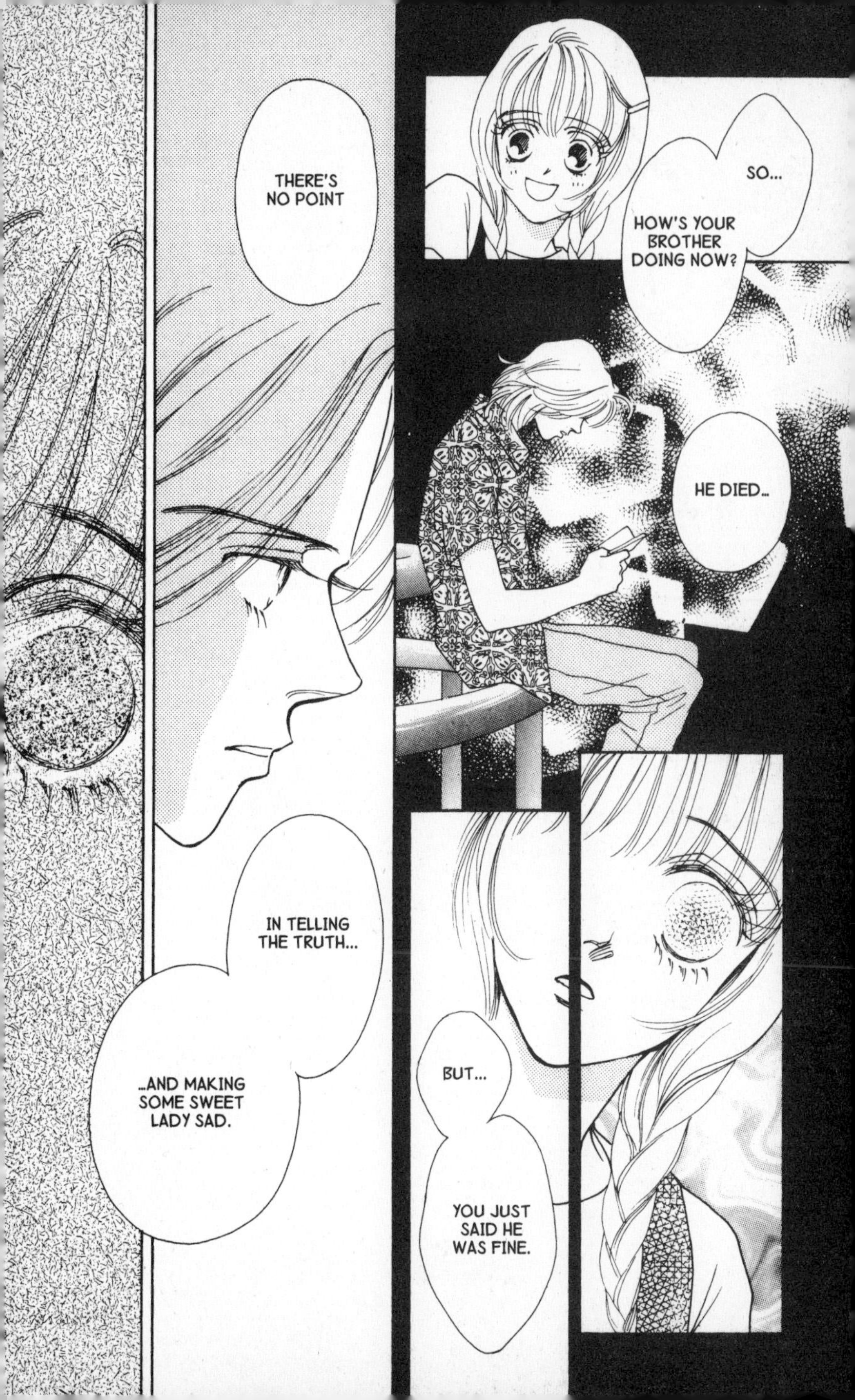
SO...
HOW'S YOUR BROTHER DOING NOW?
HE DIED...
BUT...
YOU JUST SAID HE WAS FINE.
THERE'S NO POINT
IN TELLING THE TRUTH...
...AND MAKING SOME SWEET LADY SAD.

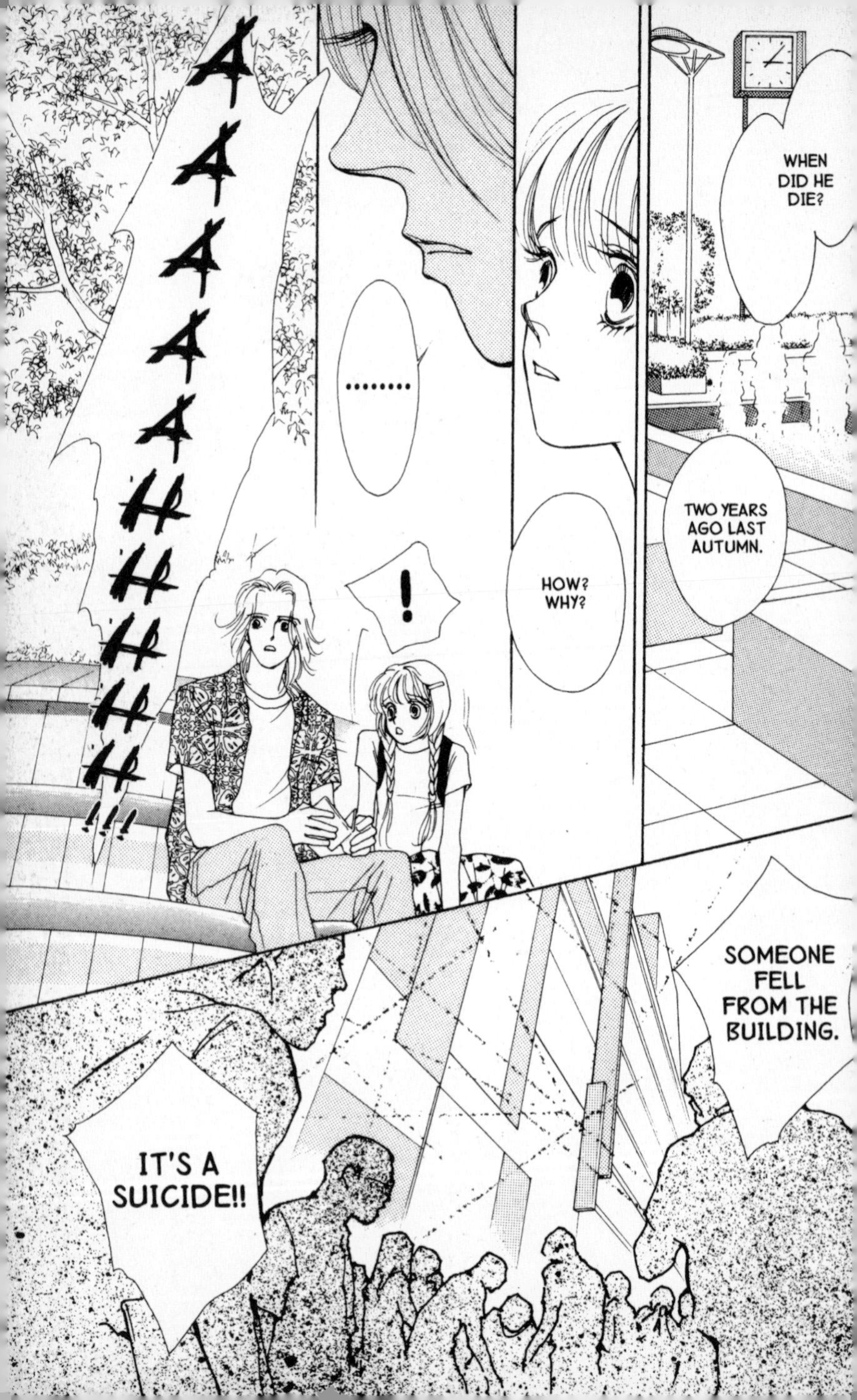
WHEN DID HE DIE?
TWO YEARS AGO LAST AUTUMN.
HOW? WHY?
....
!
AAAAAHHHHH!!!
SOMEONE FELL FROM THE BUILDING.
IT'S A SUICIDE!!

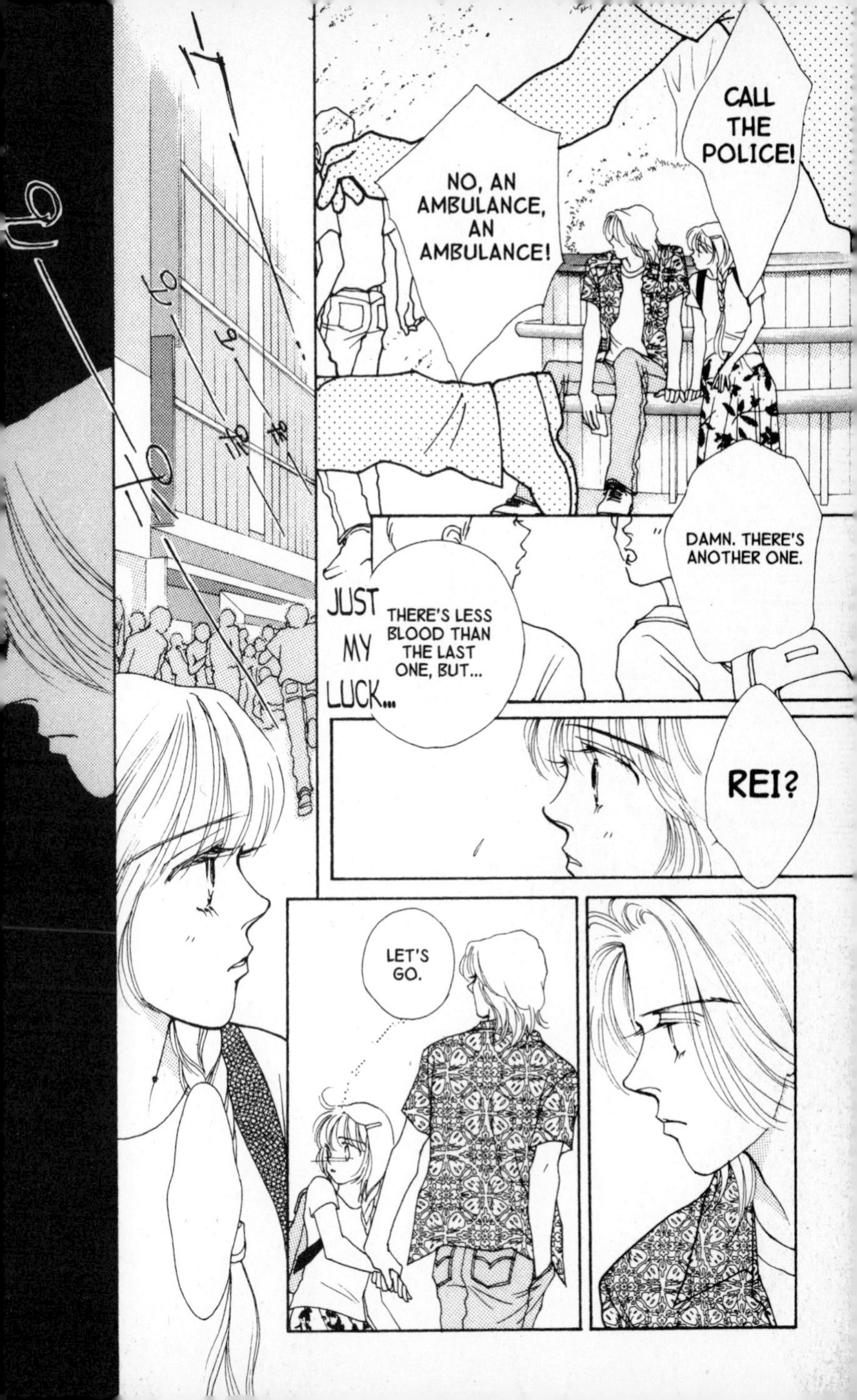
CALL THE POLICE!
NO, AN AMBULANCE, AN AMBULANCE!
DAMN. THERE'S ANOTHER ONE.
THERE'S LESS BLOOD THAN THE LAST ONE, BUT...
JUST MY LUCK...
REI?
LET'S GO.

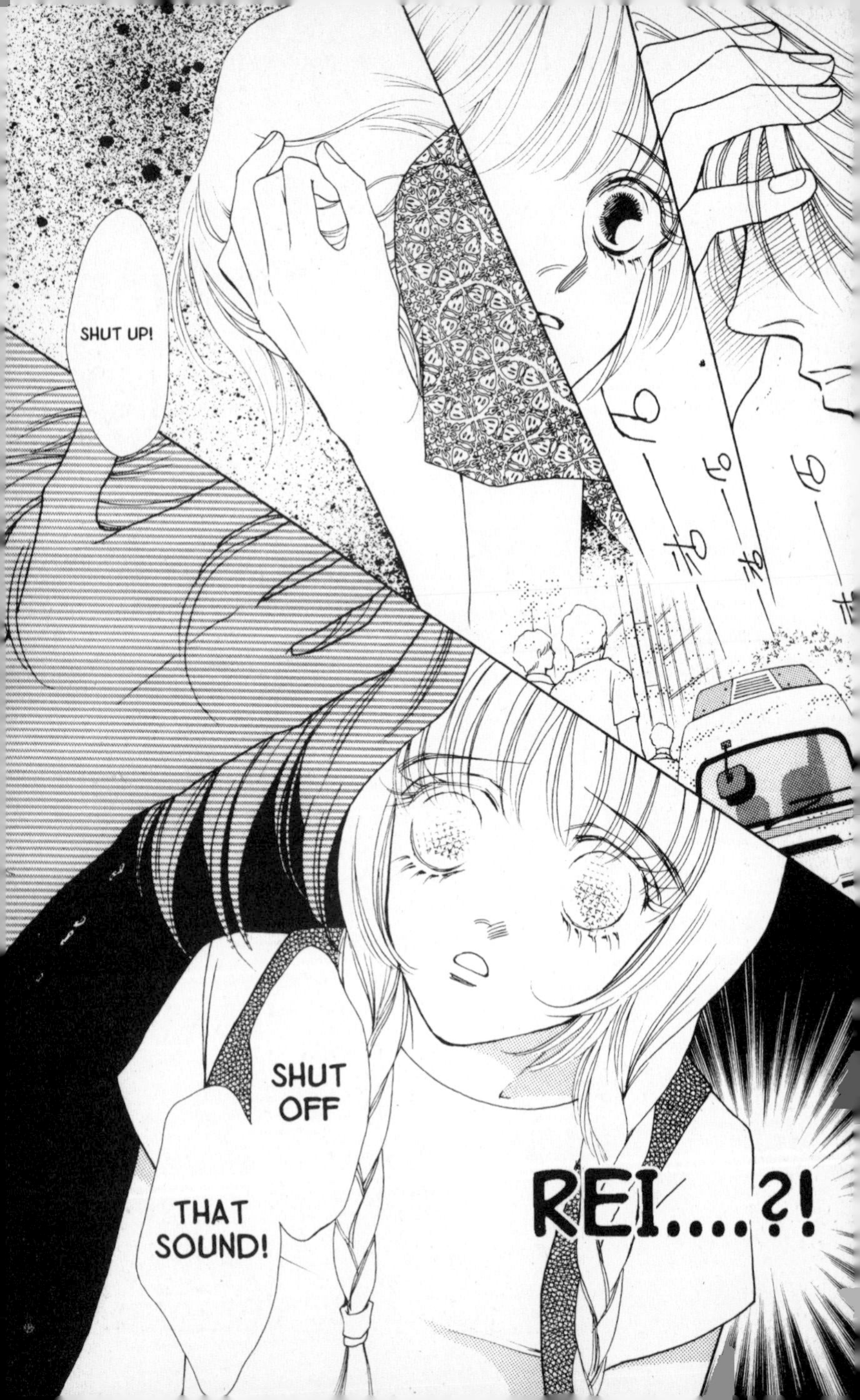
SHUT UP!
REI....?!
SHUT OFF
THAT SOUND!

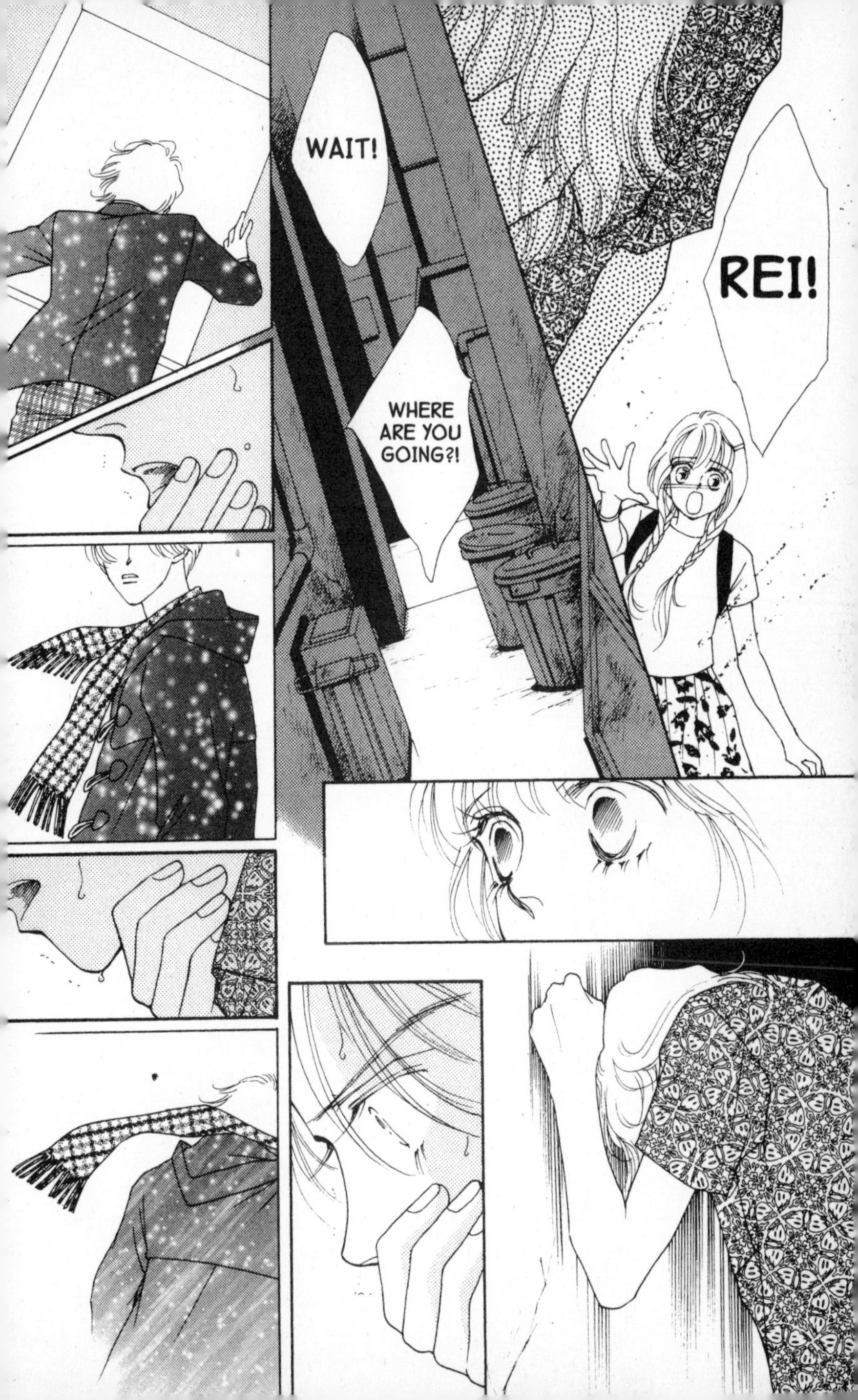
REI!
WAIT!
WHERE ARE YOU GOING?!

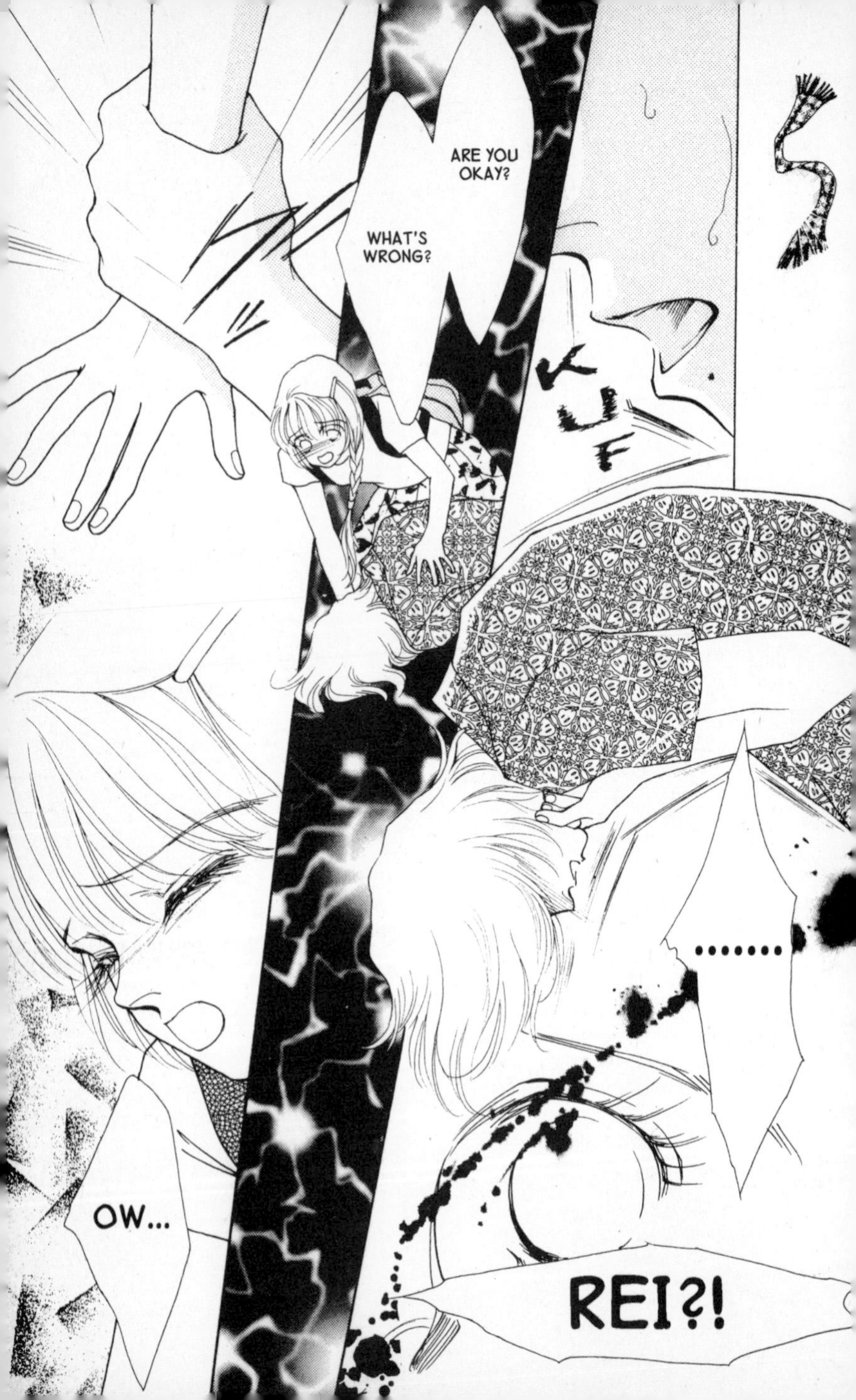
VUF
ARE YOU OKAY?
WHAT'S WRONG?
......
REI?!
OW...

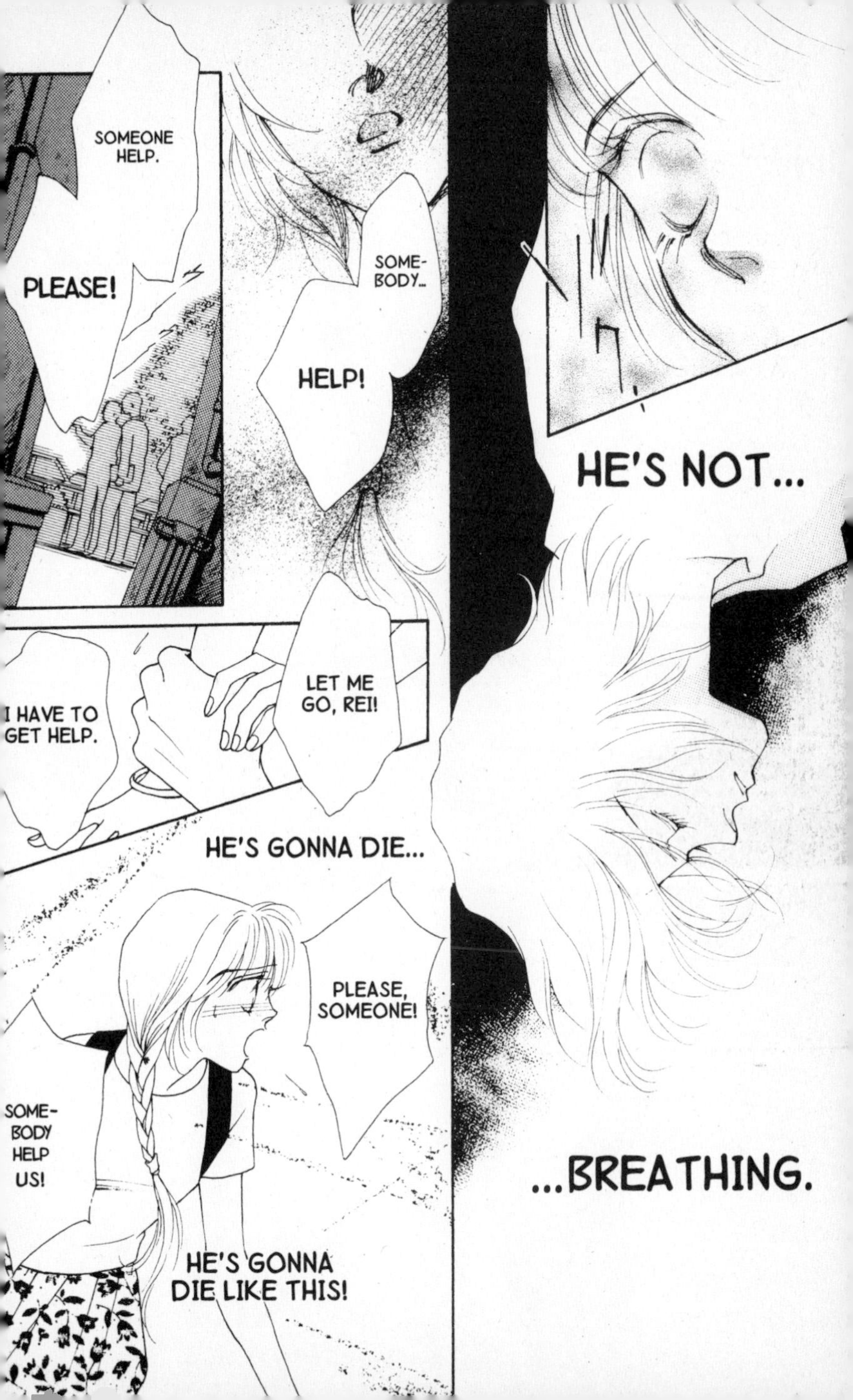
HE'S NOT...
...BREATHING.
SOME-BODY...
HELP!
SOMEONE HELP.
PLEASE!
LET ME GO, REI!
I HAVE TO GET HELP.
HE'S GONNA DIE...
PLEASE, SOMEONE!
SOME-BODY HELP US!
HE'S GONNA DIE LIKE THIS!

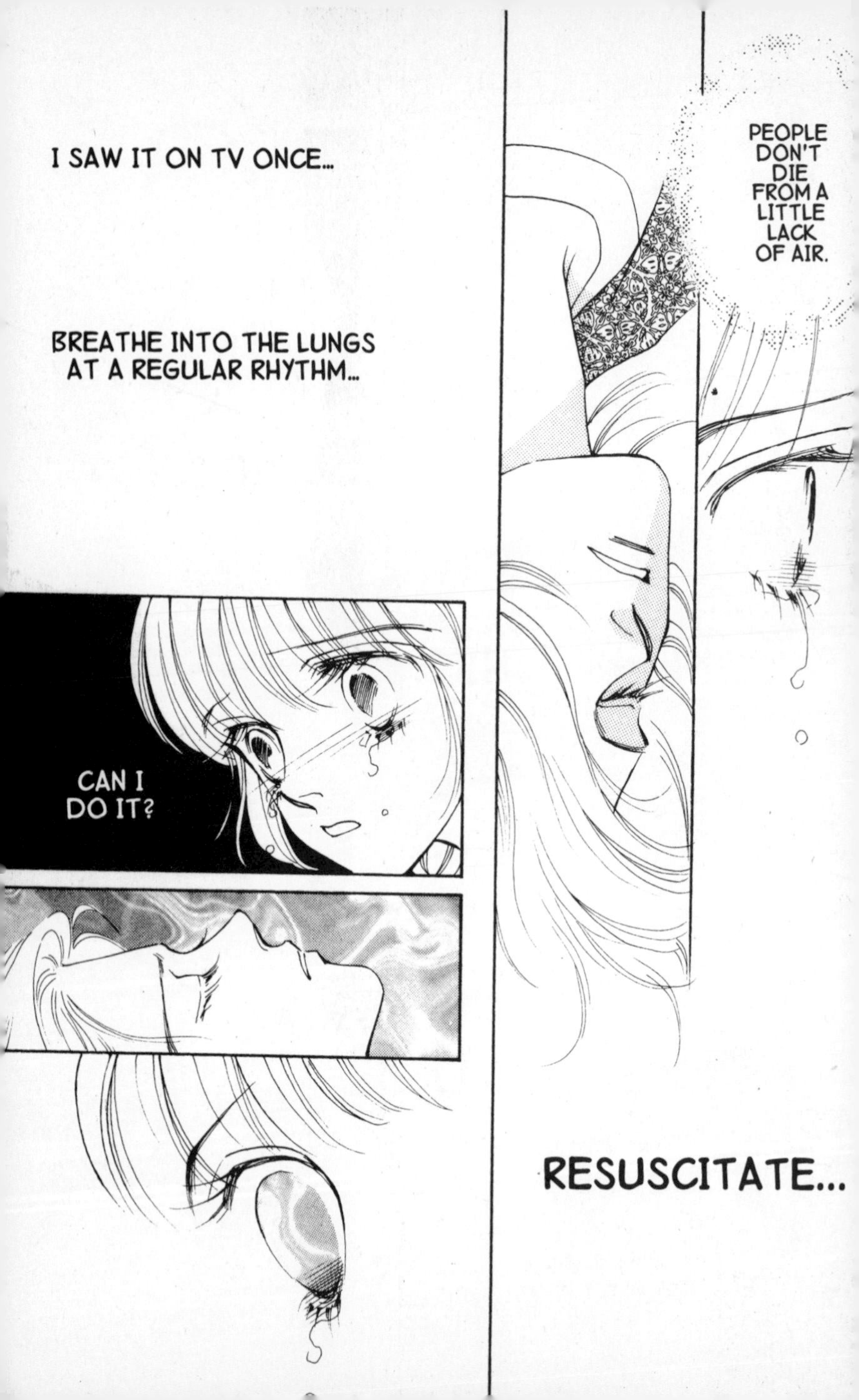
PEOPLE DON'T DIE FROM A LITTLE LACK OF AIR.
RESUSCITATE...
I SAW IT ON TV ONCE...
BREATHE INTO THE LUNGS AT A REGULAR RHYTHM...
CAN I DO IT?

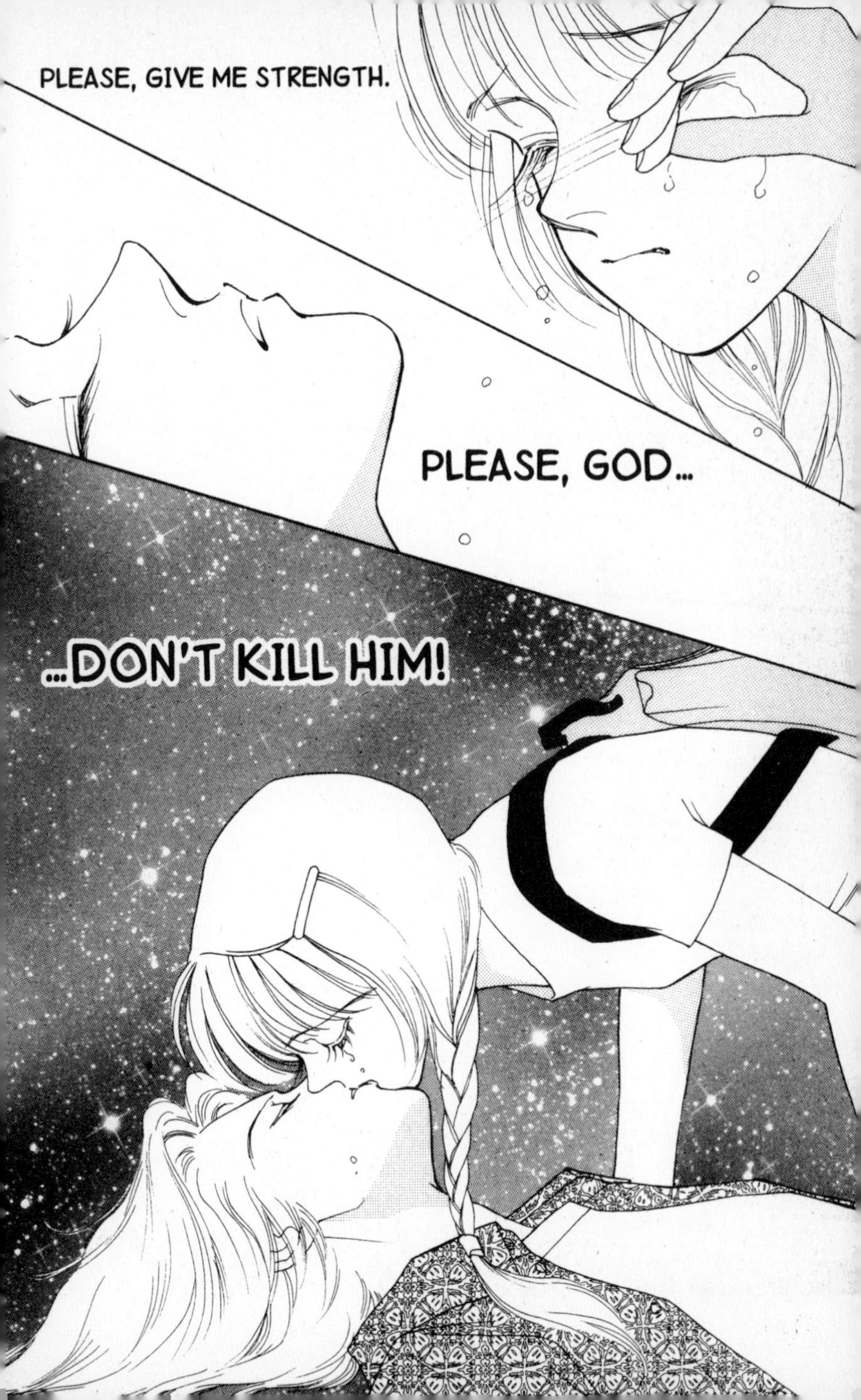
PLEASE, GIVE ME STRENGTH.
PLEASE, GOD...
...DON'T KILL HIM!

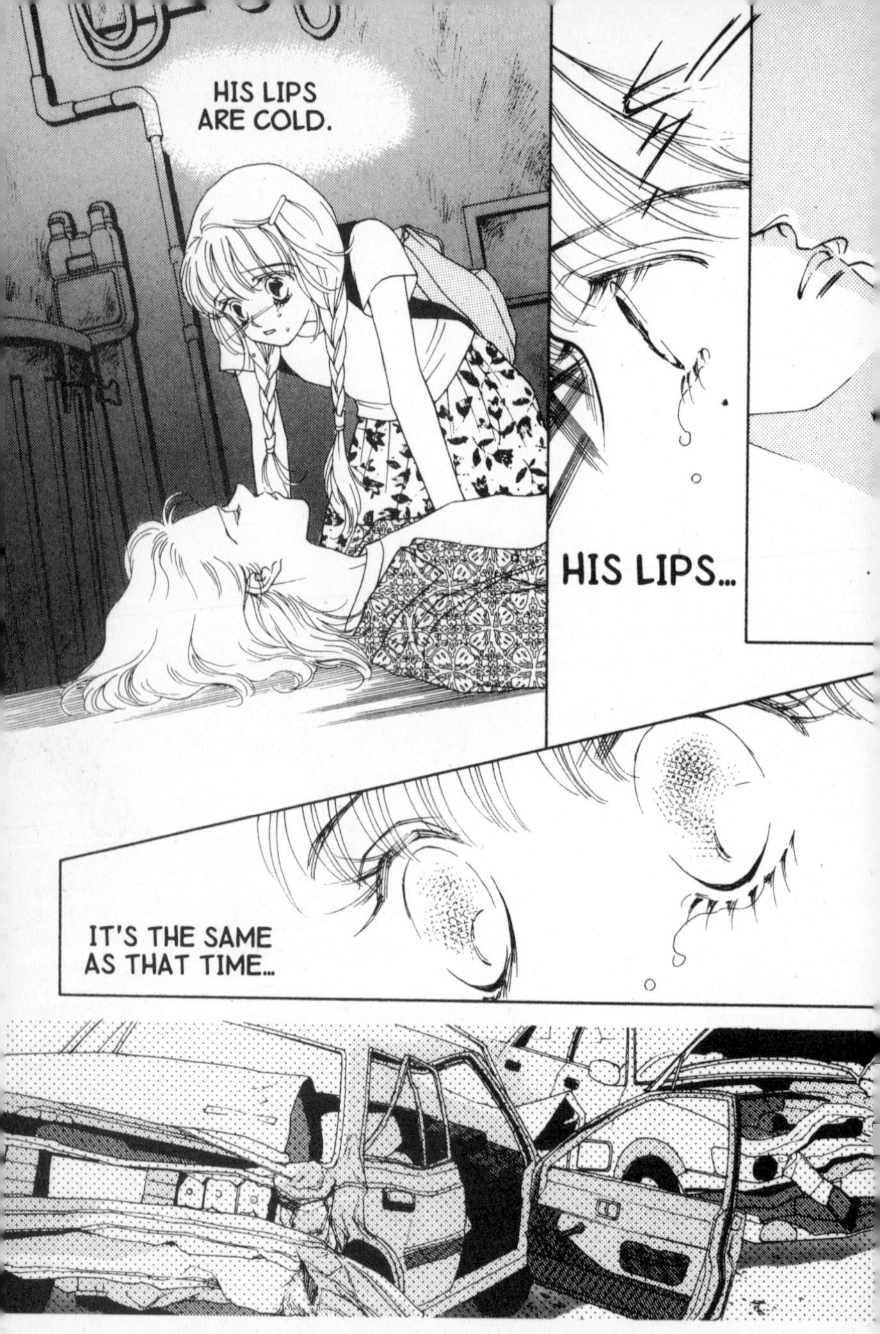
HIS LIPS...
HIS LIPS ARE COLD.
IT'S THE SAME AS THAT TIME...

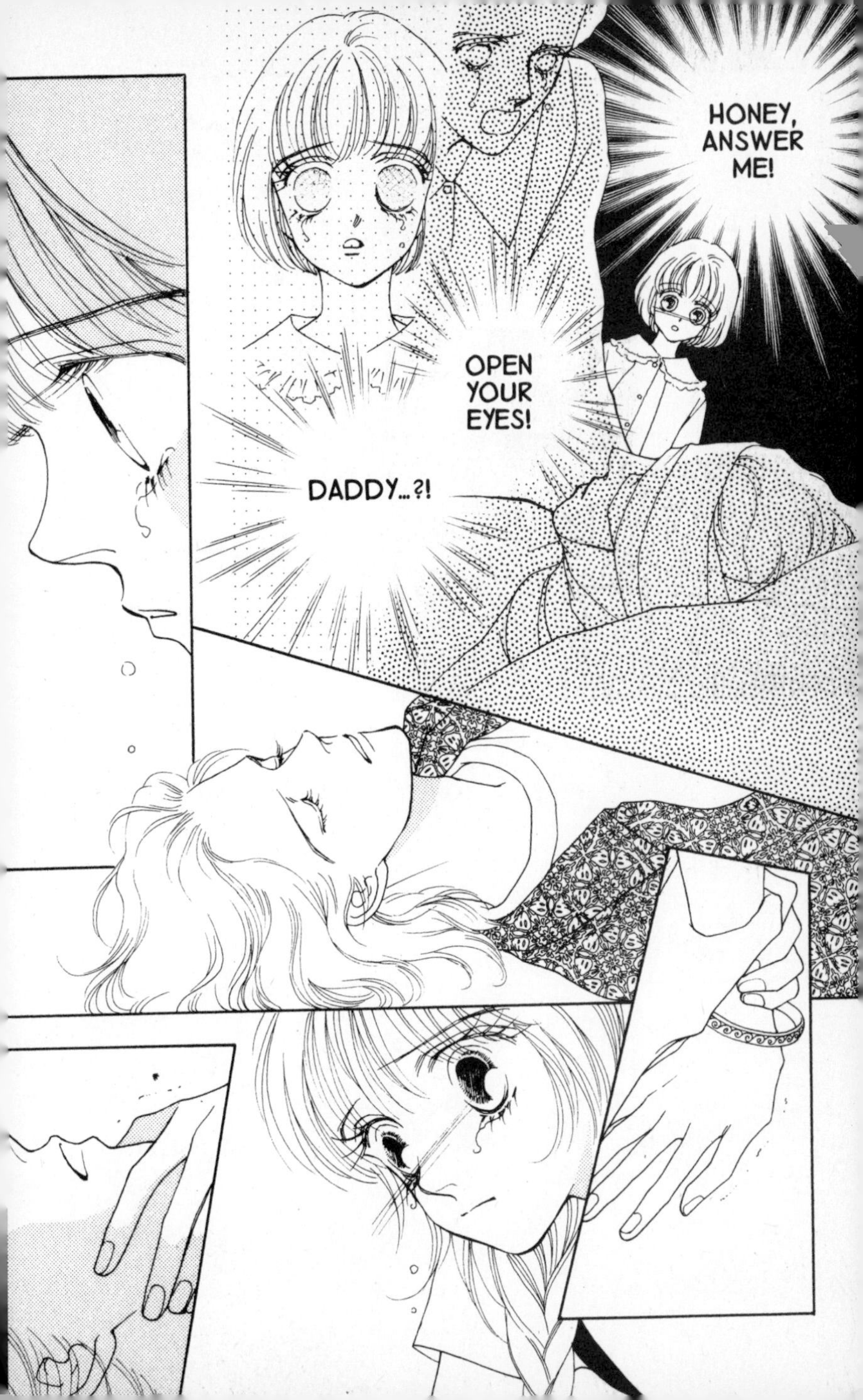
HONEY, ANSWER ME!
OPEN YOUR EYES!
DADDY...?!

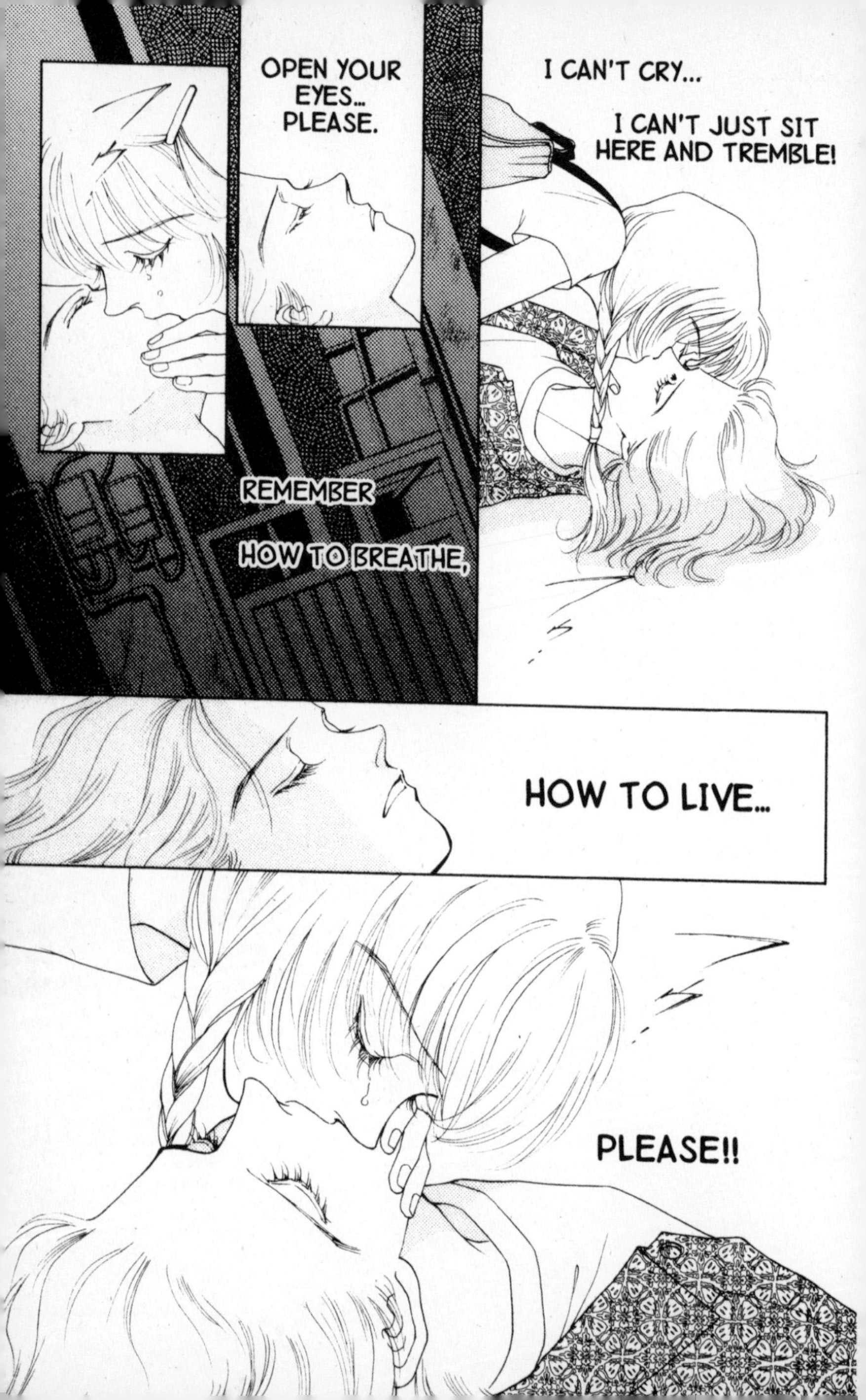
I CAN'T CRY...
I CAN'T JUST SIT HERE AND TREMBLE!
OPEN YOUR EYES... PLEASE.
REMEMBER
HOW TO BREATHE,
HOW TO LIVE...
PLEASE!!

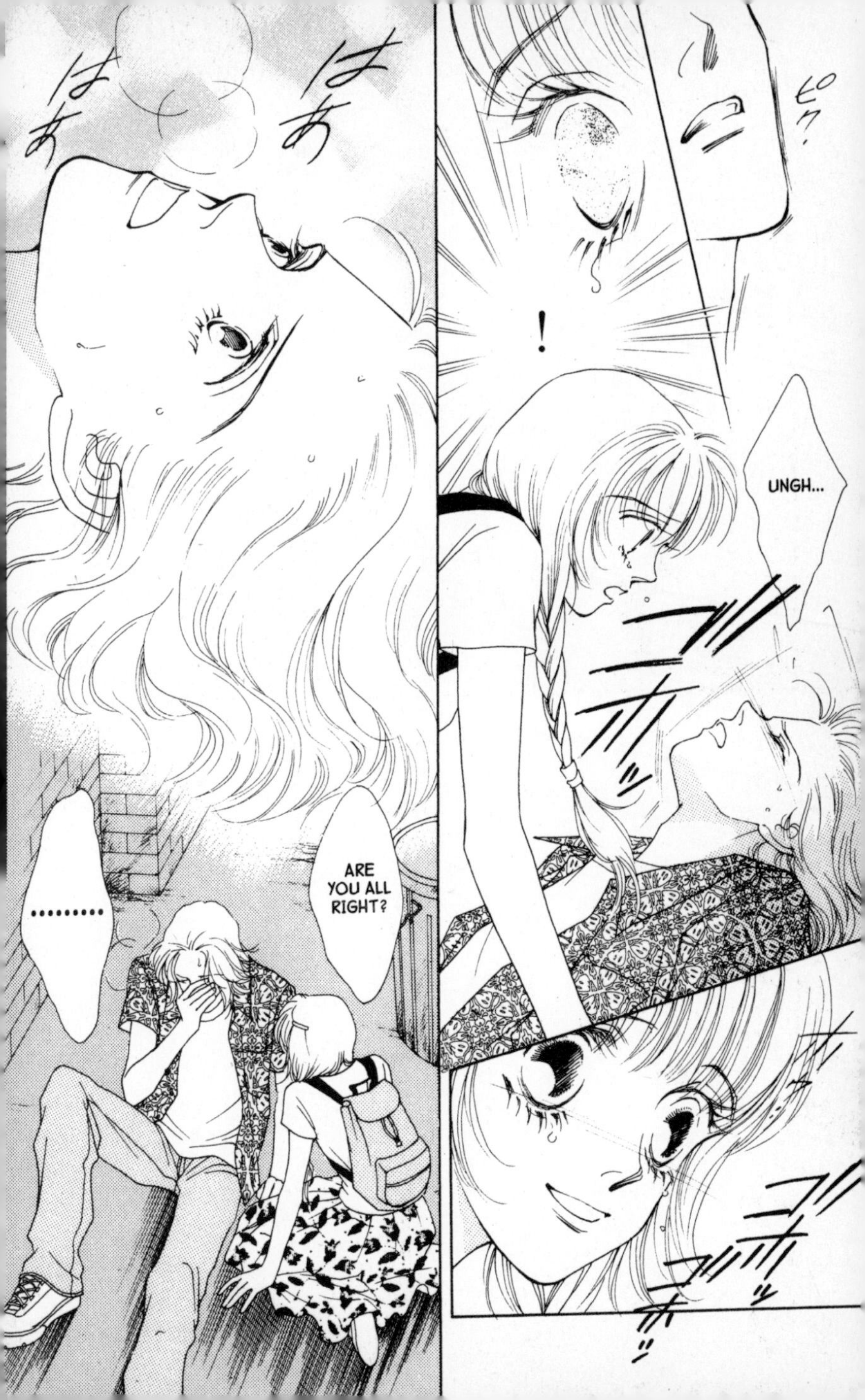
ピク
!
UNGH...
はあ
はあ
ARE YOU ALL RIGHT?
....

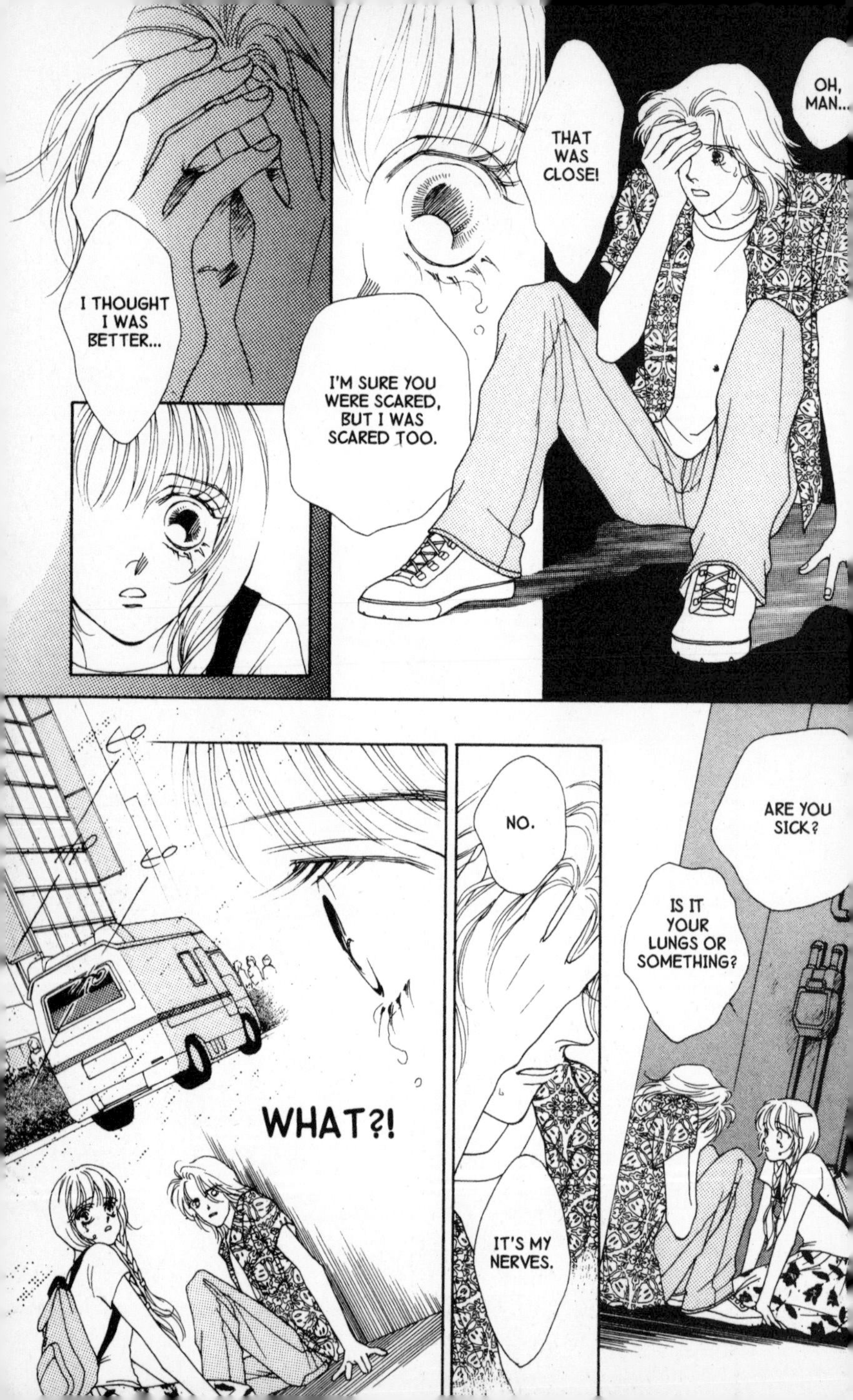
OH, MAN...
THAT WAS CLOSE!
I'M SURE YOU WERE SCARED, BUT I WAS SCARED TOO.
I THOUGHT I WAS BETTER...
ARE YOU SICK?
IS IT YOUR LUNGS OR SOMETHING?
NO.
IT'S MY NERVES.
WHAT?!

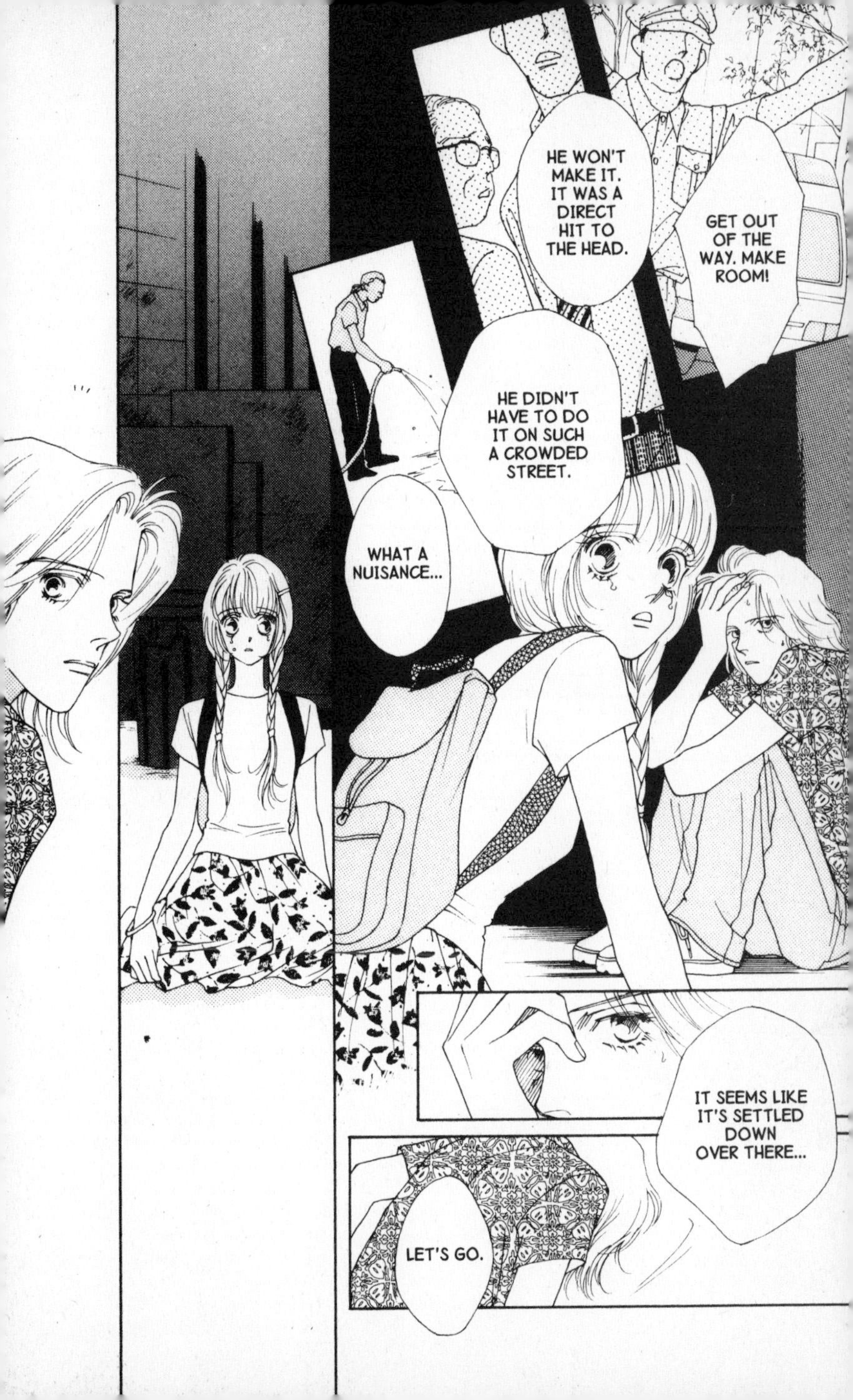
GET OUT OF THE WAY. MAKE ROOM!
HE WON'T MAKE IT. IT WAS A DIRECT HIT TO THE HEAD.
HE DIDN'T HAVE TO DO IT ON SUCH A CROWDED STREET.
WHAT A NUISANCE...
IT SEEMS LIKE IT'S SETTLED DOWN OVER THERE...
LET'S GO.

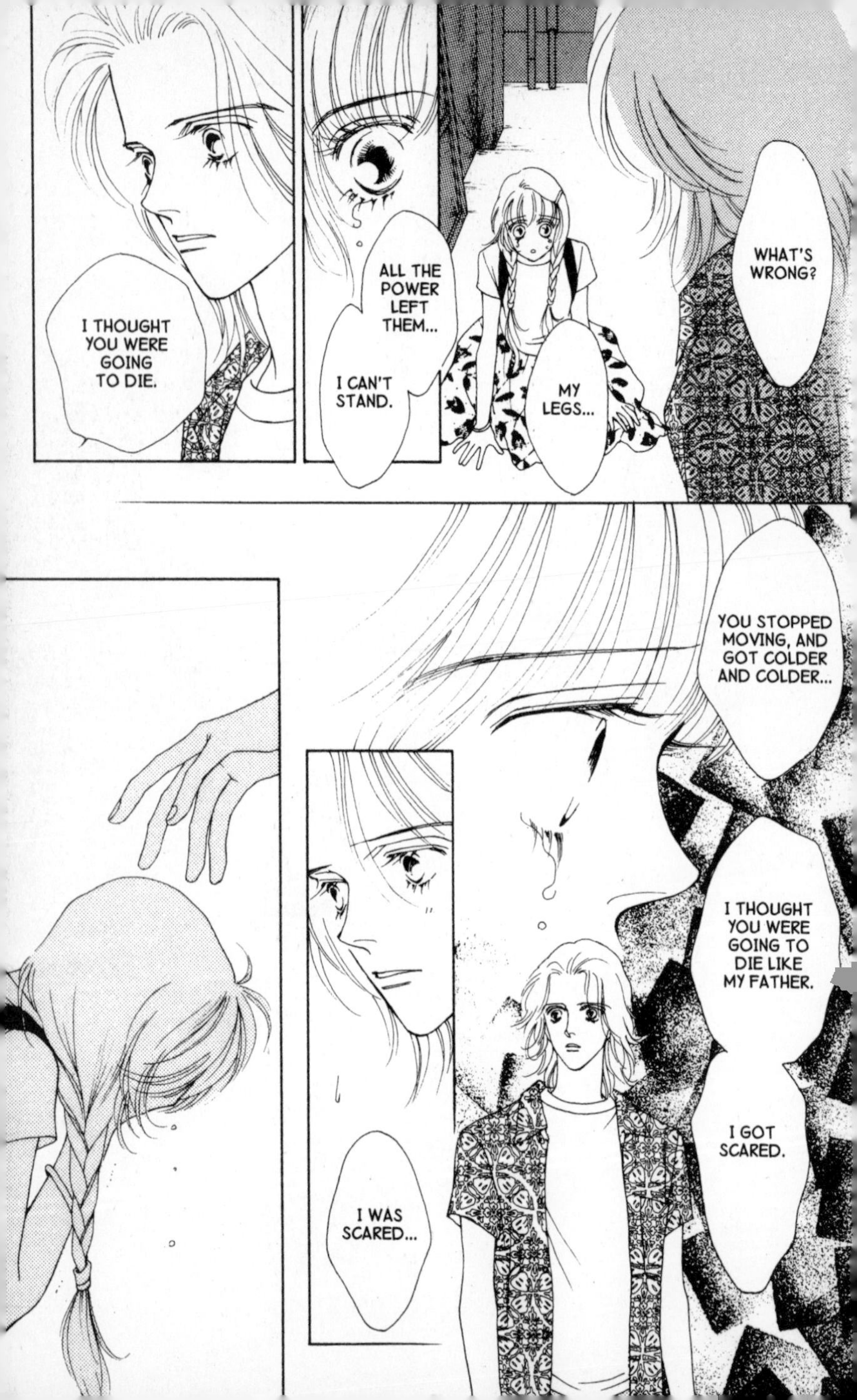
WHAT'S WRONG?
MY LEGS...
ALL THE POWER LEFT THEM...
I CAN'T STAND.
I THOUGHT YOU WERE GOING TO DIE.
YOU STOPPED MOVING, AND GOT COLDER AND COLDER...
I THOUGHT YOU WERE GOING TO DIE LIKE MY FATHER.
I GOT SCARED.
I WAS SCARED...

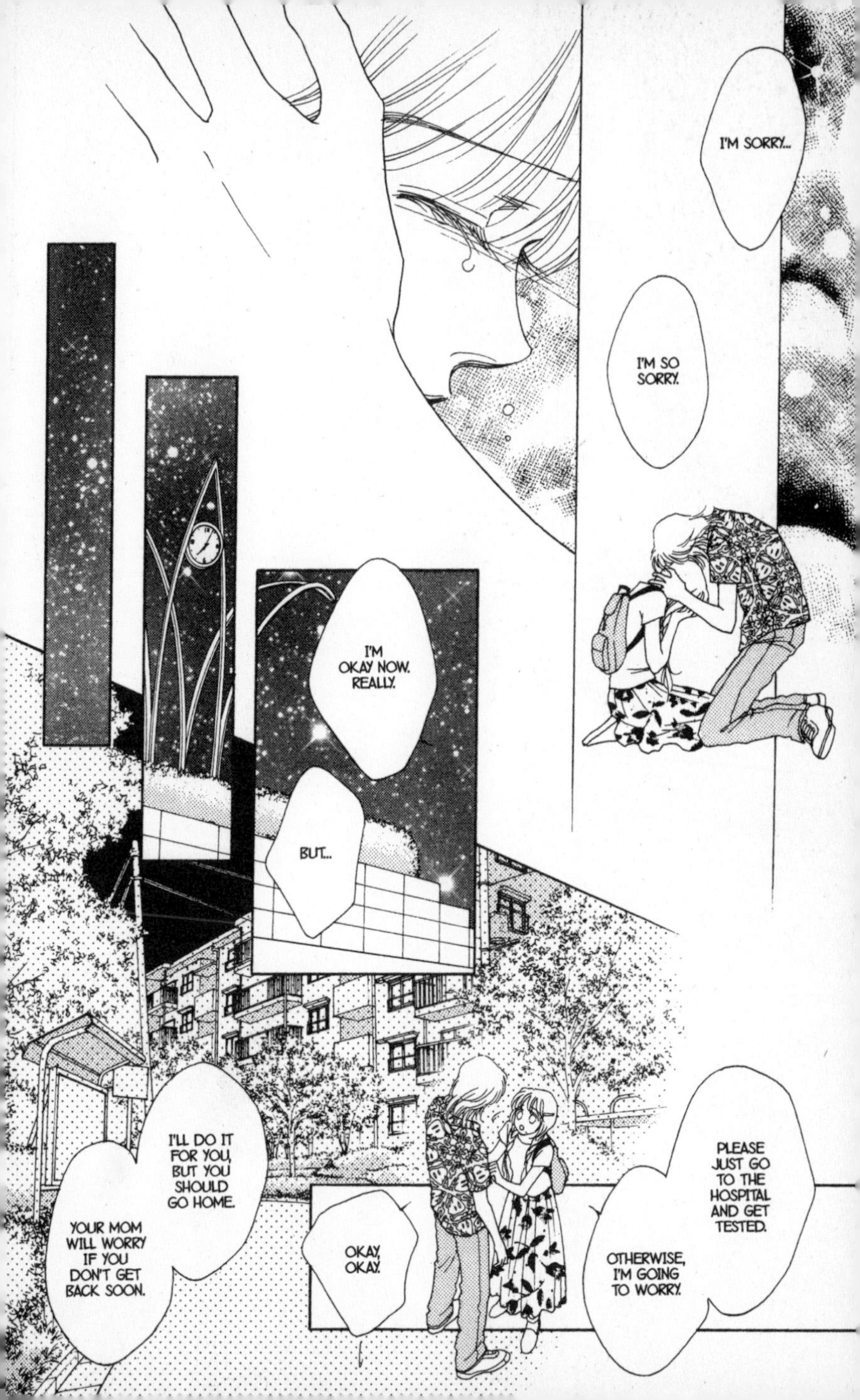
I'M SORRY...
I'M SO SORRY.
I'M OKAY NOW. REALLY.
BUT...
PLEASE JUST GO TO THE HOSPITAL AND GET TESTED.
OTHERWISE, I'M GOING TO WORRY.
OKAY, OKAY.
I'LL DO IT FOR YOU, BUT YOU SHOULD GO HOME.
YOUR MOM WILL WORRY IF YOU DON'T GET BACK SOON.

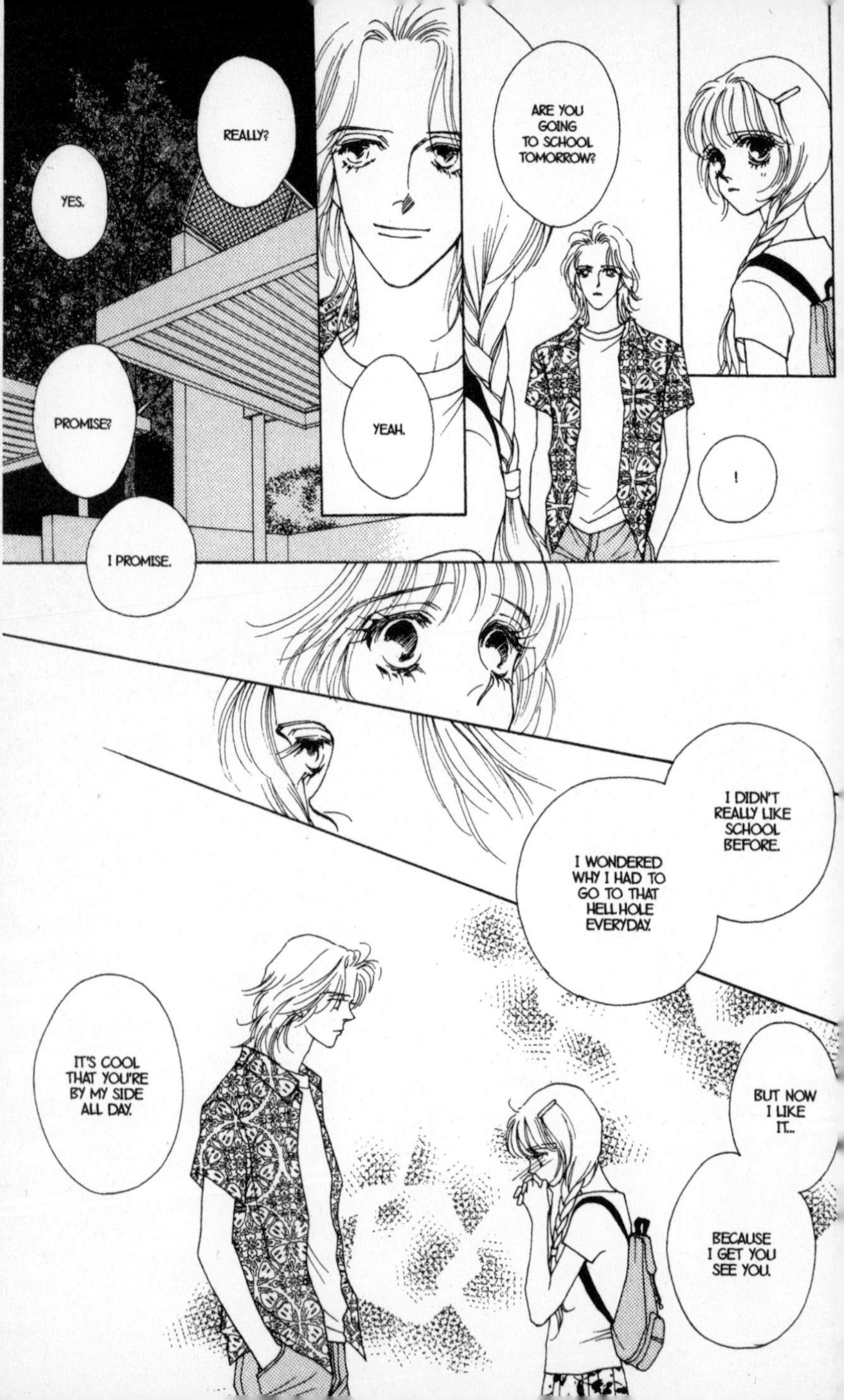
!
ARE YOU GOING TO SCHOOL TOMORROW?
YEAH.
REALLY?
YES.
PROMISE?
I PROMISE.
I DIDN'T REALLY LIKE SCHOOL BEFORE.
I WONDERED WHY I HAD TO GO TO THAT HELL HOLE EVERYDAY.
BUT NOW I LIKE IT..
BECAUSE I GET YOU SEE YOU.
IT'S COOL THAT YOU'RE BY MY SIDE ALL DAY.

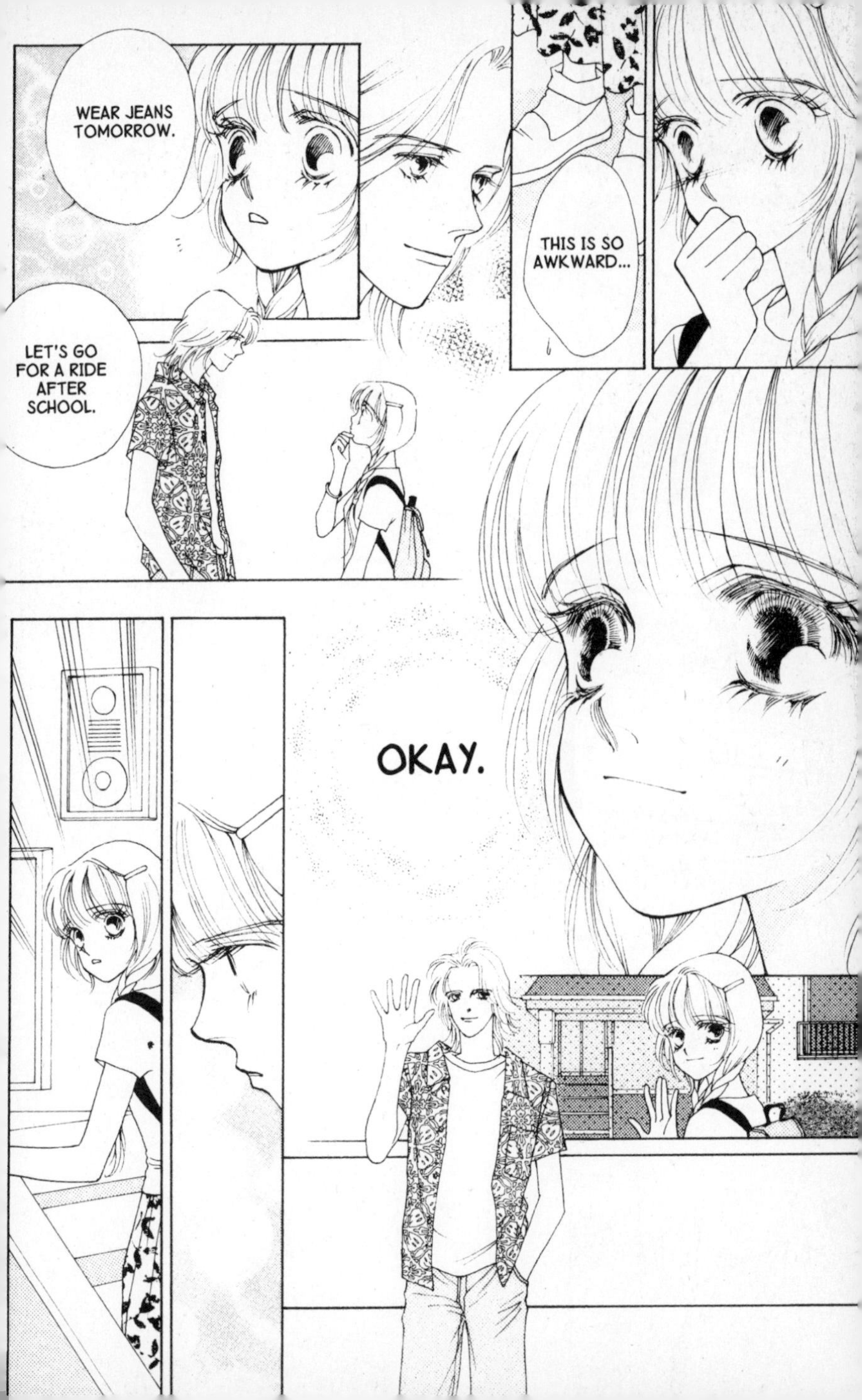
THIS IS SO AWKWARD...
WEAR JEANS TOMORROW.
LET'S GO FOR A RIDE AFTER SCHOOL.
OKAY.

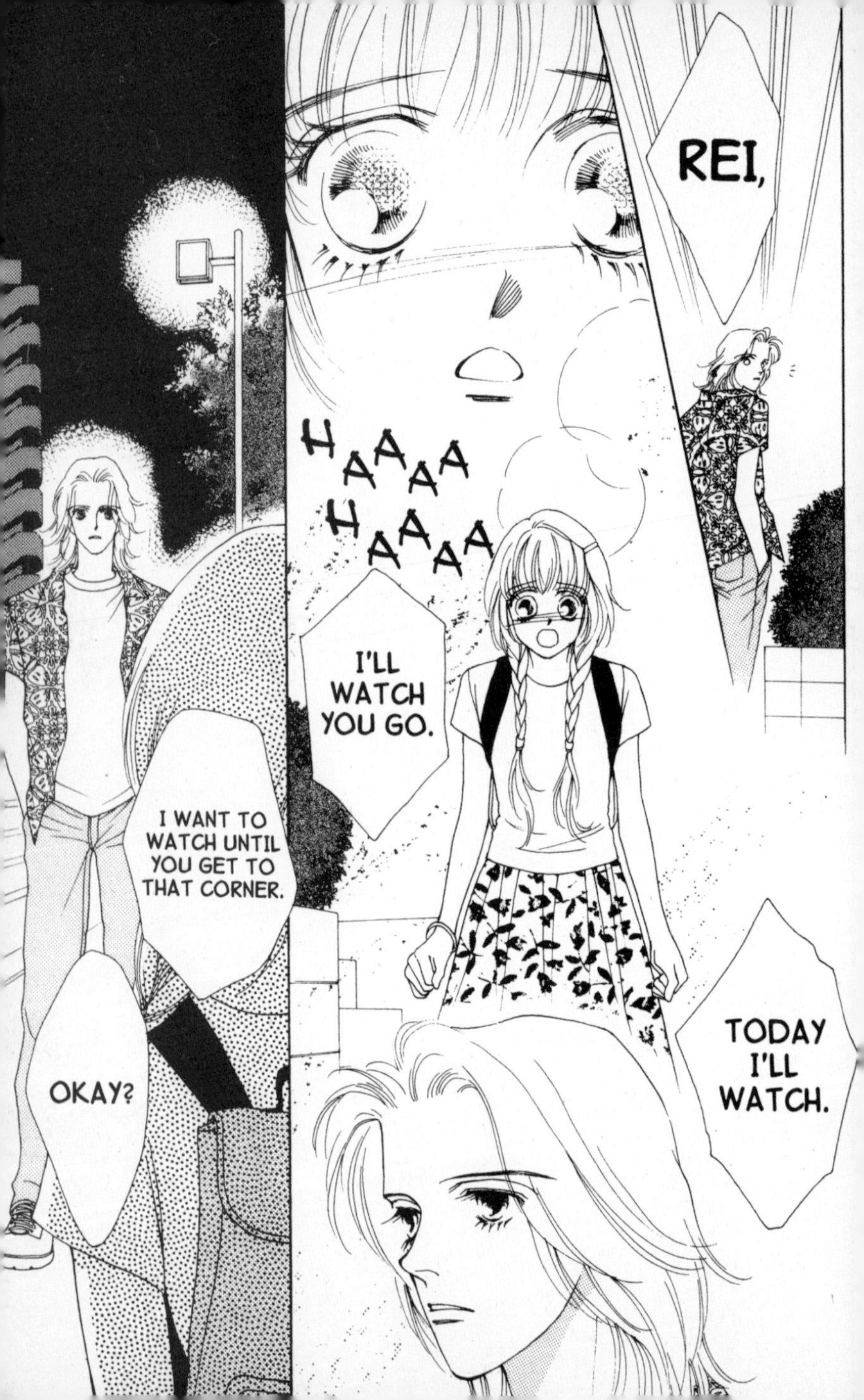
REI,
HAAAA HAAAA
I'LL WATCH YOU GO.
TODAY I'LL WATCH.
I WANT TO WATCH UNTIL YOU GET TO THAT CORNER.
OKAY?

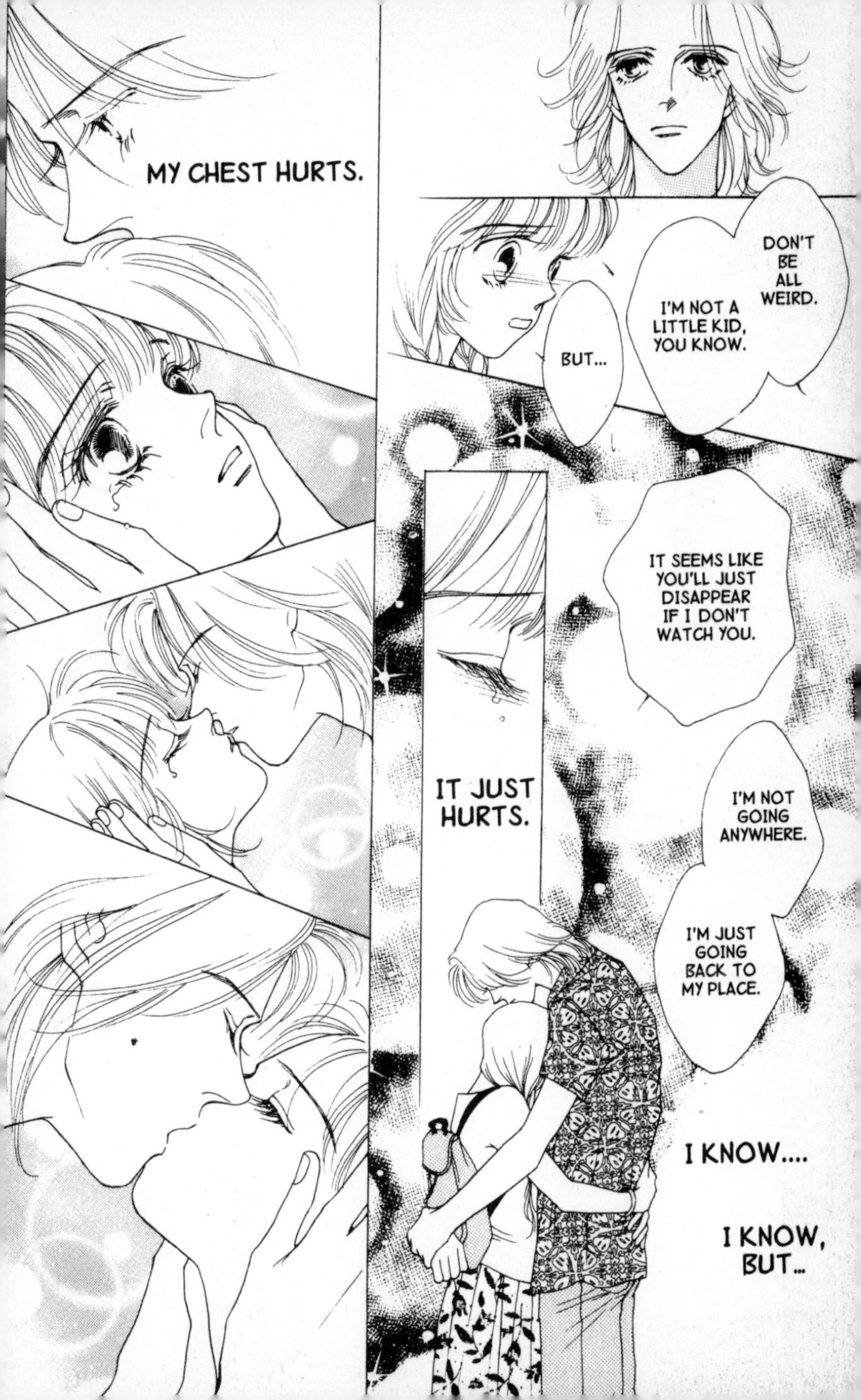
DON'T BE ALL WEIRD.
I'M NOT A LITTLE KID, YOU KNOW.
BUT...
IT SEEMS LIKE YOU'LL JUST DISAPPEAR IF I DON'T WATCH YOU.
I'M NOT GOING ANYWHERE.
I'M JUST GOING BACK TO MY PLACE.
IT JUST HURTS.
I KNOW....
I KNOW, BUT...
MY CHEST HURTS.

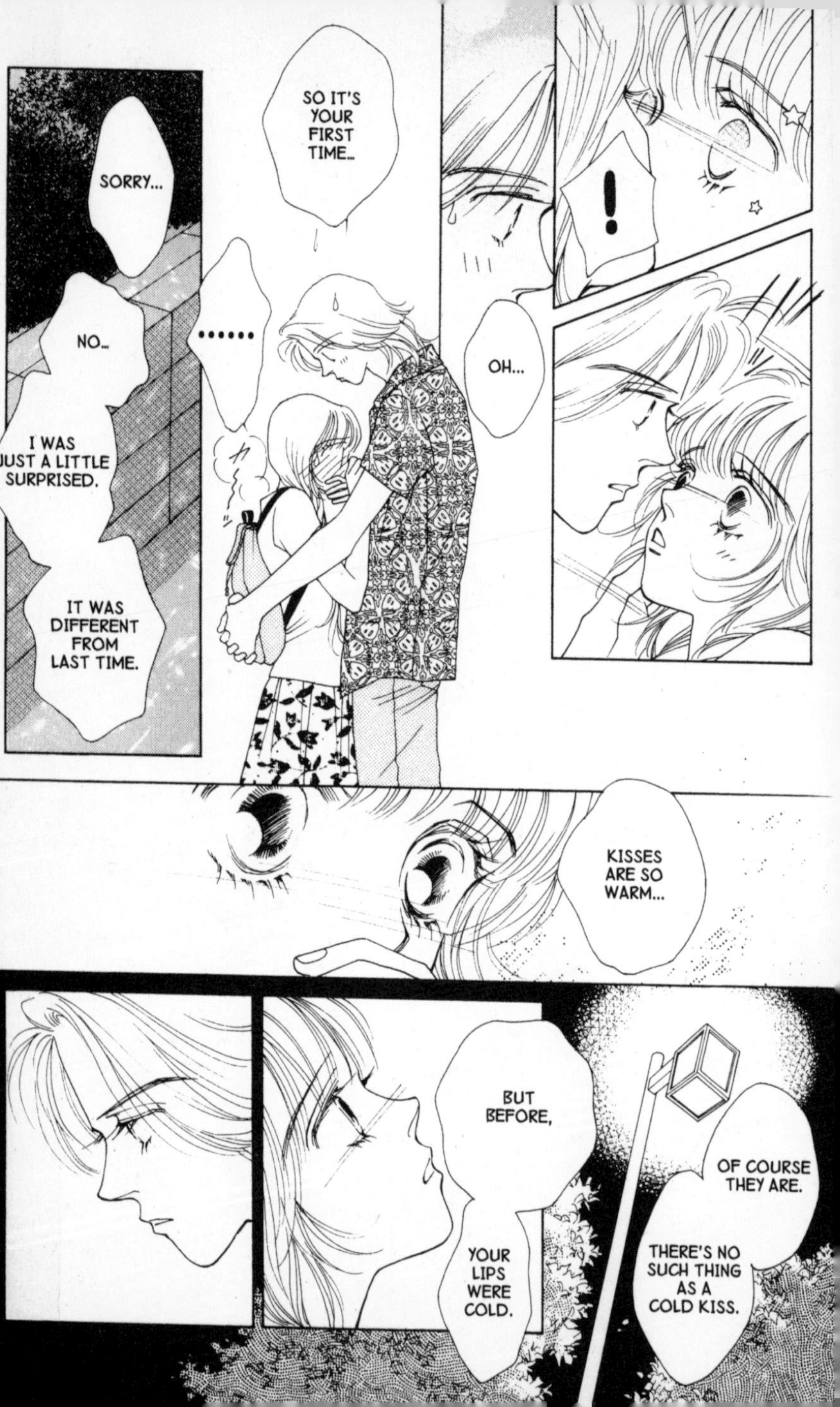
!
OH...
SO IT'S YOUR FIRST TIME...
......
SORRY...
NO...
I WAS JUST A LITTLE SURPRISED.
IT WAS DIFFERENT FROM LAST TIME.
KISSES ARE SO WARM...
OF COURSE THEY ARE.
THERE'S NO SUCH THING AS A COLD KISS.
BUT BEFORE,
YOUR LIPS WERE COLD.

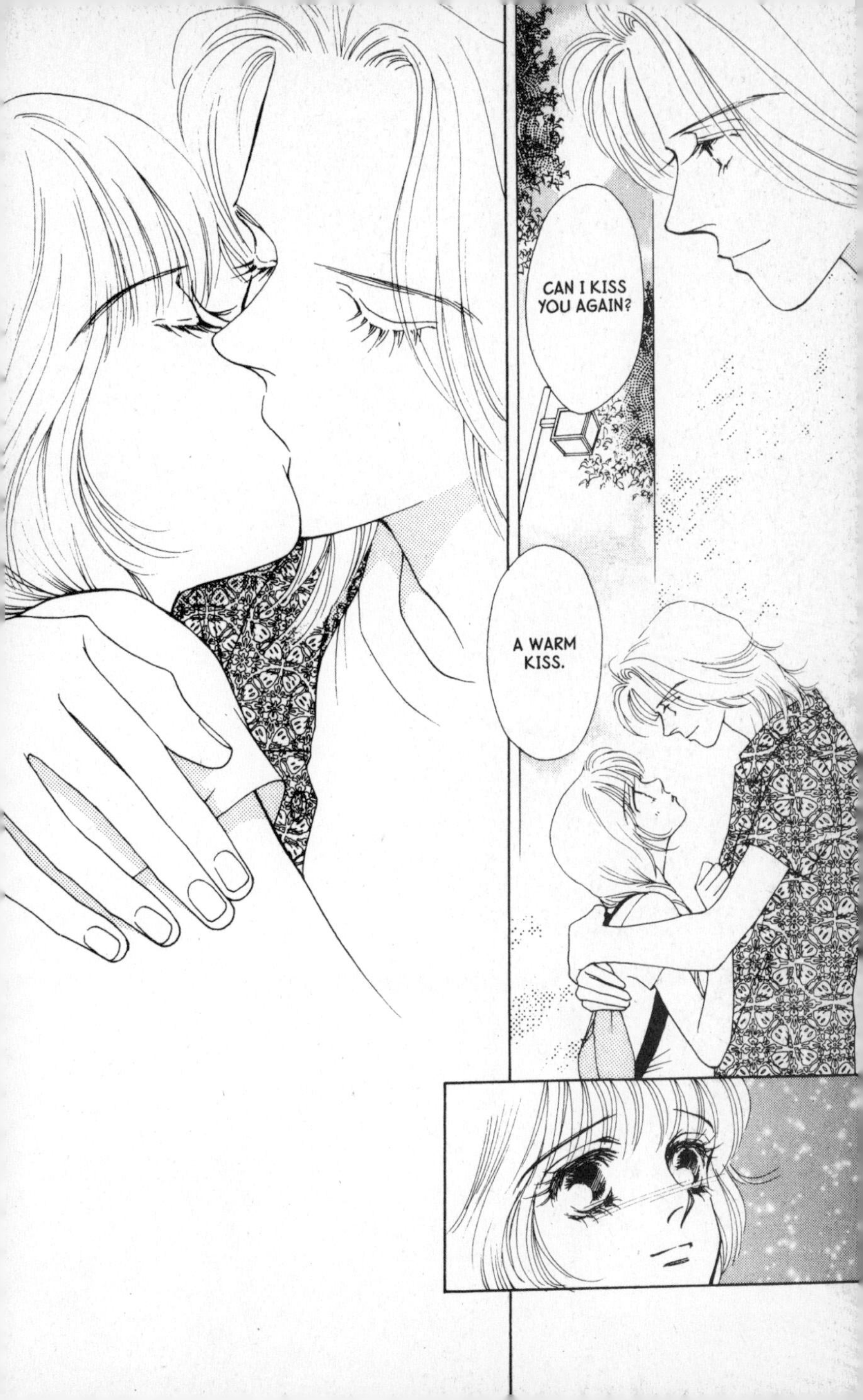
CAN I KISS YOU AGAIN?
A WARM KISS.

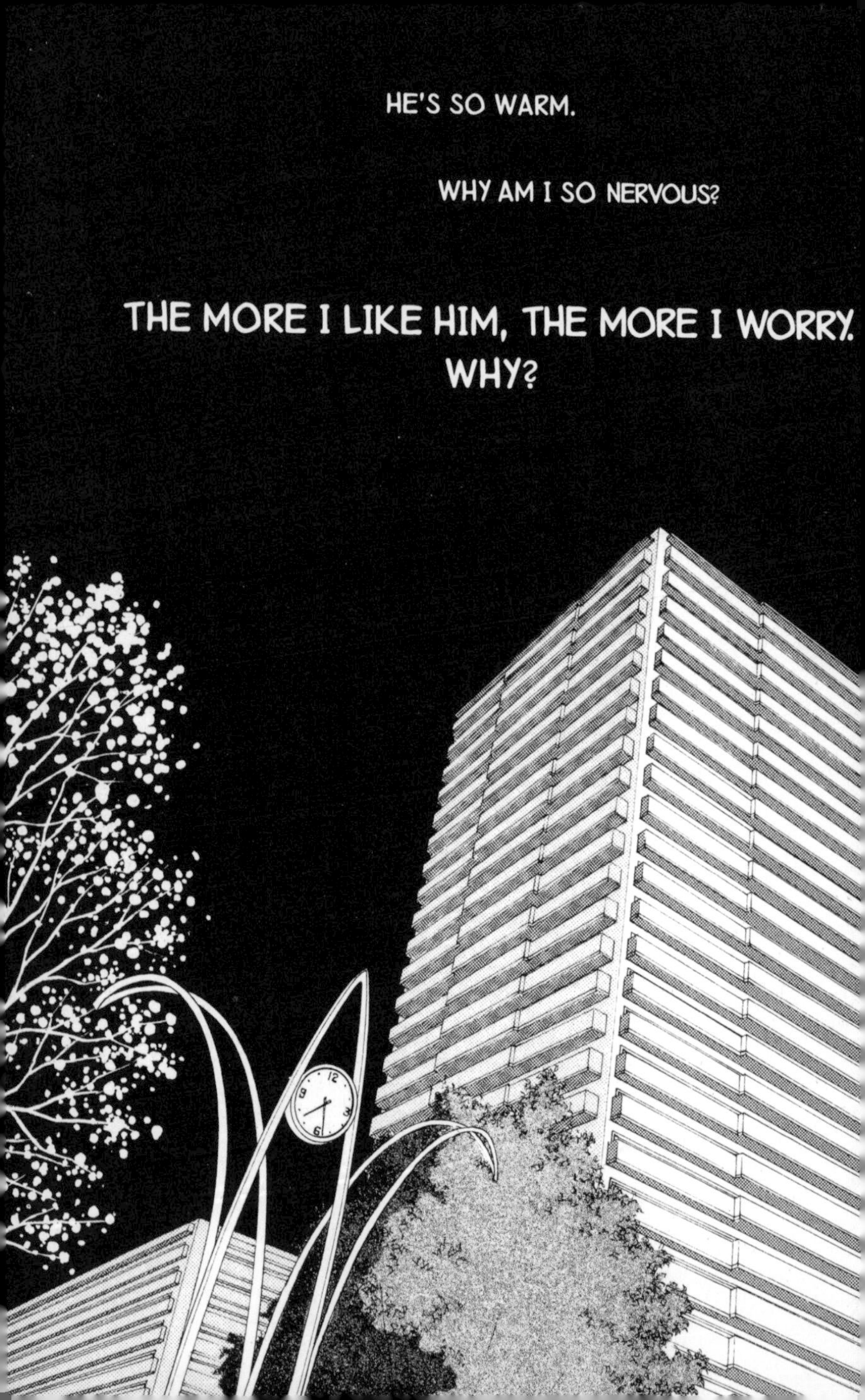
HE'S SO WARM.
WHY AM I SO NERVOUS?
THE MORE I LIKE HIM, THE MORE I WORRY.
WHY?

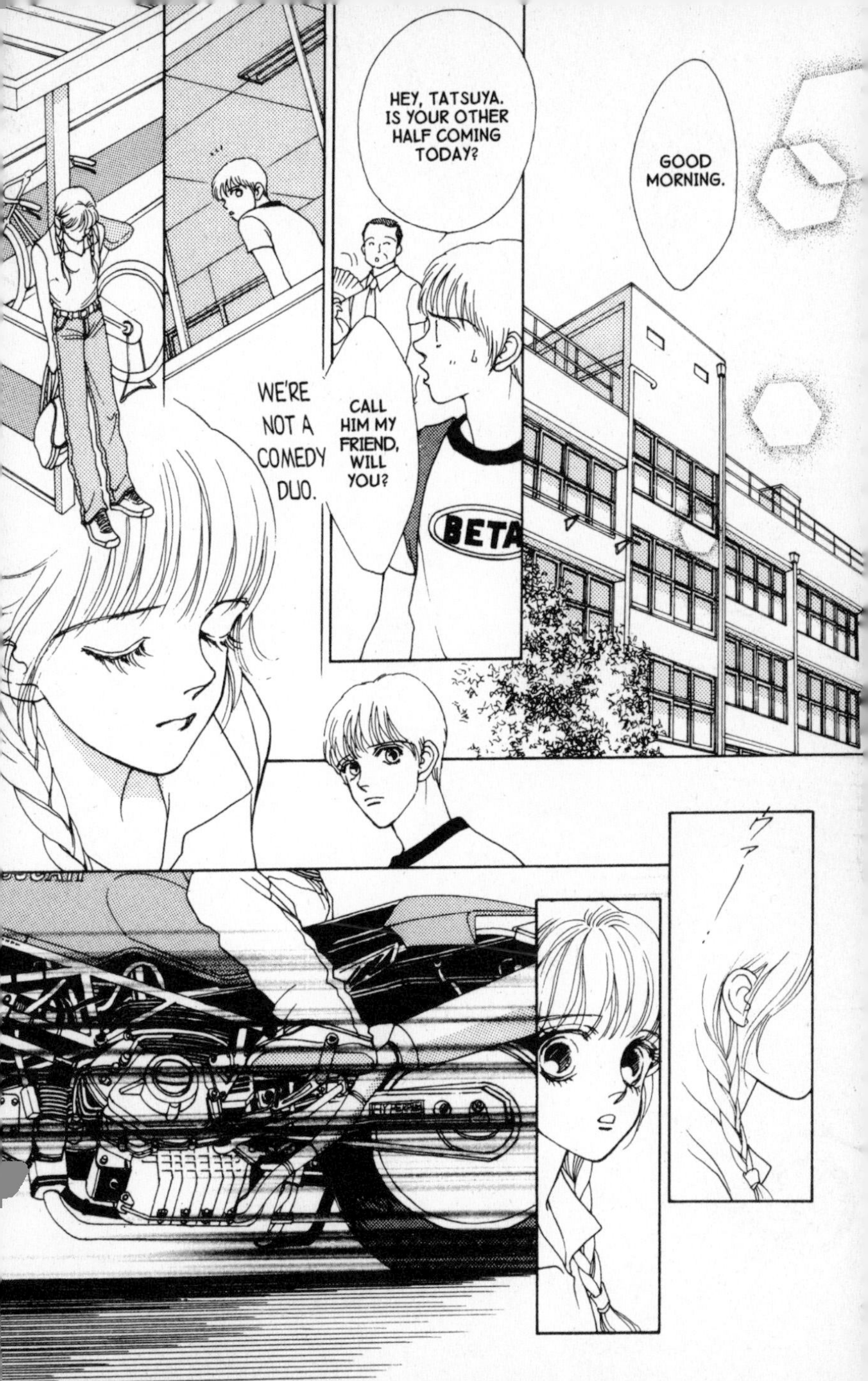
GOOD MORNING.
HEY, TATSUYA. IS YOUR OTHER HALF COMING TODAY?
BETA
CALL HIM MY FRIEND, WILL YOU?
WE'RE NOT A COMEDY DUO.

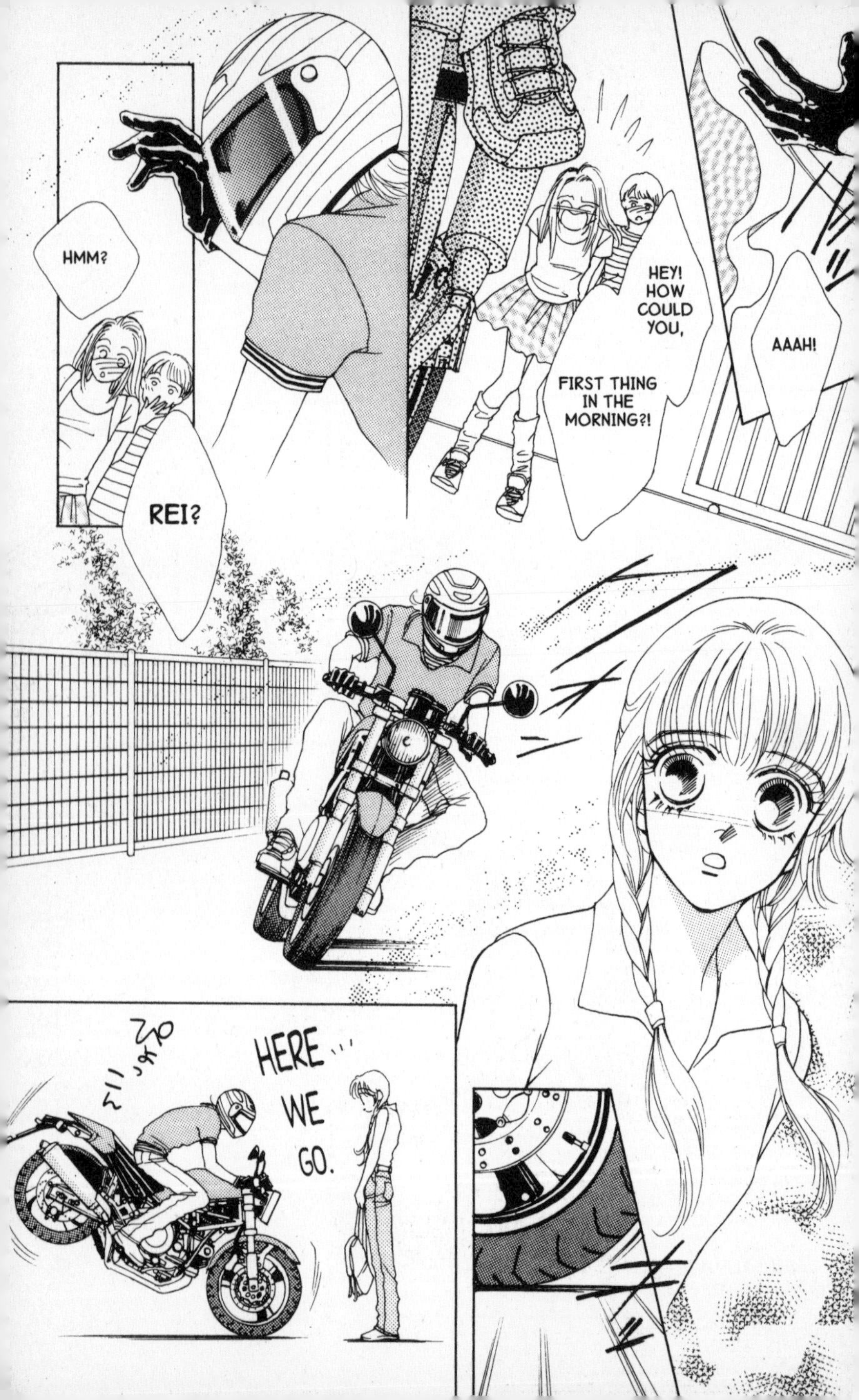
AAAH!
HEY! HOW COULD YOU,
FIRST THING IN THE MORNING?!
HMM?
REI?
HERE... WE GO.

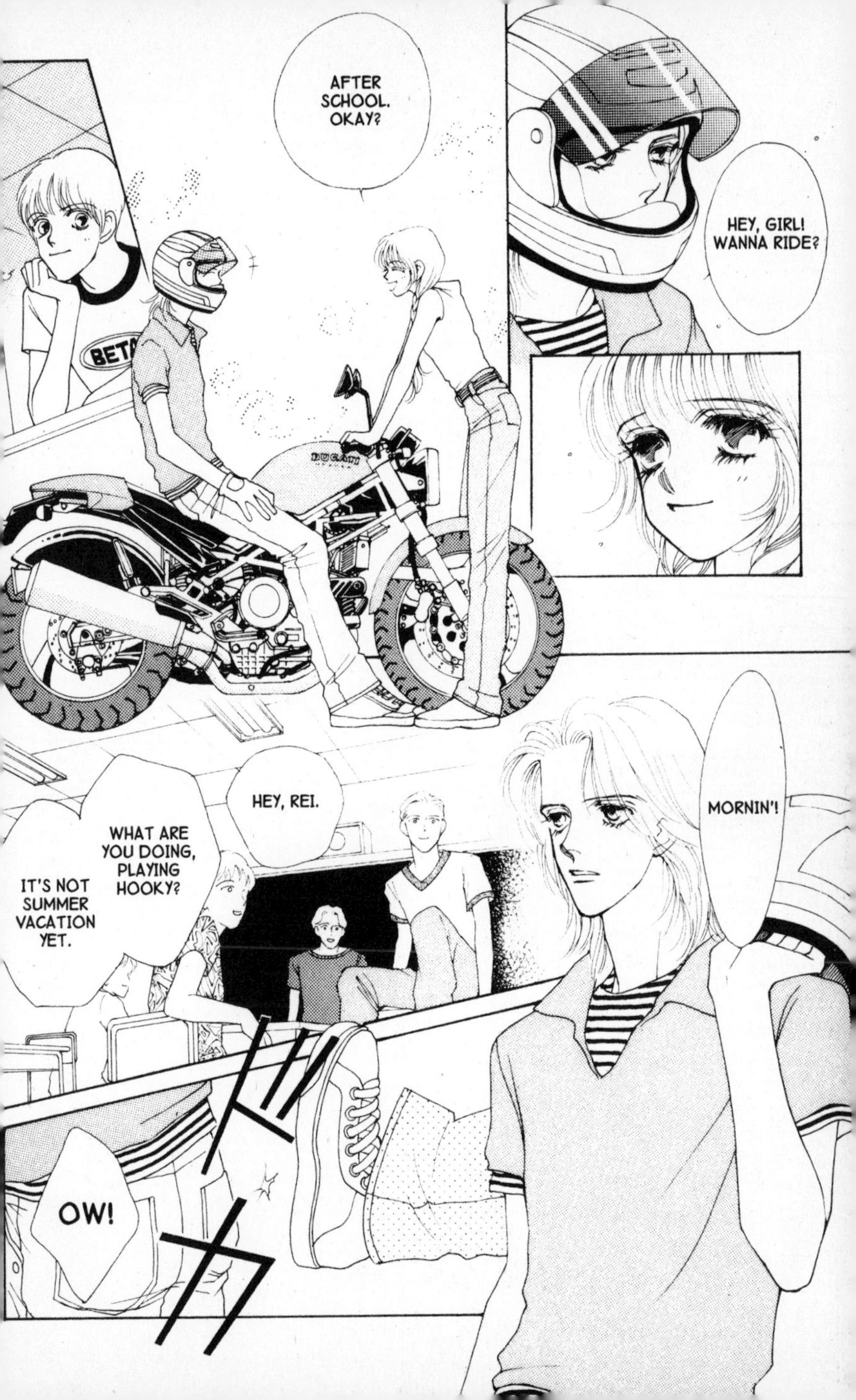
HEY, GIRL! WANNA RIDE?
AFTER SCHOOL. OKAY?
MORNIN'!
HEY, REI.
WHAT ARE YOU DOING, PLAYING HOOKY?
IT'S NOT SUMMER VACATION YET.
OW!

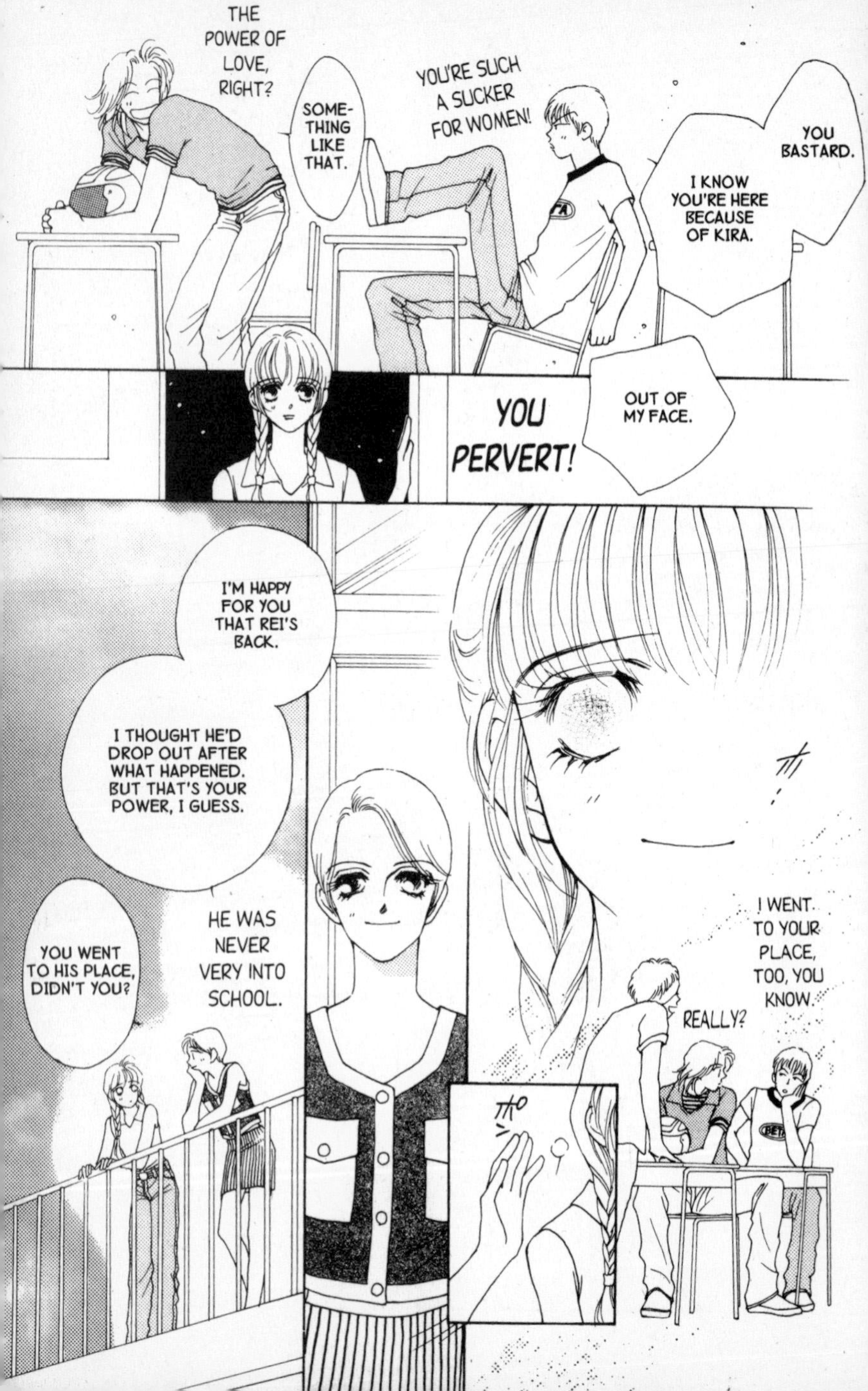
YOU BASTARD.
I KNOW YOU'RE HERE BECAUSE OF KIRA.
YOU'RE SUCH A SUCKER FOR WOMEN!
SOME-THING LIKE THAT.
THE POWER OF LOVE, RIGHT?
OUT OF MY FACE.
YOU PERVERT!
I WENT TO YOUR PLACE, TOO, YOU KNOW.
REALLY?
I'M HAPPY FOR YOU THAT REI'S BACK.
I THOUGHT HE'D DROP OUT AFTER WHAT HAPPENED. BUT THAT'S YOUR POWER, I GUESS.
HE WAS NEVER VERY INTO SCHOOL.
YOU WENT TO HIS PLACE, DIDN'T YOU?

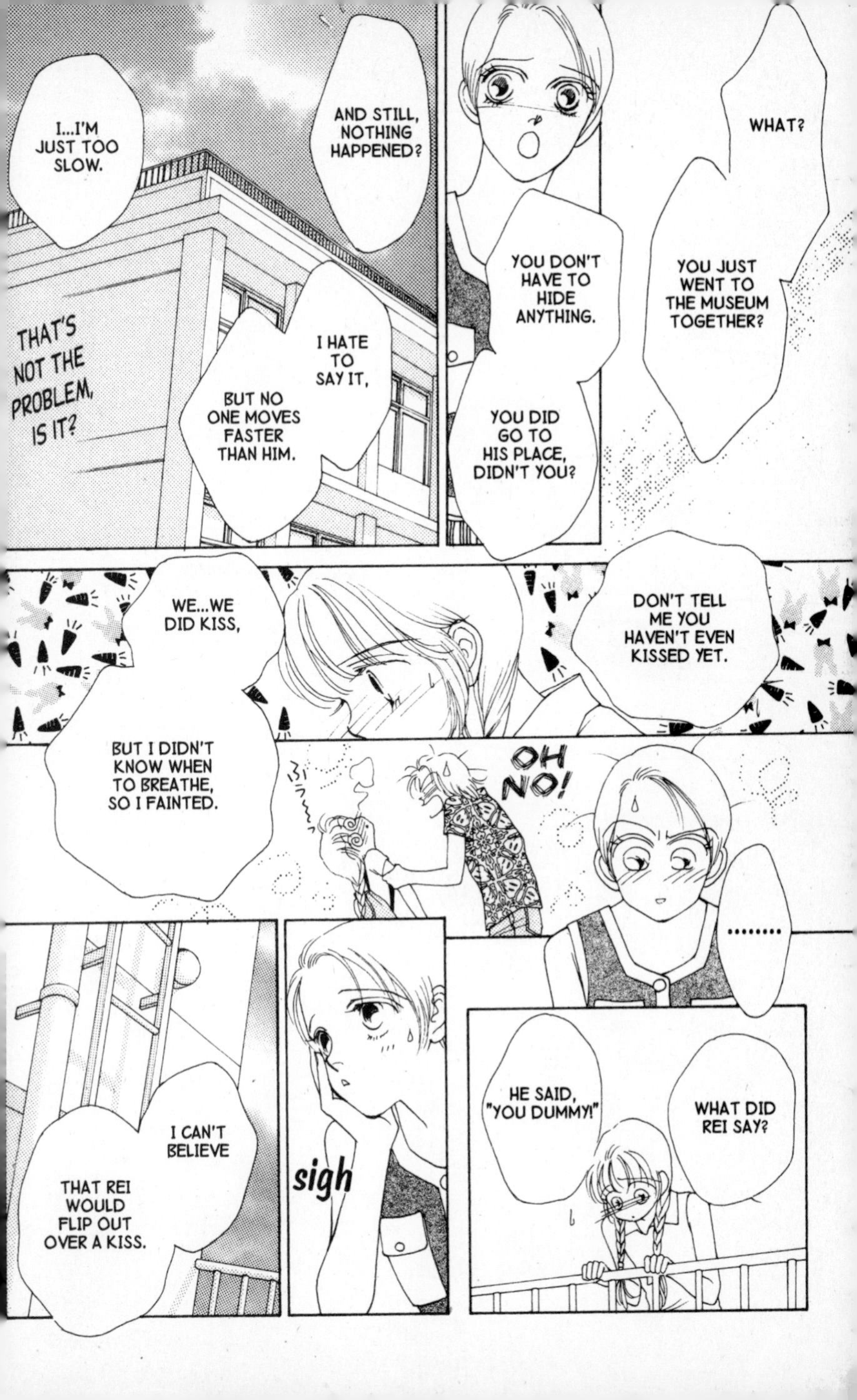

WHAT?
YOU JUST WENT TO THE MUSEUM TOGETHER?
YOU DON'T HAVE TO HIDE ANYTHING.
YOU DID GO TO HIS PLACE, DIDN'T YOU?
AND STILL, NOTHING HAPPENED?
I...I'M JUST TOO SLOW.
I HATE TO SAY IT,
BUT NO ONE MOVES FASTER THAN HIM.
THAT'S NOT THE PROBLEM, IS IT?
DON'T TELL ME YOU HAVEN'T EVEN KISSED YET.
WE...WE DID KISS,
BUT I DIDN'T KNOW WHEN TO BREATHE, SO I FAINTED.
....
OH NO!
WHAT DID REI SAY?
HE SAID, "YOU DUMMY!"
sigh
I CAN'T BELIEVE
THAT REI WOULD FLIP OUT OVER A KISS.

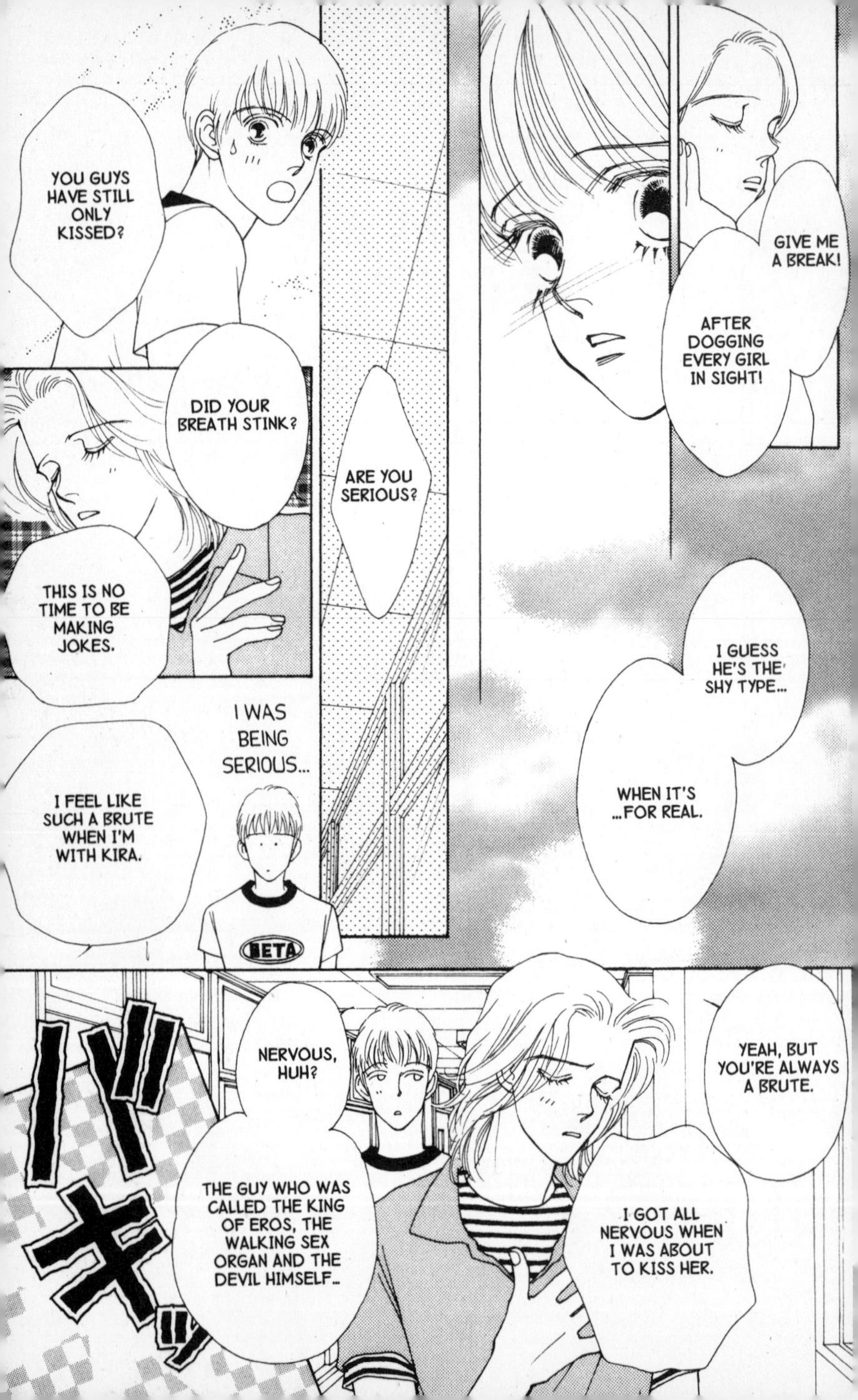
GIVE ME A BREAK!
AFTER DOGGING EVERY GIRL IN SIGHT!
I GUESS HE'S THE SHY TYPE...
WHEN IT'S ...FOR REAL.
ARE YOU SERIOUS?
YOU GUYS HAVE STILL ONLY KISSED?
DID YOUR BREATH STINK?
THIS IS NO TIME TO BE MAKING JOKES.
I WAS BEING SERIOUS...
I FEEL LIKE SUCH A BRUTE WHEN I'M WITH KIRA.
YEAH, BUT YOU'RE ALWAYS A BRUTE.
I GOT ALL NERVOUS WHEN I WAS ABOUT TO KISS HER.
NERVOUS, HUH?
THE GUY WHO WAS CALLED THE KING OF EROS, THE WALKING SEX ORGAN AND THE DEVIL HIMSELF...
バキッ

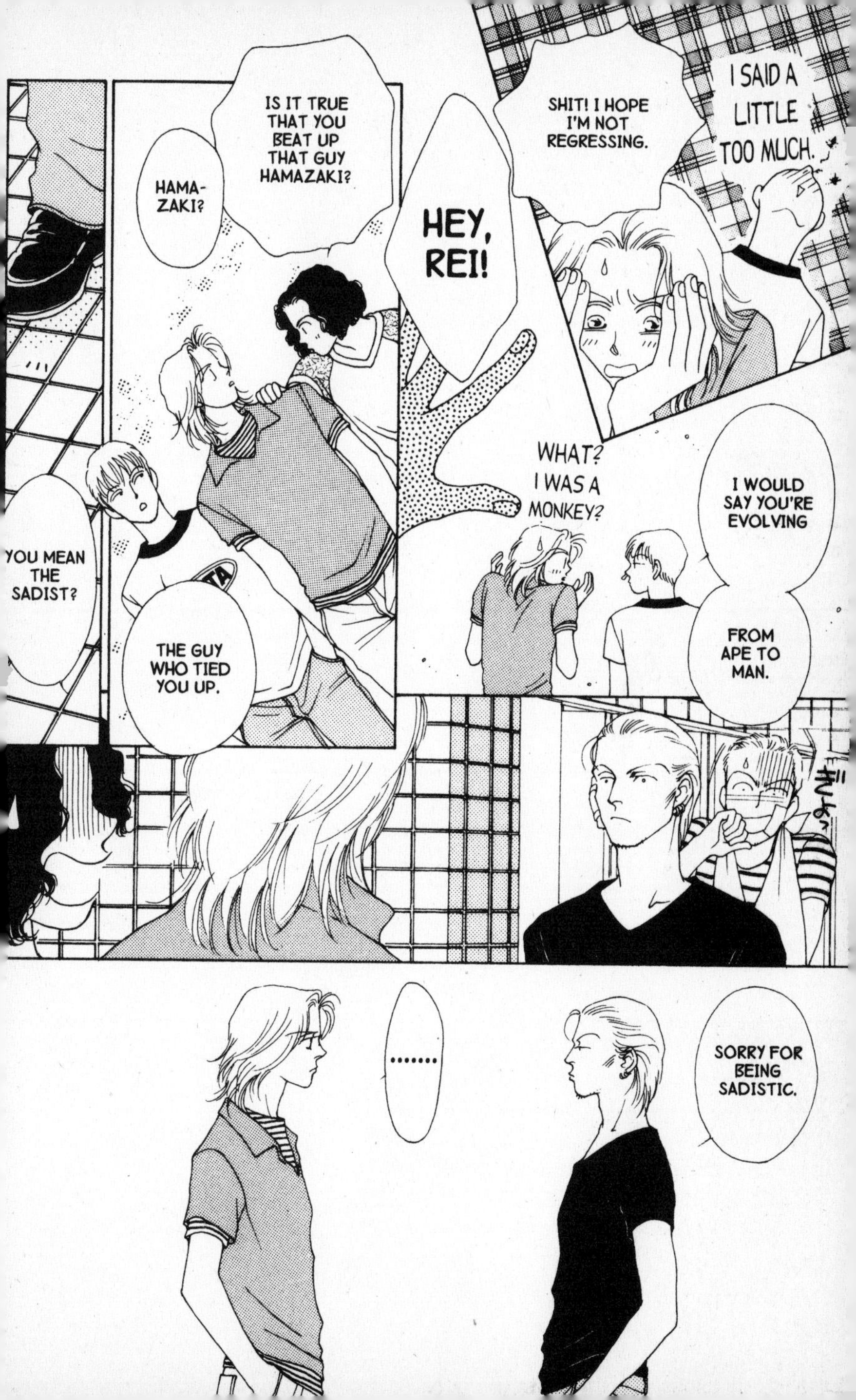
I SAID A LITTLE TOO MUCH.
SHIT! I HOPE I'M NOT REGRESSING.
WHAT? I WAS A MONKEY?
I WOULD SAY YOU'RE EVOLVING
FROM APE TO MAN.
HEY, REI!
IS IT TRUE THAT YOU BEAT UP THAT GUY HAMAZAKI?
HAMA-ZAKI?
YOU MEAN THE SADIST?
THE GUY WHO TIED YOU UP.
SORRY FOR BEING SADISTIC.
....

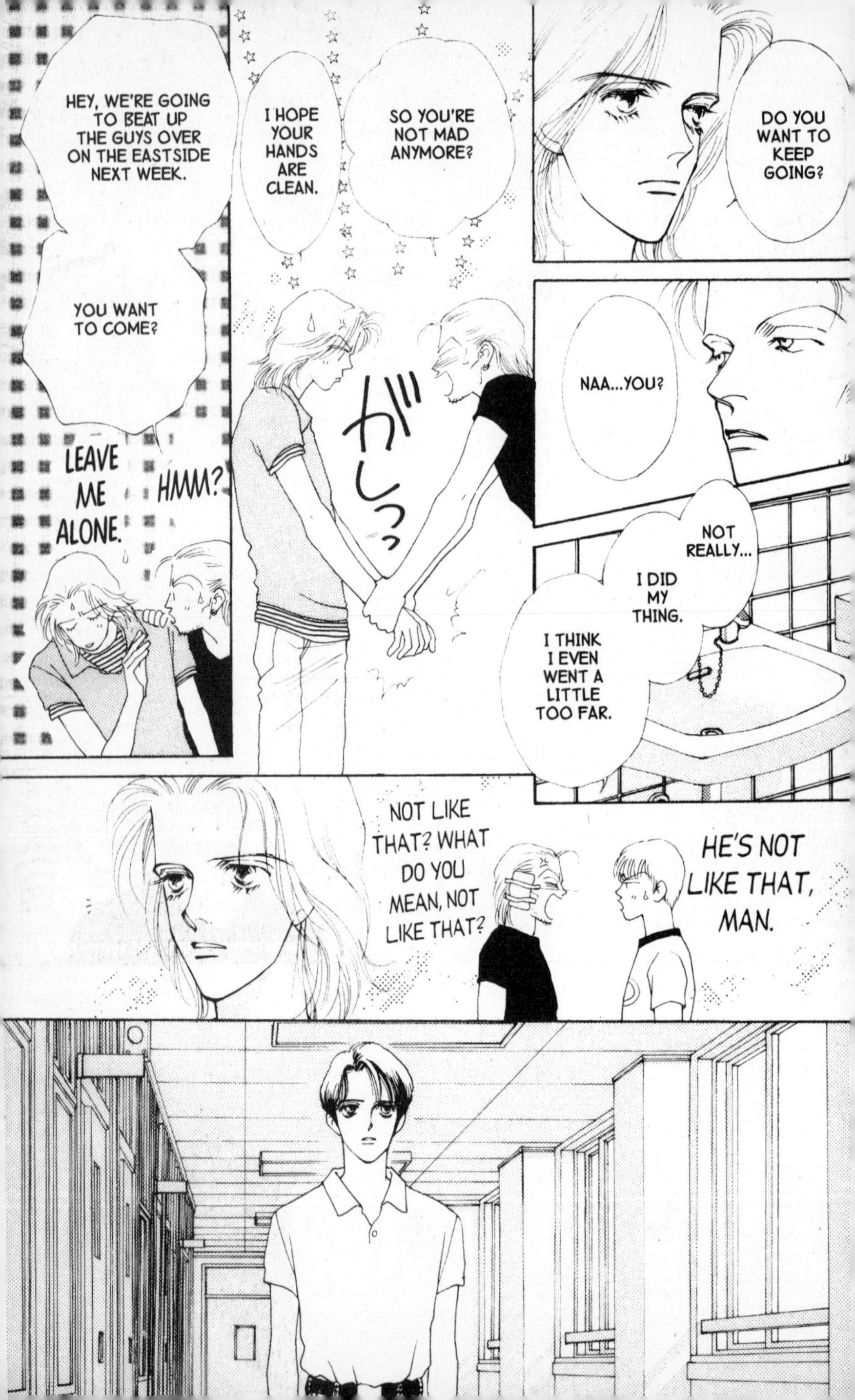
DO YOU WANT TO KEEP GOING?
NAA...YOU?
NOT REALLY...
I DID MY THING.
I THINK I EVEN WENT A LITTLE TOO FAR.
SO YOU'RE NOT MAD ANYMORE?
I HOPE YOUR HANDS ARE CLEAN.
がしっ
HEY, WE'RE GOING TO BEAT UP THE GUYS OVER ON THE EASTSIDE NEXT WEEK.
YOU WANT TO COME?
HMM?
LEAVE ME ALONE.
HE'S NOT LIKE THAT, MAN.
NOT LIKE THAT? WHAT DO YOU MEAN, NOT LIKE THAT?

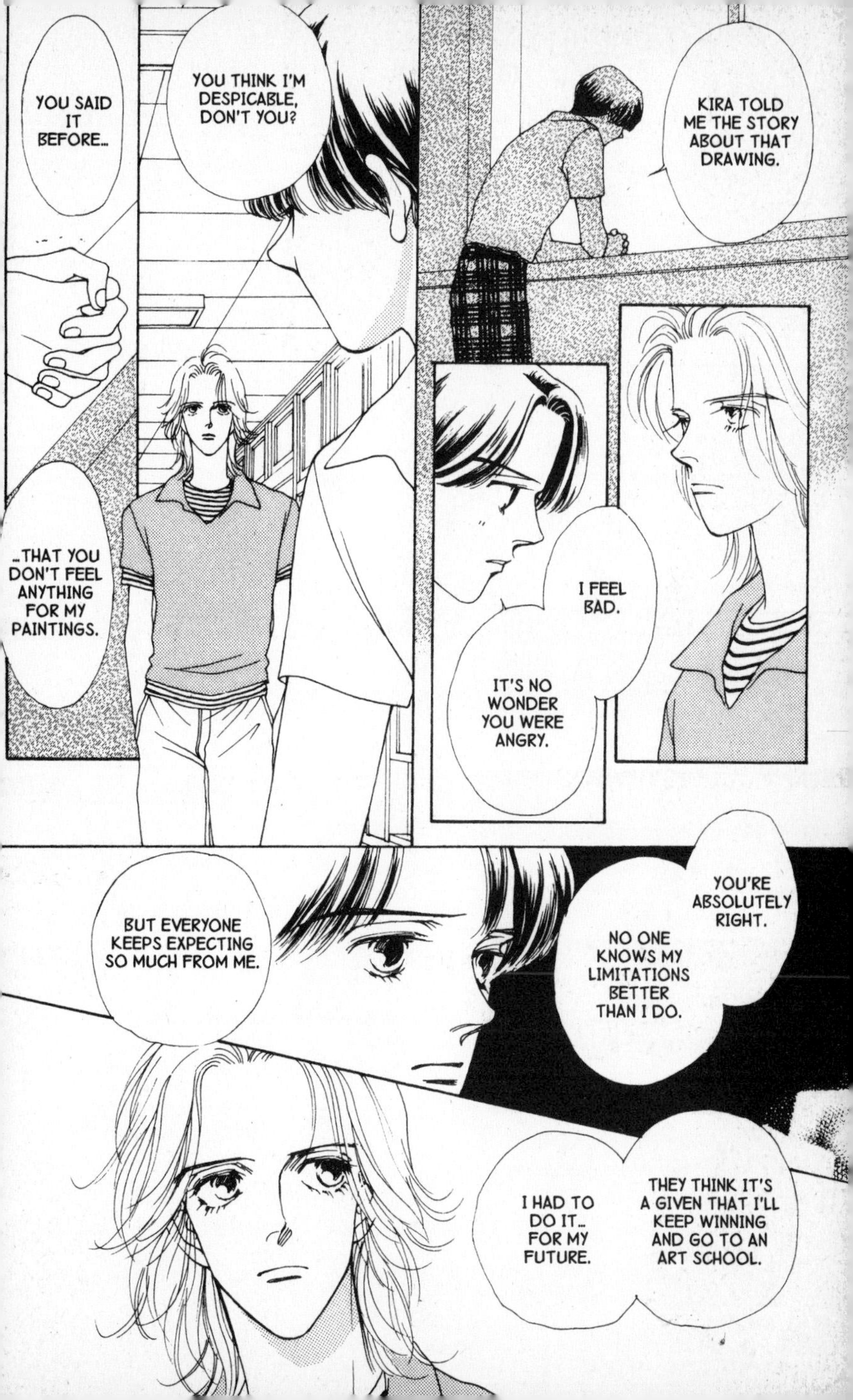
KIRA TOLD ME THE STORY ABOUT THAT DRAWING.
I FEEL BAD.
IT'S NO WONDER YOU WERE ANGRY.
YOU THINK I'M DESPICABLE, DON'T YOU?
YOU SAID IT BEFORE...
...THAT YOU DON'T FEEL ANYTHING FOR MY PAINTINGS.
YOU'RE ABSOLUTELY RIGHT.
NO ONE KNOWS MY LIMITATIONS BETTER THAN I DO.
BUT EVERYONE KEEPS EXPECTING SO MUCH FROM ME.
THEY THINK IT'S A GIVEN THAT I'LL KEEP WINNING AND GO TO AN ART SCHOOL.
I HAD TO DO IT... FOR MY FUTURE.

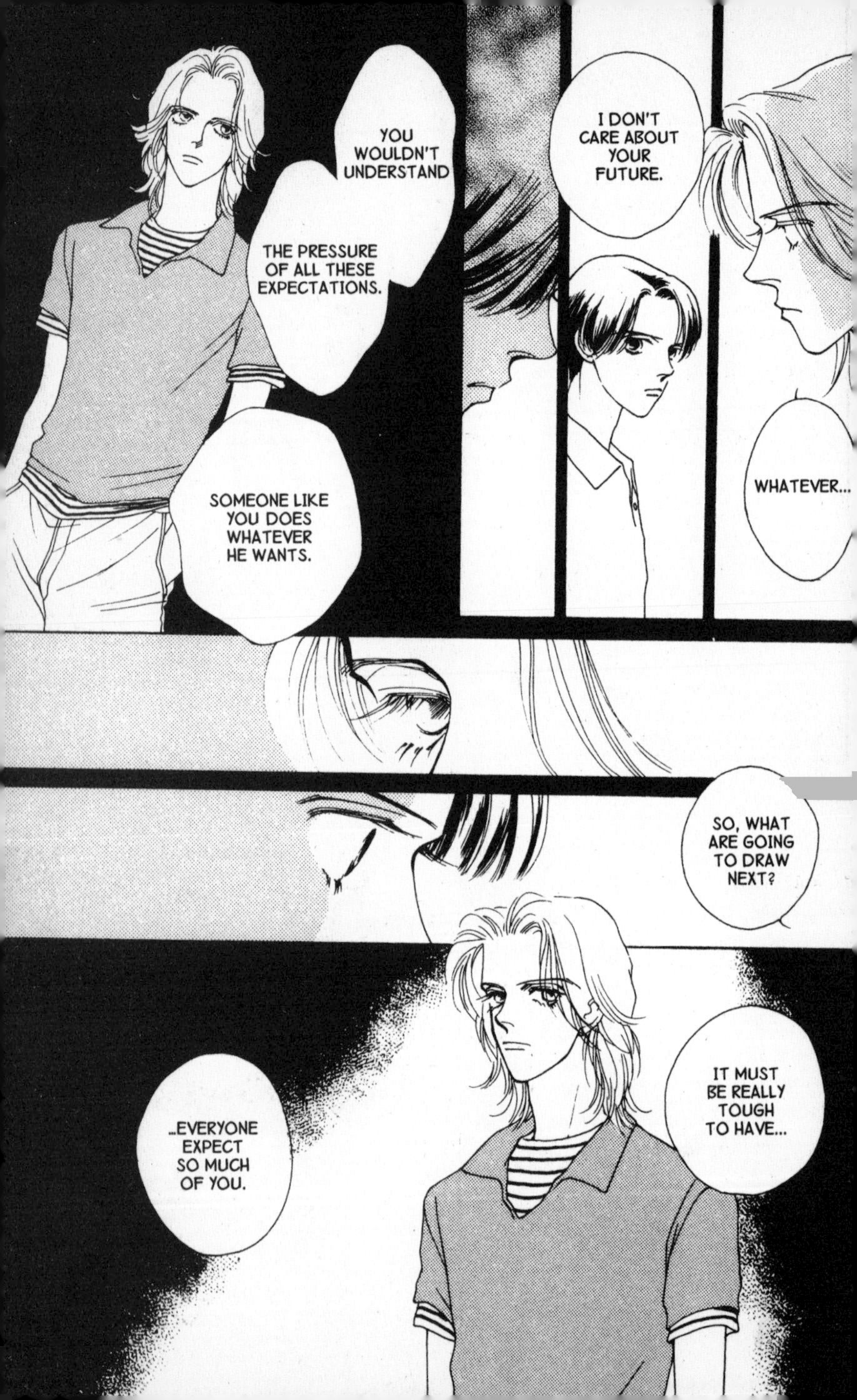
I DON'T CARE ABOUT YOUR FUTURE.
WHATEVER...
YOU WOULDN'T UNDERSTAND
THE PRESSURE OF ALL THESE EXPECTATIONS.
SOMEONE LIKE YOU DOES WHATEVER HE WANTS.
SO, WHAT ARE GOING TO DRAW NEXT?
IT MUST BE REALLY TOUGH TO HAVE...
...EVERYONE EXPECT SO MUCH OF YOU.

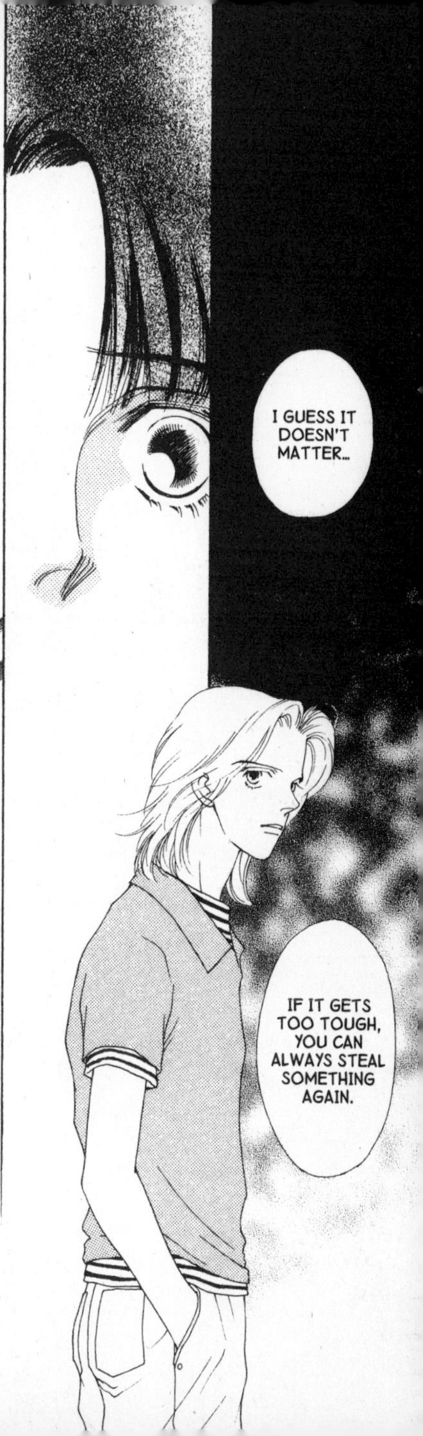
I GUESS IT DOESN'T MATTER...
IF IT GETS TOO TOUGH, YOU CAN ALWAYS STEAL SOMETHING AGAIN.
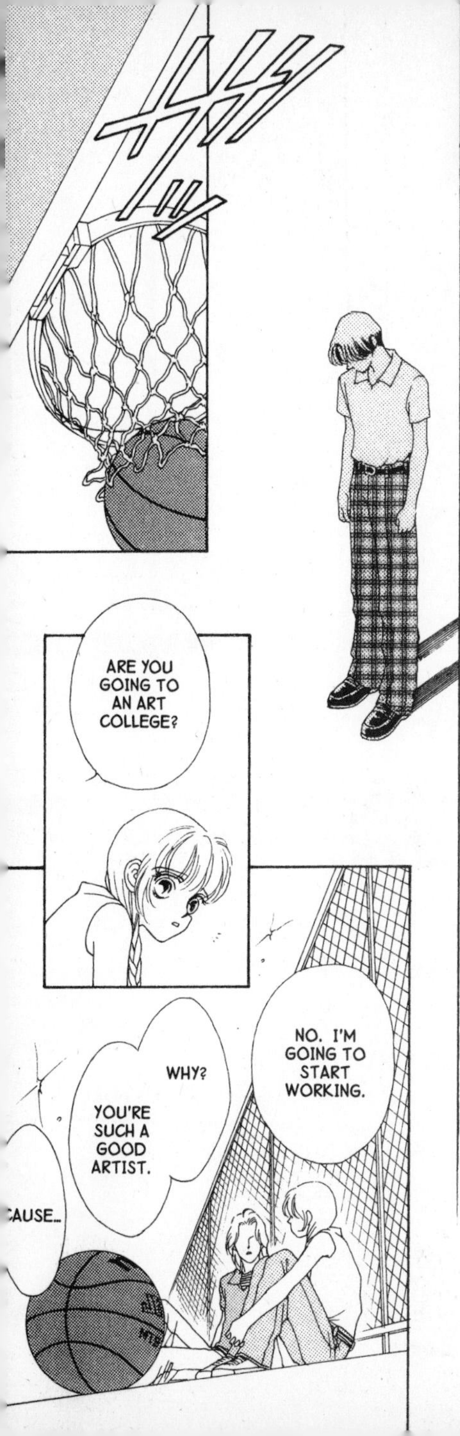
ARE YOU GOING TO AN ART COLLEGE?
NO. I'M GOING TO START WORKING.
WHY?
YOU'RE SUCH A GOOD ARTIST.
CAUSE...

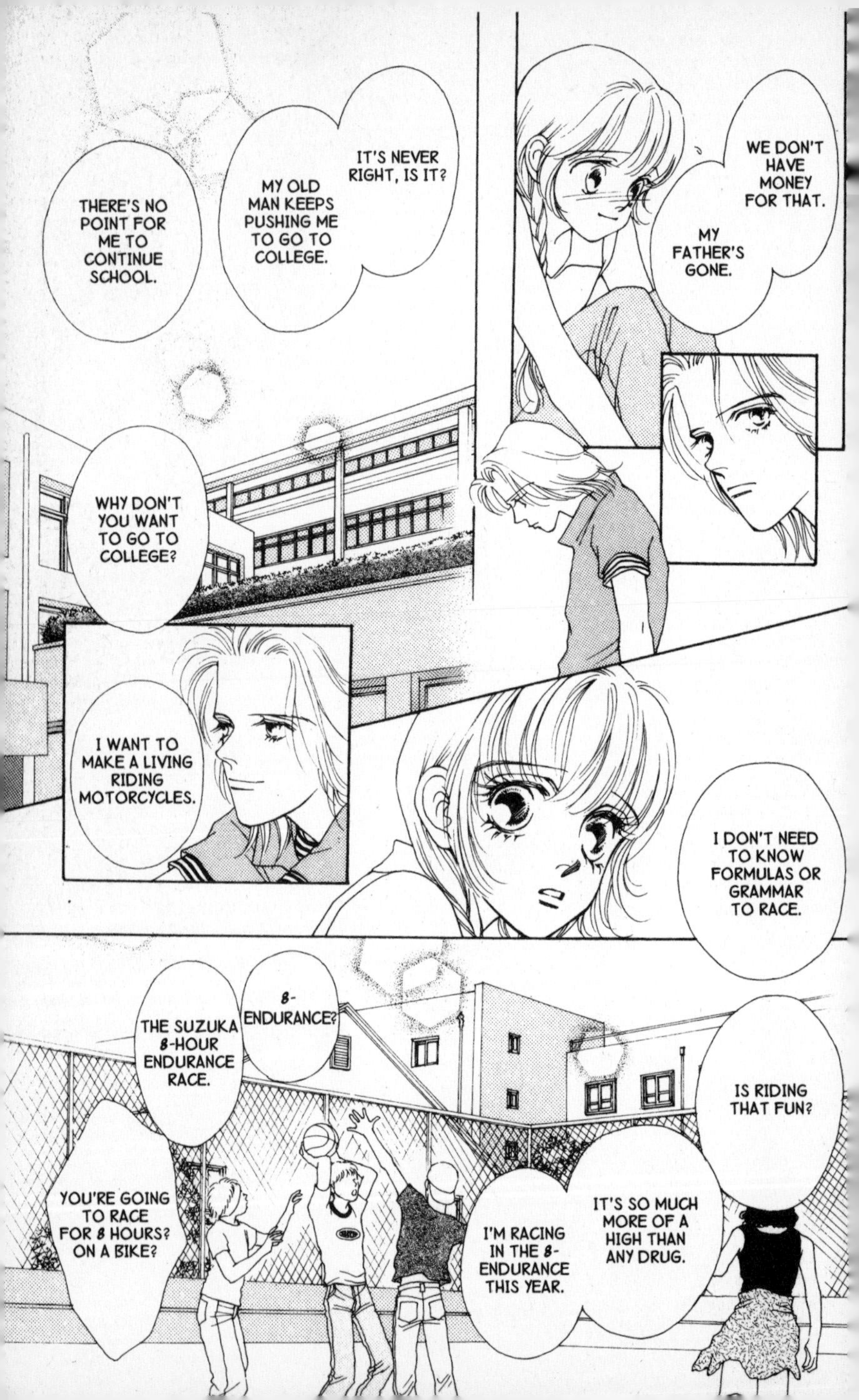
WE DON'T HAVE MONEY FOR THAT.
MY FATHER'S GONE.
IT'S NEVER RIGHT, IS IT?
MY OLD MAN KEEPS PUSHING ME TO GO TO COLLEGE.
THERE'S NO POINT FOR ME TO CONTINUE SCHOOL.
WHY DON'T YOU WANT TO GO TO COLLEGE?
I DON'T NEED TO KNOW FORMULAS OR GRAMMAR TO RACE.
I WANT TO MAKE A LIVING RIDING MOTORCYCLES.
IS RIDING THAT FUN?
IT'S SO MUCH MORE OF A HIGH THAN ANY DRUG.
I'M RACING IN THE 8-ENDURANCE THIS YEAR.
8-ENDURANCE?
THE SUZUKA 8-HOUR ENDURANCE RACE.
YOU'RE GOING TO RACE FOR 8 HOURS? ON A BIKE?

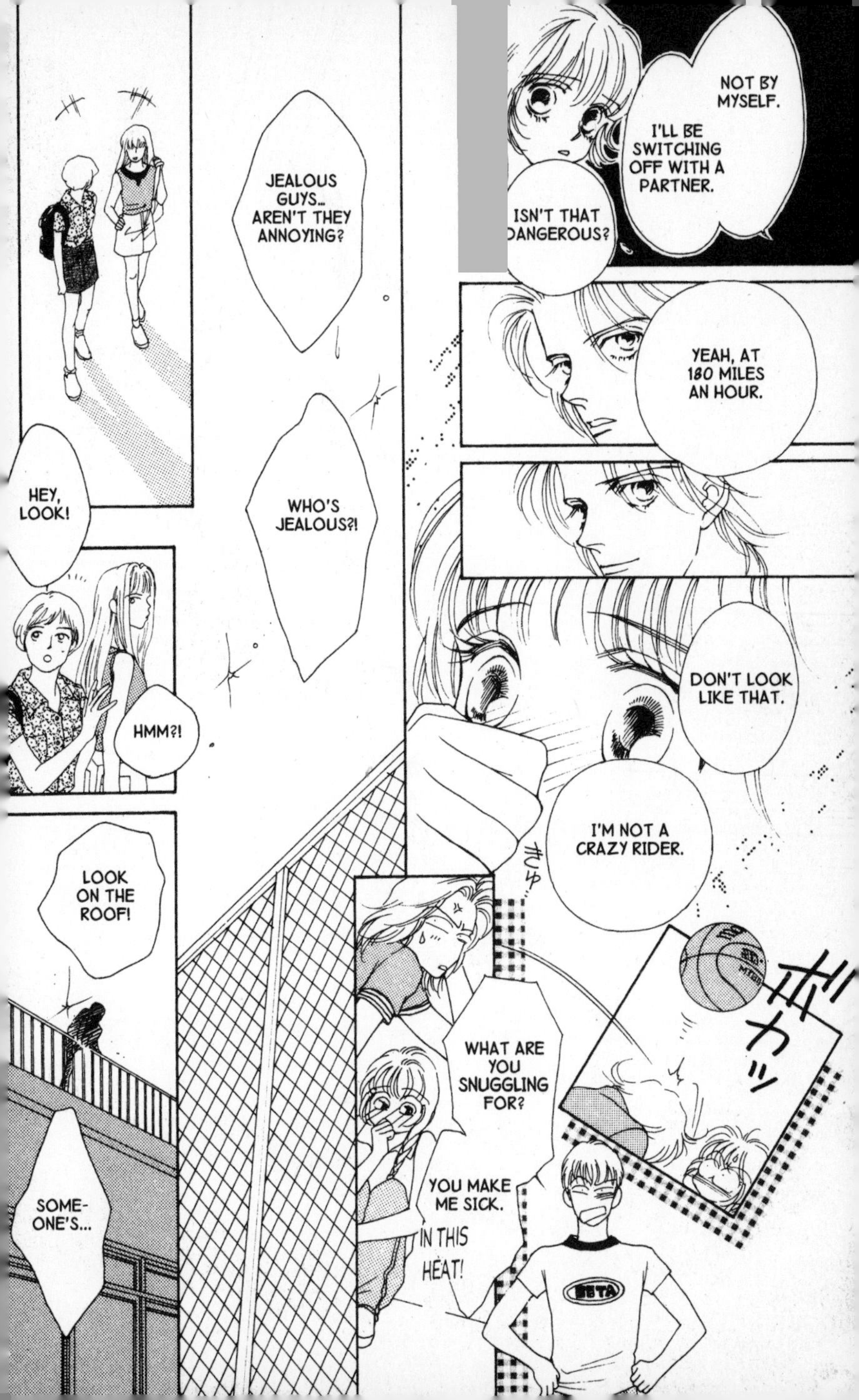

NOT BY MYSELF.
I'LL BE SWITCHING OFF WITH A PARTNER.
ISN'T THAT DANGEROUS?
YEAH, AT 180 MILES AN HOUR.
DON'T LOOK LIKE THAT.
I'M NOT A CRAZY RIDER.
きゅ…
ボカッ
WHAT ARE YOU SNUGGLING FOR?
YOU MAKE ME SICK.
IN THIS HEAT!
JEALOUS GUYS... AREN'T THEY ANNOYING?
WHO'S JEALOUS?!
HEY, LOOK!
HMM?!
LOOK ON THE ROOF!
SOME-ONE'S...

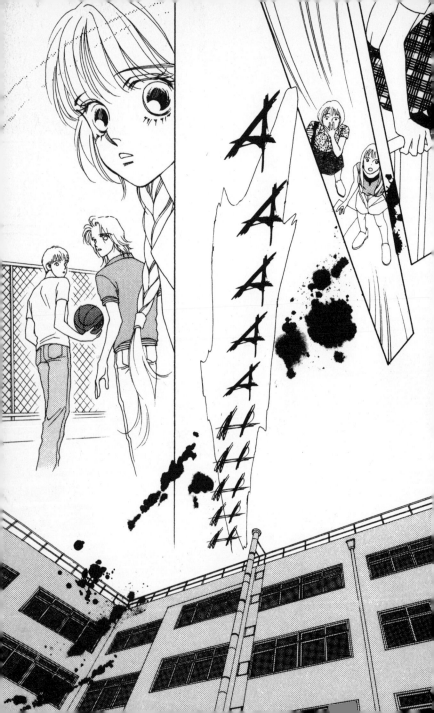

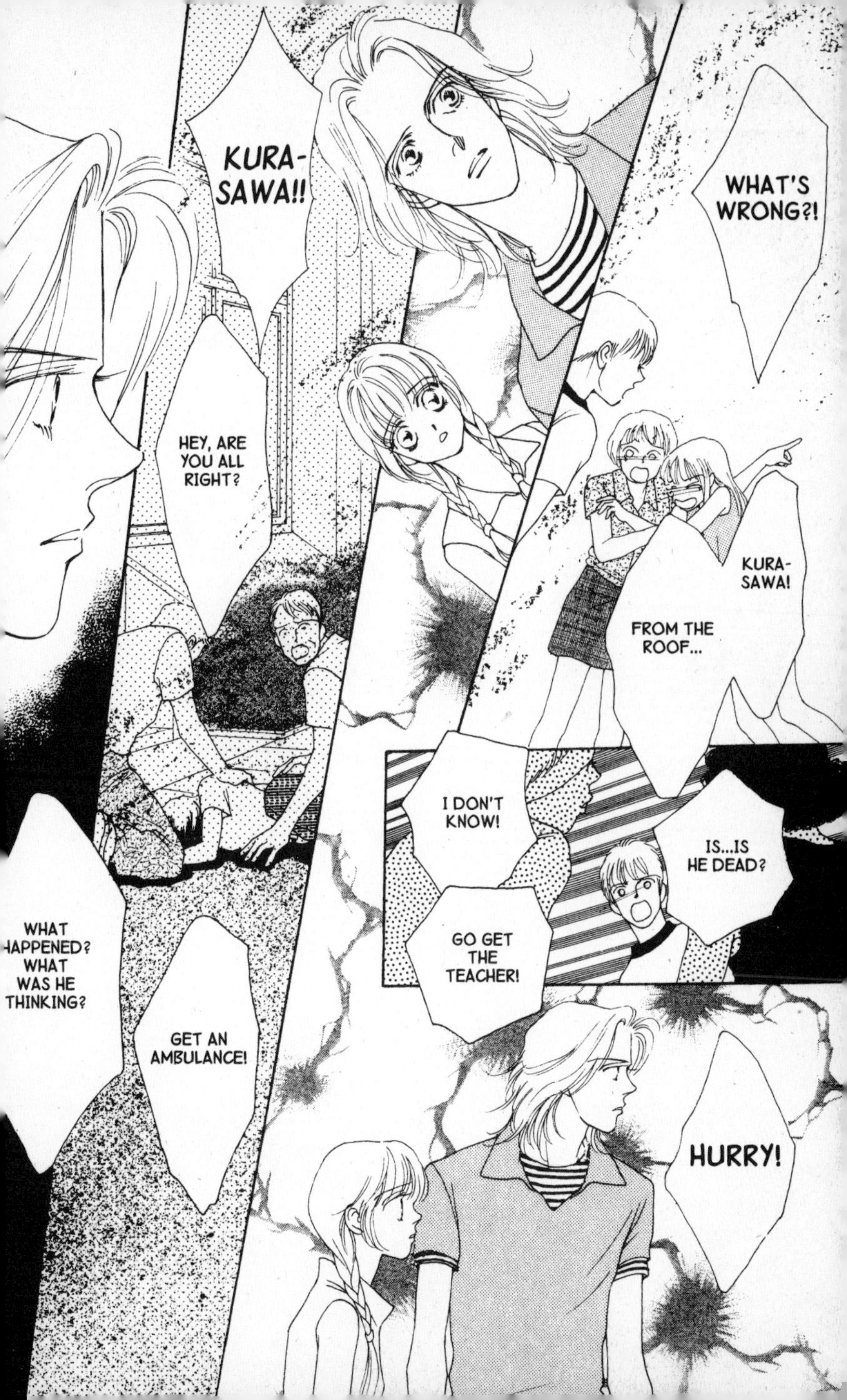
WHAT'S WRONG?!
KURA-SAWA!
FROM THE ROOF...
KURA-SAWA!!
IS...IS HE DEAD?
I DON'T KNOW!
GO GET THE TEACHER!
HEY, ARE YOU ALL RIGHT?
GET AN AMBULANCE!
WHAT HAPPENED? WHAT WAS HE THINKING?
HURRY!

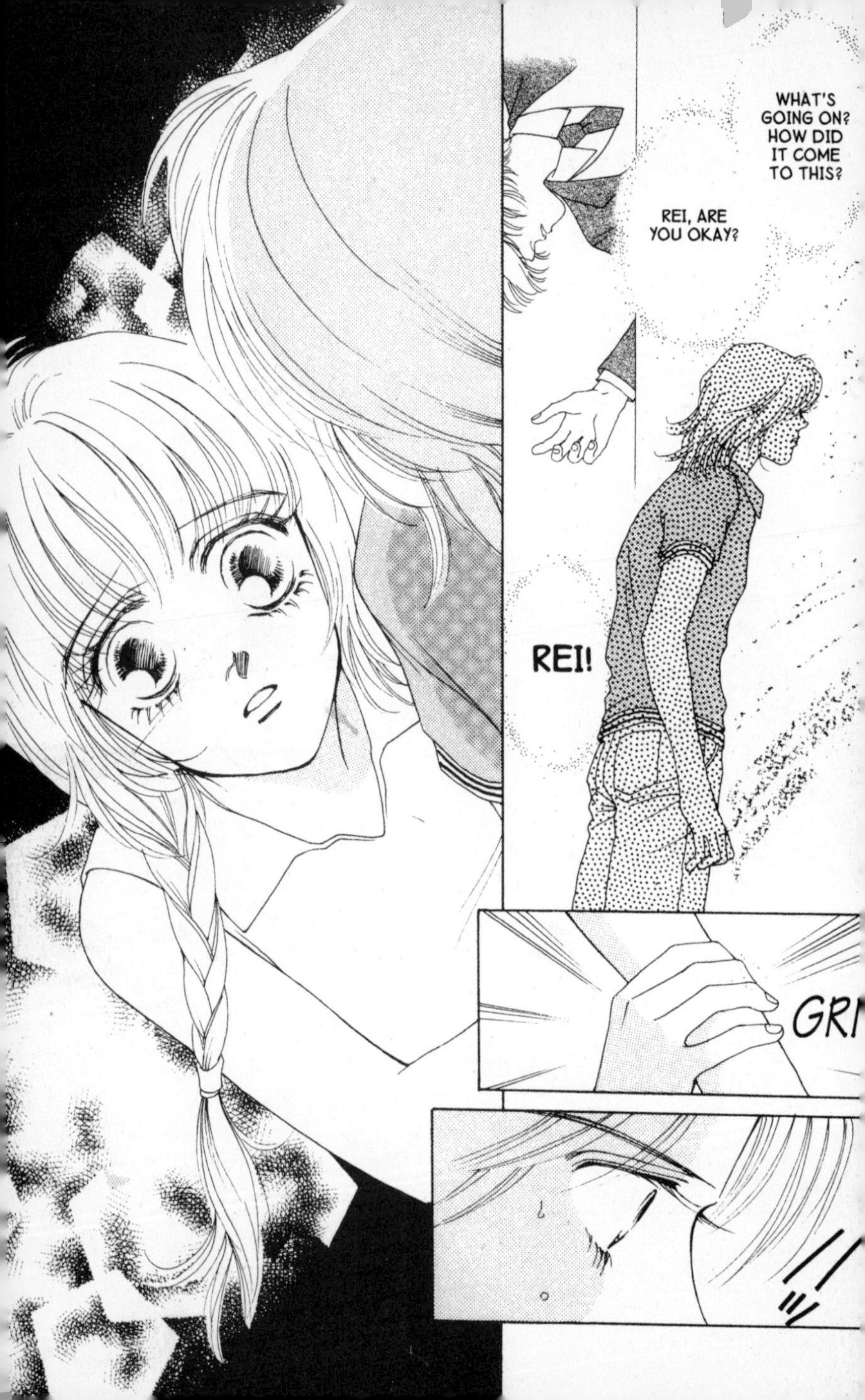
WHAT'S GOING ON? HOW DID IT COME TO THIS?
REI, ARE YOU OKAY?
REI!
GRI

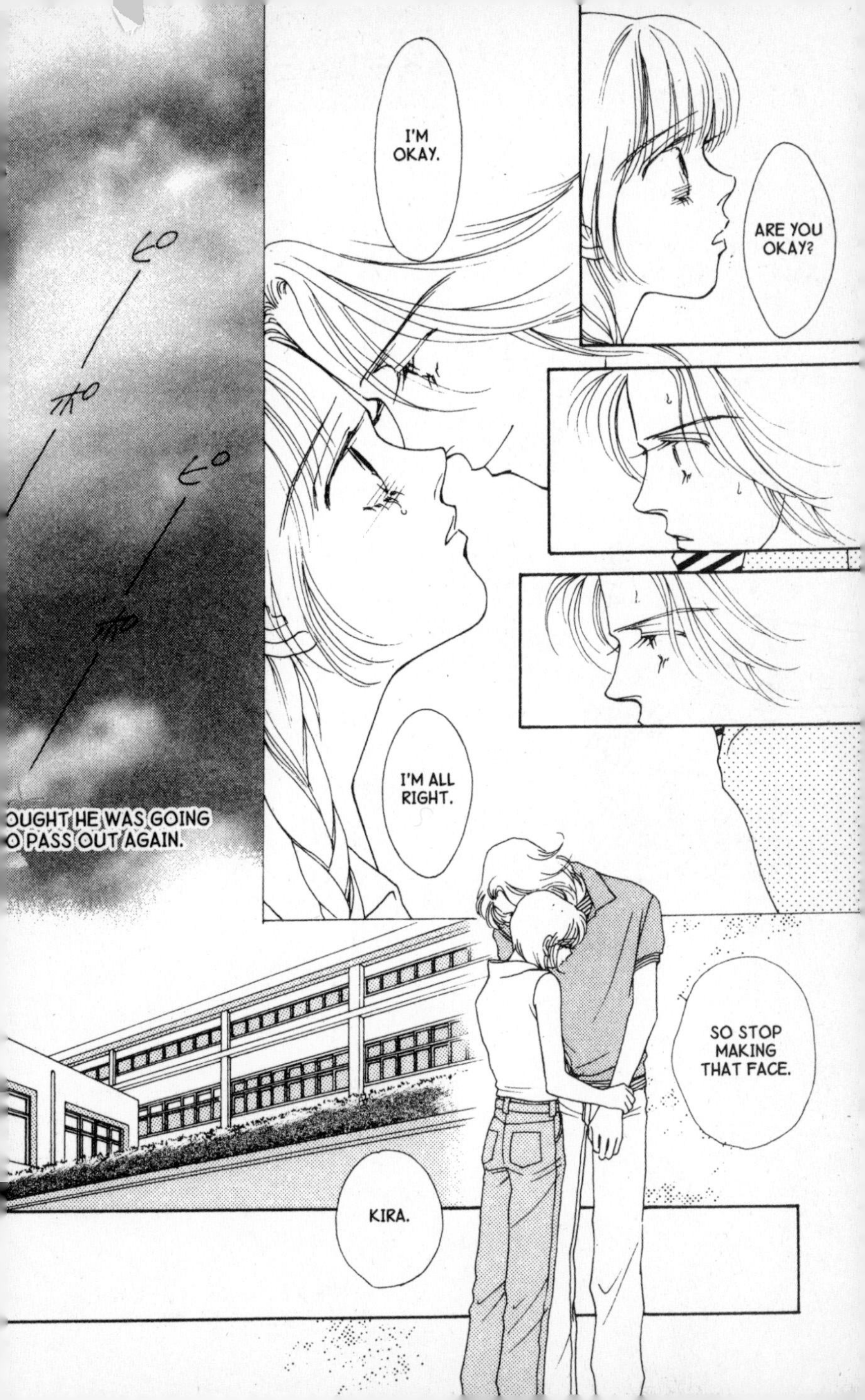
ARE YOU OKAY?
I'M OKAY.
I'M ALL RIGHT.
SO STOP MAKING THAT FACE.
KIRA.
ピーポー
ピーポー
OUGHT HE WAS GOING
O PASS OUT AGAIN.

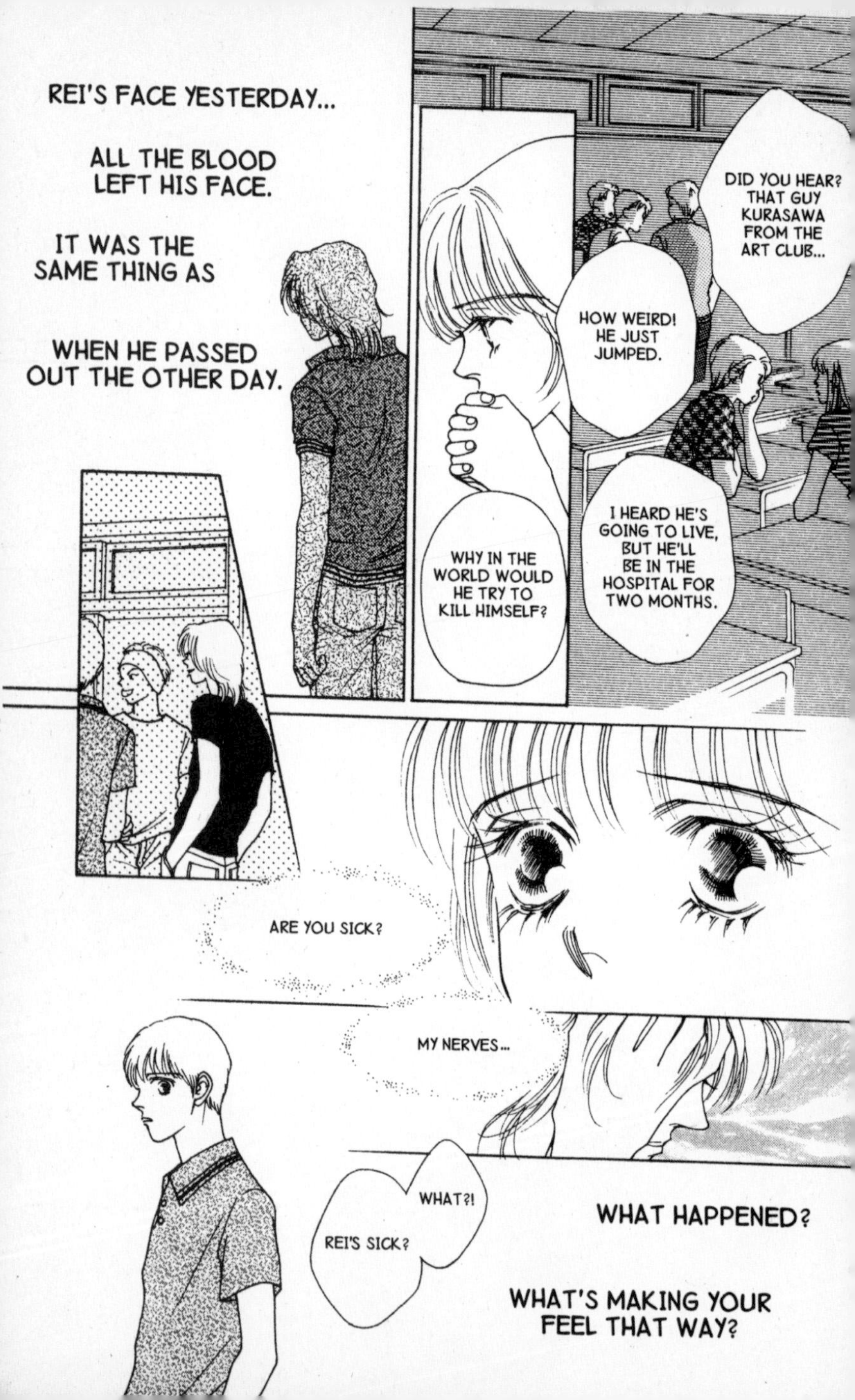
DID YOU HEAR? THAT GUY KURASAWA FROM THE ART CLUB...
HOW WEIRD! HE JUST JUMPED.
I HEARD HE'S GOING TO LIVE, BUT HE'LL BE IN THE HOSPITAL FOR TWO MONTHS.
WHY IN THE WORLD WOULD HE TRY TO KILL HIMSELF?
REI'S FACE YESTERDAY...
ALL THE BLOOD LEFT HIS FACE.
IT WAS THE SAME THING AS
WHEN HE PASSED OUT THE OTHER DAY.
ARE YOU SICK?
MY NERVES...
WHAT HAPPENED?
WHAT'S MAKING YOUR FEEL THAT WAY?
WHAT?!
REI'S SICK?

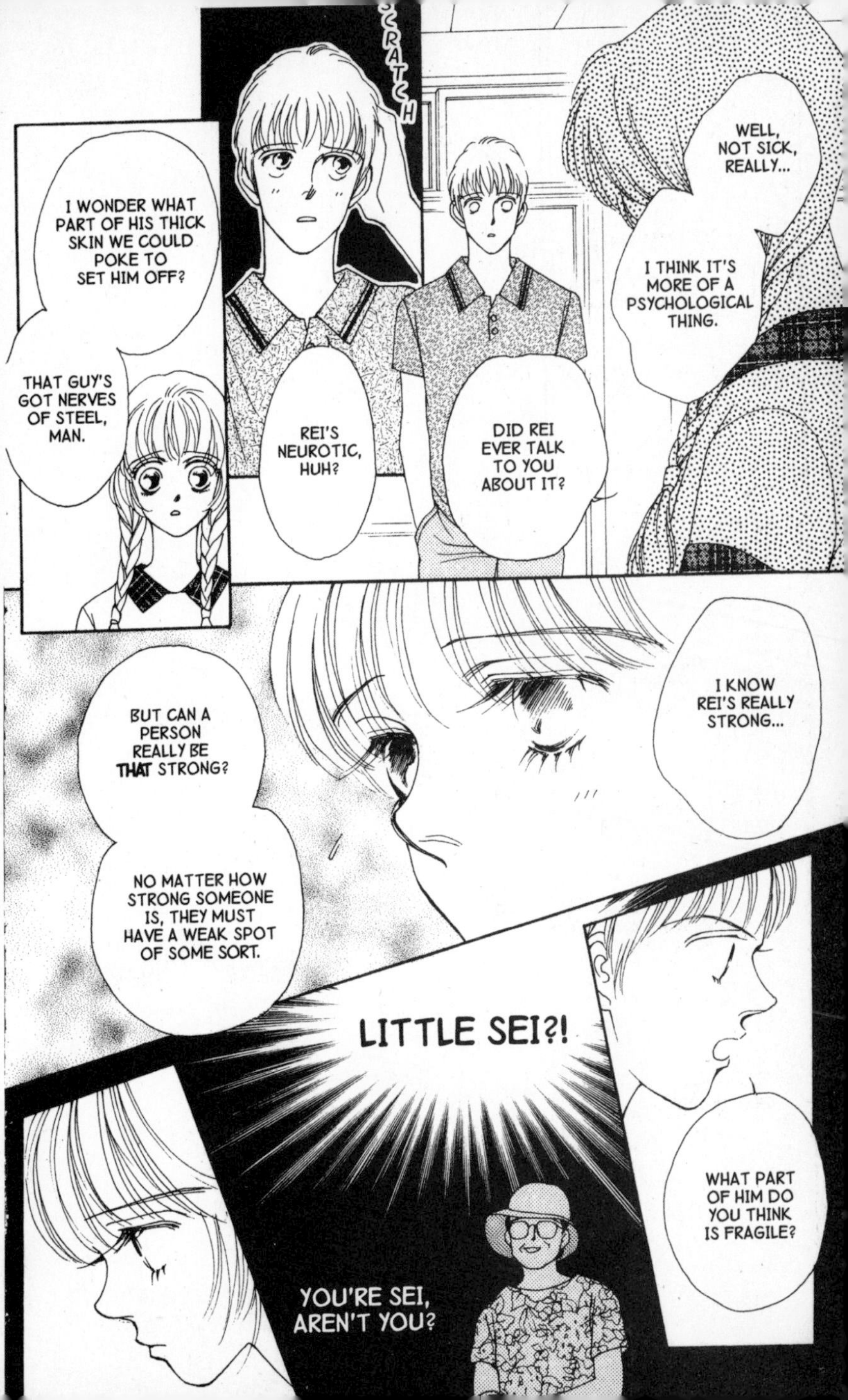
WELL, NOT SICK, REALLY...
I THINK IT'S MORE OF A PSYCHOLOGICAL THING.
DID REI EVER TALK TO YOU ABOUT IT?
SCRATCH
REI'S NEUROTIC, HUH?
I WONDER WHAT PART OF HIS THICK SKIN WE COULD POKE TO SET HIM OFF?
THAT GUY'S GOT NERVES OF STEEL, MAN.
I KNOW REI'S REALLY STRONG...
BUT CAN A PERSON REALLY BE THAT STRONG?
NO MATTER HOW STRONG SOMEONE IS, THEY MUST HAVE A WEAK SPOT OF SOME SORT.
WHAT PART OF HIM DO YOU THINK IS FRAGILE?
LITTLE SEI?!
YOU'RE SEI, AREN'T YOU?

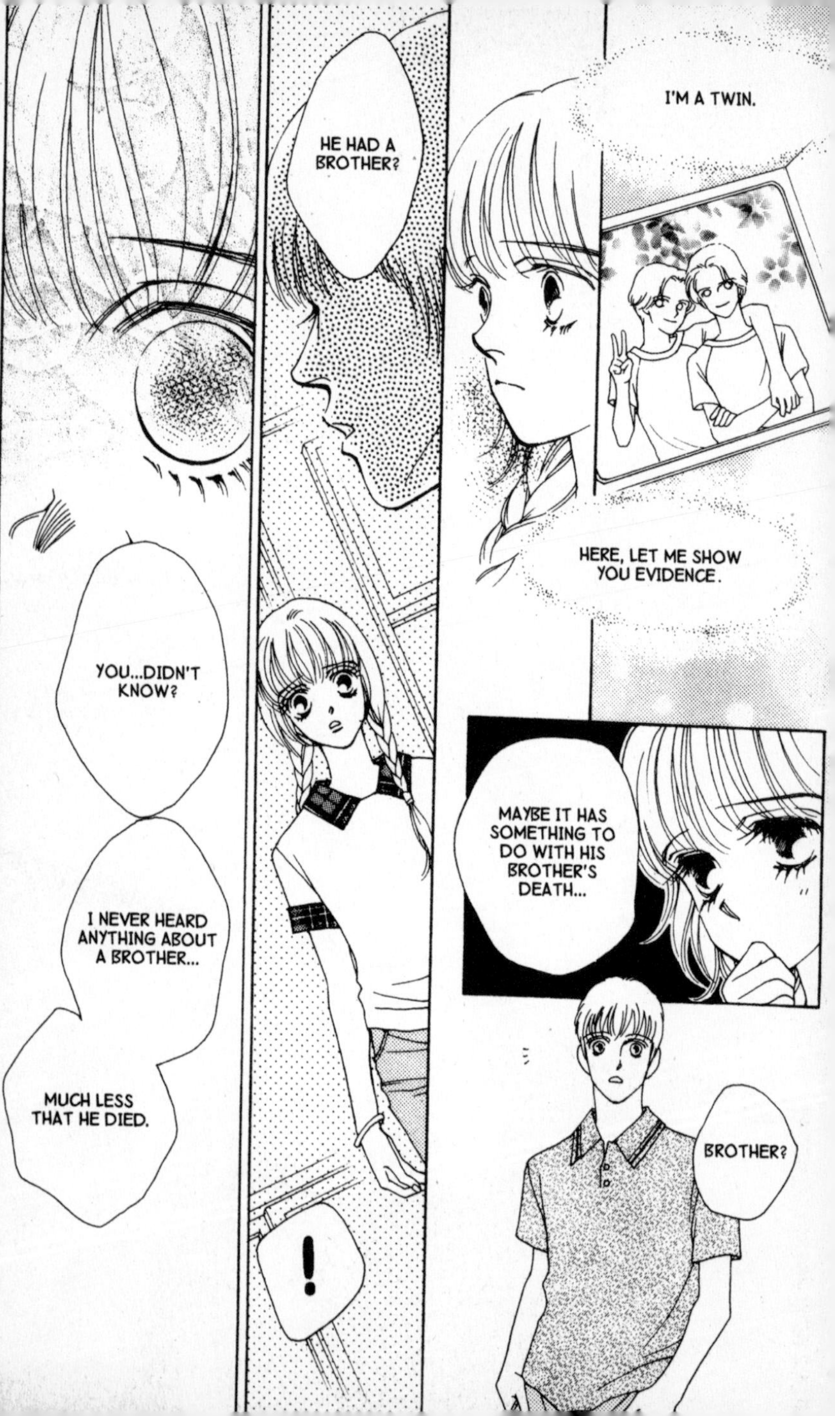
I'M A TWIN.
HERE, LET ME SHOW YOU EVIDENCE.
MAYBE IT HAS SOMETHING TO DO WITH HIS BROTHER'S DEATH...
BROTHER?
HE HAD A BROTHER?
!
YOU...DIDN'T KNOW?
I NEVER HEARD ANYTHING ABOUT A BROTHER...
MUCH LESS THAT HE DIED.

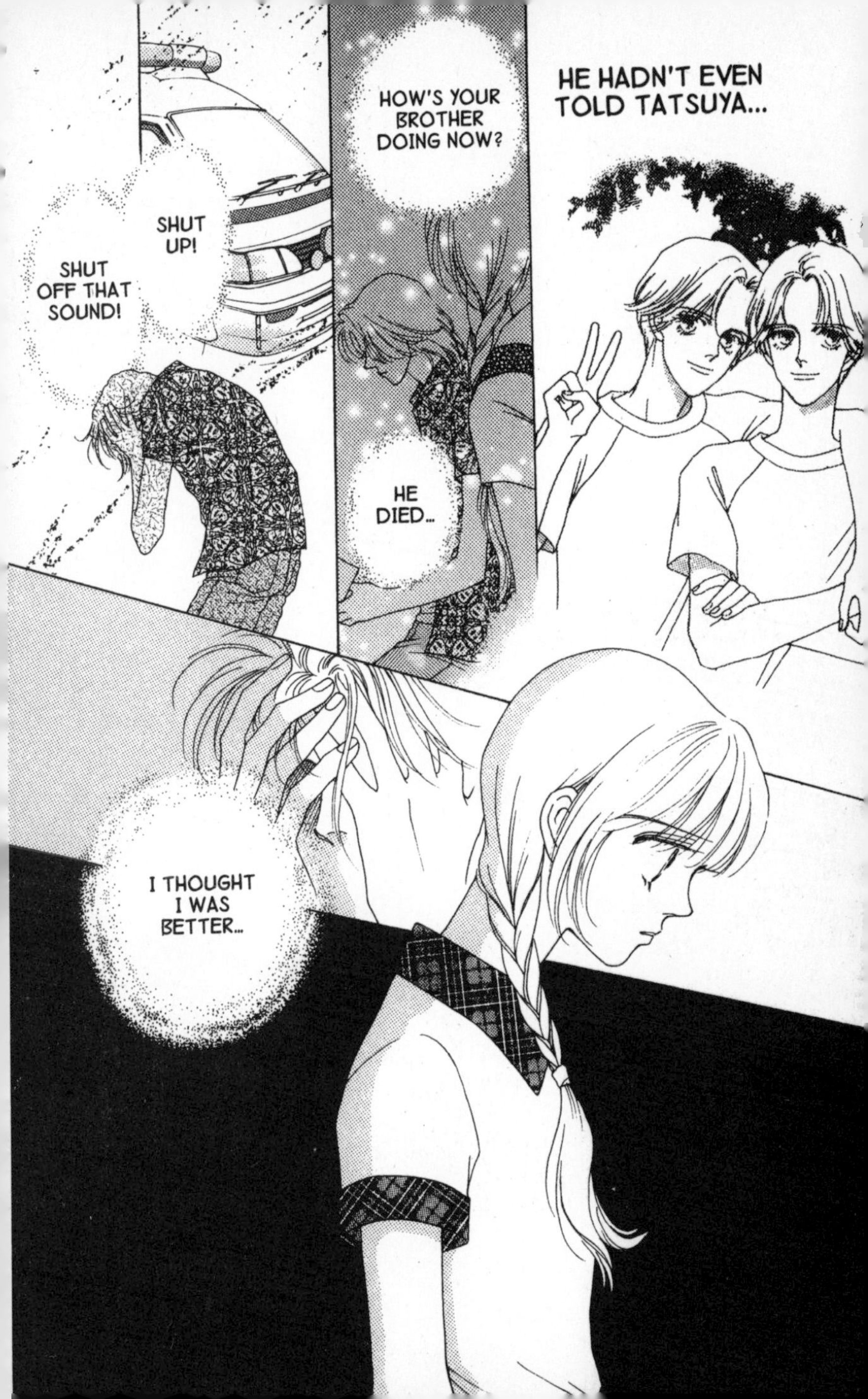
HE HADN'T EVEN TOLD TATSUYA...
HOW'S YOUR BROTHER DOING NOW?
HE DIED...
SHUT UP!
SHUT OFF THAT SOUND!
I THOUGHT I WAS BETTER...

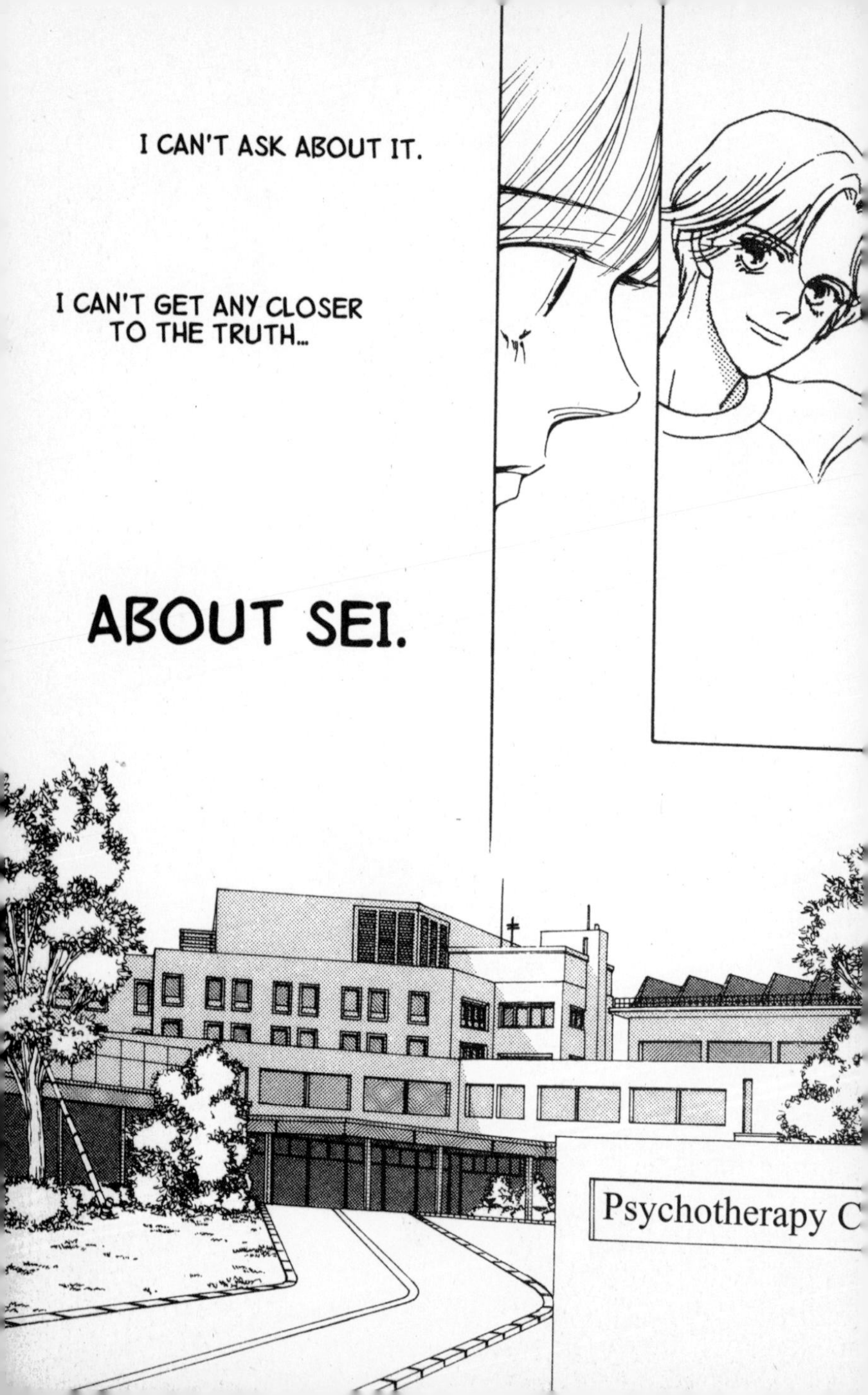
I CAN'T ASK ABOUT IT.
I CAN'T GET ANY CLOSER TO THE TRUTH...
ABOUT SEI.
Psychotherapy C

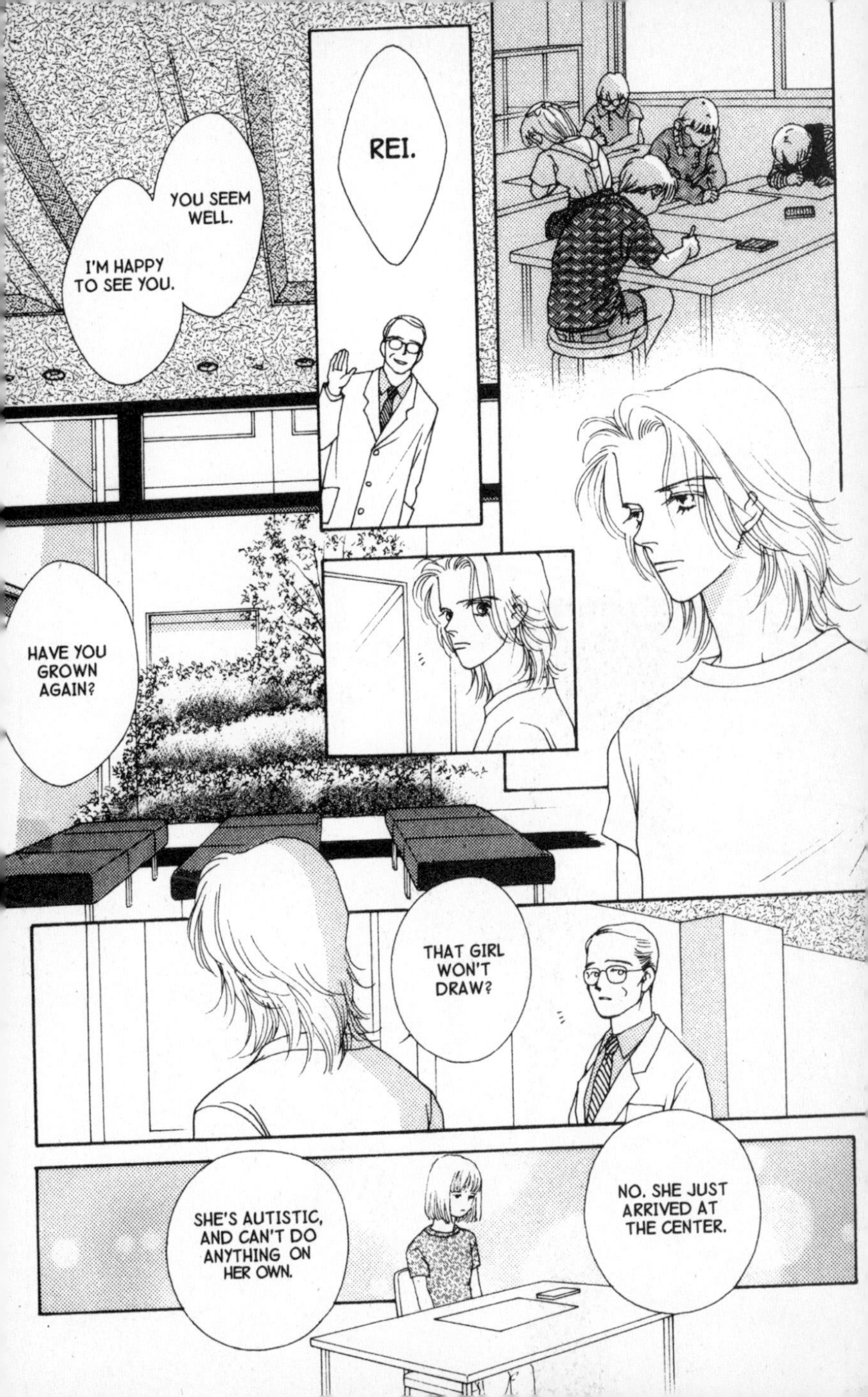
REI.
YOU SEEM WELL.
I'M HAPPY TO SEE YOU.
HAVE YOU GROWN AGAIN?
THAT GIRL WON'T DRAW?
NO. SHE JUST ARRIVED AT THE CENTER.
SHE'S AUTISTIC, AND CAN'T DO ANYTHING ON HER OWN.

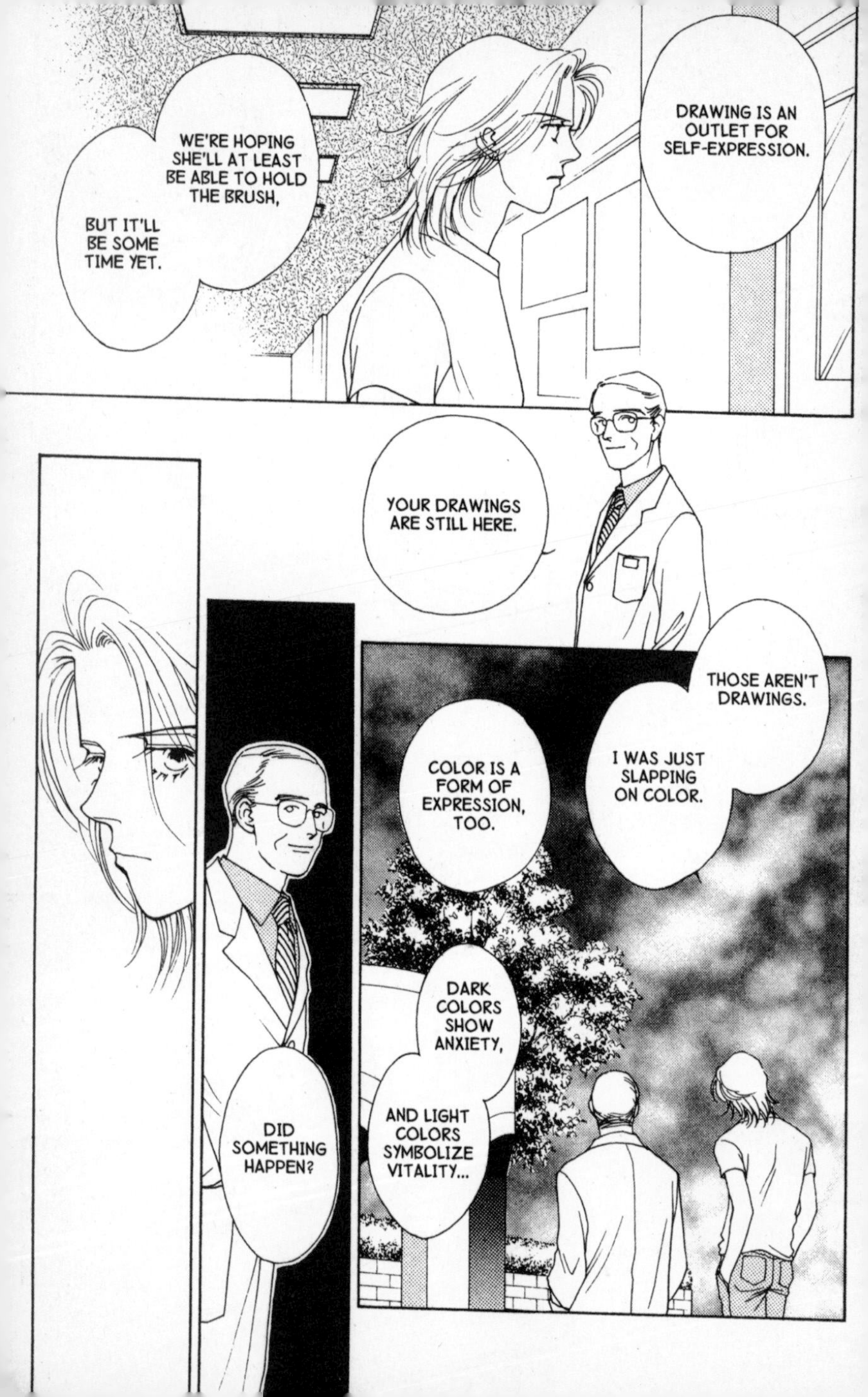
DRAWING IS AN OUTLET FOR SELF-EXPRESSION.
WE'RE HOPING SHE'LL AT LEAST BE ABLE TO HOLD THE BRUSH,
BUT IT'LL BE SOME TIME YET.
YOUR DRAWINGS ARE STILL HERE.
THOSE AREN'T DRAWINGS.
I WAS JUST SLAPPING ON COLOR.
COLOR IS A FORM OF EXPRESSION, TOO.
DARK COLORS SHOW ANXIETY,
AND LIGHT COLORS SYMBOLIZE VITALITY...
DID SOMETHING HAPPEN?

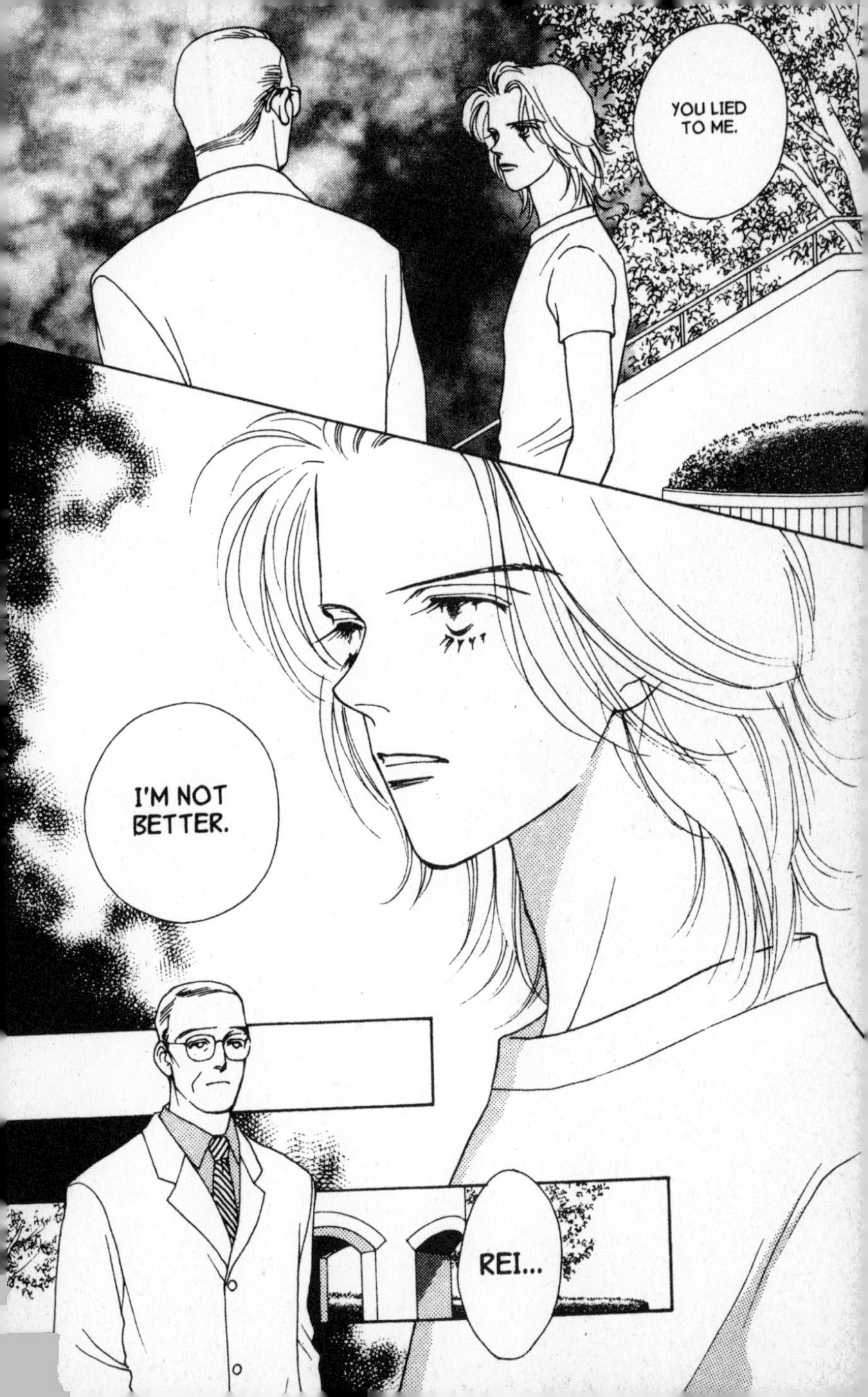
YOU LIED TO ME.
I'M NOT BETTER.
REI...

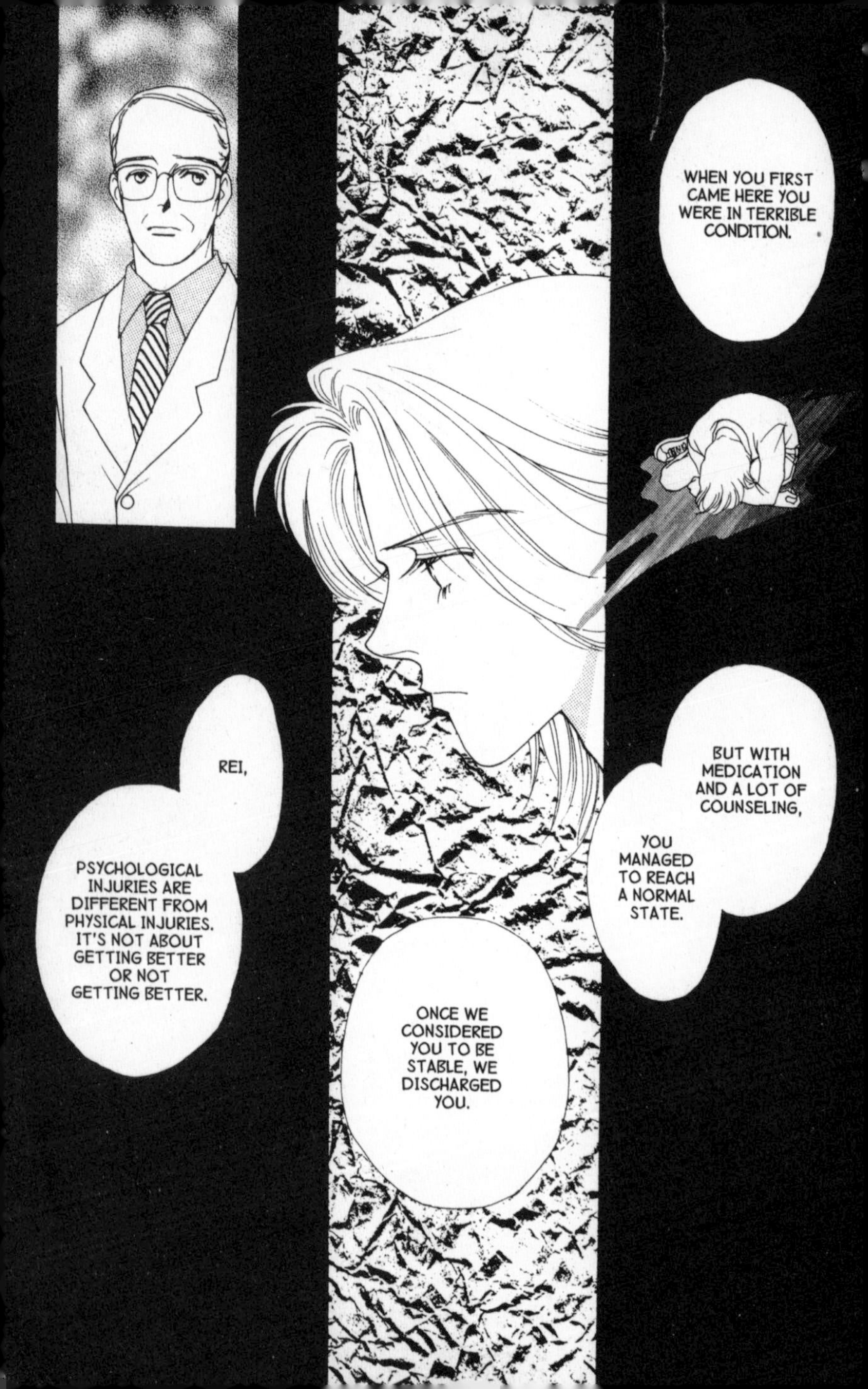
WHEN YOU FIRST CAME HERE YOU WERE IN TERRIBLE CONDITION.
BUT WITH MEDICATION AND A LOT OF COUNSELING,
YOU MANAGED TO REACH A NORMAL STATE.
ONCE WE CONSIDERED YOU TO BE STABLE, WE DISCHARGED YOU.
REI,
PSYCHOLOGICAL INJURIES ARE DIFFERENT FROM PHYSICAL INJURIES. IT'S NOT ABOUT GETTING BETTER OR NOT GETTING BETTER.

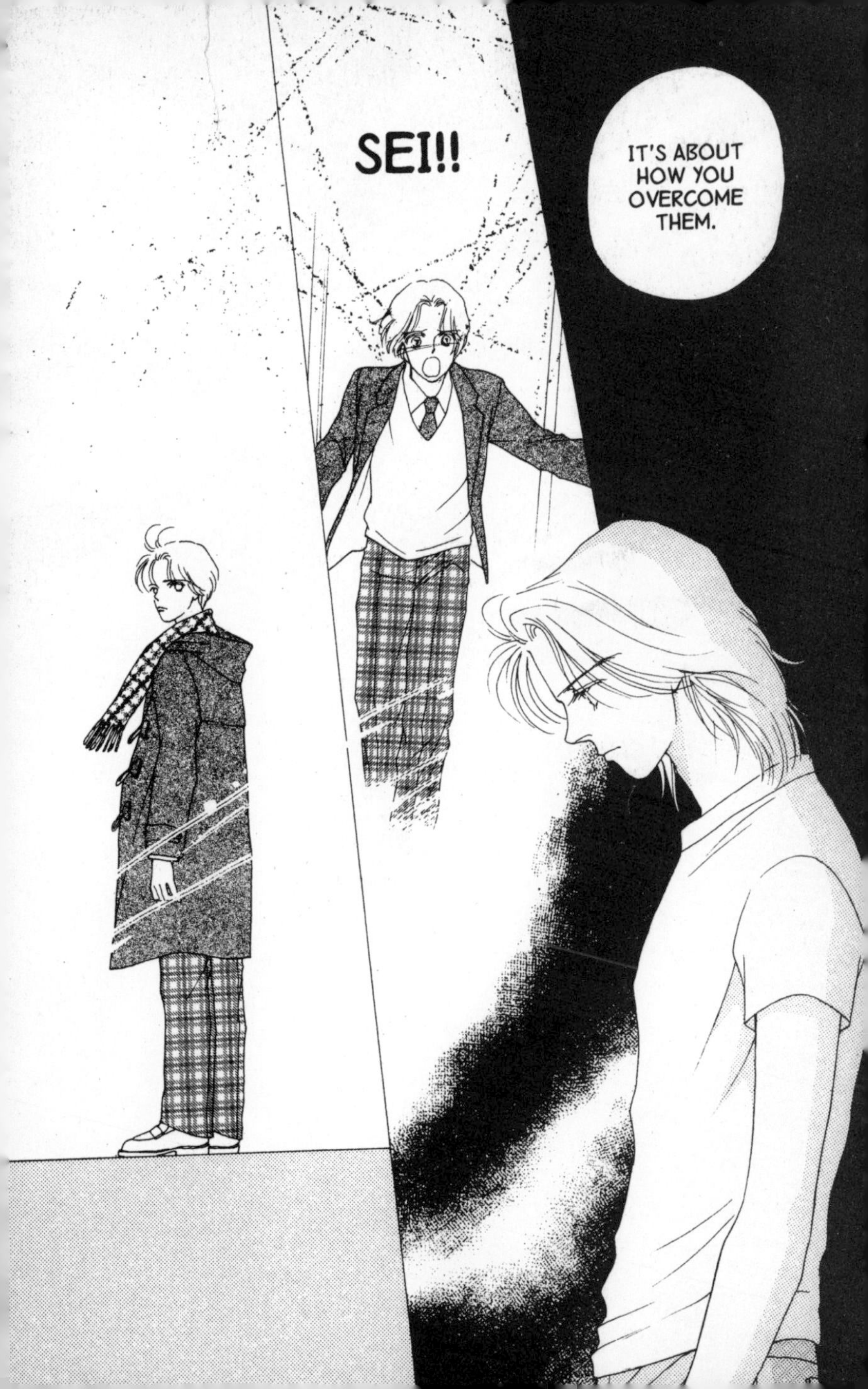
IT'S ABOUT HOW YOU OVERCOME THEM.
SEI!!

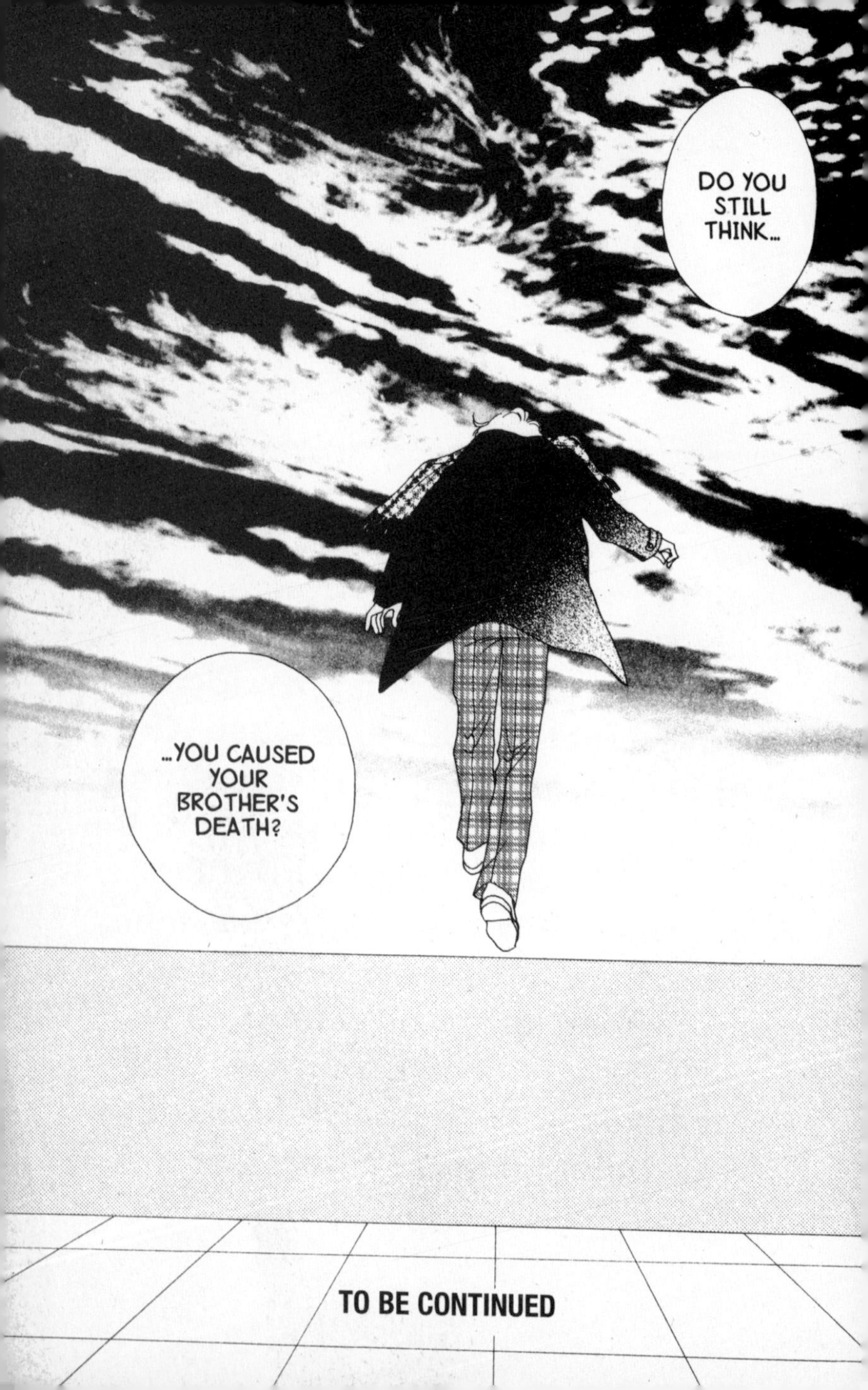
DO YOU STILL THINK...
...YOU CAUSED YOUR BROTHER'S DEATH?
TO BE CONTINUED

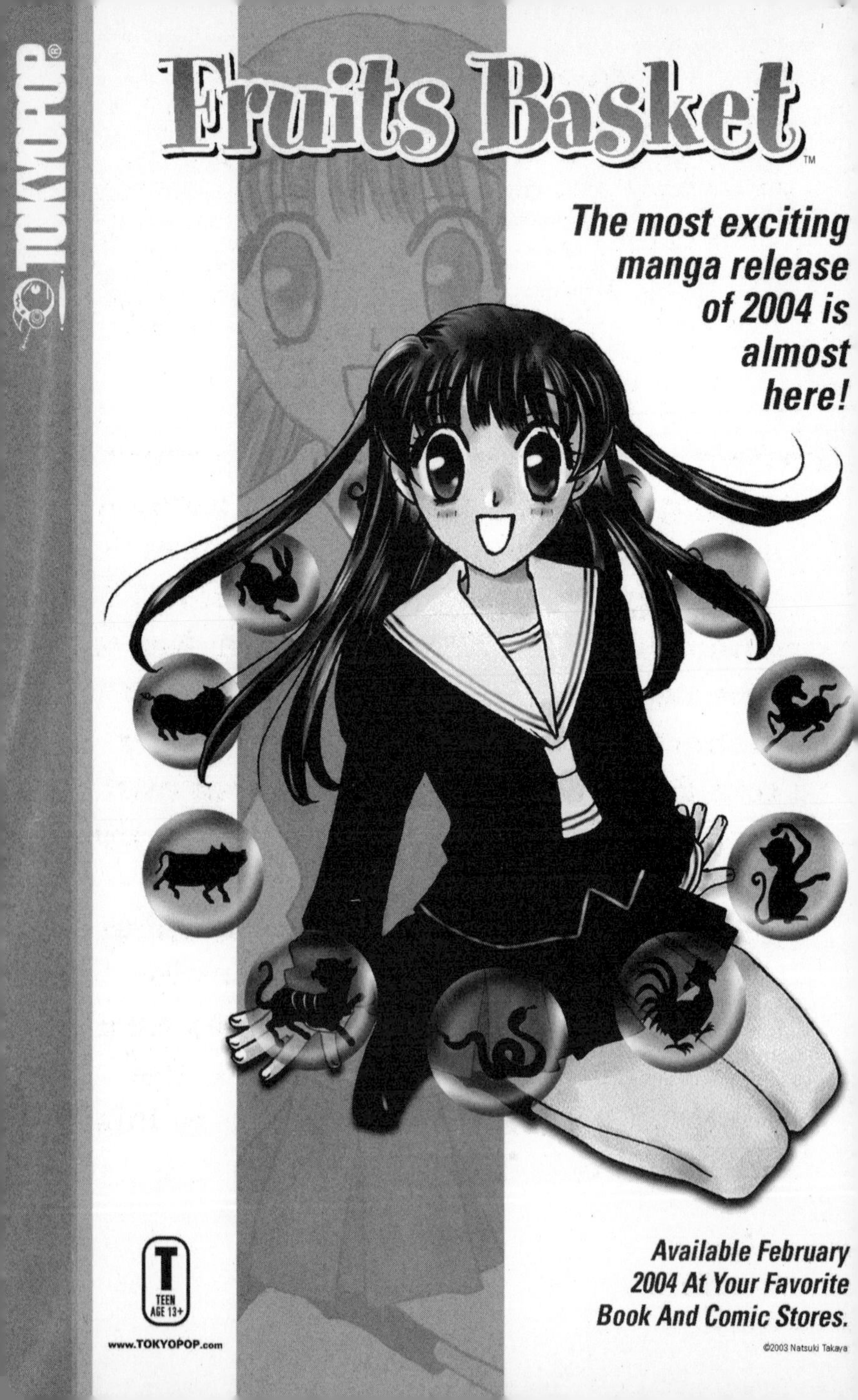
TOKYOPOP
Fruits Basket
The most exciting manga release of 2004 is almost here!
T TEEN AGE 13+
www.TOKYOPOP.com
Available February 2004 At Your Favorite Book And Comic Stores.
©2003 Natsuki Takaya

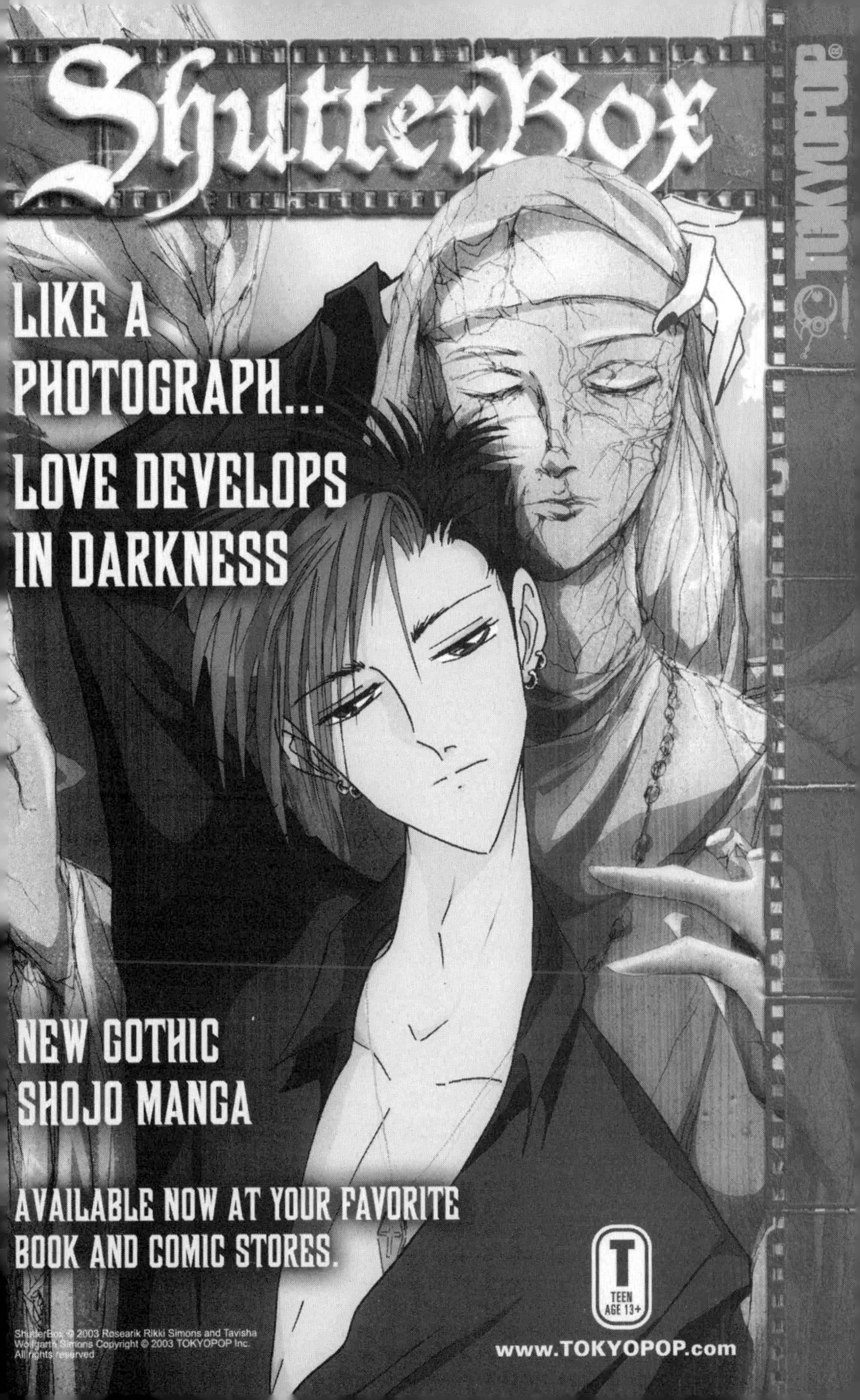
ShutterBox
TOKYOPOP
LIKE A PHOTOGRAPH...
LOVE DEVELOPS IN DARKNESS
NEW GOTHIC SHOJO MANGA
AVAILABLE NOW AT YOUR FAVORITE BOOK AND COMIC STORES.
T
TEEN AGE 13+
ShutterBox © 2003 Rosearik Rikki Simons and Tavisha Wolfgarth Simons Copyright © 2003 TOKYOPOP Inc. All rights reserved
www.TOKYOPOP.com

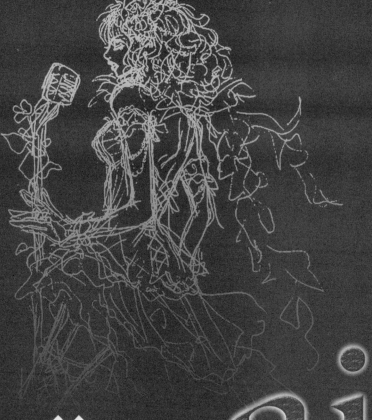

Princess ai

Courtney Love & D.J. Milky
put their spin on celebrity and fantasy.

www.TOKYOPOP.com

©2004 TOKYOPOP Inc

Manga coming in Summer of 2004

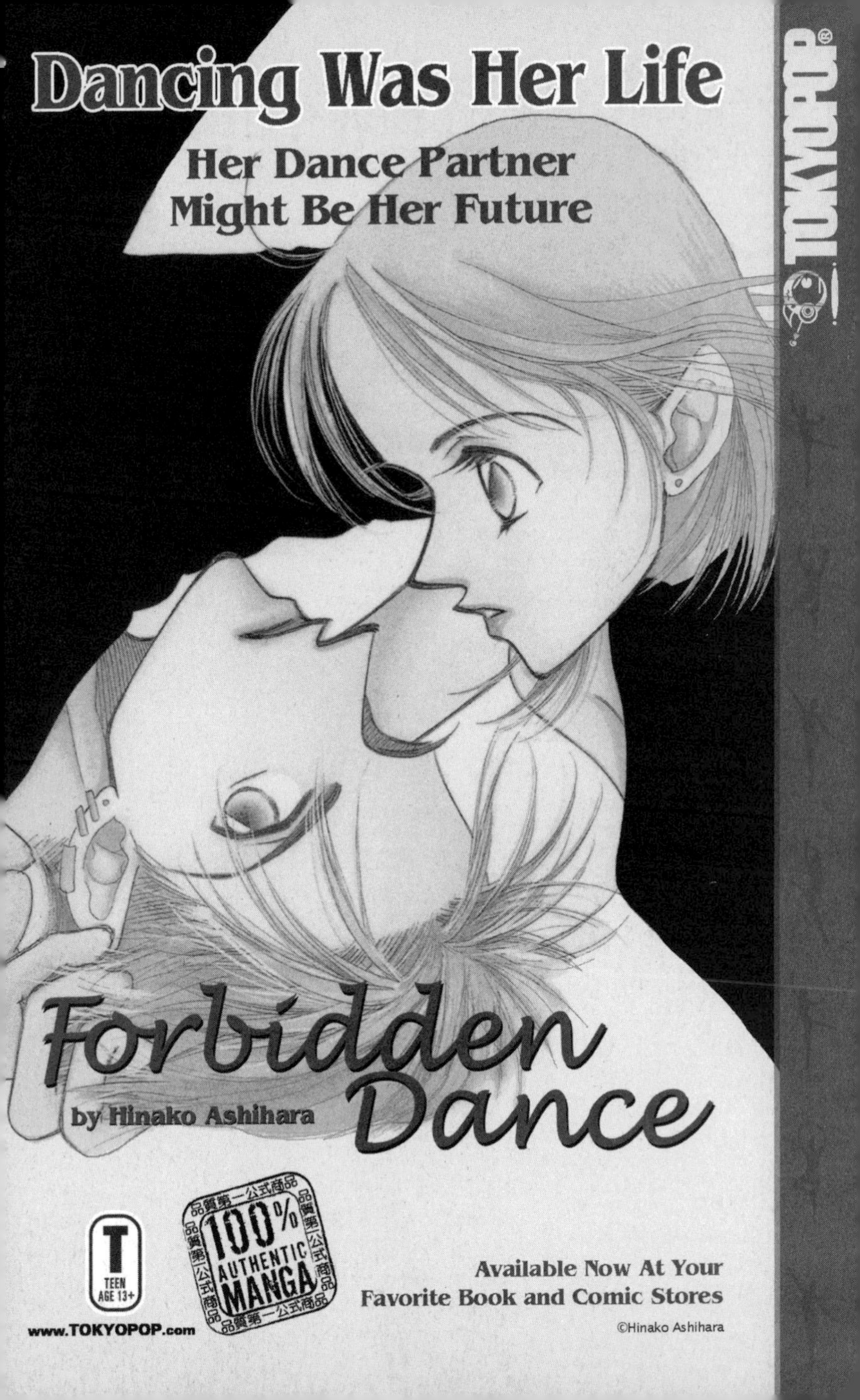
Dancing Was Her Life
Her Dance Partner
Might Be Her Future
TOKYOPOP®
Forbidden Dance
by Hinako Ashihara
T
TEEN
AGE 13+
100% AUTHENTIC MANGA
品質第一公式商品
Available Now At Your
Favorite Book and Comic Stores
www.TOKYOPOP.com
©Hinako Ashihara

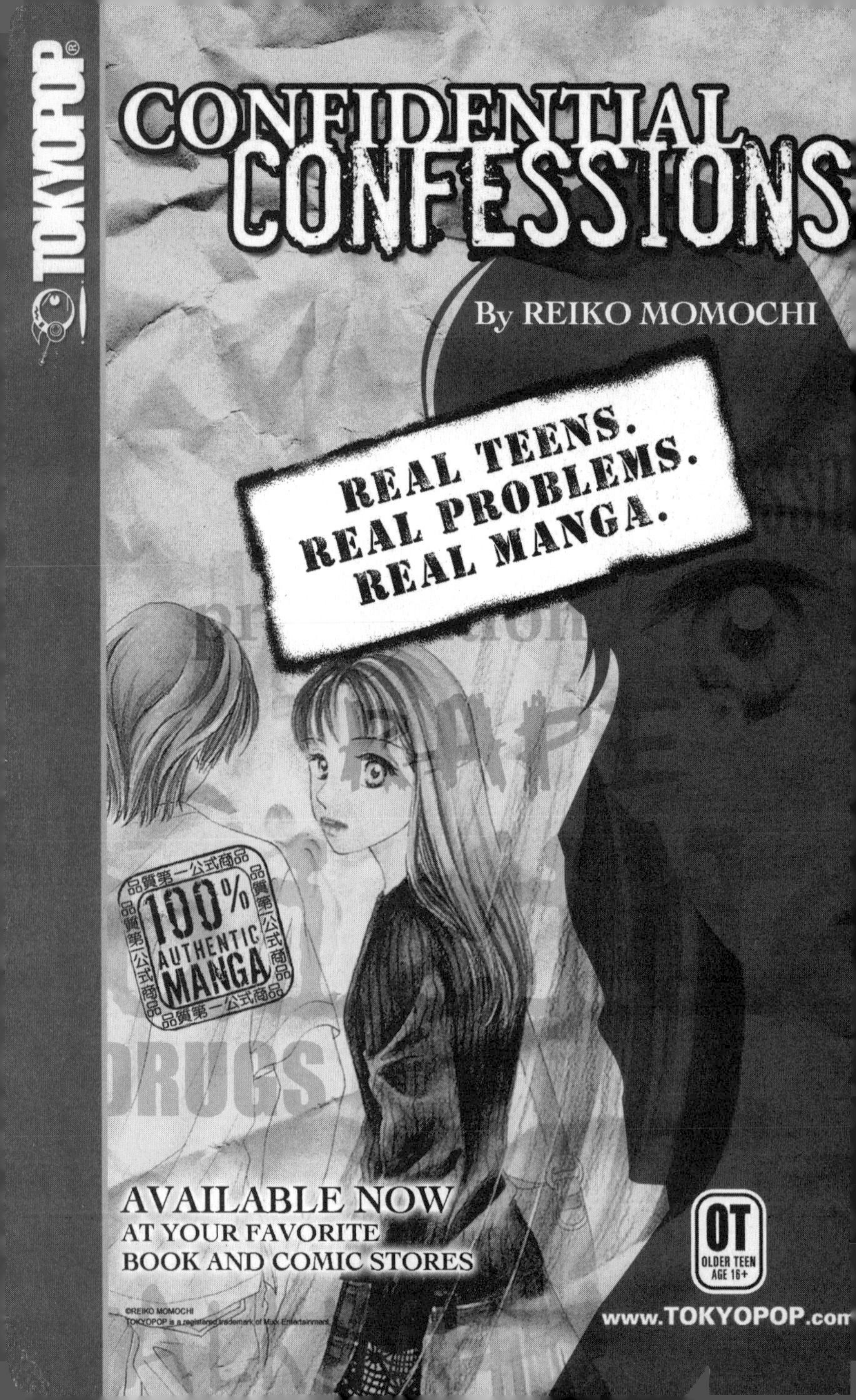
TOKYOPOP
CONFIDENTIAL CONFESSIONS
By REIKO MOMOCHI
REAL TEENS.
REAL PROBLEMS.
REAL MANGA.
100% AUTHENTIC MANGA
品質第一公式商品
DRUGS
AVAILABLE NOW
AT YOUR FAVORITE
BOOK AND COMIC STORES
OT
OLDER TEEN
AGE 16+
©REIKO MOMOCHI
TOKYOPOP is a registered trademark of Mixx Entertainment
www.TOKYOPOP.com

STOP!

This is the back of the book.
You wouldn't want to spoil a great ending!

This book is printed "manga-style," in the authentic Japanese right-to-left format. Since none of the artwork has been flipped or altered, readers get to experience the story just as the creator intended. You've been asking for it, so TOKYOPOP® delivered: authentic, hot-off-the-press, and far more fun!

DIRECTIONS

If this is your first time reading manga-style, here's a quick guide to help you understand how it works.

It's easy... just start in the top right panel and follow the numbers. Have fun, and look for more 100% authentic manga from TOKYOPOP®!